kathakali
❦❦❦ dance-drama

Kathakali, the distinctive dance-drama of Kerala in south-west India, is comprehensively presented and illuminated in this unique book. During these performances heroes, heroines, gods, and demons tell their stories from traditional Indian epics. The four *kathakali* plays included in this anthology, translated from actual performances into English, are:

- *The Flower of Good Fortune*
- *The Killing of Kirmira*
- *The Progeny of Krishna*
- *King Rugmamgada's Law.*

One of the few books published on this genre, and based on extensive first-hand research, the book:

- explores *kathakali*'s reception as it reaches new audiences both in India and the west
- includes two case studies of controversial *kathakali* experiments
- explores the implications for

Each play has an introduction and is illustrated by stunning photographs taken during performances. A comprehensive guide to *kathakali* stage conventions, make-up, music, acting, and training is also provided, making this an ideal volume for both the specialist and the non-specialist reader.

Phillip B. Zarrilli is Professor of Theatre and Performance Studies at the University of Surrey. He is the author of *The Kathakali Complex* (1984) and the editor of *Acting (Re)Considered* (Routledge 1995).

kathakali dance-drama

where gods
and demons
come to play

phillip b. zarrilli

With Translations by   V.R. PRABODHACHANDRAN NAGAR,
M.P. SANKARAN NAMBOODIRI AND
PHILLIP B. ZARRILLI

London and New York

First published 2000
by Routledge
11 New Fetter Lane, London EC4P 4EE

Simultaneously published in the USA and Canada
by Routledge
29 West 35th Street, New York, NY 10001

Routledge is an imprint of the Taylor & Francis Group

Designed by Chantel Latchford
Typeset by 🅣 Tek-Art, Croydon, Surrey
Printed and bound in Great Britain by Butler and Tanner Ltd, Frome, Somerset

British Library Cataloguing in Publication Data
A catalogue record for this book is available from the British Library

Library of Congress Cataloging in Publication Data
Zarrilli, Phillip B., 1947–
    Kathakali dance-drama : where gods and demons come to play/
Phillip B. Zarrilli.
        p.   cm.
    Includes bibliographical references and index.
    1. Kathakali.   2. Kathakali plays.   I. Title.
PN2884.5.K36Z38   1999
792'.0954'83–dc21   99-26482
                                                                          CIP

ISBN 0–415–13109–x (hbk)
ISBN 0–415–19282–x (pbk)

for

mozie and larry

೪೪೪

with thanks
for their love, inspiration,
and guidance

and for kor

contents

❧❧❧

part iii
contested narratives: new plays, discourses, and contexts

illustrations

꿏꿏꿏

PLATES

(Note: all photographs are by the author except as otherwise noted.)

preface

ჯგჯგჯგ

Kathakali dance-drama is a distinctive genre of South Asian performance which developed during the sixteenth and seventeenth centuries in the Malayalam speaking coastal region of south-west India known today as Kerala State (Figure 0.1). Like Japanese *noh* and China's *jingju* (Beijing Opera), *kathakali* has become internationally known during the past thirty to thirty-five years as troupes regularly tour throughout the world as part of government-sponsored international cultural exchanges or through private initiative. The vast majority of these performances have been *kathakali*'s dance-drama versions of episodes from the Indian epics (Mahabharata and Ramayana) or stories from the *puranas* – encyclopedic collections of traditional stories and knowledge. While there is a long history of 'experimentation' with content and technique, recent performances of new *kathakali* have brought increasing attention to and arguments about the place and role of experimentation and change in *kathakali* performance today.

This book takes account of *kathakali* as a distinctive 'traditional' genre of dance-drama performance particular to India's south-west coast, its entry into the transnational flow of global cultures as it is performed for tourists within Kerala and for new audiences in India and the West, *and* how *kathakali* interacts with and responds to contemporary politics in Kerala where the first democratically elected Communist state government came to power in 1957. Based on extensive ethnographic research in Kerala, India, conducted between 1976–77 and the present, this book articulates the dynamic set of relationships between dramatic/performance text(s), techniques and structures of performance, and reception among *kathakali*'s multiple audiences. It describes and analyses how the same *kathakali* performance can appeal to *kathakali*'s highly sophisticated connoisseurs whose reception is a refined aesthetic 'of the mind,' as well as make a seven-year-old child break into tears. The book is based on observation of performances, archival research at *kathakali* schools and institutions, extensive interviews with *kathakali* actors and appreciators, collaborative work on translations of the *kathakali* plays included in the volume, and the experience of training in *kathakali* techniques.

Although the theoretical and methodological backdrop for *When Gods and Demons Come to Play* is similar to my earlier study of *kathakali*, *The Kathakali Complex: Actor, Performance, Structure* (1984a), this book focuses on texts-in-performance by including four plays in translation with introductions and commentaries, and two case studies of *kathakali* experiments – none of which appeared in my first book. For the general reader, I provide an introduction to *kathakali* make-up, stage conventions, music, and acting. For those most interested in details of technique, I refer the reader to *The Kathakali Complex*.

A NOTE ON TRANSLATION

Whenever possible we have attempted to keep close to the word order of the Malayalam texts; however, it has often been necessary to alter the word order of the text for clarity in translation. This is especially true of the third-person descriptive *sloka* which string together long lists of phrases which modify the subject. For example, in the first *sloka* of *The Progeny of Krishna*, the subject, Hari (Vishnu in his manifestation as lord Krishna), is not found until the fifth line. Four modifying phrases begin the *sloka*. In our translation we often place the subject first, followed by the modifiers. For the individual watching the video performance of one of the plays-in-translation, this transposition for ease of reading results in a substantial difference in word order between the text in translation and the (video) performance. An exact correlation would only be possible in a literal word-by-word translation.

In Chapters 5-8, two types of notes on the plays in performance are included. Those essential for a non-specialist's understanding of the play are given as footnotes. Technical or textual notes of interest to specialists are given as endnotes.

VIDEOGRAPHY OF KATHAKALI

Since this book and its translations focus on *kathakali* in performance and context, it is accompanied by five videocassettes entitled an 'Introduction to *Kathakali* Dance-Drama,' and videodocuments of the four translated plays-in-performance. Taken together the translations, editorial notes, commentary, and videodocuments are intended to allow the reader to understand how an 'original' literary text is brought into performance today.

While working on this project in Kerala, India during 1993, I collaborated with the newly founded Centre for Documentation of Performing Arts in Killimangalam, Kerala and its organizers, Kunju Vasudevan Namboodiripad, Vasudevan Namboodiripad, M.P. Sankaran Namboodiri, and K.K. Gopalakrishnan. With the permission of all of *kathakali*'s senior artists, we documented as many well-known *kathakali* plays as we could fit into seven all-night performances staged both inside and outside the Killimangalam village temple. All the performances were attended by large and appreciative local audiences. It was an exciting and unprecedented documentation event which produced a collection of videos of the top artists in their best-known roles for use in translations such as these, for research, and for educating future generations of *kathakali* performers. The first night of actual documentation on 13 May, 1993, began with the official inauguration of the Killimangalam Centre for Documentation of the Performing Arts. Three of the plays translated here (*The Flower of Good Fortune*, *The Progeny of Krishna*, and *King Rugmamgada's Law*) were performed at Killimangalam between May and August 1993. The Centre for Documentation of the Performing Arts holds copyright on all videos made during this period of documentation.

The fourth play included here, *The Killing of Kirmira*, was recorded in 1996 at a staging organized by Drishyavedi in cooperation with the University of Wisconsin-Madison Kerala Summer Performing Arts Program. Like the performances at Killimangalam, this one was free, open to the public, and attended by a large and enthusiastic audience at Tirtapatta Mandapam located at East Fort in the heart of 'old' Thiruvananthapuram near the main temple. Complete information on the availability of the videos, including a list of artists involved, is included in the Appendix.

Figure 0.1   *Location of Kerala within India*

Cheruthuruthy is the home of the Kerala Kalamandalam. Guruvayur is where Krishnattam is performed. Irinjalakuda is home to both *kathakali* and *kutiyattam*. Kochi is the major port city where 'tourist' *kathakali* is regularly performed. Thiruvananthapuram is the capital city where Margi is located.

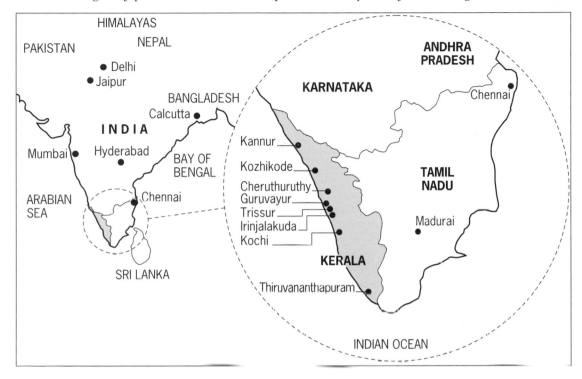

acknowledgments

Beginning with my first trip to Kerala in 1976–77, *kathakali* actor-dancer M.P. Sankaran Namboodiri (former Principal, Kerala Kalamandalam), and scholar/critic/connoisseur Vasudevan Namboodiripad (former Superintendent, Kerala Kalamandalam) have provided constant inspiration and guidance for me as I studied/sweated, enjoyed, and learned to appreciate *kathakali*. In 1993 I also began working with Professor Prabodhachandran Nayar of the University of Kerala, and we were able to spend countless hours together working on translations, talking about the pleasures of *kathakali*, and watching favorite performances. I owe these three individuals in particular a great deal for the little I am able to say about *kathakali*.

I thank the Kerala Kalamandalam teachers and administrative staff for welcoming and assisting me over the years of my research, and for offering institutional affiliation in 1976–77, 1993, and 1996. I also wish to thank Margi – a remarkable private cultural organization in Thiruvananthapuram responsible for a revival of training and interest in the traditional arts in southern Kerala, especially *kathakali*, *kutiyattam*, and *nangyar kuttu*. In particular, I want to acknowledge the late D. Appakoothan Nair for the precious time we spent together, and for his keen and incisive intellect. Although we often disagreed, it was always a disagreement with space for listening and friendly arguments. The current treasurer of Margi, Rama Iyer, and all its members and artists deserve my

continuing thanks for welcoming me over the years to their homes and performances. Ganesha Iyer's wisdom, memory, and insights have been shared with grace and charm.

During 1993, Kunju Vasudevan Namboodiripad, along with all his family, provided the logistical and organizational support to undertake video and photographic documentation of a number of all-night performances – all of which were sponsored by the Centre for Documentation of the Performing Arts, Killimangalam, Trissur District, Kerala. To Kunju, Vasudevan, Vimala, and their entire extended family, many thanks for all their efforts in bringing together the most senior artists to document their performances for the future education of *kathakali* actor-dancers and appreciators. And thanks to all the artists who agreed to have their performances documented for the Centre, including among many others Kalamandalam Gopi Asan, Ramankutty Nayar Asan, Padmanabhan Nayar Asan, and Kummaran Nayar Asan.

Thanks also to the leadership and members of Drishyavedi, another important cultural organization in Thiruvananthapuram, Kerala, which organized *kathakali* performances for the University of Wisconsin-Madison Summer Performing Arts Program in 1993 and 1996, and which were also documented for this project.

I also wish to express my thanks to Annette Leday, David McRuvie, and Iyyamgode Sreedharan for opening their rehearsals to me, and for the hours we spent talking about their work. They have been more than generous.

K.K. Gopalakrishnan and Sharon Grady offered their advice, support, assistance, as well as still photographs taken at all the performances commissioned in 1993. During 1993, Dr Jose George did yeoman service by assisting me with translation. I thank him for his company, patience, and keen insights into Kerala culture.

Some of the chapters in this book are revisions of previously published essays, or chapters in books. Part of Chapter 2 was originally published as 'A Tradition of Change: The Role of Patrons and Patronage in the *Kathakali* Dance-drama' in *Arts Patronage in India: Methods, Motives, and Markets*, edited by Joan Erdman (1992). Parts of Chapters 3 and 4 are a revision of several chapters from *The Kathakali Complex*. The commentary on *The Progeny of Krishna* in Chapter 7 was first published as 'An Ocean of Possibilities: From *Lokadharmi* to *Natyadharmi* in a *Kathakali Santanagopalam*' in *Comparative Drama*, Vol. 28, 1, 1994, and is published with the permission of the editors of *Comparative Drama*. Part of Chapter 4 was originally written for publication in *By Means of Performance*, and published in 1990. Part of the commentaries in Chapters 6 and 8 were originally published in *When the Body Becomes All Eyes* . . . and are published with the permission of Oxford University Press. Chapter 9 originally appeared in *Critical Theory and Performance*, edited by Janelle Reinelt and Joseph Roach, and is published with the permission of the University of Michigan Press. Chapter 10 originally appeared as 'Contested Narratives on and off the *Kathakali* Dance-Drama Stage' in *Modern Drama* (35, 1992), and is published with the permission of the University of Toronto Press.

A number of colleagues have commented on my work over the years and offered very helpful constructive criticism. Among them I wish to thank in particular Professor Joan Erdman (Columbia College and the University of Chicago), Professor Peter Claus (California State University-Hayward), and Professors V. Narayana Rao, David Knipe, and Kirin Narayan at the University of Wisconsin-Madison.

I want to acknowledge with great thanks, several grants which provided opportunities to work on parts of this manuscript. During 1993 I was in Kerala for seven months on a Guggenheim Fellowship, a senior Fulbright research fellowship, and with supplemental support from the University of Wisconsin-Madison. In 1995 I was able to work on the final draft of translations of the three plays through the support of the Asian Cultural Council. And in 1996 I was able to spend two months in Kerala revising the final manuscript with a short-term senior research fellowship from the American Institute of Indian Studies.

I would especially like to thank Talia Rodgers at Routledge Press for her patience and confidence through the writing and editorial process, and Deborah Procter for her critical reading of much of the final draft.

ক৶৶৶ **1**

an 'ocean of
possibilities'

Kathakali dance-drama is
like a vast and deep
ocean. Some may come
to a performance with
their hands cupped and
only be able to take away
what doesn't slip through

their fingers. Others may
come with a small vessel,
and be able to drink that.
And still others may
come with a huge
cooking pot and take
away so much more!

KATHAKALI AND ITS MANY AUDIENCES

My paraphrase of this highly reflective story
about *kathakali* and its relationship to its
audiences was told to me during my 1993 trip to
Kerala, India, by my friend and colleague, V.R.
Prabodhachandran Nayar – a life-long
appreciator of *kathakali* and Professor of
Linguistics at the University of Kerala. Sitting on
the veranda of his wife's family home on a quiet
back street in Thiruvananthapuram, the capital
city of Kerala, he told me this story as we
continued our work of translating *The Progeny
of Krishna (Santanagopalam)* – a *kathakali* play
text (*attakatha*, literally, 'enacted story')
authored by Mandavappalli Ittiraricha Menon
(c.1747–94).

I had selected *The Progeny of Krishna* as the
first play for us to translate for all the 'wrong'
literary reasons. As Prabodhachandran Nayar
explained when wearing his dual hats of linguist
and appreciator of good Sanskrit and Malayalam
poetry, *The Progeny of Krishna* simply 'isn't great
poetry. There's too much repetition, and the
vocabulary is meagre. It's just not rich!' In fact,
such 'bad' poetry was *The Progeny of Krishna*
that Prabodhachandran Nayar had never read a
printed version of the text before I convinced
him to read it with me. As a text on the page,
The Progeny of Krishna simply cannot compare
to the poetic richness and beauty of the four

formative kathakali texts (*Bakavadham,
Kirmiravadham, Kalyanasaugandhikam,* and
Kalakeyavadham) by Kottayam Tampuran
(c.1645–1716), or Unnayi Variyar's (c.1675–1716)
much heralded four-part version of the
Nala/Damayanti story. Variyar's *Nalacaritam* in
particular has been singled out as 'the highest
peak in *kathakali* literature' (George 1968: 102),[1]
and therefore, along with the Kottayam plays,
finds its way into the required syllabi of
Malayalam literature courses and/or critical
editions and commentaries.

Although Prabodhachandran Nayar had never
read the text of *The Progeny of Krishna* before,
he knew the text-in-performance by heart and,
like some other life-long appreciators among a
Malayali audience, might be heard humming the
well-loved if simple language beautifully set to
appropriate musical modes (*ragas*). Quite simply,
even if he did not think much of the poetry of
the play, he loved attending a good performance.
Moreover, he cherished a life-long set of
memories of *The Progeny of Krishna* in
performance – from those sponsored in family
house compounds or local temples as an
auspicious act by childless couples hoping to
secure future progeny, to performances of the
renowned actor-dancer Krishnan Nayar, whose
genius left its stamp, along with Kunju Nayar, on
contemporary interpretations and conventions
for acting the main role of the Brahmin.[2]

What struck me most about the performances of *The Progeny of Krishna* that I saw at village temples during 1993 were the many levels of appreciation and pleasure available to audiences attending this 'vast and deep ocean' of performance. Those who showed up with their 'huge cooking pots' were like 78-year-old Ganesha Iyer – life-long connoisseurs educated by years of attendance to respond with appreciation and/or criticism to the nuances and virtuosity of each performance. As Ganesha Iyer explained to me:

> From six years of age I was taken to see *kathakali* performances by my father and older brothers. I've read all the plays, can appreciate performances, and point out all the defects! But real appreciation requires critical study and drawing on knowledge of actors and other experts.

Traditionally known as being '*kathakali* mad,' connoisseurs like Ganesha Iyer used to travel far and wide during the 'season' from January through April/May to attend as many performances as possible by their favorite actor-dancers. The ideal connoisseur is knowledgeable in Sanskrit, enculturated into the finest nuances of each poetic text, and able to appreciate and criticize each performer's style and approach to performing particular roles. Today he is known as a *rasika* ('taster of *rasa*') or *sahrdaya* – one whose heart/mind (*hrdaya*) is so attuned and able to respond intuitively to a performance that he is able to 'take away so much.'

But also in attendance were children and the child-like – those with little to no education in *kathakali*'s nuances – who came with 'cupped hands' only able to drink what did not 'slip through their fingers' or could be held in their 'small vessels.' This drama's pleasures included:

1   interest in the story and its drama of a couple's love and loss of their children;
2   empathy for the main character of the Brahmin;
3   enjoyment of the beautiful musical modes to which the text is sung;
4   raucous laughter at the Brahmin's all too human foibles;
5   a sense of devotion (*bhakti*) for Krishna;
6   a sense of affirmation that human suffering is subsumed within the workings of lord Vishnu's cosmic 'play.'

Although from a literary point of view *The Progeny of Krishna* was the '*wrong*' play to translate, from a folkloristic point of view foregrounding performance context and effect,[3] *The Progeny of Krishna* was a good candidate for translation because its pleasures are accessible and popular.

Another good candidate would have been the very popular play *The Killing of Duryodhana* (*Duryodhanavadham*) by Vayaskara Aryan Narayanan Moosad (1841–1902). This enacts that part of the Mahabharata in which the Pandavas achieve victory over their cousins, the Kauravas, when their leader, Duryodhana, is killed on the great Kurukshetra battlefield. In a discussion, Prabodhachandran Nayar vividly recalled the response two popular scenes used to elicit from their audiences. In the scene at court, the Pandavas seek to defuse the impending crisis, which will lead to a division of their property, by making an increasingly meagre set of requests of Duryodhana. The first request is for him just to give them 'five villages' to rule. Duryodhana refuses with a simple 'no.' The second request is for 'five houses' to which he again responds 'no.' And the final request is for only 'one house' to which he also responds 'no.' At this moment during some performances in the past, a member of the audience occasionally stood up to proclaim, 'Then I will give!'

A second example of commonplace audience–performer interaction which Prabodhachandran Nayar recalls is the electrifying scene of banishment at Duryodhana's court, especially when the title role of Duryodhana was played by the once popular southern actor Mankulham Vishnu Namboodiri. As the scene opens, the hand-held curtain is lowered to reveal Duryodhana at his court accompanied by his family and counselors – his brother Dussassana, as well as the strong Karna and wise Bhisma. He announces that Krishna will soon arrive, but that absolutely no one at court should show Krishna any respect at all.

> When Mankulham Vishnu Namboodiri acted the role of Duryodhana, he used to make the audience part of the play! He'd just told no one in the court to stand when Krishna arrived. And then, when Krishna comes onto the stage, many in the audience would stand!

During the run-up to Indian Independence in 1947 and immediately after, for those in the audience active in the nationalist movement, this simple act of defiance to the authority represented by Duryodhana symbolized their resistance to British colonial rule.

In a separate discussion of this play's popularity, life-long connoisseur G.S. Warrier recalled another resonance that made *The Killing of Duryodhana* so popular in the 1930s and 1940s:

> Among Nayars . . . the request to 'give a portion of the kingdom' was precisely the situation they faced at the time since Nayar extended families were deciding whether and how to divide their property!

Warrier's reference is to the effect that changing socio-economic conditions and colonial legislation about marriage and property rights were having on large, matrilineal Nayar families. Before the development of a marketplace economy, these families lived on commonly owned property under the leadership of the eldest male. Changes in marriage and inheritance patterns were causing these families to divide their 'kingdoms' (householding) into ever smaller parcels.

Unfortunately, descriptions of such immediate responses and popular pleasures that make *kathakali* such a 'vast and deep ocean' for its indigenous audiences have often been missing from accounts of *kathakali*, including my own, which have problematically represented *kathakali* either as a 'classical' performing art or as an art exclusively intended for its patron-connoisseurs.[4] *Where Gods and Demons Come to Play* is intended to reveal some of *kathakali*'s numerous pleasures and 'attractions.' As Prabodhachandran Nayar comments:

> At old feasts there were always supposed to be sixty-four items served with rice. *Kathakali* is like that – it's got sixty-four attractions. If you like one thing, you can fix your attention on that!

THE HISTORY OF KATHAKALI IN KERALA: A BRIEF OVERVIEW

At the historical moment of its emergence as a distinct genre of performance in the late sixteenth and early seventeenth centuries, *kathakali* was given its present name, which literally means 'story play' and refers to the performance of dramas written by playwright-composers in highly Sanskritized Malayalam. Like most traditional modes of storytelling and performance in India, *kathakali* plays enact one or more episodes from regional versions of the pan-Indian religious epics (*Ramayana* and *Mahabharata*) and *puranas*, the 'bibles of popular Hinduism' (De Bary 1958: 23).[5] In *The God of Small Things*, Kerala-born contemporary novelist Arundhati Roy describes in vivid prose the 'secret' of these 'Great Stories' adapted for *kathakali* performance, and their popular appeal:

> the secret of the Great Stories is that they *have* no secrets. The Great Stories are the ones you have heard and want to hear again. The ones you can enter anywhere and inhabit comfortably. They don't deceive you with thrills and trick endings. They don't surprise you with the unforeseen. They are as familiar as the house you live in. Or the smell of your lover's skin. You know how they end, yet you listen as though you don't. In the way that although you know that one day you will die, you live as though you won't. In the Great Stories you know who lives, who dies, who finds love, who doesn't. And yet you want to know again. *That* is their mystery and their magic.
>
> (1997: 229)

As discussed in detail in Chapter 2, *kathakali* was given birth, nurtured, patronized, and increasingly refined by its traditional patrons – those 'non-polluting' high-caste ruling and/or landholding extended families, especially titled royal lineages of Nayars (Samantans) and the highest ranking Namboodiri brahmins. These castes were most directly charged with and invested in the sensibilities and socio-political order reflected in the epic and puranic literatures enacted on the *kathakali* stage.

By the end of the eighteenth century, most of the distinctive performance techniques and conventions that still characterize *kathakali* as a regional genre of performance had evolved. On a bare outdoor stage cleared of underbrush and defined only by a temporary canopy of four poles with cloth hung overhead, using only a few stools and properties, three groups of performers collectively create *kathakali* performances: actor-dancers, percussionists, and vocalists. Traditionally an all-male[6] company of actor-dancers drawn originally from the ranks of martial practitioners pledged to death in service to their patron-rulers, the performers use a highly physical style of performance embodied through years of training to play its many and varied roles. Each role is easily identifiable to many in a Malayali audience since each character type has its own distinctive make-up, elaborate costume, and characteristic behavior. The actor-dancers create their roles by using a repertory of dance steps, choreographed patterns of stage movement, an intricate and complex language of hand gestures (*mudras*) for literally 'speaking' their character's dialogue with their hands, and a pliable use of the face and eyes to express the internal states (*bhava*) of each character. The percussion orchestra consists of three types of drums (*centa, maddalam, and itekka*) each with its own distinctive sound and role in the ensemble, and brass cymbals which maintain the basic rhythmic cycles around which the dance-drama is structured. The two on-stage vocalists play the basic time patterns on their cymbals and sing the entire text, including both third person narration and first person dialogue, in a vocal style characterized by elaboration and repetition.

A *kathakali* performance traditionally served as a pleasurable form of education into these well-known stories and their implicit values and meanings. As Wendy O'Flaherty argues

> Myths are not written by gods and demons, nor for them; they are by, for, and about men. Gods and demons serve as metaphors for human situations . . . Myth is a two-way mirror in which ritual and philosophy may regard one another. It is the moment when people normally caught up in everyday banalities are suddenly (perhaps because of some personal upheaval) confronted with problems that they have hitherto left to the bickerings of the philosophers; and it is the moment when philosophers, too, come to terms with the darker, flesh-and-blood aspects of their abstract inquiries.
>
> (1976: 8–9)

One of the major 'macrostructural narratives'[7] that informs *kathakali*'s staging of these mythic stories is the notion of 'divine play' (*lila*). Norvin Hein explains the theological significance of this central notion of 'play' in Hindu thought:

> [*Lila* . . . is] the central term in the Hindu elaboration of the idea that God in his creating and governing world is moved not by need or necessity but by a free and joyous creativity that is integral to his own nature. He acts in a state of rapt absorption comparable to that of an artist possessed by his creative vision or that of a child caught up in the delight of a game played for its own sake.
>
> (in Sax 1995: 13)

In addition to God's creative dimension, *lila* also refers to the various forms or incarnations the divine takes 'in order to sustain and protect the world; thus, the *lilas* of such deities as Rama and especially as Krishna are the subject of much devotional art and literature' which have been adapted and 'elaborated by various Indian religious traditions' including Vaishnava, Saiva, and Sakta (Sax 1995: 4).

In Kerala, the Krishna cult and the fundamental theological concept of *lila* grew in importance between the sixth and ninth centuries as part of the Alvar devotional (*bhakti*) movement throughout Tamil country. Spurred on by such early devotional works as the Malabar (Kerala) King Kulashekhara's collection of hymns (*Mukunda Mala*), by the twelfth century the movement was ensconced in Kerala's Vaishnavite temples, where Jayadeva's popular Sanskrit work *Gitagovinda* was introduced. It was sung and danced to allow an audience to enter a devotional as well as aesthetic experience of the amorous 'sport' (*lila*) of Krishna's love-play with Radha (Varadpande 1982: 87ff.). In 1650 the deep devotionalism of Jayadeva's original work inspired the ruler of Kozhikode, Manaveda, to compose and stage a cycle of eight dance-dramas (*Krishnagiti*) in Sanskrit and based, like the *Gitagovinda*, on the life of Krishna. The genre eventually became known as *Krishnattam* (Krishna's dance) and was performed only within the confines of the Guruvayur temple as an offering to the primary deity, Lord Krishna. The eight dramatic episodes are traditionally performed on eight consecutive nights, beginning with the birth of Krishna, continuing through Krishna's absorption into his divine form (Mahavishnu), and concluding on the ninth night with the repetition of the drama of Krishna's birth, symbolizing and actualizing for devotees Krishna's eternal presence.

Unlike *Krishnattam*, which restricted itself to performances of Manaveda's eight plays enacting the life and grace of Krishna, when *kathakali* was given birth it drew on a wide range of epic and *puranic* sources. The serious 'sport' of all the gods and their agents became the cosmic backdrop against which traditional *kathakali* performances are staged. *Kathakali*'s temporarily sanctified theatre space is visited by a colorful array of epic and puranic players from demons, demonesses, and demon-kings to epic heroes and heroines, priests and brahmins, and even the gods themselves (Agni, Indra, Siva, Vishnu, etc.). There are also the agents of the gods such as Sudarsana Cakra (Vishnu/Krishna's divine weapon, appearing in *The Killing of Kirmira* and *The Progeny of Krishna*), Chitragupta (agent of Yama, the god of death, appearing in *The Progeny of Krishna*), or Nandikeswara (the gatekeeper of Siva's abode). All these characters are festooned in (more or less) larger-than-life costumes, head-dresses, and symbolic full-face make-up as they enact these cosmic scripts.

Always implicit, this notion of divine play is occasionally explicit, as in *Kiratam* by Irrattakulangara Rama Varier (1801–45). *Kiratam* enacts that part of the Mahabharata in which the epic hero, Arjuna, goes to the Himalayas to perform penance to lord Siva as he seeks to secure from him the divine *pasupata* weapon needed to help the princely Pandavas in their forthcoming battle with the Kauravas. After Arjuna's journey to the Himalayas, he performs a series of austere meditations (*tapas*). Although Siva is pleased with Arjuna, he wants to test him. He disguises himself as a Hunter (Kirata) and engages Arjuna in a dispute of wills and arms over which of them killed a wild boar. Arjuna is gradually stripped of all his weapons and subdued by Siva-in-disguise. Recovering from his defeat, Arjuna returns to his austerities, realizing that the Hunter was Siva-in-disguise. Asking Siva's forgiveness, Arjuna is blessed by Siva and his wife, Parvati, and given the divine weapon. This and other tests are instigated by the gods as part of their cosmic 'play.' As Arjuna sings of Siva in *Kiratam*, 'By means of your "play," you protect the whole universe!'

As in *Kiratam*, this cosmic script is sometimes enacted by the gods themselves when they come to the stage to return cosmic 'law' to its rightful order. This is the case in both *The Progeny of Krishna* and *King Rugmamgada's Law* where it is lord Vishnu himself who intercedes at the end of each play to set 'right' an imbalance created by his own divine 'sport.' But more often than the gods themselves, it is their heroic agents such as Arjuna, Bhima and Rama, who are called upon to set things 'right.' Among the many manifestations of this cosmic play are the *kathakali* dance-dramas with 'killing' ('*vadham*') in their titles such as *The Killing of Kirmira* (*Kirmiravadham*), *The Killing of Duryodhana* and *The Killing of Narakasura*. It is traditionally at dawn at the end of an all-night performance that the act of killing a demon such as Kirmira, an anti-hero like Duryodhana, or a demon-king such as Narakasura in a one-on-one combat concludes these cosmic dramas.[8] Even in plays without 'killing' in their titles[9] some killing still takes place. For example, in the full-length version of *The Flower of Good Fortune* the heroic Bhima encounters two demons on his journey. In order to accomplish his mission of collecting the 'flowers of good fortune,' he first dispatches Jatasura, and in the penultimate scene he kills Krodhavasa. As David R. Kinsley persuasively argues, when faced with combat 'one gets the impression that the gods are really never in trouble at all, that they condescend to battle the demons simply because it is part of some cosmic script or because they enjoy it' (1979: 49).

Another major 'macrostructural narrative' implicit in these ubiquitous 'killings' in *kathakali* is the royal obligation of the South Asian king to conduct warfare. In India, kingship has long been understood to play an essential role in the maintenance of political and cosmic order. In spite of the fact that the 565 kingdoms or 'princely states' that existed in India at the time of Independence in 1947 disappeared within a year or two of that date, as Chris Fuller asserts, kingship has retained

a central importance in Hinduism and Indian society. In the traditional Hindu worldview, as expounded most clearly in textual sources, kingship is seen as a vital institution; a society without a king is unviable and anarchic . . . [A]ll sources agree that the king's first responsibility is to protect his kingdom and subjects, by guaranteeing their safety, prosperity, and well-being . . . [T]he order of the kingdom is itself part of the sociocosmic order or *dharma*, and it is ultimately preserved by king and deity together, rather than the king alone.[10]

(1992: 106)

One of the major duties of the king was to conduct warfare, which, as Chris Fuller has convincingly argued, 'is a reiteration of the idea that an ordered cosmos is created by sacrificial destruction' (1992: 124–5). In medieval Kerala with its fragmentary, segmented state structure, battle was a 'dominant metaphor for conceptualizing relations of spiritual and socio-political power' (Freeman 1991: 588). The royal obligation to sacrifice oneself on the battlefield and to at least attempt to symbolically expand one's kingdom led to an almost constant state of warfare between and among its petty rulers (see Zarrilli 1998: Chapter 2). As we shall see in several of the plays translated in this book, this royal obligation to conduct warfare as an act of sacrificial destruction is reflected in the concerns and actions of *kathakali*'s epic heroes. As represented in most *kathakali* plays, the 'heroic' is an idealized state of being/doing dramatically marked by the necessity of the hero's sacrificial acts of blood-letting, usually accomplished by the end of the performance when he 'kills' one or other demon or demon-king. As detailed in Chapter 2, and several of the commentaries in Chapters 5-8, the concerns, trials, and tribulations of *kathakali*'s epic heroes can be read as reflecting the concerns and problems of its traditional patrons – those charged with upholding the 'kingdom.'

By the time *kathakali* crystallized its basic performance structure and techniques at the end of the eighteenth century, its all-night performances of 30- to 40-page texts had become one of the most popular forms of entertainment. Performances took place at least seasonally if not more frequently sponsored by royal households, by wealthy landholding families in celebration of a wedding or a birth, and/or as part of annual temple festivals. *Kathakali*'s popularity derived not only from its enactment of familiar stories in the local language of Malayalam (although still heavily Sanskritized) with its recognizable cast of characters, but also from its accessibility to large audiences when performed as a regular part of annual Hindu temple festivals. G.S. Warrier described for me his memories of attending *kathakali* during his childhood:

> From the tender age of six or seven, I saw *kathakali*. The temple across the road had a ten-day festival, and on four of those days there were *kathakali*. There was also a Krishna temple within fifteen miles of my village, and it was a real center for *kathakali*. The Ambalapuzha Raja was there, and they had a *kathakali* yogam (company) for training. In those days there used to be crowds of 3,000 to 4,000 at a performance! So we learned to appreciate that way.[11]

Since Kerala's largest high-caste temples limited entry to only the 'non-polluting' castes, Kerala's mode of enacting Sanskrit dramas (*kutiyattam*), and *kathakali*'s immediate precursor, *Krishnattam*, were only seen by the gods, for whom they were performed as visual sacrifices/offerings, and by the high castes. In contrast, *kathakali* has, with a few exceptions, always been performed *outside* the walls of temples, or in palace or family house compounds. Consequently, it was accessible to many more, if not 'all', people.

Accessibility is relative and context specific. Although *kathakali*'s performances outside the temples were theoretically 'accessible,' 'all' were not welcome and would not have felt welcome, especially in the front rows where high caste connoisseurs sit, men to the right and women to the left. As Robin Jeffrey explains,

> Old Kerala was a place of boundaries and constraints – boundaries on where particular people might go; constraints on what they might do. People lived in discrete groups which connected with others in regulated, symbolic ways.
>
> (1992: 19)

Some of the most obvious and restrictive constraints were those placed on mingling of genders and castes. Substantive/pollution-based notions of caste were based on the concept that an individual born into a particular caste possessed, by virtue of one's birth, a more or less polluting 'substance.' Exchanges of food and/or bodily based fluids, and the amount of distance that needed to be maintained between individuals of differing castes/substances were therefore defined and restricted by one's birth into a particular caste. These notions lingered into the early twentieth century.

> [A]t the base of these many little pyramids [of caste], families of slave castes, usually Pulayas or Parayas, did the heavy work of paddy cultivation and were treated virtually as beasts . . . In the eighteenth century, Pulayas who polluted their superiors might be killed, and as late as 1904, a Nayar was reported to have killed a Pulaya with a spade after the Pulaya had approached and 'polluted' him. All groups ruthlessly preserved ritual purity.
>
> (Jeffrey 1992: 20)

Given the strict rules of distance pollution and bans against intermingling, exchange and cooking of food, and touch, we can be sure that audiences at *kathakali* performances taking place at temples or in family house compounds were governed and constrained by these rules and conventions, and did not mix across either boundaries of gender or the caste-based line of 'pollution.'[12]

Although the largest number of *kathakali* performances today continue to be organized as part of temple festivals during the dry festival season from mid-December through May, the large and enthusiastic audiences it once attracted are becoming the exception rather than the rule. One such exception is the annual Vishwambhara Krishna Temple festival performances during March–April in Kottakkal. Kottakkal is well known to *kathakali* lovers because a *kathakali* troupe and training institution has been patronized there since 1939 when the P.S.V. Natyasangham was established by Vaidyaratnam P.S. Varier – visionary philanthropist, artist, physician, businessman, and founder of one of the largest and best known Ayurvedic medical factories and clinics in India, the Kottakkal Ayurveda Sala. Like other years, when I was there in 1993 the week-long March festival boasted all-night performances every evening, featuring all the top *kathakali* 'stars', such as Gopi Asan in the title role of Karna in *Karnasapatham* (playing opposite the ageing but still popular Kottakkal Sivaraman in the role of his mother, Kunti); Padmanabhan Asan in the role of Ravana in *Balivijayan*. Each evening connoisseurs arrived early to get a seat on the ground just in front of the stage, to have the best view of the nuances of the performances to follow, and an eager and enthusiastic audience of well over 2,000 gradually filled and overflowed the cleared performance area immediately outside the temple compound. Many if not all of the audience stayed until dawn.

In contrast are the ever-diminishing audiences at temple festivals lesser known for sponsorship of *kathakali* and where no 'stars' are playing. At several performances I attended in 1993, such as one at the Narasimha Temple near Kottayam, by midnight as few as twenty people remained in the audience, and only a handful among them were attentive to the performance.

In addition to temple sponsorship, *kathakali* is performed monthly in a few of Kerala's major towns and cities under the sponsorship of cultural organizations such as the Trissur Kathakali Club in central Kerala, the Trivandrum Kathakali Club, Drishyavedi, and Margi in the capital city of Thiruvananthapuram.[13] These and other private cultural organizations began to be founded in the 1960s by groups of civic-minded connoisseurs of the traditional arts to fill what was perceived as a vacuum in the regular public presentation of Kerala performing arts, especially *kathakali*. Most performances sponsored by *kathakali* clubs and cultural organizations are given in large, proscenium-style regional theatres and are attended by fifty to several hundred paying spectators – primarily *kathakali* aficionados who attend monthly to see their favorite performers in particular roles.

KATHAKALI AS CONTESTED TERRITORY

Although *kathakali* continues to hold many different pleasures and is appreciated in many different ways by its audiences in Kerala, it is one form of cultural practice which, like other modes of expressive culture, is increasingly contested territory today. One arena of contestation is simply for the attention of the Malayali public. In 1993, I was waiting for the 'Parasuram Express' to the capital (Thiruvananthapuram) at the Shoranur Junction railway station near Cheruthuruthy, where the internationally-known Kerala State Arts School (Kerala Kalamandalam) is located, when a well-dressed 21-year-old college student of computer science, Mohan, approached me and started a conversation in English. It was raining heavily – typical during the south-west monsoon which begins every June and lasts until August. Mohan asked what I was doing in Kerala. I explained I had been coming to Kerala for twenty years, and that I was conducting research and writing on *kathakali* dance-drama.

Surprised, Mohan asked, 'are people in the United States really interested in this art?' I explained that although very few people knew about *kathakali*, those interested in non-Western theatre and dance wanted to know more. I asked if he was interested in *kathakali*. Mohan smiled ironically,

> Oh, no, I'm not interested in *kathakali* at all. Most people my age aren't interested at all. We'd rather go to films or watch television.

I asked if anyone in his family attended *kathakali* performances. He proudly explained that his father had never been interested in *kathakali* and therefore never went. Almost apologetically, Mohan added:

> My mother was raised in a [relatively high-caste] family that enjoys *kathakali* and attends performances whenever she comes here [to her family home] with my uncle and aunt, as well as my cousin who is my age. They all love *kathakali* and go to performances often.

Today *kathakali* dance-drama must compete for the attention and imagination of young Malayalis like Mohan and his cousin with an increasingly diverse set of enticing entertainments – from the numerous popular films churned out by the massive Indian/Malayalam film industries, to the flood of Western films (everything from Stallone action films to X-rated movies), to television (introduced to Kerala in 1983), to a variety of new popular entertainments from modern drama to 'mimics parade' – solo stand-up routines in which young men enact phenomenally accurate impressions of everything from animals to popular singers, cinema stars, or political personalities. Unlike Mohan's cousin, who is

being 'educated' by his family into appreciation of *kathakali*, an increasing number of young people from families that would traditionally have been likely to attend and appreciate *kathakali*, like Mohan, seldom if ever attend *kathakali* today. As Prabodhachandran Nayar commented in a discussion:

> The trend [toward featuring popular performances] has resulted in totally forgetting the gods at many temple festivals by replacing *kathakali* with dramas, mimic shows, etc. The divine may still be there, but increasingly it is being buried under more and more layers. Temple festivals used to be measured by the number of nights on which *kathakali* was being performed!

In the late twentieth century, *kathakali*'s existence has become part of what South Asian anthropologist Arjun Appadurai and historian, Carol Breckenridge call 'public culture':

> a zone of cultural debate . . . characterized as an arena where other types, forms, and domains of culture are encountering, interrogating and contesting each other in new and unexpected ways.
>
> (1988: 6)

As a genre, *kathakali* is increasingly open to a variety of modes of contestation over everything from its potential audiences to its content and representations, performance techniques, modes of appreciation and reception, or performance contexts both in Kerala and abroad. Mohan and his cousin experience the type of social and personal 'realities' described by ethnographic historian James Clifford:

> the world's societies are too systematically interconnected to permit any easy isolation of separate or independently functioning systems . . . Twentieth century identities no longer presuppose continuous cultures or traditions. Everywhere individuals and groups improvise local performance from (re)collected pasts, drawing on foreign media, symbols, and languages.
>
> (1988: 230)

Consequently, the public culture terrain which *kathakali* inhabits in the late twentieth century is contested by an increasingly diverse group of 'producers of culture and their audiences' (Appadurai and Breckenridge 1988: 6–7) who make use of quite different discursive and critical narratives in shaping their versions of *kathakali*. This is as true of 'learned' discourses about *kathakali* such as this one, as of the more 'local' world *kathakali* artists and connoisseurs inhabit in Kerala, where the discourses of elite scholars of cultural studies and history around issues of gender, class, race, and identity are only beginning to circulate and make their impact felt.

Inhabiting a 'world dominated by the media, by consumption, and by global cultural flows' (Appadurai and Breckenridge 1995: 3), *kathakali* is constantly being (re)created and (re)positioned by and/or for its many different actor-dancers, critics, scholars, sponsors, audiences, administrators, as well as politicians, thereby making available an increasingly heteronomous set of images, discourses, experiences, structures, knowledges, and meanings for them all. Some of these constantly shifting (re)positionings have been an inevitable and often violent result of socio-economic and/or political reforms resulting from British colonial rule, while others are arguably less 'benign.'

As discussed in Chapter 2, perhaps the most abrupt and radical historical shift in the history of *kathakali* has been the loss of traditional patronage resulting from rapidly changing socio-economic circumstances brought by continuing British colonial rule in the late nineteenth and early twentieth centuries. New institutional structures for the support of *kathakali* were necessarily established in 1930 when the well-loved contemporary Malayali poet Mahakavi Vallathol Narayana Menon founded the now internationally known Kerala State School of the Arts, Kerala Kalamandalam, in order to ensure that future generations of performers would receive training under the best master teachers. Institutions like the Kalamandalam have had to develop new ways of organizing training which combine indigenous models with Western colonial ones. These changes have inevitably influenced all aspects of *kathakali*.

Just as *kathakali* patronage and institutional structures have shifted and changed *kathakali*, it has adapted in a variety of ways to suit the changing concerns, needs, and tastes of its traditional high-caste audience of connoisseurs, including:

1   editing all-night plays-in-performance into three-hour cameos for its 'stars' so that either one play is performed in an evening program ending at 9:30p.m., or three edited plays are performed in an all-night program;
2   writing and staging new plays based on traditional epic/puranic sources, and in the process occasionally creating new (epic) characters based more on everyday life than most roles in the repertory;
3   restaging long 'lost' scenes of plays still in the repertory in order to restore the 'original,' and/or reviving plays no longer in the repertory;
4   considerably expanding existing scenes to suit an aesthetic defined as a 'non-worldly' 'theatre of the mind' performed primarily if not exclusively for an audience of connoisseurs.

As we shall see in Chapters 2 and 3, even though some of these changes have radically altered how a full-length *kathakali* play was performed in the nineteenth or early twentieth century, they are not usually perceived as negative, but as acceptable changes legitimized from 'within' the tradition. These changes test but do not break the 'rules.' The relative 'success' or 'failure' of such changes are debated by connoisseurs and critics in terms of the degree of 'appropriateness' of content, music, technique, and acting. As we shall see in the commentary in Chapter 6, some forms of change are represented by their champions as 'improving' *kathakali*'s aesthetic and therefore are naturalized as positive.

In contrast are changes and 'experiments' in content and technique discussed in Chapters 9 and 10 – the highly controversial productions of *Kathakali King Lear* performed in 1989-90 for audiences on the international festival circuit, or the 1987 production of *People's Victory* (*Manavavijayam*) performed primarily for non-traditional leftist audiences in Kerala. These productions are perceived by many connoisseurs as transgressing the limits of what they consider 'appropriate' to the 'tradition.' To dismiss such productions as unimportant for commentary or analysis, as do many connoisseurs, because they are not 'traditional,' would implicitly reify 'traditional' *kathakali* and its epic narratives as normative and uncontested, thereby failing to situate such experiments within the complex set of historical, socio-political, cultural, discursive, and aesthetic forces at work in contemporary Kerala history. I agree with South Asian anthropologist and performance scholar Joan Erdman's observation that 'the use of performing arts for political and social messages and value transmission create questions for scholars *which arise from the performers themselves*' (1991: 113, emphasis added). While still the exception rather than the rule, controversial *kathakali* productions like *Kathakali King Lear* and *People's Victory* invite performance scholars to address issues beyond the stereotypical aesthetic and genre questions often exclusively discussed in studies of Indian performance. They invite attention to the specific historical, socio-political, and contextual issues raised by all performances, whether considered 'controversial' or 'normative,' and also to the discursive and socio-cultural formation of what is or is not considered normative or contested.

THEORETICAL FRAMEWORK AND OUTLINE OF THE BOOK

Folklorist Richard Bauman noted long ago that traditions of performance (like *kathakali*) have always stood available to participants and spectators 'as a set of conventional expectations and associations' which can be 'manipulated in innovative ways, by fashioning novel performances outside the conventional system, or working various transformations and adaptations which turn performance into something else' (1977: 34–5). As the above examples show, and as I hope to demonstrate in this book, a system of cultural performance such as Kerala's *kathakali* dance-drama is, like the concept of culture itself, not a set of fixed conventions and attributes but, rather, a dynamic system of human action constantly undergoing a process of negotiation.[14] Critical theorist Susan Bennett expands this notion of the interactive state of flux and contestation in the relationship between 'culture' and performance when she writes that

> both an audience's reaction to a text (or performance) and the text (performance) itself are bound within cultural limits. Yet, as diachronic analysis makes apparent,

those limits are continually tested and invariably broken. Culture cannot be held as a fixed entity, a set of constant rules, but instead it must be seen as in a position of inevitable flux.

> (1990: 101)

Based on extensive field research in Kerala between 1976 and the present, *When Gods and Demons Come to Play* is written as a performance ethnography of *kathakali* as one mode of cultural praxis through which knowledges, discourses, and meanings are repositioned through the practice of performance. I assume with performance scholar Margaret Drewal that both 'society and human beings are performative, always already processually under construction' (1991: 4). Anthropologist Johannes Fabian similarly asserts that '"performance" seem[s] to be a more adequate description both of the ways people realize their culture and of the method by which an ethnographer produces knowledge about that culture' (1990: 18). I use the word 'performance' as the most appropriate metaphor for an epistemology which assumes that 'ethnography is essentially, not incidentally, communicative or dialogical; conversational, not observation' (Fabian 1990: 4). Therefore, I include many different perspectives on *kathakali* from among its many producers, appreciators, and interpreters.

From this point of view, theater-making is a mode of socio-cultural practice. As such, it is not an innocent or naive activity separate from or above and beyond everyday reality, history, politics, or economics. As theatre historian Bruce McConachie asserts, 'theatre is not epiphenomenal, simply reflecting and expressing determinate realities and forces' (1989: 230); rather, as a mode of socio-cultural practice, theatre is a complex network of specific, interactive *practices* – in *kathakali* these include the practices of authorship/composition, acting/performing, patronage/connoisseurship, construction/maintenance of the appurtenances of performance, and (more recently) management and even directing. McConachie suggests that an appropriate unit of analysis in theatre history is the 'theatrical formation,' that is, 'the mutual elaboration over time of historically-specific audience groups and theatre practitioners participating in certain shared patterns of action'

(1989: 232). Chapter 2 provides a social history of the 'theatrical formation' basic to *kathakali* – the relationship between its patron/connoisseurs and performers.

Throughout the book, I (re)situate *kathakali* within the historical and socio-political particulars of each production/reception context so that the variety of subject positions from which interested discourses of theatrical practice, criticism, and reception are constructed can be identified, and the implicit ideologies of each position discussed. In this view, cultural performances are sites of cultural action which either implicitly assume, or explicitly assert, one or more discourses or meanings which can be propagated, contested, and/or protected as part of local, state, national, and/or geo-political 'social dramas.'[15] Performances of a play, the content of the drama/narrative, the genre of performance itself (*kathakali*), and/or the discursive and critical constructs through which the performance/drama/genre are discussed may become contested territory.

Although twentieth-century identities no longer necessarily presuppose continuous cultures or traditions, there are many contexts within which either 'the world' or at least some more framed and circumscribed arenas of experience are imagined and/or assumed to be continuous.[16] This is especially the case in India generally and in the world of *kathakali* in particular, where, as we shall see (especially in Chapter 2), 'tradition' is often cast in the normative role of maintaining and authorizing a specific form of continuity with an imagined and/or 'authorized' past. As South Asian scholar A.K. Ramanujan has astutely observed, 'in a culture like the Indian, the past does not pass. It keeps on providing paradigms and ironies for the present, or at least that's the way it seems' (1989: 133). Therefore, Parts I and II of this book provide an account of *kathakali*'s paradigmatic 'past' – that 'set of conventional expectations and associations' (Bauman 1977: 34) or aesthetic 'rules' constantly (re)negotiated in the present. Part I, 'Performance in the Kerala Context' (Chapters 2-4), provides an overview of the socio-cultural history of *kathakali*, and an 'ideal-typical' account (Marglin 1985) of the dance-drama in performance – of its texts, repertory, performance conventions, techniques of training, and 'traditional' aesthetic. This account is in part

an 'ideal-typical picture of the core . . . activities' (Marglin 1985), techniques, conventions, and assumptions or 'rules' which constitute *kathakali* in many, but not all, 'traditional' contexts today. It is 'ideal-typical' in that it is the account of no single school or performer, but rather is constructed from fieldwork, observation, practice, and interviews with numerous performers and at numerous schools and institutions throughout Kerala solicited under my prompting as an 'outsider.' Given the processual view adopted here, cultural performances like *kathakali* are not reducible to their obvious set of performance techniques, repertory of play texts, 'traditional' set of conventions and/or aesthetics, etc. Rather, *kathakali* 'exists' as a set of potentialities inherent in the complex set of practices, texts, discourses, representations, and constraints through which it is constantly negotiated and (re)created by means of 'tactical improvisation' (Jenkins 1992: 51), both within the 'tradition' and outside it.

Part II, 'Plays from the Traditional Repertory' (Chapters 5-8), provides for the first time in English a set of translations with commentaries of four plays-in-performance. Given the universal praise and respect among Malayalis for Unnayi Variyar's poetry in his four-part series of plays enacting the story of Nala and Damayanti (*Nalacaritam*, Parts 1-4 performed in four nights), the few translations which exist have understandably been of his plays.[17] The first English version was V. Subramania Iyer's 1977 translation, which includes an introduction to *kathakali* texts (*attakatha*), notes on the author, plot summary and commentary, and the performance manual (*attaprakaram*) which actors use to guide them in performing the plays.[18]

Of the more than five hundred *kathakali* plays written, and of the approximately fifty authored by twenty major writers which still hold 'the stage with recognizable persistence' (Paniker 1993: 21), I have selected four plays-in-performance for translation which, arguably, represent a diversity of characters, modes of staging, and range of moods and modes of aesthetic appreciation. The first two, *The Flower of Good Fortune* (*Kalyanasaugandhikam*) and *The Killing of Kirmira* (*Kirmiravadham*) were authored by Kottayam Tampuran (*c*.1675–1725) and are two of his four formative 'Kottayam plays,' based on the Mahabharata, which gave *kathakali* its name – 'story play.' After Variyar's *Nalacaritam*, the Kottayam plays are considered to have some of the best poetry in the *kathakali* repertory. Moreover, the four Kottayam plays are considered fundamental to the technical training of today's *kathakali* actor. Since technique plays such an important part in structuring performance of these plays, appreciation of the actor-dancer's technique in performance of them is a source of great pleasure to connoisseurs.

The other two plays, *The Progeny of Krishna* and *King Rugmamgada's Law*, are the only two plays authored by Mandavappalli Ittirariccha Menon (1747–94). In contrast to the Kottayam plays, which are infamous for their tight performance structure and the virtuosic technical requirements placed on the actor-dancer, both these plays feature major roles which allow great individual freedom in enacting the 'dramatic' dilemmas of the major character in each play. As such they offer different challenges for the actor-dancer, and pleasures for audiences. The content of the two plays, and others authored during the same period such as *Ambarishacaritam*, reflect the importance that devotion (*bhakti*) to Vishnu came to have in some *kathakali* plays written during this period.

Following most closely the earlier model of translation by Rajagopalan and Iyer (1975),[19] the four included here provide:

1   a translation of the literary text;
2   the interpolations (*ilakiyattam*) added to the literary text and performed by the actor-dancers to elaborate on the 'original' text;
3   annotations of the music and dance elements which shape and punctuate the ever-changing moods of the performance and make *kathakali* not simply a drama, but a dance-drama.

Written between my own reading of the plays, the extensive literature on South Asian area studies and Hinduism, and interviews and discussions with *kathakali* actor-dancers and appreciators, the commentaries allow the Western reader a glimpse of some of the meanings the plays make available to Malayali audiences and performers. These commentaries are by no means intended to be comprehensive, but to illuminate certain specific issues of history, interpretation, and context within a living tradition.

Read as a counterpoint to Parts I and II, Part III illustrates just how dynamic are both the 'internal cultural debates' within the *kathakali* world today (Parkin 1978: *passim*), and the 'external debates' in the flows of public culture. Part III provides a historical overview of *kathakali* experiments with new content and form in the post World War II and Independence era, but focuses in particular on two of *kathakali*'s most controversial 'new' productions – the 1989–90 intercultural adaptation of Shakespeare's *King Lear* (Chapter 9), performed primarily in Europe and the UK, and *People's Victory* (Chapter 10), performed exclusively in Kerala. Each experimental production in its own way exemplifies the contrasting ways in which producers, performers, critics, and connoisseurs of *kathakali* simultaneously negotiate conventional rules and expectations 'within' the tradition, a variety of transnational global flows (aesthetic, political, or institutional), and the socio-political assumptions which inform both production and reception today, as each voice justifies, decries, or applauds the 'new.' My approach is intended to allow the reader insight into *kathakali* as a complex and ever-changing system of social and aesthetic practices which both shapes and is shaped by its context(s).

BETWEEN *KATHAKALI* TEXTS AND THE ETHNOGRAPHIC PRESENT

Kathakali plays, like those of its immediate precursor, *kutiyattam*, and earlier Sanskrit dramas, are all 'anchored in the processes of their production, in the orbits of connection and influence that give them life and force' (Camaroff and Camaroff 1992: 34). It is to some of these 'orbits of connection and influence' that I turn my attention in the next chapter, since the values and behaviors reflected in *kathakali* dramas and their enactment are, following Sanskritist David Gitomer,

> neither documentary records of the ruler warrior (ksatriya) caste nor the fantasies of poets writing in isolation. They are texts of imagination that weave together traditional epic, mythology, and normative classical learning . . . [L]ike most Sanskrit texts they habitually eradicate their situatedness in time and place, being rooted in patronage they are at the same

time expressive, often in indirect ways, of the anxieties and concerns of specific royal political milieux. Out of these varied sources, the poets create the dream of an order, an ideal, playful world. It is the pleasure of the connoisseur to enter this world, the work of the scholar to understand its intersection with . . . the . . . past *and* the present.[20]

(1998: 34)

part i

❧❧❧

performance
in the kerala
context

a social history of *kathakali* patronage, connoisseurship, and aesthetics

INTRODUCTION

As a performing art, *kathakali* dance-drama shares certain general characteristics with other Indian traditions (religious, literary, etc.). All such traditions may be thought of as dynamic systems of action constantly undergoing a process of generation and degeneration. A tradition like *kathakali* exists simultaneously as (1) an inherited collection of established ways of feeling, thinking, and doing passed on through generations, and (2) the active and ongoing process of transmitting what has been handed down orally, through entrainment, enculturation, and/or written records. A performance tradition includes both the system of performance as a collection of practices and the social-structural network within which its practices are carried out. A tradition, then, is created, maintained, or changed by the dynamic interplay between what is received and what is passed on by its students, performers, craftsmen, critics, audiences, and patrons. The degree of maintenance, variation, elaboration, transformation, and degeneration within a tradition varies historically as the conventions, rules, boundaries, socio-economic realities, discursive/aesthetic principles, and the like are constantly (re)negotiated in the dynamic interplay of individual and social formations.

Traditional performing arts like *kathakali* incorporate patronage and connoisseurship

necessarily, and their social and performative histories are directly related to their patrons and connoisseurs. *Kathakali*'s creation, growth, consolidation, and maintenance as a culturally distinct performance tradition have been inextricably linked to its patronage. In this chapter I trace the social and performance history of *kathakali* in order to understand the ways in which patrons and connoisseurs have shaped the life of the tradition, its structure and techniques, its repertory, its evolving aesthetic and practice of connoisseurship, and therefore their pleasure(s). From the available historical and anthropological literature, I examine the role and place of patrons and connoisseurs within Kerala's social hierarchy, as well as within the artistic tradition in each of four phases of *kathakali* history:

1   The formative years from the origins of *kathakali* in the late seventeenth to the late eighteenth century, by which time the genre had evolved into what we recognize as *kathakali* today.
2   The mature years from the late eighteenth to the late nineteenth century, during which time there was further refining of the expressive possibilities of the genre.
3   The early modern period from when a resurgence of interest was sparked by poet Vallathol's establishment of a new

institutional form for teaching and preserving the genre beginning in the late 1920s.

4 The recent past in which some of today's connoisseurs have defined the quintessential experience of *kathakali* as a 'nonworldly' 'theater of the mind.'

In addition to identifying how patrons and connoisseurs have been directly and intimately involved in the development of many aspects of *kathakali* throughout its history, I am particularly concerned with understanding the 'cultural politics' of connoisseurship as an aesthetic discourse and as a collective social practice into which individuals are enculturated. As cultural theorist Graeme Turner argues,

> Much of the work on pleasure so far has concentrated on individual desires and pleasure, omitting those that derive from and create shared, collective experiences . . . We simply do not know how pleasure aligns with or supports us against dominant views of the world. We do not even know how texts produce all their variety of pleasure.
>
> (1992: 222)

However, any discussion of the cultural politics of art-making and appreciation must be careful not to become reductionist. As historian David Morgan asserts,

> While it would be rash to insist that . . . cultural politics is all that the disinterested contemplation of art amounts to, we should be alert to the politics of taste and suspicious of any claim for political neutrality in ranking the disinterested experience of art above . . . popular reception . . .
>
> (1998: 30)

Given the predominance of the 'word,' texts, and canonization of textuality, Western discussions of the cultural politics of pleasure or 'authority' in theater and drama have tended to be preoccupied with issues of authorship. As reflected in this and other chapters, issues of authority in *kathakali* are not primarily concerned with issues of authorship or authorial intent or privilege, but rather with other concerns and constellations of authority:

1 What is or is not considered permissible 'within' one's lineage or style of practice (*sampradaya*).

2 What is or is not considered 'appropriate' to the dramatic context.

3 One's social location within the lineage of practice, and/or within the hierarchy of social roles that constitute *kathakali*'s immediate spheres of production.

THE FORMATIVE YEARS: THE ROLE OF ROYAL PATRONS

Royal authorship and patronage are ubiquitous to the early history of *kathakali*. As briefly discussed in Chapter 1, *Krishnattam*'s cycle of eight plays were authored by Manaveda, ruler of Kozhikode from 1655 to 1658. Manaveda's cycle may have served as a model for a new cycle of eight plays known as *Ramanattam*, based on the Ramayana, and authored by Kottarakkara Tampuran (c.1625–85), the ruling prince of Elayidattu Swaroopam in southern Kerala.[1] In this earliest form of *kathakali* the actor-dancers sang their own lines. Chitra Panikkar describes its style as 'plain and rustic' with 'vigorous and fast rhythms in the dance steps' accompanied only by the horizontal *maddalam* drum and gong (*chenkala*) keeping rhythm (1993: 32). Its costuming and make-up must have been relatively simple and plain.

> Rama and Lakshmana had their faces painted blue, and demons and monkeys wore face masks. The headgear was made of palm sheath with designs painted on it, while the torso was bare.
>
> (ibid.)

Although *Krishnattam* remained a genre exclusively performed under the patronage of the rulers of Kozhikode, '*Ramanattam* spread to other parts of Kerala over a period of three decades,' including the patronage of the Vettom Tampuran in northern Kerala (Panikkar 1993: 32). The name *kathakali* came into popular use when yet another ruling prince, the Kottayam Tampuran (c.1645–1716), authored a set of four plays based on stories from the Mahabharata, thereby expanding the repertory to sources other than the Ramayana.

Krishnattam, Ramanattam, and then *kathakali* could never have come into existence without royal patronage. Like the Kottarakkara, Kottayam, and Vettom Tampurans, the earliest royal patrons were from the high-ranking ruling Nayar families (see Figure 2.1), although there was also support and involvement from a few Ksatriya ruling families, such as the Venttattu Raja (Jones 1984: 18–19). These examples show that patronage was readily accepted as one role within the 'role set' assumed by royal lineages. Sociologist Robert Merton argues that any social position is characterized by a 'complement of role-relationships' or a 'role set' (1957: *passim*). During this period in Kerala's history, 'patronage' was one multifaceted role within a series of social roles constituting the 'role set' identifying a ruler as a ruler, with all the privileges, rites, powers, and responsibilities assumed by that position. The role of patron was not a passive, disinterested one but, rather, an active role in which the patron himself was often directly involved not only in providing the social and economic means necessary to realize the art, but also as author/composer of texts, ideal audience member, and, occasionally, performer.

The political and socio-economic basis of traditional patronage

From approximately the twelfth century onward, the Malayalam-speaking region of South India known today as Kerala State was divided into numerous small states – each governed by its own ruler who wielded widely different degrees of influence and power. The ruler of each kingdom aspired to expansion as part of an implicit understanding of kingship as ritual sacrifice. As Chris Fuller explains:

> the ideal Hindu kingdom is coextensive with India, the world, and the universe, and every Hindu king should strive to expand his kingdom's boundaries to the uttermost frontier. This ideal, which necessitates expansive conquest, is evoked in the classical rite of 'crossing the limit' . . . [I]t is the king's duty to make war to expand his kingdom, principally by forcing other rulers to submit to his suzerainty, rather than by annexing their territories as such. Because it brings the kingdom closer to its ideal form, military expansionism is

a harbinger of prosperity for the realm, which engenders a more perfect order, not the opposite. Furthermore, because war is classically conceptualized as sacrifice . . . military confrontation can be seen as a religiously sanctioned act necessary for the sustainment of the world. Consistent with this, to fall in battle is to die a glorious hero who is likely to be deified. Thus warfare itself is a reiteration of the idea that an ordered cosmos is created by sacrificial destruction.

> (1992: 124–5)

Anthropologist John R. Freeman explains that this form of kingship does not follow the commonplace 'conception of a single individual, occupying the unique structural center of a political organization' but, rather, is an example of '"little kingdoms"' which are 'segmentary,' and therefore exemplify a form of political authority which is 'multiplex and contestatory' (1991: 715). In this system the

> center (or centers) exhibit . . . an ideal sovereignty that is primarily ritual; but actual executive authority is distributed at many lower sites of the structure, where there are multiple, scaled down replicas of the king . . . [I]n Kerala, even a minor chieftain might be called the 'Pre-eminent King' (Rajadhiraja) in the context of his own little domain.

> (ibid.)

The four most powerful among the larger kingdoms during the period of *kathakali's* invention were the Kolathiri of Kolathunatu and Zamorin of Calicut in the north, the ruler of Cochin in Central Kerala, and the Travancore Raja in the South. Each state was divided into a number of districts (*nadu*), which in turn were divided into counties (*desam*) within which were numerous villages (*amsa*). Each district was governed by a *nadu-vali*, whose rights included criminal and civil jurisdiction and 'the right to claim military service from the Nayars under him' (Panikkar 1919: 257–8). Next in authority were the *desa-vali*. They ruled the counties and were in charge of maintenance and training of local *kalari* where training in the martial arts was given. At each segmentary level of organization, a mini-'kingdom' or locus of power and authority existed.

The right to hold land was only in possession of the highest ranking non-polluting castes (Puthenkalam 1977: 14): Namboodiri brahmins, the royal lineages (a few Ksatriya groups and the highest ranking title-holding Nayars, often called Samanthans), lesser ranking Nayar who were local rulers (*nadu-vali*), heads of villages (*desa-vali*), and temples. Those with the right to hold land did so by birth right (*janmam*) (see Figure 2.1). Those working the land did so by tenure (*kanam*), in service to landholders (Moore 1983: 28ff.; Gough 1961: 308–9).

The basic unit, 'house and land,' was a royal model ideally intended to be a self-sufficient microcosm,

> designed to contain a more or less complete set of the beings inhabiting the universe and the entire set of life-cycle events of persons who are its members . . . [T]he rest of society seems to remain solitary by means of a set of ritual relationships defined relative to it.
>
> (Moore 1982: 26)

This ideal microcosm was only realized by those at the very top of the hierarchy, Namboodiri Brahmins, the aristocratic or ruling lineages, or large temples dedicated to pan-Indian puranic deities. Each house and its land provided for

> not merely subsistence, but the conduct of cultural activities (temple maintenance, festivals); and was not satisfied merely with things, but required persons of all kinds (i.e., *jatis*) who were either granted along with the land (e.g. the Cerumans) or encouraged to settle on it (e.g. the Ilavas and artisans).
>
> (Moore 1982: 142)

Each basic unit, house and its land, ideally supported and thereby patronized all rituals and cultural activities associated with the necessities of maintaining both socio-economic and cosmological equilibrium, from the sponsorship of the ritual life and annual temple festival to the training of men-at-arms ready to defend the unit.[2]

Whether held by proprietary birth right (*janmam*) by a Namboodiri brahmin, Ksatriya, or one of the Nayar lineages, or by a temple, the basic unit 'house and its land' supported (i.e.,

'patronized') those cultural activities associated with the ritual necessities of maintaining the unit as a microcosm. Many of the performing arts of the region prior to the emergence of *Ramanattam/kathakali* were ritual arts, i.e., each was an integral part of a daily/calendrical cycle of ritual propitiation, or life-cycle or crisis ritual performances intended to prevent or alleviate disaster and disease (such as smallpox). Such arts were supported by the interdependent network of castes in service to a particular house (or temple) and its land. As this hierarchy and the rights and responsibilities granted those of high rank illustrates, the role of arts patron for genres like *Krishnattam, Ramanattam,* and *kathakali* was an exclusive privilege restricted to those at the very top of the political and socio-economic hierarchy.

Even the most aesthetic and literarily developed traditions of Kerala theater, *kutiyattam*, was integrated into the socio-economic, *jati*, and ritual network of pan-Indian Puranic temples. Performers were drawn from the ranks of the Ambalavasis, intermediate ranking temple service castes, specifically *cakyars, nambyars,* and *nangyars*. Patronage, as financial support of the network of performers and artisans necessary to put on performances, was part of the obligation of the temple as a base-unit, 'house and its land.' Only those temples had the right and duty to maintain performers and hold calendrical performances as 'visual sacrifices' for the primary deity of the temple (Richmond and Richmond 1985: 54; Jones 1967; Raja 1964; Richmond and Richmond 1978).

Likewise, both the right and socio-economic means to conceive, originate and organize, and patronize a performance genre such as *Ramanattam/kathakali* or *Krishnattam* would only have been appropriate for those whose positions in the hierarchy accorded them the 'rights and duties,' wealth, and network of service castes necessary to realize a particular type of performance. Unlike patronage of yearly temple festivals required to propitiate deities under a family's jurisdiction, and unlike a Namboodiri or Nayar extended household (*taravadu*) commissioning a necessary ritual such as *pampin tullal* (serpent worship) to ensure fertility and prosperity (Neff 1987), there was initially no obligation to patronize *Ramanattam/kathakali*. At first patronage must have been taken on for a variety of reasons, such as: personal devotion (*bhakti*) inspired by a general

Figure 2.1 *The Kerala caste hierarchy*

Most sources generally agree with the following ordering of castes, listed by decreasing status as follows:[3]

Non-polluting high castes (only the following 'non-polluting' castes were traditionally allowed entry into large and well-known 'restricted entry' temples dedicated to pan-Indian puranic deities such as the Krishna temple at Guruvayur and Sri Padmanabhaswamy [Vishnu] Temple at Thiruvananthapuram)
> Namboodiri Brahmins
>> landlords of large estates
>> lower sub-castes owning smaller estates, temple priests, physicians, household priests, cooks, other 'foreign' brahmins (from Tamil Nadu, Karnataka, or Andra Pradesh)
> Ksatriyas (the 'princely' castes)
> Samantans (and other titled royal lineages of the indigenous Nayars)
> Ambalavasis (temple servants)
> Nayars
>> middle-ranking retainers
>> various specific lower-ranking serving sub-groups including those who served in brahmin kitchens, servants to Namboodiris or rulers, bearers, washermen, barbers and midwives, or funeral priests

Higher polluting castes
> Kammalas (artisan castes including carpenters, stone-carvers, blacksmiths, brass and coppersmiths, and goldsmiths)
> Tiyyas, Izhavas or Thandans, Chovans (tenant farmers, toddy tappers)
> Kaniyans (astrologers and agricultural laborers)

Lower polluting castes
> Mukkuvans and Aryans (fishermen)
> Pulayas or Cherumans (Harijan 'out-castes')
> Parayas

increase in Vaishnavite (Rama and Krishna) devotion (Jones 1983: 15); a means of accentuating the traditional role of royal patrons as protectors of the social order; and/or engagement in an activity appropriate to one's status, and therefore as a means of enhancing that status and 'prosperity.' Patronizing the arts was one of many ways to acquire 'good fruits' for both family and kingdom (Moore 1983: 159–68), thereby helping to ensure general prosperity.

Prompted by such motivations, *Ramanattam/kathakali* was brought to the stage within the pre-existing socio-economic network of the Kerala unit, 'house and land.' Among those *jatis* in service to royal Nayar lineages who fostered the art were middle ranking Nayars. They were 'vassals' (*adiyar*) and formed the ruler's retinue (*akampadi*) – established by taking a vow to death to serve the ruler (Zarrilli 1998). The relative power and rank of royal lineages was partially based on the number of Nayar soldiers in service to that ruler. Those Nayars forming an *akampadi* held land as tenants (*kanakkaran*) in return for service to their lords. Special titles were conferred on some Nayars, such as Panikkar (teacher of the martial art), or Kurup (martial master).[4]

These Nayars, trained in the highly energetic indigenous martial art (*kalarippayattu*) and expected to actualize *vira* (heroism) on the battlefield, became the first performers of *Ramanattam/kathakali* as well as *Krishnattam* (Zarrilli 1984a: 53–5). From their intensive life-long training, begun at the age of seven or eight, they already possessed an embodied basis from which much of the dance-drama choreography and its energetic (*tandava*) qualities were created. The early patrons established a new social role, 'actor/dancer', as an additional appropriate role in the set of roles associated with these middle-ranking Nayar soldiers. Eventually, the role 'actor-dancer' was dissociated from that of Nayar martial practitioners and became a primary *jati*-specific activity open to a larger group of similarly ranked service castes, but primarily associated with middle-ranking Nayars.

Musicians and drummers were already in service to ruling families and/or their temples. Properties and costumes could easily be crafted by the artisan castes in service to the rulers. The only other people needed to complete a troupe were bearers to carry accoutrements for performances outside the house/palace or temple compounds and washermen to care for the costumes – both *jati*-specific tasks for which traditional lower sub-caste ranks already existed. The basic needs of performers and artisans and their families were provided for according to the pre-existing model of tenancy and service, ritually confirmed by the offering of gifts (*kayca*) (Moore 1983: 273ff.) and/or titles. Special ceremonial gifts were given in recognition of high achievement (Jones 1983: 31). As long as this socio-economic infrastructure remained stable, the means of supporting the newly established artistic 'tradition' were within the rights, means, and duties of land-holding royal lineages.

The initial evolution of *kathakali* into what eventually became a virtuosic dance-drama depended on close artistic collaboration between royal patrons and their Nayar soldiers-turned-performers. The royal patrons possessed the literary capabilities and aesthetic sensibilities which shaped the art as it developed; the performers, in service to a ruler, possessed the embodied ability to realize in performance what their patrons desired.

Patron as author

The first *kathakali* royal patrons were also authors of the first plays. However, not all plays in the post-Kottayam Raja period were authored by royal or elite patrons. The patron could be author and/or patronize those with literary skills. What are the regional models for royal authorship, especially of drama?

The precedent for kingly patronage and authorship is found in the early examples of two South Indian kings, Saktibhadra and Kulasekhara. Saktibhadra authored the ninth to tenth-century Sanskrit play, *Ascarayacudamani* (Jones 1984: x, 3–4) and Kulasekhara authored three eleventh- to twelfth-century Sanskrit dramas (Unni 1977).

Selected acts from these plays are still performed today as part of the *kutiyattam* temple–theater tradition. No further royal dramatists appear in the region until the emergence of *Ramanattam/kathakali* and *Krishnattam*.

In the interim, however, from the *manipravalam* literature of the thirteenth to the late fifteenth centuries, we know that rulers wrote poetry and were patrons of court writers and scholars (K.R. Nair 1971: 215–16). *Kathakali* plays (*attakatha*) were stylistically molded from a combination of the court-supported *manipravalam* tradition and the 'cantable song mold.' As discussed in Chapter 3, from their inception the plays were characterized by a high degree of poetic conceit and the assimilation of Sanskrit (Chaitanya 1971: 96). The early royal dramatists were competent in the use of Sanskrit, following a tradition of learning continued in many courts of the petty principalities from the thirteenth through the seventeenth centuries.

The association of Sanskrit learning with the ruling aristocracy is in part attributable to the close relationship between ruling castes and the ritually purer and higher ranking Namboodiri brahmins of Kerala. The legacy of Nayar/ruling class authorship as well as the eventual involvement of Namboodiris in *kathakali* is not surprising given the interdependency that existed between them. The Namboodiri practice of primogeniture, a method of inheritance assured by allowing only the eldest son to take one or more wives within his own caste, led to the requirement that all other males either remain celibate or form relationships with women from the ritually less pure but nevertheless high-ranking matrilineal royal castes (Mencher 1966b: 188). The years of interdependence affected the royal lineages.

> Namboodiri skill in Sanskrit was fostered by the local rulers who often helped subsidize Vedic sacrifices, recitations, etc. Furthermore, it was often a Namboodiri who taught Sanskrit to the children of ruling families. It should be noted in passing that, because of the close relationship between the Namboodiris and the matrilineal castes in Kerala, there was a far greater Sanskritic influence among non-Brahmins than has been noted on the east coast. Nayars, especially in Central Kerala, where the

Namboodiris were most concentrated, were strongly influenced by the daily customs of Sanskrit education; in consequence the Nayars of Kerala were far more literate than their equivalents on the east coast.

(Mencher 1966b: 187)

We should not imagine that Sanskrit education went beyond the highest-ranking ruling Ksatriya and Nayar families, nor would it have been considered appropriate for the majority of Nayars in the mid- and lower-range service *jatis* to have learned Sanskrit – at least until it became important and necessary for performance.

Although this structural relationship of interdependence and Sanskritic influence existed from the inception of *Ramanattam*, at first the performance tradition had little appeal for Namboodiris. It was only after the prince of Kottayam authored his plays, richer in poetic beauty than the *Ramanattam* cycle, that Namboodiri interest and patronage developed (Jones 1983: 22). Once their interest had been aroused, Namboodiri patronage was of course possible since they possessed both the appropriate rank and the socio-economic means to provide support for the art. As land-holders, the largest Namboodiri households could support new artists either by recruiting from the ranks of their own service castes, or by bringing new individuals into their service. Thus, we find early in *kathakali* history that Namboodiri patrons often brought to their households Nayars in service to royal families who had previously trained in the art, as exemplified by the case of Nanu Menon, nephew of Vellattu Chattu Panikkar (Jones 1983: 28). Namboodiri interest and patronage brought gradual changes to *kathakali*, strengthening its movement toward literary, poetic, and aesthetic refinement.

Patron as *rasika*/connoisseur

As mentioned earlier, the eight cycle plays in *Krishnattam* and *Ramanattam* focus on narrating the stories of their central devotional figures – Krishna and Rama. As M.P. Sankaran Namboodiri explained in a discussion,

all eight of the Ramayana plays are not so concerned with expressing *bhava*. Even the interpolations (*ilakiyattam*) are oriented

toward telling the story. These interpolations primarily fill in the details of what happens in the story.

The expansion of the repertory with the addition of the Kottayam plays and concurrent changes initiated in performance by the Kottayam Tampuran attracted Namboodiris because, in part, it shifted emphasis from dramatizing narrative to creating further opportunities for aesthetic realization, especially with expansion of opportunities to explore the erotic (*srngara*) and heroic (*vira*) sentiments in these plays.

Given the vagaries and bellicosity of the exercise of power in medieval Kerala, it is not surprising that one of the central anxieties and concerns for *kathakali*'s ruling, landholding patron–connoisseurs was that of exploring the nature of 'the heroic.' As explained further in Chapter 3, the heroic state is embodied by *kathakali*'s 'green' (*paccha*) make-up type – a class of characters which includes divine figures like Krishna, kings such as Nala and Rugmamgada, the five Pandava princes (most importantly Yudhisthira, Arjuna, and Bhima) of the Mahabharata, and Rama. The predominant 'green' color of the make-up reflects this character's basic moral uprightness, inner refinement, and calm inner poise – the 'royal

Plate 2.1 A kathakali *performance photograph from early in the twentieth century showing* pacca *(heroic/green) and* minukku *(radiant/shining) costumes and make-up typical of the period. The heroic character is probably being played by the famous actor/teacher Ittiraricha Menon Asan*

sage' of Sanskrit drama whose task as a Ksatriya is to uphold *dharma*. Within the basic type, characters range from Arjuna, Nala, and Rugmamgada, who most 'fit' the ideal, to Bhima who is something of a 'misfit.' *Kathakali* plays become arenas for playing out and reflecting the existential dilemmas that confront not only these epic heroes as they attempt to fulfill their duty, but also their everyday counterparts – the Nayars, Ksatriyas, and Namboodiris – by whom and for whom the performances were created.

As represented in most *kathakali* plays, the 'heroic' is a state dramatically marked by the hero's sacrificial act of blood-letting, usually accomplished through one-to-one combat/warfare when one or another demon, demon-king, or flawed epic villain is dispatched before the end of the performance. Fuller's assertion, noted earlier, that 'warfare itself is a reiteration of the idea that an ordered cosmos is created by sacrificial destruction' (1992: 124–5) is played out time and again on the *kathakali* stage, traditionally toward the end of the play at dawn when the killing takes place. The predominance of the ritual of battle with its numerous killings in the *kathakali* repertory is further evidence in support of Freeman's assertion that medieval Kerala battle contained a 'dominant metaphor for conceptualizing relations of spiritual and socio-political power' (1991: 588). During *kathakali* performances when stage blood is used for the disembowelment of Dussassana by Bhima, Hiranyakasipu by Narasimha, or the disfigurement of Simhika followed by the killing of Kirmira, *kathakali* can especially be seen as reflecting Kerala's 'harvest of war' where 'blood becomes the central metaphor for the essential fertilizing fluid of life' through 'the cutting of heads' or disembowelment, thereby promoting 'the health and fertility of the kingdom' (ibid.: 289). But as we shall see in Chapters 5–8, when we explore specific plays in performance, the *kathakali* stage is equally a place where these great epic heroes (often miserably) fail to fulfill both their duty and the behavioral ideals required of their station in life.

As patrons, the royal and ritual elite, including Namboodiris who became involved in the art, also played the role of ideal audience members – a role gradually defined as that of the *rasika*/connoisseur whose taste and appreciation

had to be cultivated through education. However, we need to keep in mind that even with this gradual shift toward aesthetic refinement, *kathakali* as a 'story theater' continued to appeal to a relatively broad spectrum of the population which would have been in attendance.

Patron as artistic innovator

Like Kulasekhara (Unni 1977: 189, 193–4) before them, the first *Ramanattam/kathakali* royal patrons were not only authors but also innovators, helping to shape the dance-drama in its formative years. As early as the patronage of the Vettom Tampuran a number of innovations were made in *Ramanattam*, including changing the blue make-ups of Rama and Lakshmana to emerald green, providing gilded crowns rather than the original painted palm sheath headdresses, replacing masks with painted facial make-up for the demons and monkeys, employing two singers to deliver the text and restricting the actors to speaking through hand gestures, and introducing the cylindrical *centa* drum and the cymbals (*ilattalam*) to the music ensemble (Panikkar 1993: 32).

Early in the eighteenth century Kottayam Tampuran in collaboration with his senior actor, Vellattu Chattunni Panikkar, introduced numerous other innovations. Given the increased emphasis on the expression of *bhava* in his four plays, they were careful to select *ragas* which would accentuate the mood of each section of the performance score; they increased the variety of rhythmic patterns and speeds used in performance, including slower tempos so that 'the action itself [could be] made more subtle and stylized'; and they further refined make-up and costuming, especially by adding the white rice-paste border (*chutti*) and using bright red for the lips to contrast with the dark green face and further accentuate facial expression (Panikkar 1993: 34; Jones 1983: 22–4).

During the final half of the eighteenth century the efforts of three patrons helped to crystallize *kathakali*'s basic parameters of performance and 'come of age.' Patron/performer Kaplingattu Namboodiri and the senior actor in his troupe, Ittiri Panikkar, together expanded the system of hand gestures by drawing on *kutiyattam*, and introduced the use of the important Sanskrit manual of gesture language (*Hastalaksanadipika*) as a sourcebook for *kathakali* (Jones 1983: 30–1). The patronage of the princes of two of the three largest and most powerful kingdoms in Kerala – Kartika Tirunal Rama Varma Maharaja (1724–98) of Travancore and Vira Kerala Varma (1766–1828) of Kochi (Cochin) – brought their artistic and financial resources to *kathakali*. Until he became Maharaja of Kochi in 1810, Vira Kerala Varma authored numerous plays. Kartika Tirunal Maharaja authored seven *kathakali* plays, of which *Rajasuyam* and *Narakasuravadham* remain in the popular repertory today.[5] Along with the four plays (*Rugminiswayamvaram*, *Poothanamoksham*, *Ambarishacaritam*, and *Paundrakavadham*) written by his nephew Aswati Tirunal Rama Varma (1756–94), and other new plays of the period such as *Ravanotbhavam* by Kallekkulangara Raghava Pisharody (1725–93) and *Balivijayan* by Kalloor Nambudirippad (1797–1835), the late eighteenth-century repertory popularized such very dynamic (*rajasic*) 'knife'-type anti-heroes as Ravana in *Ravanotbhavam* and *Balivijayan*, Narakasura in *Narakasuravadham*, Jarasanda in *Rajasuyam*, and Sisupala in *Rugminiswayamvaram*, whose 'amorous scenes and scenes of valour became more effective in the hands of these *rajasic* characters' (Panikkar 1993: 35). Part of what made these anti-heroes popular was the introduction and development of such specialized virtuosic interpolations as Ravana's lengthy enactment of penance (*tapassattom*), Narakasura's imaginative mimetic peacock dance (in *Narakasuravadham*), the playing of multiple roles, the lengthy descriptions of gardens, forests, and the heavens. No doubt such innovations and the growing emphasis on subtlety of expression in *kathakali* were prompted in part by Kartika Tirunal's study and expertise in the formative encyclopedia of Sanskrit dramaturgy, the *Natyasastra*, and the writing of his own Sanskrit treatise on aesthetics and dramaturgy, *Balaramabharatam* (Namboothiry 1983).

The formative seventeenth and eighteenth centuries during which *kathakali* was born, developed, and crystallized were periods of extreme military and political conflict prompted by colonial incursions into Kerala, beginning with the Portuguese in the late fifteenth century and continuing with the arrival of the Dutch, French, and English. But the traditional socio-economic infrastructure of 'house and land'

outlined previously remained basically intact. The political map of the region was most seriously affected by the Muslim invasions from Mysore in 1732 under Haydar Ali and Tippu Sultan. Their victories brought great social and political displacement and disruption as ruling families of northern Kerala fled southward (Kareem 1973; Gough 1952: 78). By the time the British vanquished Tippu Sultan, evicted the Muslim invaders from Kerala in 1792 and established their own political supremacy, the northern rulers were bereft of real political and temporal power since their armies were disbanded. The area became the Malabar District of Madras Presidency, governed by a British Collector. Displaced royal families who had fled the area were allowed to return to their lands. In both Kochi and Travancore, the maharajas continued to rule, but under the supervision of the British.

It was significant for *kathakali* patronage in the central (Kochi) and northern (Malabar) regions of Kerala that displaced royal lineages were allowed to return to their lands, and therefore to their place in the socio-economic order. In spite of the upheaval

> all the royal lineages maintained their high rank and power as important landlords, together with most of the ritual paraphernalia of their former office. Such a state of affairs was possible because the British contact had not yet radically changed the economy of Malabar.
>
> (Gough 1952: 78–9)

In Malabar, as Mencher summarized the situation, the Namboodiris in particular were little affected:

> the replacement of the traditional political structure by a new one did not in any way curtail their wealth. They were supplanted, but without land reform or any threat to their ownership of property.
>
> (1966b: 190)

The basic unit, 'house and land,' remained intact. Wealthy landholders could continue the patronage of traditional ritual and aesthetic performances they had heretofore supported, and even decide to take on patronage anew of *kathakali* by creating their own troupes (*kaliyogam*).

The situation in Travancore, southern Kerala, was quite different. There Martanda Varma Maharaja came to the Travancore throne in 1729 and reshaped the political realities of the area. During his reign (until 1758) he conquered the area from Cape Comorin to the borders of Kochi, forcing submission of all Nayar chiefs in the area, and annexing their lands.

> Their land was the principal source of their economic power, and Martanda Varma's action more or less destroyed it. By annexation is meant the transfer of *janmom* rights from individual chiefs to the Travancore state, thus reducing them to *kanamdars* of the state . . . Martanda Varma's policies were an entirely new phenomenon in Kerala . . . he laid the foundations of a modern bureaucracy.
> (Fuller 1976: 18)

In Travancore, Martanda Varma's consolidation of power and wealth made it economically, socially, politically, and aesthetically possible for future rulers like Kartika Tirunal Maharaja and others to become model royal patrons, operating with a degree of largess hitherto impossible in smaller petty principalities.

Whether in Travancore with its concentration of wealth and power, Kochi in central Kerala, or in north Malabar where, in spite of political flux and warfare, the basic socio-economic unit of 'house and land' remained intact, among royal and Namboodiri households until the late nineteenth century not only was there still sufficient wealth, but also the desire to patronize and appreciate *kathakali*.

The development of distinctive styles

One of the hallmarks of the crystallization of a tradition or genre of performance is the development of distinctive 'styles' or lineages of interpretation, practice, and performance. Japanese *noh* theater eventually produced five different 'schools', each of which continues to follow its own unique style of performance. In *kutiyattam*, lineages of performers (male *cakyars* and female *nangyars*) differ in the nuances of treatment of particular texts in performance. Like *kutiyattam*, in *kathakali* lineages of transmission from teacher to disciple are known as

sampradayam – defined as a 'traditional doctrine; a family secret' (Gundert 1872: 1040); 'a particular cultural tradition' established 'when a *guru* or set of *gurus* is recognized by a series of disciples . . . who in turn become *gurus* to the next generation' (Singer 1966: 108); and in *kathakali* as a 'particular teacher student descent group' (Jones 1983: 31). By the early to mid-nineteenth century, a number of distinctive *kathakali sampradayam*, each with their own noted actors, had developed (*Kadattanadu*, *Takayi*, *Karipuya*, etc.), but chief among them were the following two which provide the basis for the two major styles still practiced today:

1 Drawing on selected elements of both *Ramanattam* and the earlier *Kalladikkotan* styles of performance and under the strong influence of *kutiyattam*, 'Nalanunni' developed the distinctive *Kidangoor* style in Travancore,[6] southern Kerala. He did so under the patronage of Utram Tirunal Maharaja (1815–1861), the next enthusiastic patron in the line of succession to the Travancore throne after the death of Kartika Tirunal in 1798. It was during this period that *kathakali* in the south developed its emphasis on the expressive use of the face (*rasabhinaya*) in performance of *bhava*, exemplified in its concentration on developing the slow tempo in performing love scenes.

2 A 'new' composite style, *Kalluvayi*, was developed by Unniri Panikkar in 1850 under the patronage of the famous Namboodiri brahmin household at Olappamanna Mana in central Kerala. This household began patronizing its own troupe (*kaliyogam*) in 1843. This style synthesized elements of the *Kallatikkotan* and *Kaplingadan* traditions. This style continued under the patronage of Olappamanna Mana until 1905 when its troupe had to be disbanded; however, via the lineage of Ittirarissa Menon and then Pattikkantodi Ramunni Menon, this style eventually became the predominant style at the newly established Kerala Kalamandalam. It became noted for its distinctive emphasis on 'technical virtuosity' demanded by performance of the four Kottayam plays.
(Panikkar 1993: 35–7)

THE 'MATURE' YEARS:
THE ROLE OF THE RASIKA/SAHRDAYA/
CONNOISSEUR AMONG PATRONS

Royal patronage and involvement remained the mainstay of *kathakali* throughout the mid- to late-nineteenth century where rulers and/or wealthy landholding families continued to patronize *kathakali* because it had become a tradition, and/or because they took an active interest in the art. For example, the Travancore royal family continued to patronize *kathakali* since it was considered an honor, privilege, and tradition. Utram Tirunal Maharaja (b. 1815), who ruled Travancore at mid-century, authored one *kathakali* play (*Simhadhuvajacaritam*), but is best known for the fact that he himself performed on stage, and used the treasury's largess to provide support not just for one major troupe, but also for a minor second troupe until his death in 1861.

By the mid-nineteenth century all the identifiable elements which still constitute *kathakali* today (described in Chapter 3) were fully developed. The period is looked upon by many connoisseurs as *kathakali*'s aesthetic 'zenith' and 'most glorious phase' (Panikkar 1993. 44, 35) since performers and connoisseurs focused increasing attention on refinements of technique, make-up, costuming, etc., and subtleties of expression. Allowable changes took place within an increasingly narrow range than was the case when *Ramanattam* was first performed. Increased attention to the subtleties of performance and refinement, whether focused on stylistic and technical virtuosity as in the Kalluvayi style, or on *rasabhinaya* in the evolving Kidangoor/Travancore style, also began to focus on how particular actors within the 'galaxy of star performers' approached and interpreted particular roles for which they became well-known, such as Kochayyappa Panikkar's fame in 'knife' and 'black' (female) roles, or Itichenna Panikkar's achievements in 'green' heroic roles (Panikkar 1993: 38). These developments meant increased attention to, as well as scrutiny of, the nuances of acting whatever the particular *sampradayam*, and to creating new opportunities for the actor to demonstrate his virtuosity for an appreciative audience of connoisseurs.

Although Sanskrit is ubiquitous in the development of the Malayalam language *per se*, as well as in the development of *kathakali*, there can be no doubt that this trend toward refinement was part of a gradual process of further 'Sanskritization' of *kathakali* performance and its aesthetics of reception. Increased attention to the poetic beauty of textual composition first introduced by Kottayam Tampuran in his four plays, Kartika Tirunal Maharaja's study of Sanskrit aesthetics (*Balaramabharatam*), the engagement of more Namboodiris in patronage of the genre, the performative elaboration of plays like Unnayi Varryar's *Nalacaritam* with its focus on the lead character (Nala's) interior state, and the increasing influence of *kutiyattam* in the further refinement and development of *kathakali*, all contributed to this process of 'Sanskritization.' The result was a social and aesthetic process which gradually created mutually interdependent, idealized models and practices of virtuosic performance and connoisseurship based on the fundamental Sanskrit concepts of actualizing a *rasa/bhava* aesthetic through *auchityam-bodham*, or a 'sense of appropriateness.'

Although stories from the epics and *puranas* have always provided the basis for the composition of *kathakali* plays, as Chapters 3 and 4 illustrate in detail, what gradually gained precedence were the increasingly numerous opportunities for virtuosic modes of performative elaboration of the text, such as the late eighteenth-century development of plays focused on 'energetic' 'knife' characters such as Ravana and Narakasura. *Kathakali*'s various modes of elaboration expand the dramatic text and allow the various artists to display their virtuosic artistry within the prescribed limits of the form. The purpose of these elaborations is to challenge the expressive capabilities of the performers, and simultaneously to allow its patrons-as-connoisseurs to savor and relish *rasa* – the sap, juice, flavor, color, or residual essence appropriate to the character's situation in the context of the drama. The actor embodies each state of being/doing (*bhava*) through his cultivated ability to 'become' the character (see Chapter 4), and the music ensemble helps create and support each state through rhythm and musical modes, thereby serving as the vehicle to carry forward (*abhinaya*) the audience's pleasure as they taste and savor each *rasa*. As explained in more detail below, precisely how *kathakali* shapes and structures this experience is unique, and therefore the particular pleasures afforded the *kathakali* connoisseur are different from those of *kutiyattam*, or any earlier version of Sanskrit drama in performance.

It may be helpful at this point to provide one recent historical example of this process of elaboration on the dramatic text. Pattiyakkantoti Ramunni Menon (1881–1949) is considered one of the consummate *kathakali* actors and teachers of the twentieth century in the Kalluvayi style. One of his hallmark performances was the introduction of a new interpolation (*ilakiyattam*) into his performance of the role of Bhima in Kottayam Tampuran's *The Killing of Baka*. The play enacts the story of the Kauravas' attempt to have the exiled Pandava brothers killed in a fire. Ramunni Menon himself composed the 'text' which was inserted into his performance of Scene 4 of the play. The immediate dramatic context into which he set his interpolation is the moment when Dharmaputra (eldest of the Pandavas, also known as Yudhisthira) tells his brother Bhima of the trap that has been set for them. Given Bhima's character, he responds with rage (*krodha bhava*) to Dharmaputra's news. In Kottayam Tampuran's text, Dharmaputra begs Bhima to be patient. Bhima begins to recall all the cruel deeds of the Kauravas, and his fury begins to mount. It is at precisely this moment that Ramunni Menon introduced his interpolation in order to expand performatively on Bhima's internal mental struggle over their situation. The relatively one-dimensional nature of Bhima's mental state of fury in the dramatic text is expanded and further complicated. At the beginning of the interpolation Bhima asks himself, 'Why should I be patient?' The specific mood of the first line is despair over their situation. But with the enactment of each line, Bhima's fury begins to abate, and is replaced by forlornness. Seemingly pacified, Dharmaputra leaves Bhima alone. In his solitude, as Bhima reflects on their condition, his fury once again begins to grow until he reaches a point where he decides that the Kauravas must be completely destroyed.

Ramunni Menon's interpretation exemplifies the increasing focus in *kathakali* on virtuosic elaboration of the complexities of the 'internal' state of being of its major characters. When

performing this interpolation, the actor's challenge is to subtly expand on Bhima's overt fury by passing through a stage of reflective despondency. He momentarily resigns himself to his fate and to following his elder brother's orders; however, for Bhima-as-Bhima, this state does not last too long since it is characteristic for him to allow his (demonic-like) state of fury to erupt, as it eventually does in this context.

This and other interpolations discussed in Chapters 3 and 4 illustrate *kathakali*'s openness to change within the limits of what is judged 'appropriate' to the performance tradition and context of the drama, as well as the process by which such innovations become part of a text's performance history within a particular lineage (*sampradayam*) of practice. When Ramunni Menon first introduced this interpolation in performance, he did so as a recognized senior master playing a major role (*adyavasanan*) in the production; however, there was no guarantee that his interpretation would have been applauded by the connoisseurs in attendance at the first performance. When the interpolation was greeted with enthusiasm, it became part of how Rammuni Menon taught the role to his students. When he became lead teacher at the Kerala Kalamandalam, his interpolation became an essential part of how he taught such great actors as Kalamandalam Krishnan Nayar and Ramankutty Nayar to perform the role of Baka in *The Killing of Baka*, and it also became part of what an audience of connoisseurs expect to see and experience when attending a performance today.

As distinct lineages of practice and styles developed, the 'sense of appropriateness' guiding *kathakali* actors was imbibed first and foremost from one's teacher(s) and the traditional method of playing each role taught in training, as well as from observing senior actors playing a role on stage and one's own understanding of what is appropriate in the dramatic context. The degree to which performers feel constrained by, and responsible for, creating only what they consider appropriate to the context is well illustrated in the great *kutiyattam* actor Guru Ammannur Madhava Chakyar's recent account of how and why he 'modified slightly' his enactment of Bali's death scene in *The Killing of Bali* (*Balivadham*).[8] After recounting his family's traditional right to perform the play, he recalls how

Of all the actors I saw in my childhood, Kitangur Rama Chakyar, who took the role of Bali [monkey-king of Kishkindha killed by Rama's arrow in a fight with his brother, Sugriva], remains indelibly engraved in my memory. His Bali was unrivalled indeed.

(Venu 1989: iv)

Eventually, as he grew older and matured as an actor, 'the rare fortune of acting Bali descended on me,' and he was

emboldened to [make the slight modification] by the training I received from Bhagavatar Kunjunni Tampuran of the royal family of Kodungalloor. I went to Tampuran, who had done deep research in the art of drama, to learn the art strictly according to the principles laid down by Bharata [author of the authoritative *Natyasastra*]. I was his student for two years. He taught me also the minute details of climacteric breathing. This particular training took about forty days. The various *Svasas* [breaths or internal winds] . . . are controlled, one after another, appropriately to make [Bali's] death-throes realistic. This is the essence of my modification.

(Venu 1989: v)

The paradigmatic (aesthetic) past is always present for the *kutiyattam* as well as the *kathakali* actor each time he approaches any important role on stage.[9]

THE EARLY MODERN PERIOD:
THE ROLE OF PATRONS AND PATRONAGE
IN A TIME OF CRISIS

If the period until the mid-nineteenth century was *kathakali*'s heyday, then the run up to the turn of the century from approximately 1860 was a troubling period of transition – an almost schizophrenic set of ups and downs during which the seeds for the demise of the basic unit, 'house and land,' and therefore of *kathakali* patronage were sown. The growth of English education preparing a new generation for places in the shifting socio-economic order of British colonial India introduced many in the younger generation, especially among Nayar families (Fuller 1976), to

changing sensibilities, often to the disparagement of indigenous Indian social, cultural, and artistic traditions such as *kathakali*, which was represented by some as a 'dumb show.'

After the death of Utram Tirunal Maharaja in 1861 and nearly a century of lavish royal patronage and involvement in *kathakali* at the Travancore court, a string of successors took little interest in the art. Chitra Panikkar reports that Utram Tirunal's immediate successor

Ayilyam Tirunal was more interested in Carnatic music and dances by women . . . [and therefore] disbanded the palace *kaliyogam* and restricted its function to staging twenty performances a year in the Padmanabhaswami Temple at Thiruvananthapuram . . . His successor Visakhom Tirunal, who ruled for a short period, considered Western civilization superior to Indian. His successors, in turn, Sree Moolam Tirunal and Sree Chitra Tirunal, were indifferent to *kathakali* but continued with it because they did not want to discontinue a tradition.

(1993: 38)

Even though patronage at the Travancore court was on the wane, there was a general proliferation of new plays and troupes. More than fifty new plays were authored, although only four continue to be considered noteworthy by today's connoisseurs (Panikkar 1993: 38). The largest number of troupes ever founded during one period (twenty-five) were established and patronized by landholding families; however, many of these were short-lived, some only surviving a year or two. Both these developments reflect the fact that *kathakali* continued to be just as important, if not even more important, to its potential patrons and connoisseurs who struggled to support it even as their households were undergoing the traumatic fluctuations of significant socio-economic change during this period.

More indirect but important was how changing attitudes toward social customs such as marriage and the absolute authority of the eldest male (*karanavan*), who ruled extended family households, combined with socio-economic, political, and legal reforms at the turn of the century to undermine the fundamental unit, 'house and land,' and thereby lead to a rapid decline in *kathakali* patronage in the early twentieth century. Caste-based social reform movements such as the establishment of the Nayar Service Society in 1914, new forms of Malayalam popular literature such as short stories and novels addressing issues of social reform, and political movements began to question many traditional practices such as arranged or child marriages, and the disparities and injustices of Kerala's feudal, hierarchical caste-based social order. Specific changes included British-influenced reforms of marital and inheritance laws, and the attendant parcelling and partition of property between family members, both of which directly undermined the concentration of wealth in many extended upper-caste families. By the 1920s, legislative and social reform brought the virtual if not yet absolute demise of the old socio-economic order based on the unit, 'house and land.' Many if not all royal and landholding households could no longer afford to patronize troupes. There is no doubt that with a few notable exceptions such as the *kaliyogams* at Poomooli Mana, Manjeri, Kadathanad,

> By 1923 *kathakali yogams*, performers, and performances were in distress . . . [T]he art was badly in need of money, patronage, and revival.
>
> (Panikkar 1993: 38–41;
> see also Nedungadi 1990)[10]

New forms of institutional patronage and management

Into this increasing vacuum stepped the great Malayali poet, Mahakavia Vallathol Narayana Menon.[11] Steeped equally in the distinctiveness of his Kerala cultural heritage and pride as a staunch member of the swelling nationalist movement, Vallathol recognized the urgent need to find new means of support for *kathakali* before it would languish further from lack of patronage and/or interest. Expressing his concerns over the future of *kathakali* as the '"greatest treasure of the Keralites" culture trove' to the head of the Manakulam royal household near Trissur and his nephew Sri Mukunda Raja, they launched a plan to establish a new organization for the future of *kathakali*, the Kerala Kalamandalam. Their efforts began with a

series of very successful ticketed fund-raising performances in 1923, 1924, and 1925 in Alleppey, Trissur, and Kozhikode, Kerala. In 1928, they continued their fund-raising efforts with a national lottery, which eventually raised Rs. 75,000. This amount was (barely) sufficient for an official opening of their new institution, the Kerala Kalamandalam, on 9 November 1930 at its first site in a private building belonging to Sri Mukunda Raja's uncle.

The Kerala Kalamandalam was initially organized and administered by a society registered under the Cochin Registration of Literary and Scientific and Charitable Societies, Act II. Vallathol served as President, and M. Mukunda Raja as Secretary. Although plagued during these early years by an ongoing acute shortage of funds and several relocations, Vallathol nevertheless managed to attract some of the best teachers and performers of the art, including the great Guru Kunju Kurup, Sri Ambu Panikkar, Koppan Nayar, Pattikkamthodi Rammunni Menon, Kavalppara Narayanan Nayar, and Kadambur Gopalan Nayar – all teachers of acting. Equally outstanding members were selected in music and drumming.

By founding the Kerala Kalamandalam, Vallathol sought to establish a new institutional and patronage framework to support traditional *kathakali* teaching and performance, and to bridge the gap created by a decline in patronage by wealthy landholding families. The gap that the Kalamandalam filled is evident in the story that one of today's best known senior actors Vadakke Manalath Govindan (Gopi Asan) tells of his own training:

> Before I started *kathakali* training I studied *ottantullal* for a short period. This was [in 1944] at age 8 under Parameswaran Nambeesan, the elder brother of the famous *kathakali* singer (late) Neelakandhan Nambeesan. Due to certain personal reasons, I had to discontinue *ottantullal* after one year. Later on I was taken to Koodallur Mana – a prestigious, rich Namboodiri family in my village. At that time a *kathakali kalari* was conducted by one Thekkinkattil Ravunni Nayar – a very famous *kathakali* actor and the first disciple of Pattikkamthodi Ramunni Menon. I joined that *kalari*. All my

expenses were met by the Namboodiri family. After one year I performed my *arannettam* (inaugural performance) as Kusa, son of Sita, in *Lavanasuravadham*. Again, due to my bad luck, my *kathakali* training had to be terminated. Then I went to a formal academic education in a nearby school. After one year, on the advice of the above Kalamandalam Neelakandhan Nambeesan, I was asked to come for an interview at the Kalamandalam (in 1951) where I was selected at a student. Thus I began my training at Kalamandalam.

(joint interview conducted by M.P. Sankaran Namboodiri in 1993)

Vallathol knew intuitively that his goal of preserving *kathakali* could only be realized by rekindling interest in and appreciation of the art at a local level among Malayalis as a marker of their identity, at a 'national' level as a marker of a distinctively Indian national identity, and at an international level by gaining recognition for *kathakali* as one 'classical' art among the world's great classical arts. Faced with a continual shortage of funds, Vallathol took the Kalamandalam troupe on tour to other parts of India with a 1932 performance at the Mysore palace (Menon 1978: 79–80) as well as abroad – a step which was both bold and fraught with difficulties.[12] From meagre savings made while touring, and on a permanent site acquired from the then Government of Kochi on the banks of the Bharathapurzha River in the village of Cheruthuruthy, Trissur District, in 1936 classes opened in a set of new buildings.

In spite of the recognition brought by national and international tours, and its initial success in teaching *kathakali* to a new generation of young performers, with no permanent financial subsidy, a meagre income, and paltry public donations, the Kalamandalam simply could not meet operating costs. In 1941 the Kerala Kalamandalam was officially handed over to the Government of Kochi; however, poet Vallathol remained in control as President, Art Director, and head of a governing committee.

It was not until the visit of then Prime Minister, Pandit Jawaharlal Nehru, to the Kalamandalam in 1955 for the Silver Jubilee Celebrations that more substantive financial assistance and national recognition came to the economically troubled Kalamandalam. Nehru donated one lakh of rupees toward the institution's further development. At the same time the Central Sangeet Natak Akademi in New Delhi also made grants to the institution. In 1957, on Vallathol's special request, the Kalamandalam was placed under Kerala State government management, and under the direct control of the District Collector, Trissur. An advisory committee was established, an executive officer was appointed to administer the institution on a day-to-day basis, the student body and teaching staff were expanded, and Kerala State subsidies for the institution were substantially raised. Riding the initial wave of heady enthusiasm which was part of Kerala State's initial formation as a distinctive socio-linguistic and political entity, this decision of state government sponsorship seemed not only necessary at the time, but also right.

Since then the Kalamandalam has existed as a grant-in-aid institution under the management of the Kerala State government. Each year the government makes a lump sum grant, with supplemental income made from performances. In 1963, the Kalamandalam was reconstituted as an Academy of Arts and began to offer training in other arts, including *ottantullal*, *Mohiniattam* (already on offer at this time), *bharatanatyam*, and classical music. *Kutiyattam* training was added later as a course of study. In 1973, a new, expanded campus known as 'Vallathol Nagar,' was opened on thirty-two acres east of the village of Cheruthuruthy. The student body expanded, as did the campus, from four students studying *kathakali* at its inception to today's student body of well over one hundred.

Today the administration of the Kalamandalam is in the hands of a General Council with members drawn from other state academies, as well as members of the Lok Sabha (parliament) and Kerala State legislative assembly. An executive committee carries out the actual administration under the leadership of a chairman. The secretary and the main executive officer and treasurer are appointed directly by the current state government in office.

Since the founding of the Academy in the 1960s, the governing bodies have ensured that students receive a fundamental general education in addition to their training in a traditional performing art, and in the 1990s this took the form of gaining a pass in VII Standard, or a high school certificate. The introduction of general education was motivated by a desire to provide a sufficient level of education so that Kalamandalam graduates not finding employment as performing artists would nevertheless improve their chances of other means of employment. However, this has also meant a reduction in hours and energy available for study of *kathakali* and other performing arts (Gopalakrishnan 1992b: 24–5). Most recently, the Kalamandalam is on the verge of undergoing further institutional rebirth as a 'university,' a move which has been widely debated in the local Malayalam press.

Although at the time of the founding of the Kalamandalam new forms of patronage and institutional organization were necessary to fill a vacuum, state government patronage *per se* has become a doubled-edged sword. From its founding and through the early 1980s, there is no doubt that the Kalamandalam continued to be the crown-jewel among the various new institutional forms of patronage founded to maintain and develop *kathakali*; however, as the Kalamandalam has grown in size, scope, bureaucratic complexity, and as certain changes in its goals were instituted – from strict 'traditional' training in a traditional art to multiple educational functions (degree certification as well as training) – different problems began to emerge. Some of these problems have been 'educational,' such as the shift from the more traditional mode of training under one (or perhaps two) master teacher(s), so that the student gradually embodied the distinctive style (*sampradayam*) of his teacher's lineage, to a graded curriculum where the *kathakali* student trains each year in a six year curriculum with a different teacher.

Just as vexing has been the increasing politicization of the Kalamandalam as an institution. As K.K. Gopalakrishnan explained in a recent retrospective on the Kalamandalam and its problems,

> As a State institution, Kalamandalam derives benefit, especially financial support, but it also suffers from political interference, especially when the Government changes . . . Some of the Committee members are purely and simply politicians. Regrettably, not seldom the criticisms they offer smack of politics rather than reflect a constructive approach; and, in the last decade especially, they have often revealed a streak of malice as well.
>
> (1992b: 23; see also Olappamanna Subrahmanian Nambudirippad in Nair and Panikar 1993: 48)

The fractiousness of Kerala's contemporary political scene is reflected in the anomie that has sometimes gripped the Kalamandalam in recent years – an anomie which has all too often become commonplace not just at the Kalamandalam, but also at many other government institutions. Many students, faculty, and staff are organized along political lines reflecting Kerala major political parties/factions, and classes have often been disrupted by strikes, protests, and/or boycotts. The rash of social, economic, and political problems accumulating during the 1980s have contributed to a lack of a clear and distinct vision for today's Kalamandalam and for its future, and it is difficult for even strong leaders dedicated to reform to solve what appear to be intractable problems.[13] It remains to be seen whether in today's political climate, any such state supported institution can clearly and fully accomplish the type of nascent goals that Vallathol envisioned for the Kalamandalam at its founding.

Whatever the recent problems at the Kalamandalam, there is no doubt that Vallathol's visionary founding of this institution in 1930 provided a completely new model of non-traditional patronage which inspired others.[14] The Sri Muthappan Kathakali Yogam was founded in 1938 by P.M. Kunhi Raman, a trustee of the Sri Muthappan Temple in Parassinikkadavu, Kannur District, and historically patronized a very small troupe and local training in the 'northern' style of *kathakali*. In 1939, philanthropist, physician, artist, and businessman Vaidyaratnam P.S. Varier founded a small but important *kathakali* performing company and training institution, the P.S.V. Natyasangham. Along with his other charitable enterprises, the Natyasangham is well subsidized from the profits of the Arya Vaidya Sala – Kerala's most profitable and well-known Ayurvedic medical factory and hospital. Two schools/companies drawing their inspiration and teaching style from the early Kalamandalam model were the Unnayi Warrier Smaraka Kalanilayam (1955) and F.A.C.T. Kathakali School, Udyogmandal (1965). Each has a quite different form of organization and patronage: the first as an independent non-profit cultural organization run by an administrative committee of fifteen; the second as a 'Cooperative Society' at Udyogmandal set up under the inspiration of the then managing director of Fertilisers and Chemicals, Travancore, Ltd. (F.A.C.T.).

Arguably today's most visible, well organized and funded, and important *kathakali* training and performance company is Margi[15] – the distinguished private non-profit cultural organization originally founded in 1969 under the leadership of D. Appukuttan Nair. At first Margi limited its activities to preparing selected publications on Kerala's classical arts, and to presenting regularly scheduled stage performances of *kathakali* and other traditional Kerala performing arts in the capital city, Thiruvananthapuram, since the organizers perceived that 'there was a vacuum' and need for such performances. In 1974, Margi modestly began to expand its program from sponsorship of *kathakali* and other traditional performances to the establishment of its own teaching and performance company in the 'southern Kerala style.' Some assistance came in part from Kerala government subsidies, and instruction began when Mankulam Vishnu Namboodiri was hired as the first regular teacher, bringing with him two students of acting. By 1976 the school/troupe consisted of the artistic director who taught four students of acting several times each month, a junior actor/teacher who took full responsibility for the day-to-day training of the students, and teachers of *centa*, *maddalam*, vocal music, and a part-time make-up artist. Training and housing for students and teachers were provided in quarters managed by the Devaswam (temple) Board of Travancore in the old East Fort area of the city near the main and quite grand Vishnu temple, the Sri Padmanabhaswamy Temple.

As more and more financial and political problems began to plague the state-supported Kalamandalam during the 1980s and as its vision and collective energy seemed to dissipate in internal disputes and struggles, Margi, quite in contrast, flourished. It was something of an artistic 'coup' when Margi hired the extraordinary actor Kalamandalam Krishnan Nayar in 1980 to teach Margi's students as a master–teacher in residence once per month. Noted for his expertise in roles requiring an understanding and embodiment of the nuances of facial expression and depth of psychological interpretation of roles, Krishnan Nayar's teaching until his death in 1990 helped solidify and legitimize Margi's role as a teaching and performance institution specializing in the southern style. Furthermore, the predominantly male and most active members of Margi are aged over fifty-five, retired, and living on pensions; therefore, they are able to devote their free time to their interest in *kathakali* and other traditional arts. Since its members and leaders were all volunteers motivated by their knowledge and/or love for *kathakali*, their collective energy can be focused solely on artistic goals free from the (overt) political pressures faced by the Kalamandalam with its political appointees, paid staff, etc.

THE RECENT PAST:
CONTEMPORARY CONNOISSEURSHIP AND
A 'THEATER OF THE MIND'

In this final section of the social history of *kathakali*, I analyse Margi's institutional, discursive, and performative construction of *kathakali* aesthetics, reception, and connoisseurship in order to understand how these formations both construct and are constructed by contemporary 'cultural politics' of Kerala.

Perhaps the most important long-term result of the breakdown of traditional patronage has been the disruption of the process of artistic and creative interaction which developed between learned, high-caste patron/connoisseurs and the *kathakali* artists in their service. However inconsistent the process may have been, and however dependent on the idiosyncratic interest of individual rulers/landholders, the development and refinement of *kathakali* artistry within particular lineages of practice through the end of the nineteenth century owed much if not all to this process of interaction. The founding of the Kalamandalam temporarily sutured this rupture as long as those in administrative positions at the Kalamandalam remained learned literary figures like Vallathol himself, or individuals like

Vasudevan Namboodiripad (long-term superintendent) whose knowledge of both Sanskrit aesthetics and *kathakali* meant that there was mutual respect between senior artists and institutional leaders.

Sensing that *kathakali* was becoming artistically moribund and unable to explore its creative potential due to the breakdown in this relationship, Margi has modelled its most recent creative process on the interaction between patron–author/connoisseurs and artists of the past. It brings together learned scholar/connoisseurs like Ganesha Iyer with the performance skills and imagination of its artists in order to 'restore the arts to their former glory by enabling revivals, creative elaborations through a poetic treatment, etc.' and to do so by providing 'a constant challenge to the creative talents of the artistes in every production and performance' (Damodaran 1996: 5). When Margi received a major grant from the central government of 5 lakhs rupees in 1991, it redefined itself as operating as a *kaliyogam*, and has been able to support full-time *kathakali* and *kutiyattam* troupes in which

> continuous training and performance go on side by side throughout the lifetime of the artistes [who remain] together as a well knit cohesive unit, which leads to high level production values.
>
> (Damodaran 1996: 5)

More than any other contemporary *kathakali* organization, Margi self-consciously and assiduously attempts to reproduce as closely as possible the kind of creative stimulation and interaction which fostered new developments in the history of *kathakali* and *kutiyattam*, and therefore represents itself as restoring 'the standard of *kathakali* performances to its days of glory' (see Warrier in Nair and Paniker 1993: 49).

Margi views and represents itself as counteracting the 'general decline in the popularity of classical arts' through its self-conscious program of reviving complete *kathakali* and *kutiyattam* plays or scenes of plays no longer performed (Damodaran 1996: 1). To counteract the editing and shortening of plays in performance (see Chapters 3 and 4), Margi has returned to the original dramatic texts, and in 1995 presented two of the original four Kottayam plays in their entirety: *The Flower of*

Good Fortune lasted for six nights, and *The Killing of Baka* for eight.[16] Margi's versions not only 'restored' the scenes seldom if ever performed today, but also added new opportunities for elaboration, thus making them even longer than usual.

Another of Margi's major goals has been to elaborate further on Unnayi Varryar's four-part series of plays, *King Nala's Law* (*Nalacaritam*), by conducting detailed research on the play and its sources guided by life-long Sanskrit scholar Ganesha Iyer. Based on this research and working rehearsals, they drew on 'related literature' to develop and/or expand upon interpolations in each of the four plays (Damodaran 1996: 2). The results have included publication of performance manuals for the new, expanded versions, and public performances in which the four parts of the play have been extended to twelve nights of performance each.

Also during 1995, Margi revived three of the original eight *Ramanattam* plays no longer in the active repertory, including *Vichinnabhishekom*, *Kharavadham*, and *Sethubandhanam*. For some scenes detailed performance scores (*attaprakaram*) were prepared. The results were twelve nights of performance for *Vichinnabhishekom*, ten for *Kharavadham*, and ten for *Sethubandhanam*. All of these revivals and further elaborations are accomplished through a two-part process. Ganesha Iyer and Appukutthan Nair study the dramatic text, refer to any/all relevant *puranic* source material which might be elaborated, and prepare new texts for interpolation into the dramatic text. At daily rehearsals the scholar/connoisseurs work with the actors as they go through each section of the text and/or a new interpolation, and work out the details for its performative elaboration, always guided by the fundamental principle of what is considered 'appropriate' to the context. The increasingly well-known actor of female roles Margi Vijayakumar said with great admiration of his interactions with the learned Ganesha Iyer: 'Swami. If *you* were an actor on stage knowing as much as you do, you would never leave the stage!'

Margi's 1990s vision has increasingly focused on providing ongoing, life-long training for a small company of performers, and informed exploration of *kathakali*'s aesthetic potential by catering 'not to the interest of the masses, but to rare discerning *rasikas* possessed of an aesthetic clairvoyance in judging histrionics' (Warrier, in Nair and Paniker 1993: 52). Most of Margi's 'experimental' revivals or performative elaborations are staged either in their intimate indoor performance area, or in their small outdoor theater with perhaps twenty to a maximum of forty members and the odd occasional visiting dignitary or foreigner in attendance. In either of these intimate spaces,

> The audience can closely observe the subtle expressions of a performer's eyes and face, and the very slow movements of the body, for which Margi has earned a reputation.
> (see Warrier in Nair and Paniker 1993: 52)

Margi's self-conscious attempt to resurrect what it interprets as the aesthetic and artistic essence of *kathakali*'s past in the present is very much a part of a general post-colonial South Asian search for and reclamation of its own distinctive indigenous aesthetic and heritage over the West which began in the 1970s, and is reflected in the pan-Indian search for a 'theater of roots' (Awasthi 1989). Margi is an organization whose philosophy and institutional practice epitomize this trend, and its garnering of difficult to secure grants, both government and private, exemplify the success of their endeavor. There should be no doubt that Margi has been rejuvenating *kathakali* with a renewed sense of the possibilities for the imaginative engagement of its actors and connoisseurs alike in issues of interpretation and reconstruction. As Marlene Pitkow points out, this is nowhere more in evidence than in Margi's 'enlightened view' of the importance of further developing the potential in female roles in the repertory (1998: 112). As Margi Vijayan enthusiastically explained to me in a 1993 interview about Margi's further elaboration and reconstruction of traditional texts such as *Nalacaritam*, 'Before I simply performed what was in the written text. Usually incidents happen one after another. We have to show hand-gesture after hand-gesture, rushing through! But now, here, there is no rush, no time limitation. We have time to think!' It is clear that the actors involved with Margi are relishing the new opportunities and creative challenges offered them.

Expanding on the concept of appropriateness, and drawing on other traditional aesthetic concepts in order to define itself, G.S. Warrier clearly articulates Margi's aesthetic and legitimizes it when he writes:

> The concepts of *margi* and *desi* styles as applied to arts such as music and dance have been enunciated in India from ancient times. While the *desi* style is bounded by space and time, with consequent limitations in aesthetics, *margi* transcends space and time to provide lasting and boundless rapture. Margi at Tiruvananthapuram, was an institute conceived to comply with the latter.
> (quoted in Nair and Paniker 1993: 49)

As announced in the title, the 1993 publication of the extraordinarily beautiful book *Kathakali: The Art of the Non-Worldly*, edited by D. Appukuttan Nair and K. Ayappa Paniker, articulates Margi's view of *kathakali*'s aesthetic as epitomized in the concept of the 'non-worldly.' Appukuttan Nair and Paniker assert that

> Among the various performing arts in India, and perhaps, even the world, *kathakali* is unique in so far as it is one of the farthest from earthly reality and humanism. There is no attempt at representing the mundane world in any manner – whether by imitation or otherwise. Only epic, non-human beings are chosen for the re-creation of a story for presentation on the stage. And that presentation, whether in form, colour, behaviour, or sound, is deliberately made contra-human, to exist in another world: that of the imagination of the connoisseur . . . *Kathakali* takes the connoisseur away from the transient worldly experience of pleasure to one of transcendental entrancement.
> (1993: x)

Appukuttan Nair further defines this 'non-worldly' aesthetic and how only the connoisseur can

> experience bliss which is non-dual, at which level there is no difference between beauty and ugliness; it is the realm where art and anti-art co-exist . . . This point of bliss is also the level of divine art – that is, art beyond art . . . The dualistic realm of art is not pleasing to a philosopher-

appreciator. The supreme *sahrdayan* seeks the non-dualistic variety of art, where the artiste, the art-form, and the connoisseur become one.

(ibid.: 4)

Appukuttan Nair argues that any discussion of *kathakali* must take into account 'the difference between the experience of the real world and the experience of art performed on the stage' where the connoisseur can experience this transcendental, non-dualistic world 'through its performance alone' (ibid.: 3). In one of our many lengthy discussions, Ganesha Iyer explained to me how this aesthetic operates:

> When the actor enacts certain *rasas*, they are able to create a sympathetic motion in my heart. When he enacts a sorrowful aspect, I do not experience [the emotion of] sorrow but appreciate his [artistic] expression of sorrow . . . I experience sympathetic vibration. But in some people, they may experience this as a *real* emotion . . . When a very sorrowful scene is enacted, some may weep . . . This difference may be due to having a more intellectual appreciation, and not emotional.

The aesthetic experience described here is part of a cultural paradigm which is implicitly understood, over time, to 'discipline' the practitioner's sensibilities, whether through yoga, practising a martial or performance discipline, or practising connoisseurship by attending performances. According to this paradigm, one's sensibilities begin at the grossest, physical/emotional, most external level, and through a gradual process of education and/or disciplined training one moves toward a subtler, more refined internal mode of appreciation and/or action. Appukuttan Nair concludes his own lengthy discussion of *kathakali* as a 'three-dimensional poetic art' by making the following claims:

> only a *tattwabhinivesi* (philosophically-oriented person) will be able to fully appreciate a *kathakali* performance . . . Only a select few can bring themselves to imbibe the essence of . . . [*kathakali*'s most aesthetically subtle and challenging roles] . . . While the actor puts to conscious use his innate skill which is enhanced by constant practice, the connoisseur engages

in the super-conscious act of receiving and appreciating every single aspect of the performance. He is therefore to be considered superior to the performing artiste. It is the innate poetic sensibility of the connoisseur which enables him to understand the relevance of the *eklochana* (expression of two different emotions in two eyes which is made to appear simultaneous) in *kathakali*, where two contradictory *rasas* are expressed with each eye, alternatingly and continually. The artiste, with conscious movements and regular practice, makes such an action possible, but it requires the supreme imagination of the spectator to visualize these eye movements as simultaneous. The *kathakali eklochana* is thus meaningful only when its reach extends to the learned connoisseur.

(Nair and Paniker 1993: 16–17)

Like other privileged aesthetic discourses, the discursive constructs of 'appropriateness' and 'theater of the mind' cloak themselves in the guise of what is 'natural,' 'right,' and in this case 'traditional.' There is no doubt that Margi is doing yeoman service today preserving, and I would argue even regenerating, a sense of creativity and imagination in *kathakali* interpretation and performance. Having acknowledged this, from a critical perspective, it is crucial to remember that the principles of 'appropriateness' and developing a 'theater of mind' guiding Margi reflect the ideal experience and spectatorial practices of today's educated connoisseur, and that they are therefore not 'disinterested' or 'natural' since they hide their historical construction (or reconstruction) and implicit privilege behind their elegant elaboration of a non-dualistic, transcendental mode of reception/appreciation. Part of what is left unsaid in these discursive formations is how a connoisseur/*rasika*/*sahrdayan* attains the optimal state of 'aesthetic clairvoyance,' who is left out of 'legitimate' appreciation, and what forms of experimentation are rejected out of hand and/or excluded from serious consideration.

Aesthetic appreciation is not of course in-born, but encultured and/or learned. This is nowhere better exemplified than in the story of Rama Iyer, current Treasurer of Margi. Unlike Ganesha Iyer, Prabodhadhanran Nayar, or G.S.

Warrier, who were all born into families of *kathakali* appreciators and attended performances from childhood, Rama Iyer did not really take much of an interest in *kathakali* until *after* he got involved in the administration of Margi on its founding in 1970.

> In 1970 I knew only the skeleton of *kathakali*. Before that I may have only occasionally glanced at *kathakali* and had found it boring. I was chief financial officer for Appukuttan Nayar at the government engineering office. He knew how much I loved karnatic music, and he envied my knowledge of the music modes (*ragas*). So he asked me to help out administratively with his new organization, Margi. Since at first I didn't understand what was happening during much of the *kathakali* performances, I found it boring; however, since I had an ear for music, especially when Nambisan sang, I would love the music. I also liked the dance because of the accent on rhythm. So very imperceptibly over the years, I slowly started going through the [Malayalam text of] the *padams*.
>
> (personal interview)

Rama Iyer's lack of an initial understanding and appreciation of *kathakali* also stemmed from his lack of formal education in both Malayalam and Sanskrit language, literature, and poetry. Indeed, he had never read or listened closely to *kathakali*'s play texts prior to becoming involved in Margi. He has evolved into a fairly knowledgeable connoisseur through his years of 'education' and association with Margi, and has gradually come to a point where his level of appreciation can begin to approach that of the ideal *rasika*.

One of the ways in which Margi educates its members and guests toward the ideal practices of connoisseurship outlined above is by providing an ongoing translation of either the new interpolations or the expanded ways of performing lines of the text developed during company rehearsals and overseen by Appukuttan Nayar and Ganesha Iyer. At many performances I attended during 1993, Appukuttan Nayar vividly and energetically performed his knowledge of the new segments of a performance by explaining each poetic image and its meaning as it was

performed to three or four less knowledgeable members or special guests. For some in the Margi audience, the pleasure of a performance is not simply the individual pleasure of experiencing/tasting *rasa* and appreciating the actor's performance, but also the collective social pleasure of openly displaying and/or being educated into a state of knowledge and understanding. One of the ideal pleasures performed by Appukuttan Nayar and others is the connoisseur's ability to simultaneously recognize, understand, and therefore be able to explain to the less initiated the nuances of *kathakali*'s complex poetic images and references, especially in its interpolations.

As an individual with much less knowledge than that of Appukuttan Nayar or Rama Iyer, I too have always needed such translation and explanation, whether during or after a performance, so there is no question that education and enculturation into the nuances of *kathakali* regularly takes places through such translations and is welcome to whose who seek it out. What is not at first evident in the benign representation of this interaction as 'education' or 'enculturation' is the location of expertise from the actor to the connoisseur/patron, where ultimately the connoisseur is considered 'superior to the performing artiste' (Nair and Paniker 1993: 17).

A second aspect of the 'unsaid' of these aesthetic discourses is their historical development. Although their roots certainly are in the *bhava-rasa* aesthetic first articulated in the *Natyasastra* and long associated with and developed in conjunction with Sanskrit poetics, a transcendental interpretation of this aesthetic and its reception was not developed until Abhinavagupta wrote his commentary in the twelfth century. This transcendental interpretation has been further (re)elaborated in today's discursive articulation of an indigenous aesthetic of the 'theater of the mind' appealing to the ideal *rasika/sahrdayan*; however, it should be remembered that there could have been no 'ideal' connoisseurs as defined by a 'theater of the mind' when *Ramanattam* and then *kathakali* were first given birth since, in their nascent form, they were still in formation toward the kind of refinements not crystallized until the mid-nineteenth century. The radical non-dualistic transcendentalism explicit in Margi's discourse is a contemporary historical (re) definition and crystallization of this fundamental aesthetic concept and mode of reception.

As clearly expressed by Ganesha Iyer above, the development of today's 'theater of the mind' is similar to the development in the West of an 'aesthetic of disinterestedness' (Morgan 1998: 26–9) which garners to itself exclusive power to define what that experience can and should be, where judgements of taste and acceptability are based on a cultivated consciousness and competence, and which therefore rejects the overt sentimentality of 'real tears.' When *kathakali* is discussed as a 'classical' art (most often by Westerners), it is suggested that this form is an art of the elite and educated connoisseurs to the exclusion of the everyday and mundane, and that it could be of little interest to non-connoisseurs. When *kathakali* is exclusively discussed as a 'theater of the mind' requiring a 'higher' consciousness and aesthetic sensibility, it clearly disparages the 'lower,' 'sensual,' 'worldly,' 'uneducated,' or 'everyday' modes of appreciation encompassed by the folk expression discussed in

Chapter 1, which welcomes all to the 'ocean' of possibilities of reception. It clearly leaves out or disparages many of the plays that women in particular enjoy and appreciate, such as *The Progeny of Krishna.*

Finally, for Appukuttan Nayar, some of the entailments of his definition of a 'theater of the mind' are clearly delineated in opposition to some of the recent experiments and developments in *kathakali* production that he, and Margi, vociferously oppose. In Olappamanna Subrahmanian Nambudirippad's contribution to *Kathakali: The Art of the Non-Worldly* on the Kerala Kalamandalam, he criticizes the Kalamandalam for its 'adoption of unsuitable themes for *kathakali*,' a clear reference to the Kalamandalam's involvement in the 1989 highly controversial production of *Kathakali King Lear* (Nair and Paniker 1993: 48). A complex web of political history and current cultural politics are reflected in this criticism, and are fully analysed in Chapters 9 and 10 of this book where the details of two experiments and reactions against them are delineated.

kathakali texts in performance

INTRODUCTION

Performance systems like *kathakali* are organized around the production of its 'score' for the aesthetic engagement of its publics. A performance score consists of all the units which structure the performance, as well as the conventions and techniques used to bring that structure to realization through enactment, embodiment, etc. A performance is structured by its various compositional units, including dramatic texts, choreography, composed music, scenarios which structure improvisation, etc. Performance scores vary widely in the degree to which they are 'set.' In contrast to modern, contemporary, or post-modern performance, genres like Western ballet, Japanese *noh*, or *kathakali* are often identified as 'traditional' because they have relatively 'set' scores. As discussed in Chapter 2, for aesthetic, historical, as well as socio-cultural reasons, their performance structure, conventions, and techniques change only slightly from performance to performance through elaboration, refinement, and the relatively slow process of innovation through changes in nuances of technique, adaptations in costume, etc.[1]

For genres like *kathakali* and Japanese *noh*, which construct their performances around a dramatic text, the play assumes central, but not sole, importance in the historical development of the performance score and its structure. Both *kathakali* and *noh* dramas are highly regarded

poetic works composed according to specific literary conventions. Each play is recognized as a discrete, individually authored work capable of judgement as a dramatic work on the basis of the quality, beauty, and originality of its poetic language; therefore, some *kathakali* plays like *Nalacaritam* or the four Kottayam plays (including *The Flower of Good Fortune* and *The Killing of Kirmira*) are occasionally read in their entirety and appreciated for their literary and poetic qualities. The literary and poetic conventions which guide composition of a play are one set of constraints which shape the structure of the text in performance.

But when a *kathakali* drama is brought to the stage, the literary text is only the beginning point in the construction of the performance score for the performers; therefore, a *kathakali* drama is best thought of as a 'base' text that has been added to and subtracted from over the years since its first production. Since elaboration is such a fundamental aesthetic principle, every aspect of a *kathakali* performance is shaped by a variety of modes and styles of performative and/or narrative elaboration.

In this chapter and in Chapter 4 I examine the processes by which *kathakali* texts and their 'traditional' performance scores are elaborated and brought into performance on the stage today. In this chapter I describe performance and literary conventions, techniques, and structural units, as well as the processes of editing and adaptation which guide, constrain, and affect how an 'original' play is expanded or contracted when performed. In Chapter 4 I describe the actor's process of training, embodiment, and characterization through which he elaborates the text and its basic moods, and actualizes *kathakali*'s aesthetic.

TEXTUAL CONVENTIONS AND THE PERFORMANCE SCORE

The play-text and the performance score

If you were to read a complete translation of all fourteen scenes of Kottayam Tampuran's *The Flower of Good Fortune*, and then attend a performance, you might become confused when the performance begins not with Scene 1 and the appearance of the angry Bhima before his elder brother, Dharmaputra but, rather, with Scene 9 where Bhima and Draupadi appear 'ripe for amorous games' in the forest (see Chapter 5). You might also be surprised that the performance ends at the conclusion of Scene 10 with the humbling of Bhima's pride before the wise and valorous chief of the monkeys, Hanuman, rather than continue through Scene 14 when Bhima finally returns home to deliver the 'Flower of Good Fortune' to Draupadi. You might wonder what happened to scenes 1–8 and 11–14. Although we can assume that when Kottayam Tampuran oversaw the first performance of his play sometime during the early eighteenth century it included all fourteen scenes, today you are likely to see a performance which includes between two and five of the play's scenes – either Scenes 9 and 10, or at the most Scenes 1, 9, 10, 13, and 14.

By the same token, you might be equally surprised when Scene 9 does not end as does the 'original' literary text with Bhima's declaration to Panchali:

O beautiful deer-eyed one,
without hesitation I shall fetch the
    graceful Saugandhika flowers which
    you desire . . .

Rather, the scene continues for another thirty to sixty minutes as the senior actor playing the role of Bhima holds center stage for a *tour de force* set-piece of 'mono-acting' in which he elaborates what Bhima sees on his trip through the forest, including a fight between an elephant, python, and lion. Added to the original literary text, interpolations (*ilakiyattam*) like this are so much a part of the popular 'tradition' of performing the play that it would be unthinkable not to include them; indeed, connoisseurs go to performances to watch their favorite actors performing these 'star turns.' Maintained by performers within their lineages of transmission (*sampradaya*), the interpolations are as much a part of a text's performance score as the original literary text.

Like the plays of Aeschylus or Shakespeare, texts at first performed fully in their 'original' context are often adapted and/or edited to meet the desires and needs of historically variable audiences in ever-changing contexts. In the Hellenistic period the emphasis of performance shifted from the fifth century BC Athenian festival context, where a unified program of three tragedies and a satyr play were authored and presented by competing playwright/producers, to an emphasis upon individual 'star' performers, for whose benefit the earlier Greek tragedies were adapted and modified in performance. A similar phenomenon occurred when Shakespeare's plays became vehicles for 'star' performers during the Restoration and eighteenth century theaters of England. The result was that Shakespeare's plays were not played in their 'entirety' again until the nineteenth century. Many *kathakali* plays, including the four translated here, are usually 'edited' for performance today, shortening them from all-night performances to three- or four-hour performances featuring 'star' performers in favorite roles such as Bhima and Hanuman in *The Flower of Good Fortune.* Although there are still all-night performances of single *kathakali* plays, it is more typical to attend all-night performances of three shortened plays, each focusing on scenes of interest to connoisseurs, or performance of a single shortened play that allows the audience to reach home at a reasonable time rather than staying for an all-night performance.

Kathakali's 'typical' performance structure and score

To summarize, the performance score for each *kathakali* play is structured not only by the sub-units of the dramatic composition to be performed, but also by the other compositional units of performance (interpolations and set pieces of choreography), which elaborate upon specific moments in the dramatic narrative. Figure 3.1 is a schematic figure of *kathakali*'s structure based on a 'typical' love scene between a hero and heroine in a play – Scene 9 in *The Flower of Good Fortune*. Included in the figure and briefly explained below are the textual sub-units, units of dance composition, and the interpolations which together constitute the basic structure of a *kathakali* performance score.

Textual sub-units

Kathakali plays interweave two major types of poetic composition:

1   The narrative sections of the text set in third-person, usually composed in Sanskrit metrical verses known as *sloka* (or the slightly different form known as *dandaka*), and sung by the onstage vocalists.
2   The first-person dialogue and/or soliloquy passages (*padam*) composed in a mixture of Sanskrit and Malayalam as dance music for delivery and interpretation by the actors.

The descriptive, third-person narrative passages link together sets of poetic images that modify and elaborate upon the main subject. For example, at the beginning of Scene 10 in *The Flower of Good Fortune*, the first two of the three *sloka* that begin the scene poetically elaborate on Bhima's 'lustre' and 'strength,' and also the 'terror' which he instills in all those who encounter him.

Both narrative and dialogue are set to specific musical modes (*raga*) appropriate to the mood and dramatic context; however, only the dialogue/soliloquy parts of the texts are set to specific rhythmic patterns (*tala*) and tempos (*kala*). Composers of *kathakali* plays set each scene in the musical mode and/or rhythm they consider most appropriate for capturing the mood they want to evoke in the audience. Since *sloka* are sung by the vocalists without percussion background, they allow the vocalists great freedom of interpretation outside the constraints of rhythmic pattern and speed. Unfettered by rhythm and speed, the vocalists elaborate their vocal interpretation of the poetry

on the long syllables of any word within the limits of what is appropriate to the context and musical mode. Roughly 80 percent of the *sloka* are sung without actors onstage and set the mood and narrate the context for the scene which follows. When the actors perform during the singing of a *sloka*, they enact the essence of what the singers are narrating.

All *padam* are performed by the actor-dancers, constitute the 'dialogue' of the play, and occupy a majority of a performance's duration. When *padam* are performed, the entire ensemble is involved as the lines are sung by the vocalists, the actor-dancers 'speak' each line with hand gestures as well as enact the narrative, and the percussionists set and keep the basic rhythmic structures and times within which the lines are sung/spoken/enacted. Each *padam* usually has three parts: the *pallavi* (refrain), *anupallavi* (subrefrain), and *caranam* (literally 'foot'). While the *anupallavi* may be omitted from a *padam*, there are usually several *caranam*. As we shall see in detail later, it is in the performance of the *padam* that we encounter *kathakali*'s characteristic form of repetitious double-acting of each line of the text. As a general rule, each line of a *padam* is enacted at least twice by the actor-dancer while the line is sung repeatedly by the vocalists.

Units of dance composition

Other basic compositional units which contribute to *kathakali*'s basic performance structure are the two major types of choreography described earlier:

1   The 'accentuating/linking' dances (*kalasam*, etc.), which accentuate the mood of a scene and link sections of a performance.
2   The longer pieces of set choreography like battles, which push the narrative forward, or the 'peacock' dance, which, like interpolations, takes a temporary 'time out' from the narrative to elaborate a mood in dance.

One important example of a lengthy piece of 'set choreography' is Kirmira's preparation for battle at the end of Scene 13 in *The Killing of Kirmira*. Typically performed by demon-kings, such as Kirmira or Narakasura in 'knife' make-up, this extensive piece of choreography allows the actor to enact mimetically the lengthy preparations the combatant makes before setting off to fight.

Figure 3.1   *Schematic diagram of typical* kathakali *structure*

This is a schematic diagram of Scene 9 between Bhima and Panchali from *The Flower of Good Fortune* (Chapter 5

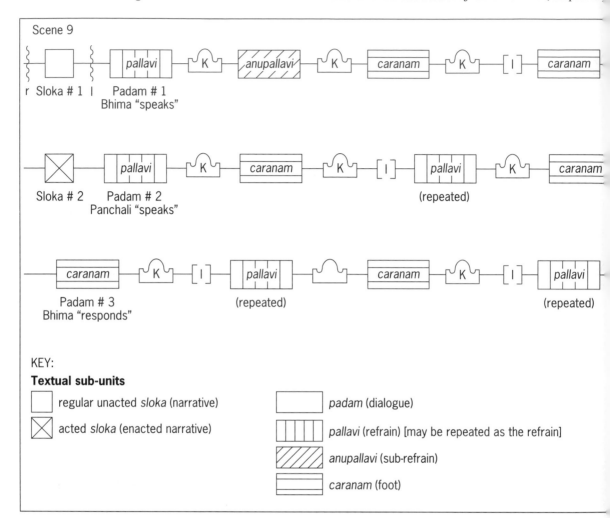

Interpolations

The third major compositional units are interpolations (*ilakiyattam*, also known as 'attam') into the dramatic text. Interpolations are of many types, and many are modelled on *kutiyattam*'s tradition of elaboration. One is a set form of soliloquy (*tante tattam*) acted by specific character types ('knife,' 'beard,' and 'black') after their entrances, such as Simhika's elaborate enactment of her 'beautification' and dressing at the beginning of *The Killing of Kirmira*. Simhika's interpolation elaborates her character's basic nature as a demoness, and therefore her

process of 'beautification' is a parody of the idealized feminine represented in the 'shining' female type. As explained further in Chapter 4, this interpolation allows the actor to explore the fine line between humor and disgust.

Another example of *tante tattam* is a soliloquy or form of mono-acting in which the character assesses the situation facing him by asking questions like, 'what does this mean?' or 'how did this happen?' One example is Hanuman's interpolation at the beginning of Scene 10 in *The Flower of Good Fortune*. With the curtain raised, the final *sloka* at the opening of the scene describes Hanuman as 'in meditation on Rama

17). It illustrates the typical linkage among textual and acting/dance sub-units which comprise the performance score.

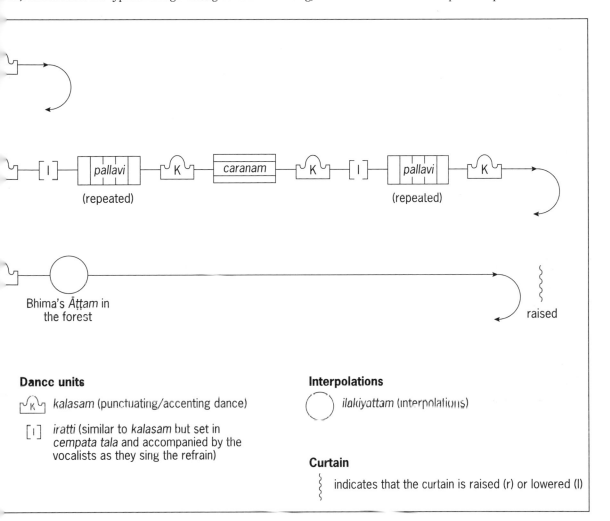

Dance units

ꕁꕅꕁ   *kalasam* (punctuating/accenting dance)

[ꕃ]   *iratti* (similar to *kalasam* but set in *cempata tala* and accompanied by the vocalists as they sing the refrain)

Interpolations

◯   *ilakiyattam* (interpolations)

Curtain

⫝   indicates that the curtain is raised (r) or lowered (l)

and performing peaceful ascetic techniques (*tapas*)' in the forest. This interpolation elaborates on the basic question Hanuman asks himself within the context of the drama, i.e., 'Why is it that my meditation is being disturbed?' A similar type of interpolation is Kirmira's mimetic enactment of his worship of and meditation on Shiva at the beginning of Scene 13 in *The Killing of Kirmira* (see p. 127).

A second general type of interpolation is 'descriptive set-pieces' of mono-acting such as Bhima's infamous mimetic *tour de force* at the conclusion of Scene 9 in *The Flower of Good Fortune* (see p. 107), or Arjuna's technical and

choreographic *tour de force* in *The Killing of Kalakeya* in which he describes the sights of the heavenly abode (*Devaloka*). Yet a third general type is the (melo)dramatic histrionic displays of inner emotional turmoil of scenes like Nala's wrenching decision to leave his beloved wife, Damayanti, at the mercy of the wild forest in *Nala's Law*, or King Rugmamgada's inner struggle over the conflict between the competing demands of duty, love for his son, and anger at the enchantress Mohini played out in *King Rugmamgada's Law* (see pp. 168–71). All these interpolations are like solo arias in an opera where the focus is on the 'star' who steps forward to command the audience's complete attention, and can last an hour or more.

Yet another form of *ilakiyattam* are those relatively unstructured improvisations involving two or three characters which explore the humorous mood through the mimetic physicalization of action. One example, discussed in detail in Chapter 7, is the interpolation in Scene 5 of *The Progeny of Krishna* in which the heroic Arjuna builds a house of arrows to protect the Brahman's wife as she prepares to deliver a child (see p. 146).

Other forms of interpolation include brief reflections or dialogues that bridge one scene to the next, especially to cover gaps created by cutting major sections of a play. For example, at the conclusion of Scene 8 in *The Progeny of Krishna*, Arjuna performs a brief interpolation that covers the gap created by cutting Scenes 9–11 (see p. 149). Similarly, the lengthy interpolation introduced into Scene 8 of *King Rugmamgada's Law* (pp. 164–5) summarizes much of the content/action of the first seven scenes of the original play which are not usually performed today.

All interpolations share the following characteristics:

1   Each is 'textualized' in the sense that the actor 'speaks' lines in gesture-language unaccompanied by the vocalists.
2   The lines he speaks may be based on and/or improvised from a previously authored text selected or composed by a patron/connoisseur, a senior actor, or improvised in the moment.
3   Interpolations have been added to the performance score because they are thought appropriate for elaborating the dramatic context, or the state of mind/being/doing of a character.
4   The 'texts' which are the basis of the interpolations are never sung by the vocalists like the literary text, but are only enacted and spoken, without repetition, in gesture-language by the actors.
5   Unlike the performative repetition of the poetry of the literary texts, the interpolations are much more 'conversational' and more like colloquial Malayalam.

As the total performance flows from one structural or compositional unit to the next, each includes opportunities for elaboration by one or more of the artists. These elaborations, performed as solo insets by a vocalist elaborating on a poetically descriptive passage of narrative, collectively during dialogue and its enactment, or with the focus on a single performer during an interpolation, are some of the reasons for *kathakali*'s complex structure and lengthy all-night duration. Over the years an author's 'original' play-text has been modified and shaped into the specific performance score now associated with the acting of that text within a particular lineage or style of performance.

A microanalysis of *kathakali's* performance structure and score in performance

Having identified each of the basic structural units of *kathakali*'s performance score, I provide here a detailed annotation or 'microanalysis' of one example of third person narrative (*sloka*), and one example of dialogue (*padam*) in performance so that the reader can gain a more detailed understanding of the nature of the *kathakali* actor's tasks in performance, and how different these are from those of the Western actor.

The sloka in performance

When *sloka* are enacted the general purpose of the enactment is for the actor to embody the essence of the mood/situation being described in the narrative. Unlike the dialogue portions of the play (*padam*), which are always acted in two parts as the actor 'speaks' the text, the acting of *sloka* is relatively straightforward, i.e., the actor performs only selected hand gestures as he embodies and conveys the state or mood being described in the narrative.

I have chosen for description the third *sloka* in performance from *King Nala's Law* (First Day). The full story of Nala follows the budding love between Nala and Damayanti from the first time they hear of each other's perfection and beauty, through Damayanti's selection of Nala as her husband, and the many trials which they confront through separation and eventual reunion. The opening *sloka* convey Nala's heroism, prowess, and beauty. In the first scene between Nala and the sage Narada (son of Brahman), Narada suggests that Nala should 'waste not your birth-right,' i.e., should begin to consider marriage.

Having implanted the idea of marriage in Nala's mind, Narada then describes Damayanti:

> In Kandinapur there lives a beauty,
> a gem among women, Damayanti by name.
> Even the gods have fallen in love with her.
> But mark me. Jewels rightfully belong to kings.
> The gods may only claim sacrifices offered in their honor.
> Perfect one, paragon among kings,
> strive to win this jewel as your wife.

There follows an interpolation in which Nala asks Narada whether he should even attempt to win Damayanti. Narada replies that certainly Nala will win her since Damayanti already knows him, and has set her heart on him and him alone. Giving a final blessing, Narada departs.

After Narada's exit Nala stays on stage to enact the following (third) *sloka* as the vocalists sing the lines through once:

> Having heard Narada's words, and the words of other travellers, Nala's mind, already immersed in thinking about Damayanti, became pained by his longing for her.

It takes the vocalists approximately one minute fifteen seconds to one minute forty-five seconds to sing through the *sloka*, depending on the amount of time the vocalist takes to elaborate freely each end syllable of a word. As the vocalist sings, the actor embodies Nala's state rather simply, employing his skills in 'interior acting' as he subtly embodies *cinta bhava* – a state of being best translated as 'reflecting.' Nala's active state of 'reflection' is about his love for the beautiful heroine, Damayanti – an act which causes him 'pain' because he is unsure whether his budding love will be assuaged.

Since acting this *sloka* is not as 'set' or fixed as enacting *padam*, the actor works within the 'sense of appropriateness' (*aucitya bodham*) for a refined heroic character such as Nala, and assumes a physical attitude of thoughtful reflection. Nala's state is subtly conveyed through the actor's almost exclusive use of his eyes and facial expressions, both of which must be infused with Nala's response to what Narada has just communicated to him. For example, while the vocalist elaborates a long end syllable, such as 'having heard' (*srutva*), the actor may reflect in his own mind on Narada's advice, 'waste not your birth-right,' by thinking, 'Narada

said, waste not your birth-right; therefore, it is time to think of my own marriage.'

At the culminating point in the Malayalam verse, and as the on-stage vocalist slowly sings, 'it happened, his mind was pained by sorrow,' on a quick catch breath the actor moves his right hand to his chest as his eyes look up at the sky, and then, slowly following the trajectory of the gradual exhalation of his breath, his eyes trace a line downward toward the ground as he heaves a deep sigh, and his facial expression assumes a pained sorrow (*soka bhava*). The actor playing Nala then lingers thoughtfully on his beloved, taking sufficient time to allow this performative elaboration of the *sloka* and Nala's inner mental state to be relished by connoisseurs.

While the performance of this particular enacted *sloka* is relatively 'free' and depends on the actor's interpretation of the inner state of the character, other enacted *sloka* are by degree more 'set' and do not take as long to perform.[2]

Dialogue (*padam*) in performance

The line of dialogue selected for description and analysis is taken from the opening love scene of *Prahlada's Law* (*Prahladacaritam*) between the demon-king Hiranyakasipu (in *katti* make-up) and his wife, Kayati (*minukku*). I have selected this line for analysis because it is typical of opening love scenes for *katti* characters, is set in the slowest rhythmic pattern (*patinna kala*), and therefore takes a relatively long time to perform. So slow are such scenes that they are referred to as *patinnattam*, or 'performing in a slow tempo.'

The line to be analysed is the first line of the first *padam*. Hiranyakasipu is speaking to Kayati. The Malayalam line and translation follow (Figure 3.2).

In order to understand how this line of text is performed, we will assume that the text *per se* is the 'baseline' for performative interpretations and elaborations of the entire ensemble of performers. Like all lines in a *padam*, there are two parts to its delivery: in the first delivery of the line, as the vocalists sing the line through, the actor enacts what might be called the 'subtext' of the line; in the second delivery of the line, as the actor 'speaks' each word of the line in gesture-language, the vocalists sing the line over and over again through a set number of

Figure 3.2 *Performance of dialogue (*padam*), Chart 1: first delivery of a line from* Prahladacaritam, Parts A and B

Part A: Immediately below is the text of the line in both Malayalam and English. Below each Malayalam word or syllable is a literal translation. Following the literal rendering of the line is a more readable translation of the poetry.

	Manini	*mar*	*mauli*		*ratna*	*me*
Beautiful lady		(plural ending) -ies	head	jewel		vocative case ending showing direct address
	mania	*seela*		*ketal*	*lum*	
(one possessing implied) noble		mannered		listen	please	

"Oh jewel among beautiful ladies; oh, noble mannered one, please listen."

Part B: The second part of the figure provides an annotation of the actor's performance of the line via notation of the rhythmic cycles performed by the percussion ensemble, approximate elapsed time, and a description of the actor's performance.

Tala	Vocalist sings	Elapsed time	Description of actor's performance
Cycle 1	maninimar	30–45 seconds	Looks at the face of the heroine through the use of facial gestures which elaborate on erotic (*srngara*) *rasa*. Here the actor can free-associate in terms of what he imagines, mainly through the movement of the neck and eyes. Although technically looking at the heroine, the actor is actually seeing an imaginary Kayati since the actor playing Kayati is within his peripheral vision only.
Cycle 2	mauli ratname	30–45 seconds	He now sees his wife's breasts and shows how this arouses his passion. He sees her breasts with his eyes, and then shows his appreciation of the wealth of her beautiful breasts by flickering his eyelids and moving the eyes in a figure of eight pattern. Her breasts are so full that there is no visible cleavage between them.
Cycle 3	maniaseela	30–45 seconds	Up to the middle of this cycle the actor keeps the same basic *bhava* of passion, but then in the second half (last 16 *matras*), his eyes begin to move down toward his wife's feet.
Cycle 4	ketallum	30–45 seconds	At the end of this cycle his eyes reach her feet, and he does a take with his head and eyes. Having looked her fully down, his eyes, during the first half of this cycle (first 16 *matras*), slowly come up along her body. Then, in the second half of the cycle, the actor moves his face/head as he attempts to draw his wife's attention to the fact that he is about to speak.

rhythmic cycles. In performance of course these two parts of the performance of one line flow one into the other.

Part I: first delivery of a line

During the first delivery of the line the vocalists sing the entire line in four cycles of *tala*. In the Kerala Kalamandalam style of acting this scene, during the first delivery of the line the actor playing Hiranyakasipu allows his gaze to pass over his wife, the heroine, moving from her head to her feet, and back again. Figure 3.2 shows each rhythmic cycle, the vocalists' words sung within each cycle, the approximate elapsed time, and the actor's enactment of the line.

This first delivery of the line of a *padam* might best be described as a 'pre-acting' of the line. It establishes the general mood. Usually the actor embodies the primary state or mood (*bhava*) which is assumed for the entire line, i.e., what we often call 'subtext' in Western acting. For this particular line from *Prahlada's Law* there is an interesting variation. Although the line itself is rather straightforward as Hiranyakasipu addresses his wife, 'Oh jewel among beautiful ladies; oh, noble mannered one, please listen,' in the Kerala Kalamandalam tradition of performing this line the actor responds with passion as he sees his wife's beauty. Because this example is not as straightforward as most other lines, it illustrates the significance of the nuances of interpretation involved in delivering each line of a text.

Part II: second delivery of the line

After setting the overall mood for performance of the line, during the second delivery of the line a general principle guides the vocalists – they repeat as often as necessary each cycle of *tala*, and the accompanying segment of the line of the text set to that *tala*, until the actor/dancer has had sufficient time to complete 'speaking' each word of the line. Since the performance of any particular hand gesture varies in the amount of time and space used for its performance, more complex hand gestures set in slower tempos, like this line, literally take longer to perform. When performing this line set in a very slow tempo, the slow action accentuates the mood of the erotic, the absorption of each image, and the creation of an erotic ambiance for the amorous exchange between husband and wife.

As annotated in Figure 3.2, the first delivery of this line takes one complete cycle of *tala* to perform, '*maninimar*,' another cycle for '*mauliratname*,' etc. During the second delivery the text temporarily does not move forward, but is simply repeated while the actor performs each hand gesture. For this line, a second repetition of each cycle of *tala* allows the actor enough time to 'catch up' to the singing. In performance, then, there is a constant, dynamic interplay between the musicians and actor/dancers as they move toward each moment of congruence which marks the completion of each segment of a line's performance.

In Figure 3.3, the *tala* cycle, vocalist's words, approximate elapsed time, and a description of the actor's performance are annotated.

The total elapsed time for performance of this one line is approximately six minutes (Figure 3.4). During these six minutes the musicians, vocalists, and actors collectively create a series of elaborations on the 'base line' of the text. As noted earlier, the primary mood/state (*bhava*) for this entire line is the erotic, and not passion, as was embodied in the first delivery of the line. But in the second delivery of the line, the actor playing Hiranyakasipu shifts his mood from an emphasis on passion to an embodiment of Hiranyakasipu's appreciation of Kayati's character and beauty.[3]

The double-performance of each line of a *padam* illustrates *kathakali*'s most complex and densely packed mode of performative and aesthetic elaboration. For tightly structured plays, each line of a *padam* is not simply 'said' once, but delivered as a series of cyclical waves of sound/vocal and acted/embodied expressions repeated at least twice. The performative strands of each phrase of a *padam* are woven around one another, and the audience experiences the combined efforts of the percussionists keeping and/or elaborating the basic rhythm, the vocalists singing the text, and the actor/dancers embodying the text. The moments of final congruence of all these performative strands come together at the completion of the pre-acting of Part I and the full 'speaking' of Part II of each section of a *padam*.

In Chapter 4 I provide an analysis of how the actor interprets, embodies, and enacts these textual sub-units and interpolations which are the essence of *kathakali* as a dance-drama, and provide *kathakali*'s actors with their greatest challenges as performers.

Figure 3.3 *Performance of dialogue* (padam)*, Chart 2: second delivery of a line from* Prahladacaritam

Tala	Vocalist sings	Elapsed time	Description of actor's performance
Cycle 1	maninimar	30–45 seconds	The actor shows the *mudra* for beautiful lady. The single *mudra*, 'beautiful lady,' actually consists of a series of gestures. It takes one full cycle of *tala* for the actor to perform this *mudra* sequence.
Cycle 2	maninimar	30–45 seconds	Now the actor shows the plural ending, i.e. 'ies' and thus catches up with his gestural telling of the full meaning of the word, 'maninimar.' This plural ending also takes the full cycle to perform.
Cycle 1	mauli ratname	30–45 seconds	In the course of the performance of 'mauliratname,' the actor takes three *mudras* to perform the text. The three *mudras* are spread over the two cycles allotted to the singing of 'mauliratname.' The first *mudra* performed is 'head,' which the actor shows literally. The *mudra* for head takes a relatively short time to perform. The actor performs the *mudra* for head during only the first half of the first cycle, or 16 *matras*. The second *mudra* the actor performs is 'ratna' (jewel). This *mudra* takes a relatively long time to perform so the performance of jewel begins during the second half of the first cycle of the singing of 'mauliratname' and continues through the first half of the second cycle (another 16 *matras*).
Cycle 2	mauli ratname	30–45 seconds	The last half of this second cycle is given over to the performance of the third *mudra* required to say, 'mauli ratname'. The vocative ending is shown in these last 16 *matras*, or second half of this cycle. Once again the actor catches up by the end of this second cycle with the singers in the performance of all three *mudras* for 'mauli ratname.'
Cycle 1	maniaseela	30–45 seconds	'Maniaseela' requires four *mudras* to perform. The first *mudra*, 'mania' (noble), takes this entire first cycle to perform.
Cycle 2	maniaseela	30–45 seconds	The second cycle includes the performance of the three *mudras*. 'Seela' (mannered) takes the first half, or 16 *matras*, of the cycle. The second half of the cycle is again divided into halves. The first 8 *matras* are given to performance of 'one who possesses' while the last 8 *matras* are taken to perform, 'Oh, you.'
Cycle 1	ketallum	30–45 seconds	'Ketallum' has two *mudras*. The first *mudra*, 'keta' (listen), takes this entire first cycle of 32 *matras* plus the first quarter or 8 *matras*, of the second cycle below. This is the longest of any of the *mudras* for this line, running through a total of 40 *matras*, or $1^{1}/_{4}$ cycles.
Cycle 2	ketallum	30–45 seconds	The last three quarters of this cycle are taken to perform 'lum' (please listen).

Figure 3.4   *Summary: performance of a line from* Prahladacaritam

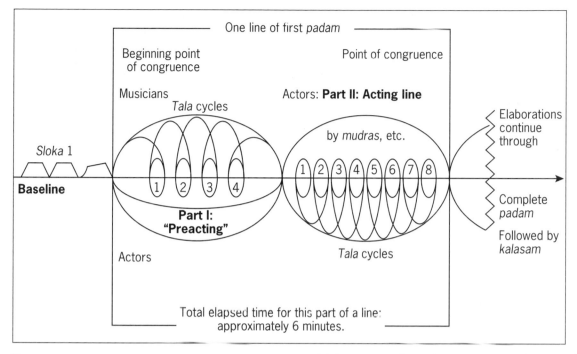

PERFORMANCE CONVENTIONS

Performance space and context

The *kathakali* actor performs in many different spaces and contexts today. The earliest *kathakali* performances took place outdoors within the compounds of family houses, or just outside the walls of temples. A simple rectangular space is cleared on the ground (Figure 3.5) for the stage measuring approximately 20 to 30 square feet (1.8 to 2.7 square metres) 4–5 feet (1.2–1.5 metres) in width and 5–6 feet (1.5–1.8 metres) in length). Poles are erected at each corner of the rectangle, and cloths are spread over and behind the poles, to create a defined acting area. The audience gathers on three sides, with the largest concentration in front; women sit to the left, and men to the right, with a passageway between to separate them. Patrons, guests of honor, and connoisseurs sit closest to the stage. Around the outer perimeter vendors set up tea or food stalls.

City and town performances sponsored by cultural organizations are usually performed on proscenium stages such as Sri Kartika Tirunal Theater, Thiruvananthapuram, which serve multiple purposes from the staging of modern dramas, to music or dance concerts, to political speeches and rallies. The playing space is large compared to the traditional outdoor space. With a raised stage and fixed seating, proscenium theaters lack the intimacy of the traditional audience-actor relationship.

One theater especially designed to preserve the intimacy of the traditional audience-actor relationship is the *Kuttampalam* Theater (Figure 3.6) located on the campus of the Kerala Kalamandalam (the Kerala State Arts School). Designed by D. Appukuttan Nair, this graceful and unique theater combines elements drawn from the *Natyasastra* (the encyclopedic collection of information on Sanskrit drama and theater), Kerala's specially constructed theaters (*kuttampalam*) in which acts of Sanskrit drama are staged within temple compounds in the *kutiyattam* style, and traditional Kerala temple architecture (Jones 1967; Panchal 1984). By keeping the theater open to cross-breezes with its temple-like lath walls, and only slightly raising the polished wood stage from the main audience seating where the audience sits on the floor, it captures both the traditional audience-actor relationship and keeps the space open to cooling breezes.

Figure 3.5   *Traditional outdoor performance*

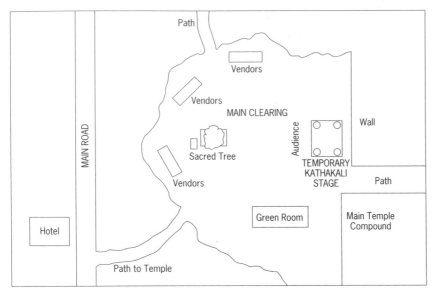

Performances were traditionally held outdoors at local temples, or in the courtyards of high-ranking, land-holding family house compounds. This diagram shows the arrangement for outdoor performances at a temple in Palakkad District, Kerala. The stage and green room are set up just outside the walls of the main temple compound in the clearing surrounding the large sacred banyan tree.

Before the introduction of electricity, outdoor performances were held all night under the stars, lit solely by the large oil lamp (*kalivilakku*) at center stage. With its multiple, flickering wicks, the lamp emits a yellow-hued light which dances across the faces and hands of the actors casting shadows. The actor-dancers necessarily concentrated their acting and dancing near the downstage lamp since this was the only source of illumination. The focus of attention was usually on the actor's faces and hands since little light fell on their feet and legs. The vocalists stand upstage center facing the audience where they keep rhythm on their cymbals and sing the entire text, while the drummers stand stage right of the actors.

Simple conventions govern entrances and exits. Direct entrances or exits are made either from upstage right or left. A number of entrances involve various uses of *kathakali*'s hand-held curtain (*tirassila*). The simplest method is when the curtain is lowered by the two stage attendants revealing the characters onstage, as when Bhima and Draupadi are revealed at the opening of Scene 9 of *The Flower of Good Fortune* (see p. 105). A more decorative use of the curtain is when it is partially lowered to give the audience an initial glimpse (*nokku*) of a character about to make his entrance – most often an heroic character (*pacca*). The most complex and exciting use of the curtain is the 'curtain look'

(*tiranokku*) used by the non-heroic characters such as the demon-king Ravana (a 'knife', *katti* character), bearded characters (whether the valorous 'white beard' Hanuman or the 'evil' 'red beard' Dussassana), hunters, demonesses such as Simhika, or animals. For these entrances a set piece of choreography is performed as the curtain is manipulated to accentuate the character's inner-nature before he is finally revealed.

Highly theatrical entrances are also made through the middle of the audience, such as the demoness Simhika's entrance in *The Killing of Kirmira* after her breasts and nose have been cut off (see p. 105), or Narasimha's entrance in *Prahlada's Law* before he kills the demon-king Hiranyakasipu. Reminiscent of the elaborate pyrotechnics that accompany a deity's dynamic and powerful entrance when possessing his human vehicle during traditional ritual performances such as *teyyam* or *mudiyettu*, stage attendants light the character's way with torches onto which they throw resins creating jumping flames, sparks, and smoke.

With the introduction of electricity, almost all performances today are lit with neon tubes and/or larger electric lights. The oil lamp is still lit at center stage for the ritual inauguration of the performance and to sanctify the stage space; however, the general illumination of the entire stage area means that both musicians and actor-

Figure 3.6 *Theater plan of the Kuttampalam Theater located in Cheruthuruthy at the Kerala Kalamandalam, Kerala State Academy of the Arts*

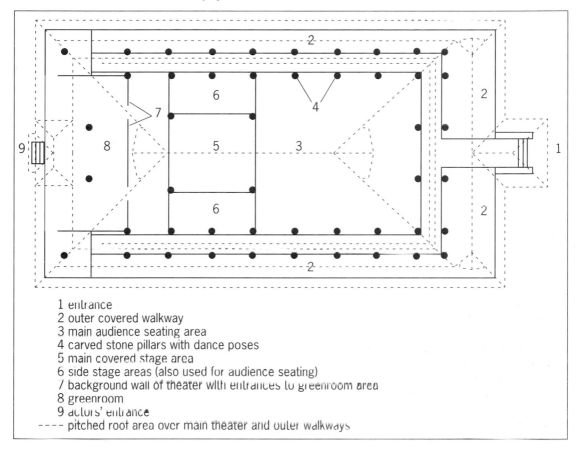

1 entrance
2 outer covered walkway
3 main audience seating area
4 carved stone pillars with dance poses
5 main covered stage area
6 side stage areas (also used for audience seating)
7 background wall of theater with entrances to greenroom area
8 greenroom
9 actors' entrance
- - - - pitched roof area over main theater and outer walkways

dancers are constantly lit, and many of the entrances once made from the dark are fully visible today.

Use of the stage is governed by several conventions. When two characters are onstage, the socially accepted pre-eminence and 'cleanliness' of the right side over the left is reflected on the *kathakali* stage where the stage right (audience left) side of the stage is always the side of respect. The character of higher status is normally stage right, and the character of lower status to his left. For example, when Bhima and Pancali are revealed at the opening of Scene 9 in *The Flower of Good Fortune*, as husband Bhima is stage right, and Panchali to his left (see p. 105).

Exceptions occur. In *The Flower of Good Fortune*, since Hanuman is Bhima's elder brother and therefore of higher status, he would normally be stage right with Bhima to his left (see p. 109). However, when Hanuman transforms himself into an old monkey and therefore assumes a lower status in disguise, he blocks Bhima's path through the forest by lying stage left. Bhima's powerful entrance from upstage right emphasizes Bhima's overweening pride – humbled by the end of the scene. Until Hanuman reveals his true identity as the son of Vayu and Bhima's elder brother, Hanuman remains stage left; however, at the very moment of Hanuman's revelation of his true form, Bhima immediately moves stage left, and Hanuman takes stage right. When the two characters exit at the end of their scene, Hanuman exits upstage right, and Bhima upstage left.

Another exception to the conventional rule that social hierarchy governs use of the stage is when a theatrical role that is of 'lower' social

Figure 3.7   *Traditional all-night structure of a performance*

Approximate Clock Time	Description
6.30–7.00 p.m. dusk	ANNOUNCEMENT OF PERFORMANCE (*kelikottu*) Percussion announcement notifying the village that a performance will take place.
8:00 p.m.	RITUAL AND PERFORMANCE PRELIMINARIES 1 Lighting of the bronze oil lamp at center stage (*kalivilakku*). 2 Percussion interlude: first section features the *maddalam* accompanied by the cymbals, then the *cen ta* (*aranukeli*). 3 First preliminary dance (*totayam*) performed behind the hand-held curtain. 4 Singing of the opening verses (*vandana slokas*) to further sanctify the performance. 5 Second preliminary dance (*purappatu*): meaning 'going forth,' this dance traditionally features two dancers (occasionally more) costumed as the two major characters in the play that follows. It is the immediate prelude to the evening's play. 6 Vocal and percussion composition (*mel appadam*) in which the drummers and vocalists display their artistic skills. The vocal portion lasts approximately 45–60 minutes as verses from Jayadeva's *Gita Govinda* are sung. In the final section the drummers perform a complex and competitive structured improvisation.
10.00 p.m.	PERFORMANCE OF TEXT
5.00–6.30 a.m. (dawn)	CLOSING VERSES/DANCE The ritual conclusion of the performance is invoked through singing a final set of verses and dancing a brief concluding dance (*dhanasi*).

status is a 'major' role played by a high ranking senior actor. In *The Killing of Narakasura* the demon-king Narakasura challenges the god Indra to a fight. Although Indra is of higher status than the demon-king, he enters stage left, and the entire scene is played with Narakasura stage right and Indra stage left. Since Narakasura is considered one of the major 'knife' (*katti*) roles in the repertory, and Indra is a somewhat minor role played by a junior actor, the actor's seniority and 'real life' social/theatrical rank take precedence over the rank of the characters in the drama.

Time and order of performance

Kathakali performances traditionally lasted all night, from dusk when the opening drum call (*keli*) announced a performance to dawn when the closing verses and dance brought the

performance to its ritual conclusion (Figure 3.7). The percussion announcement and performance preliminaries would take two to three hours, and the all-night performance of the play would not begin until approximately 10.00 p.m. The early announcement at dusk gave villagers ample notice of the forthcoming performance.

The opening and closing rituals frame and mark the performance from everyday life. The lighting of the oil lamp, as well as the singing of the invocatory verses, sanctify the space for the performance which follows. The closing rituals – singing of final verses and dance (*dhanasi*) – and not the ending of the drama *per se*, bring the performance to its ultimate conclusion.

The two preliminary dances (*totayam* and *purappatu*) allow young students to gain necessary experience as they perform the two major set pieces of choreography essential to their training in dance technique and choreography. The long vocal/percussion composition (*melappadam*) provides vocalists and percussionists ample opportunity to display their consummate musical skills for the enjoyment of the audience. The lengthy time it takes to perform a single *kathakali* drama illustrates the complexity of the performance score.

Both the order and the time of performance have been substantially altered over the last thirty to forty years. While there are still occasional performances where all the preliminaries are included, the majority of today's performances shorten the preliminaries to as little as fifteen minutes by including only the lighting of the lamp, the singing of the opening verses, and a very brief percussion composition. Especially at monthly performances in Kerala's towns for its *kathakali* club programs, with preliminaries shortened and a play edited so that only the favorite scenes featuring the top actors are performed, the evening can begin at 6.00 p.m. and the audience can catch a bus home by 9.00 or 9.30 p.m. for dinner and a full night's sleep.

Basic make-up types

> In your natural form enter the stage circle. Cover your own identity with colours and trinkets. (Kale 1974: 58; Ghosh, vol. II 1962: 15)

Kathakali's highly colorful costuming and make-up are part of the process which 'transforms' the actor into a wide variety of idealized and archetypal character types, each of which is individualized by the specific dramatic context, as well as the specific choices individual actors make in playing each role. The stylized costumes and make-ups have evolved into their present forms from several sources including *kutiyattam*, ritual performances (*mudiyettu* or *teyyam*), artistic conventions, the martial tradition (*kalarippayattu*), and traditional daily dress. From the first entrance of each character, audiences educated to the conventional make-up types know what general type of character and behavior to expect.

There are seven basic make-up types:

1 'green' (*pacca*);
2 'ripe' (*payuppu*);
3 'knife' (*katti*);
4 'beard' (*tati*);
5 'black' (*kari*);
6 'radiant' (*minukku*);
7 'special' (*teppu*),

and the occasional use of masks for selected characters. White usually frames either the entire face, or sets off intricate designs applied to part of the face when using white rice-paste. The thick white border framing the entire face for 'green' and 'knife' types is the *cutti*, whose size and width have gradually changed during the twentieth century from a relatively narrow 38mm (1.5 inch) frame to today's wide frames cut from thick white paper. Today's wider white frames and bulbous skirts give the characters a rounder, fuller appearance than at the turn of the last century.

'Green' (pacca)

This class of characters includes divine figures like Krishna and Vishnu in *The Progeny of Krishna*, kings like Rugmamgada in *King Rugmamgada's Law*, and epic heroes such as Rama, Bhima, Dharmaputra (Yudhisthira), Arjuna, etc. They are the most refined among the male characters, being upright, moral, and ideally full of a calm inner poise – 'royal sages' modelled on the hero (*nayaka*) of Sanskrit drama whose task as a *kshatriya* is to uphold sacred law. As Barbara Stoller Miller explains, kings are 'royal sages' because 'the king's spiritual power is equal to his martial strength and moral superiority. He is a sage (*rsi*) by virtue of his discipline (*yoga*), austerity (*tapas*), and knowledge of sacred law (*dharma*) . . . The ideal royal sage is a figure of enormous physical strength and energy who also has the power to control his senses' (1984: 8–9). Within this idealized type, characters like Arjuna, Nala, Rama, and Rugmamgada most 'fit' the ideal, while Bhima is something of a 'misfit' since when onstage he nearly always behaviorally and temperamentally tests the limits of the ideal, especially when he becomes 'furious.'

The white outer frame (*cutti*) sets off the green base, reflecting this type's basic inner refinement. The stylized mark of Vishnu is painted on the forehead with a yellow base and markings of red and black. The soft curving black of the eyebrows and black underlining of the lower lids extend to the side of the face, framing the eyes.

The lips are brilliant coral red. The most characteristic colors of the outer garments are the upper red and lower white skirt, with orange and black stripes. Two side panels accentuate the red motif for the lower body. The entire picture of the 'green' type is dignified with elaborate use of decorative upper-body accessories. Below the skirt the actor-dancer wears a set of bells strapped to each leg just below the knee.

While the majority of characters in this class wear the highly jewelled medium size crown (*kiritam*), a few wear a special vase-shaped crown with a short tuft of peacock feathers on top, and have costumes with different colors. Decorated with silver, this special crown (*muti*) is worn by Krishna, Rama, and Lakshmana. Given the traditional association of Krishna with the color blue, Krishna wears a blue upper garment and a skirt of bright mustard-yellow.

'Ripe' (payuppu)

The same basic facial design of the 'green' make-up is used for four divine characters in a special category known as 'ripe': Balarama, Brahma, Shiva, and Surya. The base color of green is replaced by orange-red. In place of Vishnu's markings on the forehead, Shiva's make-up also includes his third eye in the center of his forehead. The colors of the costumes are usually red and blue, while accessories and ornaments, including crowns, are like the regular 'green' characters.

'Knife' (katti)

'Knife' refers to this type's distinctive stylized mustache. Like the ten-headed demon-king Ravana, and Kirmira in *The Killing of Kirmira*, these characters are arrogant and evil, yet have some redeeming qualities – usually a streak of nobility. They wear the same facial-frame as the 'green' characters, as well as the same shape and size crown. The make-up base is green and the costume identical to that of the heroic 'green' type, indicating that they too are high-born, but their arrogance and evil is illustrated through the upturned red mustache framed by white rice-paste. This same motif is carried through by the red pattern above the eyes and eyebrows, again sharply set off by white rice-paste. The final indications of their evil nature are the two white, bulbous protrusions of the nose and forehead.

'Beard' (tati)

All characters in this set of types wear stylized 'beards' with a special color that indicates their underlying nature and behavior.

'White beard' (vella tati)

White beards represent a higher, divine type of being. Hanuman, the wise and valorous chief of the monkeys who appears in *The Flower of Good Fortune*, is the main character in this group. His monkey face is suggested by the red, white, and black patterns of the delicate design. The facial mask is extremely expressive since the slightest gesture is accentuated, especially of the cheeks and eyes. The small patch of green on Hanuman's nose illustrates his pious and virtuous nature. His most identifiable features are his white beard, furry white coat, and distinctive wide-brimmed head-dress. Hanuman's lower costume and accessories are similar to those of the 'green' characters, but with the addition of the 'gold' chest plate.

'Red beard' (cuvanna tati)

Red beards are generally evil, vicious, and vile. Characters included in this type are epic characters like Dussassana of the Mahabharata whose evil is manifest in the act of disrobing Draupadi at court, and demons such as Krodhavasa who appears in the full version of *The Flower of Good Fortune*. The eyes are encased in black, and framed by a white mustache which extends up to the ears. The black lips set off the ferocious mouth, while the nose and forehead knobs are even larger than those of the 'knife' characters. Perhaps the most distinctive characteristic of the red beards is their huge crown. Although the same basic shape and style as the crowns of 'green' and 'knife' types, the red beard crown is much larger and framed with red on its border. While the accessories and colors are similar to the 'green' type, the upper garment is a heavier, furrier material, suggesting the gross and unrefined nature of the type.

Exceptions to the general type are Bali and Sugriva, the two great monkey chiefs of the Ramayana. Although costumed as red beards since they are part animal, part human, they are basically good and serve Rama's just cause.

'Black beard' (karutta tati)

Black beards are as evil as red beards but, like the character Kattalan (Shiva as the hunter in disguise in *Kiratam*), they are also by nature schemers. Their make-up is very close to that of the red beards except that the lower part of the face is black rather than red, and the face is framed by the black beard. The upper skirt is black, while the lower skirt is a dark blue. The head-dress is an unusual bucket shape, and a distinctive stylized 'flower' appears on the nose. As primitive beings, like the hunter Kattalan, they are associated with the forest.

'Black' (kari)

Here are included the demonesses such as Simhika in *The Killing of Kirmira*. Very close to the black beard, the demonesses are also dressed in black, wear the bucket-shaped head-dress, and also add oversized comic false breasts. Their jet black faces are offset by patches of red, outlined in white rice-paste, with the addition of dotted patterns of white rice-paste suggesting the make-up of the village goddess Bhagavati, traditionally associated with small-pox. The demonesses are shape-changers capable of transforming themselves into beautiful maidens in order to deceive and trick their prey. They are therefore often considered the most grotesque of the *kathakali* characters, and are a vivid and direct contrast to the idealized females in the 'radiant' category.

'Radiant' or 'shining' (minukku)

This class includes both idealized female heroines, such as Sita in the Ramayana, Panchali in *The Flower of Good Fortune*, the Brahman's wife in *The Progeny of Krishna*, or Mohini in *King Rugmamgada's Law*, and the purest and most spiritually perfected males, including brahmans, holy men, and sages. The base make-up for this class is a warm yellow-orange, hence the term 'radiant' or 'shining.' Costumes for this class are close to traditional everyday dress. Since men play female roles, they don a long-sleeved upper garment, wear a white lower cloth, and then suggest the traditional female hair by wrapping a colorful cloth around a false top-knot worn slightly to the left on the actor's head. Holy men wear the typical saffron yellow and a special crown, while brahmans, like the main role in *The Progeny of Krishna*, wear a simple lower cloth as

well as an upper cloth tied over the head. When demonesses such as Simhika in *The Killing of Kirmira* appear in disguise, they appear as idealized beautiful maidens in the female version of 'radiant' make-up and costume.

'Special' (teppu)

The final category is a catch-all class which includes approximately eighteen characters from the active repertory of plays that do not fit any of the above types. Included here are the special bird-style make-ups and costumes of such famous characters as Garuda, Jatayu, and Hamsa (the goose in *Nalacaritam*); the goddess Bhadrakali who appears in *Daksa's Sacrifice* with a pock-marked face (white rice-paste spots), an ingeniously painted red tongue, and row of upper teeth which makes it appear that her upper lip is missing; the fantastic man-lion incarnation of Lord Vishnu appearing in *King Prahlada's Law*; and such comic village female stereotypes as Vriddha, the midwife character in *The Progeny of Krishna*, and Manthara, the comic old woman character added to the P.S.V. Natyasangham company's version of *The Complete Ramayana*. Since each of these characters and their make-ups are unique and do not 'fit' the normative categories, they exemplify *kathakali*'s flexibility.

Masks

A few *kathakali* animal characters wear masks, or appear in a mask after being transformed. A monkey mask is used for Bali's son, Angada, who appears at the conclusion of *The Killing of Bali* as his father, Bali, lies on the verge of death in the arms of his brother, Sugriva. In *Daksa's Sacrifice*, after treating Siva with contempt, Brahma's son, Daksa, is beheaded by Siva's emissaries, Virabhadra and Bhadrakali. When Brahma prays to Siva for Daksa's forgiveness, Daksa is restored to life, but his own head is replaced with that of a goat – here in the form of a goat mask.

The meaning of types

Kathakali's basic make-up types reflect South Asian assumptions about the substantive nature of the person. It is traditionally assumed that one's fundamental nature and behavior are determined by one's *gunam* – the material substance, property or quality with which one is born, including goodness or truth (*sattva*), passion (*rajasa*), and darkness (*tamasa*). As Marvin Davis observes, they are the

> 'Stuff' of which the universe is made. Together they are the constituent elements of all matter; not the attributes of matter, but the three modes in which matter itself is constituted.
>
> Physical nature and behavioral codes are not . . . distinct and separate features . . . Hindus regard the natural and the cultural as cognitively non-dualistic features.
>
> (1976: 6–8)

Although one's fundamental *gunam* is determined at birth according to the substances mixed by the couple, the specific time of birth, and the influence of the stars and the gods (Marriott 1980: 5), within each basic type the predominance of goodness, the energetic, or the dark substance will vary according to the individual.

Similar to the categories and typifications of role-types outlined in the *Natyasastra*, *kathakali*'s make-up types and characters range across the three basic substantive (*gunam*) categories, each with its 'stereotypical' behaviors and/or qualities associated with the social rank of a role. For example, the *Natyasastra* identifies/classifies its four types of heroes (*nayaka*) by 'conduct' as follows:

> the self-controlled and vehement (*dhiroddhata*), the self-controlled and light-hearted (*dhiralalita*), the self-controlled and exalted (*dhirodatta*) and self-controlled and calm (*dhiraprasanta*).
>
> (Ghosh, Vol. II, 1962: 203)

Clearly the *Natyasastra* expected all heroes to be 'self-controlled,' but there was considerable room for individuation in the quality through which such self-control was manifest in a character's behavior. What is theatrically and dramatically interesting is how a (Sanskrit or *kathakali*) playwright has created each individual character within a type by negotiating his or her inhering 'nature' in the context of a specific set of dramatic circumstances. *Kathakali* playwrights have always created their characters between two general sets of sources – the characters as they appear in the

Kerala versions of Sanskrit epic and *puranic* literatures influenced more or less by such proscriptive treatises as the *Natyasastra*, and particular local models of behavior and characterization. For too long Western scholars, following anthropologists like Louis Dumont, have problematically failed to differentiate 'individuality from individualism' – a failure which denies to non-Western cultures and societies like India 'concepts and values of individuality' (Cohen 1994: 14). Too often categories such as *kathakali*'s make-up 'types' are assumed to subsume the character. Too much emphasis is placed on the category or structure *per se* so that the category/type seems to 'erase' the individuality either of the dramatic character as written by the author, and/or as creatively played by the actor – a subject explored more fully in Chapter 4.

In *kathakali*, male characters range from the most substantively refined (*sattvika*) and pure brahmans in their 'shining' make-up; to the naturally energetic (*rajasik*), vigorous, and heroic princes/kshatriyas, who with their 'green' make-up reveal their '*sattvika*' side; to the 'mixed' category demon-kings in their 'knife' make-up who are energetic, vigorous, but also 'dark' in their use of their vigor and power; to the primarily 'dark' (*tamasa*) red-beards and black-beards – either those who are unredeemably evil and/or associated with the dark, 'uncivilized' nature of the forest. As we shall see in the commentaries on particular plays and characters in Chapters 5–8, characters like the Brahmin in *The Progeny of Krishna* or Rugmamgada in *King Rugmamgada's Law* each embody and display behaviors and/or states of being/doing which reflect the socio-cultural realities and concerns of *kathakali*'s patrons – Namboodiri brahmins and royal Nayar lineages.

Since females are by 'nature' considered impure and unrefined compared to males, females can only be compared with other females. In *kathakali* they fall within two contrasting basic types – the idealized females who conform to standardized notions of female behavior and purity as dutiful wives and heroines modelled on Sita and/or Draupadi, and therefore are as 'pure' (*sattvika*) as possible for a woman, and their opposites – the 'dark' (*kari*) demonesses who by nature are lustful, sexually charged, ugly, hysterical, and are 'dangerous' shape-changers able to transform themselves, and therefore are *tamasa* in nature. *Kathakali's* demonesses clearly reflect the basic characteristics of the fearsome goddess Kali/Bhagavati so central to Nayar identity and worship (Caldwell 1995, *passim*). As Marlene Pitkow explains, between these two extremes on a continuum is the *lalita* who appears in *minukku* make-up but is a celestial enchantress (such as Mohini) and seductress (1998: 15–16), who, in combining elements of 'two primary identities' (the *minukku* and the *kari*), becomes 'the most realistically human figure in *kathakali*.' Pitkow describes the *lalita* as

> *maya* . . . the embodiment of dread, the confusion between what someone appears to be and is in reality. The *lalita* type is also linked to the *yaksi*. Familiar to Kerala's folk tradition, *yaksis* are considered to be special types of female ghosts of unhappy women who die before having had sex or before marriage or giving birth. As *yaksis*, they return to earth in the form of seductive women to trap men and devour them . . .
>
> When she appears, the spectator knows that an appearance prescribed for one character type is being borne by a character of diametrically opposite traits. This awareness of a purely dramatic imposture reflects the *lalita's* greater psychic complexity. She alone of *kathakali* characters shows the common human experience of the disparity between appearance and perception.
>
> (1998: 16, 245)

The make-up process

The make-up and costuming process is lengthy, and takes from two to four hours depending on the complexity of the particular make-up. Specialist make-up artists apply the complex rice-paste patterns layer by layer, and the actors complete their own make-up by filling in the necessary colors. While lying before the specialist applying rice-paste, actors may use this quiet time to meditate, take in mind the character they will be playing in the evening's performance, and/or sleep (see Plate 3.1). Assistants help the actors dress and wrap the yards of starched under-cloth which give many of the characters their bulbous shape.

Once the make-up is finished, and they are outfitted in their full costumes and accessories, the actors go through several steps to complete the process. Important for all actors is the placing of a tiny crushed seed (*cuntappuvu*) under each of his eyelids. The placing of this harmless seed is a process not unlike putting in a contact lens since it causes the actor no discomfort. The crushed seed allows the whites of the actor's eyes to become reddish as the veins are exposed, thereby accentuating a character's states of being/doing (*bhava*) as revealed in his facial expressions. For actors playing either an evil 'red-beard' or 'black' character, they also place a set of fangs inside their mouths, which are revealed when the character displays his fearsome nature. But the most important final step of preparation is when the actor places the crown and/or head-covering on his head. At the moment before covering his

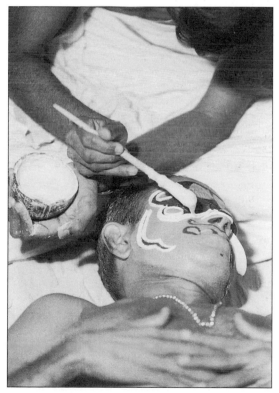

Plate 3.1 *A make-up specialist applies rice-paste to Padmanabhan Asan's face as the make-up for Hanuman is created. Hanuman appears in* The Flower of Good Fortune

head, the actor always remembers his teacher or teachers – an act of devotion and respect for his lineage of performance. Finally, just before entering the stage, the actor places the set of long silver nails on his left hand – nails which accentuate the visibility and beauty of *kathakali*'s elaborate gesture-language (*mudra*).

Properties

Kathakali's simple stage can become a palace or a forest at a moment's notice. The actor's physicalization of dramatic action and of the text's rich poetic images, supplemented by his dancing of set pieces of choreography, provoke the audience's imaginative engagement in the creation of the 'world' of the play. The only 'set piece' the actor uses is a small square wooden stool. Here the king can sit on his 'throne,' holding audience and receiving guests. For Hanuman, in *The Flower of Good Fortune*, the stool can become an extension of his physical presence as he suddenly reveals his 'divine' superhuman form to Bhima. Hanuman simply hops onto the stool, physicalizing his superhuman transformation.

Properties *per se* are few. A chariot is created through the mimetic action and dance of the performer as he simultaneously physicalizes the chariot, horse, and driver, rhythmically moving around the stage, an imaginary 'whip' in hand, driving the 'horses' to battle. If the character mounts a divine chariot taking him into the heavens, he simply steps onto the stool for the swaying, wind-driven ride heaven-ward.

Among the few properties which are not mimed are Bhima's ladle when disguised as a cook, and weapons. Stage weapons include the large mace (*gada*), bows and arrows, double-edged sword, small club (*pondi*), and sword and shield. The large mace is not actually wielded onstage, but carried on occasion by a character like Bhima to signify his superhuman strength. The sword and shield is only used by the character Yavana. Stage duels and battles are enacted through the use of swords, bow and arrow, small club, or fists. All weapons are made of wood and painted, usually red and gold.

Perhaps the most important piece of stage apparatus is the overhead canopy. Usually very colorful, it is held over the heads of some characters such as Ravana during their initial revelation to the audience behind the curtain, especially scenes emphasizing the erotic sentiment, and/or for dramatic tableaus.

Kathakali music

When composing each play the playwright/ composer selects a specific melody (*raga*) and

Figure 3.8 Kathakali *drums*

maddalam	A two-headed barrel-shaped drum approximately three feet wide used to accompany any character or situation in a drama. The right head is made of ox hide, and the left of buffalo hide. The drum is held horizontally across the player's thighs by a cloth wrapped around the waist. With thick rice-paste and lime finger-coverings, the drummer plays the right side with his right hand/fingers giving a sharp, deep, resonant sound. The left hand plays the left side.
centa	Equal in importance to the *maddalam,* this is a cylindrical double-headed drum usually played with two curved sticks, and occasionally with one stick and one hand. Both heads are made of cow hide. A long cloth allows the drum to rest on the shoulder with the main drum head vertical. The drum is tuned through the long cords holding the two heads in place. The *centa* is used to accompany all male characters when onstage. It is a versatile drum accompanying everything from the great din of battle scenes to 'weeping' when, by slightly wetting the rim of the drum and altering the tension of the head with a free hand, the stick is rubbed across the head making it 'weep' for the actor.
itaykka	A small hourglass-shaped drum (also used in *kutiyattam*). This fragile tension drum producing more muted and melodious sounds is used to accompany female characters in their 'shining' make-up.

rhythmic pattern (*tala*) to enhance the sentiment or mood of each section of the text. Changes of *raga* or *tala* often occur when there is a shift in the basic mood. *Raga* may be defined as a series of melodic modes built on a specific set of notes in the scale, and elaborated to bring together the musicians, performers, and audience in the mood the *raga* is intended to evoke. The melodic line in *kathakali* is created by the vocalists who sing the text (including *sloka*, *dandaka*, and *padam*) since there are no melodic instruments *per se* in *kathakali*.[4] The lead singer (*ponnani*) sets the mood and tempo of the entire performance, and along with the second singer creates the dynamic waves of melodic sound as their voices overlap, reinforming the emotional content and moods of the dramatic text.

Talas are the rhythmic patterns arranged in set formulas which mark time and guide the *kathakali* orchestra and actor-dancers through the performance. The percussion orchestra keeps the basic rhythmic patterns, and also elaborates on, around, and within the basic pattern. It also creates a dramatic sound environment in order to accentuate the nuances of the actor's performance, as well as developing and enhancing the overall mood of a scene. The percussion orchestra consists of the lead singer (*ponnani*) who also holds and plays the gong (*cenkila*), the second singer who assists in keeping the basic rhythmic patterns on the bell metal hand cymbals (*ilattalam*), and the three *kathakali* drums: *maddalam*, *centa*, and *itaykka* (see Figure 3.8). The lead singer serves as a kind of onstage 'stage manager' since he controls the rhythm of the entire performance on his hand-held gong.

There are six different *tala* in *kathakali* music (Figure 3.9). Each *tala* has a specific number of time units (*matras* or beats) which identify that particular *tala* as unique. Of the total number of beats in any given *tala*, only certain specific units are accented, with the remainder being unaccented. Each *tala* is arranged so that cycles of the basic pattern of accented and unaccented beats are linked one after another. For example, when performed in the 'first' or basic tempo, *cempata tala* has eight beats of which three are accented and five are unaccented. Each dance pattern (such as a *kalasam*) and each phrase of the sung dialogue portions (*padam*) of the text are set within a specific number of cycles (*talavattam*).

Each pattern or set of cycles may be played in one of three different basic speeds (*kala*):

1 slow (*vilamba* or 'first speed' *onnam kala*);
2 medium (*madya* or 'second speed' *randam kala*);
3 fast (*druta* or 'third speed' *munnam kala*).

Medium speed is a doubling of slow speed, and fast is a doubling again of medium speed. In addition, there is the very slow pattern (*patinnakalam*) used only for love scenes.

Although an oversimplification, it is generally true that certain major moods are associated with particular speeds, and that a sudden change in the basic speed of a rhythmic pattern, or a change from one pattern to another, marks a change of mood. As already noted, the slowest of the slow (*patinnakalam*) is only used for love scenes. The first or slowest of the basic three speeds is also associated with the erotic sentiment (*srngara*) or compassion (*karuna*). Medium speed is generally used to create the heroic (*vira*) or wonder (*adbhuta*). Fast speed is for the expression of fury (*raudra*) or fear (*bhayanaka*). As Leela Omchery notes, unlike South Indian concert music,

> *kathakali* musicians and instrumentalists are expected to perform – not according to their own will or pleasure, but according to the demand of the (dramatic) situation. Their aim, therefore, will be to search the various musical ways by which they can effectively express the different moods and situations in their variety and diversity. So naturally, here the musician has to elaborate those parts of the song which the character chooses for elaboration. He has to stop where the dancer concludes. Moreover his singing should be in such a way that it conveys the idea of the song and situation in their best. In short he has to cry, laugh, quarrel etc. through his music in order to encourage the actor and strengthen the situation . . .
>
> But in creating . . . a mood, the musician has to take into consideration not only the situation but also the characterization. Panchali and Surpanakha narrate the story of their molestation to others. But their expression may not be and should not be similar. Nala and Kirata express their love

Figure 3.9   Kathakali *rhythmic patterns* (tala) *(Designed by M.P. Sankaran Namboodiri)*

---

matra = number of time units in a rhythmic cycle (*tala*)
vayttari = verbal commands or vocalization of the units learned by performers syllable by syllable
. = unaccented time unit
- = rest
x = accented time unit

---

1 *cempata tala*: 8 matra

8	1	2	3	4	5	6	7	8
x	.	.	.	x	.	x	.	x

vayttari: TE]YYAM   TA   TA   TI   TI   TE[YYAM TA TA

At fast speed/tempo, the syllables change to:

x	x	x	-
TI	TI	TAI	

---

2 *campa tala*: 10 matra

10	1	2	3	4	5	6	7	8	9	10
x	.	x	x	x	x	.	x	x	.	x
TAI]		NTA	TI	NTA	TA	KITA	DHI	DHI	TI	TI TAI . . .

At fast speed:

x	-	x	x	x	x	-	x	x	-	x
TAI		NTA	TI	NTA	TA		TI	TI		TAI

---

3 *atanta tala*: 14 matra

14	1	2	3	4	5	6	7	8	9	10	11	12	13	14
x	.	x	x	x	x	.	x	x	x	x x	.	x x	x x	x
TAI]		TA	TA	TA	DHIM		TA	TA	TA	DHIM	TATA	DHIM	TATA	TAI . . .

At fast speed:

-	x	x	x	x	x	x	x	x	-	x	-	x
DHIM]	TA	TA	TA	DHIM	TA	TA	TA	DHIM		DHIM		DHIM

---

4 *pancari tala*: 6 matra

6	1	2	3	4	5	6
x	.	x	x	x	x	x
TOM]		NTA	TI	NTA	KA	TOM . . .

At fast speed: same as above.

---

5 *triputa tala*: 7 matra

7	1	2	3	4	5	6	7
x	.	-	x	-	x	-	x
DHIM]			TA	DHIM		DHIM	DHIM . . .

At fast speed: same as above.

---

6 *muri atanta*: 7 matra (half of *atanta*)

7	1	2	3	4	5	6	7	1	2	3	4	5	6	7
x	x	x			x	x	x	.	x	x	.	x	x	x
TAI]					DHIM		TAKITA		DHIM			TA		TAI . . .

At fast speed:

x	x	x	x	x	x	x
TAI		DHIM	TAKIKA	DHIM	TA	TAI

for Damayanti. But the expression of their love should not be similar even if the songs are set in the same *raga*, *tala*, etc. While singing for the noble characters the musician has to safeguard their nobility by making his expression controlled and dignified and vice versa.

(1969: 7–16)

Kathakali music is central to the creation and expression of *kathakali*'s full and wide range of dramatic moods through its melodic lines, basic rhythmic patterns, speeds of performance, and percussive accentuations. Clifford and Betty Jones have isolated some of the dominant sentiments usually associated with each basic *tala*:

cempata:	the most common *tala* covering a full range of moods, and also used for concluding scenes, especially violent battles and fights.
campa:	most often used for 'scenes of tension, agitated dispute, or battle.'
atanta:	for scenes with 'dignity and majesty.'
pancari:	for the comic, horrific, and odious, or for accompanying such specific actions as sharpening a sword.
triputa:	for scenes with sages or Brahmins, and for scenes with tension.
muri atanta:	also for comic, light-hearted, horrific, odious, as well as fast-moving scenes 'in which anger or heroism is predominant' (Jones and Jones 1970: 82).

The vocalists help create and reinforce the emotional content and moods of the text. Since he is the 'voice of the character,' the vocalist must

attack somebody at the top of his voice in wrath or . . . appeal to somebody in a tired tone of agony. Sometimes it so happens that the musician has to give expression to these different emotions through the same *raga*. He ably carries out his job not only by restricting his music to the higher or lower octaves but also by changing the tonal qualities of the same notes and phrases of the *raga*.

(Omchery 1969: 14)

Although each *raga* and *tala* was originally set by the author/composer of each play, over the years changes have occasionally been made in *raga* or *tala* for specific sections of a performance when an actor-dancer or musician thinks that a change may enhance the dramatic mood of the scene. Consequently, today's performances usually follow the *raga* and *tala* set by a particular lineage of performance and do not necessarily perform the *raga* or *tala* indicated in the literary text.

Members of the music ensemble are onstage throughout a performance. Performances minimally include two vocalists, *centa*, and *maddalam* players join and/or relieve each other during all night performances. The vocalists stand upstage center left, and the drummers upstage center right. At least one vocalist is always onstage keeping the basic rhythmic patterns with his gong or cymbals, and is accompanied by at least one, and usually two, drummers (always the *maddalam*, plus either the *centa* or *idaykka*). Especially for fast-paced scenes in which fury and fighting predominate or for Simhika's entry through the audience in *The Killing of Kirmira*, additional *centa*, *maddalam*, and cymbal/gong players may be added to create thunderous waves of sound which cascade through the cycles of *tala* bringing scenes to their climax, and often bringing performances to their conclusions. A final instrument is the conch shell – used to create auspicious moments in performance, such as Lord Vishnu's dramatic entrance at the climactic moment of *King Rugmamgada's Law* (see p. 170).

Kathakali choreography

As a dance-drama, all *kathakali* dance has been created to elaborate upon and/or accentuate the drama and its ever-changing moods; however, some dances are intended to enhance directly the immediate mood or action of the dramatic narrative, and others are 'pure' dance, especially appreciated for their stylistic elaboration. *Kathakali* dance ranges from the very strong and vigorous (*tandava*) to the soft, fluid, or languid (*lasya*). The languid is most evident in the choreography of idealized 'shining' female characters. Dramatic dances such as choreographed battles illustrate the 'strong' vigorous style of *kathakali* dance as they push forward the narrative action of the drama.

Other set pieces of choreography such as *kalasam*, which punctuate the performance of the dramatic text, help create, sustain, and/or elaborate on the dramatic mood of a scene. Longer pieces of 'set' choreography such as the 'peacock dance' in *The Killing of Narakasura* enhance the overall mood of a scene, but are also something of a 'time-out' from the dramatic narrative, since they are appreciated for their choreographic/stylistic beauty *per se*. *Kathakali* dances may be roughly categorized into the following four general types of choreography:

1   *Preliminary 'pure' dances*: the *totayam* and *purappatu* are the two preliminary pure dances traditionally performed as part of the preliminaries before an all-night performance, and an essential part of the training of the actor-dancer. The *totayam* is a lengthy piece of choreography taught during the student's first year of training. It includes all the basic non-interpretive elements of performance techniques, including foot patterns, body movement, use of the hands, and keeping time to basic rhythmic cycles. The choreography takes the student through all the basic rhythmic patterns in the basic speeds. Traditionally performed behind the hand-held curtain during the preliminaries, it served as an opportunity for young students to practise their basic dance technique.

The second preliminary dance, *purappatu*, is also a sequence of pure dance traditionally taught during the first year of training. Performed in full costume and make-up, the choreography is technically more difficult than the *totayam*, especially in combining more complex use of hand gestures with dance.

2   *Accentuating/linking dances*: as noted above, four types of choreography are closely knit into the fabric of performance of the dramatic text, serve to accentuate the dramatic mood, and link one part of the performance of the text to the next. The most important and numerous are *kalasam* – the primary dance compositions that punctuate the stanzas of the 'dialogue' passages (*padam*) of the text. These pieces of set choreography are danced according to the appropriate mood of the scene, and are accompanied only by the percussionists and not the singers. For example, at the conclusion of a passage in

which the main state of being/doing is the heroic, a *kalasam* will probably be in a fast enough tempo to accentuate the character's heroic nature. If demanded by the dramatic context, occasionally a *kalasam* is only performed by the percussionists, and not the actor-dancer. M.P. Sankaran Namboodiri provides a clear explanation of the relationship between dancing a *kalasam* and the dramatic context:

> *Kalasams* acquire their emotional import from the different rhythms, tempi, and qualities of movements. In scenes of battles and wordy challenges exchanged between opponents, the *mudra* interpretation of the dialogue lines takes a secondary place, giving all prominence to the *kalasams* which are characterized by larger and faster movements. The action is percussive and collapsing accompanied by sudden explosive release of energy. All these qualities continue to give a total impression of heroism, anger, fighting, moods, etc.
>
> In contrast to the above, in the slow-paced scenes of gentler *bhavas* like love, pathos, pity, devotion, etc. associated with major roles in *kathakali*, *kalasams* are woven out of slow, sustained, softly curving movements. There is no abrupt eruption of energy, nor are there any unexpected twists or turns. The energy flows evenly. There is a swaying but controlled quality about it. The *kalasams* reflect the tender *bhavas* in a dignified form.
>
> (1983: 197).

In addition to *kalasam*, three other types of choreography are used to elaborate upon the dramatic mood or to link elements of the performance. *Iratti* serve the same function as, and are choreographically similar to, *kalasam*; however, they are specifically set in one rhythmic pattern (*cempata tala*), and are accompanied by the vocalists as they sing the refrain in a poetic passage while the dance is performed. *Tonkaram* are like the *iratti* with a slightly different choreography. *Nalamiratti* are set in *ekatala* to a series of single beats, and used either for exits or as a dance linking part of the performance to the next.

3   *Set pieces of choreography*: some pieces of 'set' choreography like that for battles,

entrances, and entrances behind the curtain are adapted to the specific dramatic context, while others are specific to one or more plays. The latter include the well-known 'sari dance' for the entrance of female characters, and the 'peacock dance' in *The Killing of Narakasura*. The 'sari dance' emphasizes the 'erotic' mood with its languid, graceful curves and circularity. The 'peacock dance' is a choreographed, mimetic, *tour de force* elaboration (*vistarikuka*) of the demon-king Narakasura's description of the peacock's beauty as it cleans and preens itself in a garden.

4 *Improvised dances*: dance improvisations occur when senior performers elaborate on the text.

A structure and aesthetic of elaboration

To summarize, *kathakali* performances are collective and collaborative realizations of the aesthetic potential of the performance score. As the vocalists sing the entire performance text, the music ensemble provides the basic rhythmic framework accompanying each element of the performance, and each actor-dancer realizes his role by embodying/enacting the character, 'speaking' his dialogue through use of the highly codified system of hand-gestures (*mudra*), and dancing both pure and interpretive choreography as part of the role.

Kathakali's complex performance score could be described as a series of elaborations and embellishments – elaborations and embellishments on and within elaborations. The elaboration characteristic of the double performance of *padam*, the elaboration of *sloka* when performed, the vocalists' modes of elaborating while singing, and the percussionists' modes of rhythmic elaboration have all been designed and refined over the years as self-conscious challenges to the artists' collective skills. It is precisely these modes of elaboration which are savored by connoisseurs. Along with aesthetic elaboration, *kathakali*'s cyclical performance structure and all-night duration reflect South Asian assumptions about the nature of time. Mircea Eliade has noted that in India

time is cyclic, the world is periodically created and destroyed, and the lunar symbolism of 'birth-death-rebirth' is manifested in a great number of myths and rites. It was on the basis of such an immemorial heritage that the pan-Indian doctrine of the ages of the world and of the cosmic cycles developed.

(1957: 185)

I would argue that this cyclical notion of time is reflected in *kathakali*'s narrative and performance structure. The dusk-to-dawn duration is the most obvious reflection of a cyclical notion of time and cosmos, as is the underlying sacrificial/ritual notion of renewal assumed in many *kathakali* plays where 'killings' of evil demons and demon-kings are necessary to set right the cosmos by the conclusion of the 'play' (*lila*) of the gods within these plays.[5]

Lest these arguments seem tendentious, I would argue that *kathakali*'s repetitive, internal structure of performance reflects (see Figure 3.10), fundamentally, this cyclical notion of time. The most obvious structural features which are cyclical are the structure of *tala*, the rhythmic cycles which structure much of a performance, with the exception of performance of *sloka*, and the double-acting of the *padam* which necessarily employs the vocalists' repetition of the vocal text. Part of the attraction of *kathakali* is precisely the pleasure taken in the predictable waves/cycles of rhythm which lead (at best) to moments of congruence between all the performers – that space between the end of one cycle of rhythm and the beginning of the next. In these moments there can be an experiential sense of completion, consummation, return, and then continuance as the performance score progresses onward to its next phase. When lengthy interpolations are part of the performance score, there is a sense in which these are a 'time out' from the 'through line' or 'base line' of the narrative; but they always bring the connoisseur back to where he was left off, suspended momentarily in the ongoing progress of the drama – a repetition which marks a return to the character in the story.

It is to the actor's training and creative process in creating and bringing this complex structure to 'life' that we turn our attention in Chapter 4.

Figure 3.10   *Cycles of repetition and elaboration in* kathakali *performance*

Example 1: The first example below is a segment of a *padam*. This diagram is simply another way of illustrating the relationship of the performance score to the "through line" of the text. Using "maninimar mauli ratname maniaseela ketallum" as our example, and keeping in mind the two-part performance of the line, it may be seen that in terms of the "through line" of the story, Part I is a delivery of the entire line in four cycles; Part II returns us (arrow) to the beginning of this phrase of the *padam* for a second and third cyclical repetition of each word/phrase in the line: "maninimar," "mauli ratname," "maniaseela," and finally "ketallum."

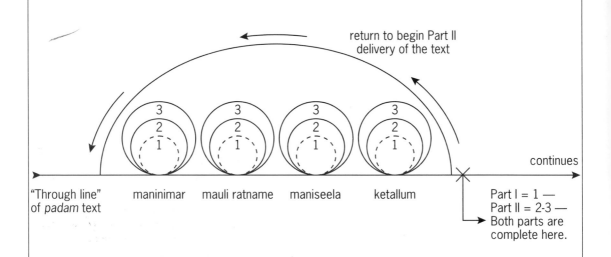

Example 2: The second example is the simpler cyclical return to the "through line" when a loop is formed for the performance of a descriptive *attam*. The *attam* is an elaboration on the text, but there is a return to the same place in the text from which the elaboration began.

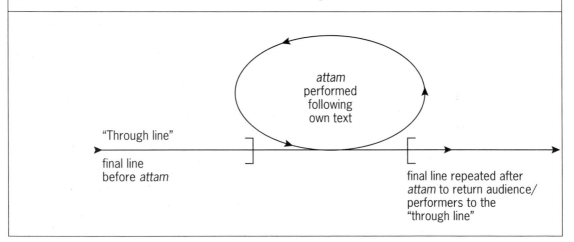

‹§›‹§›‹§› **4**

what does it mean 'to become the character'? *kathakali* actor training and characterization

[handwritten: Similarities to & differences of Stanislavsky theories of acting.]

INTRODUCTION

I always used to be in the green room watching. It was so colorful – the costumes and the make-up . . . that was in my village where they would have occasional *kathakali* performances. I was fascinated by this even from an early age . . . I thought it was something great, I was content just to sit there and watch, even though I couldn't really understand anything. Then I knew I wanted to become a *kathakali* actor.

(M.P. Sankaran Namboodiri 1976,
personal interview)

For many children the fascination of *kathakali* is first and foremost its synesthetic combination of movement, light, color, and sound which creates an epic 'larger than life' world. At most *kathakali* performances children continue to crowd around the green room, peeking inside to watch the intricate make-up process. On stage, the exciting battles, or characters like Hanuman the monkey-king in *The Flower of Good Fortune*, continue to fascinate children when, startled from his meditation by a thunderous sound, with his mimetic 'true-to-life' antics, the actor playing Hanuman tries to figure out what it is that has disturbed him. When a consummate actor like Ramankutty Nayar plays Hanuman, his interaction with the audience and the children in it never fails to bring laughter and smiles of immediate engagement as he mimetically enacts his monkey-nature by feeling an itch, scratching it, discovering and picking lice out of his hairy coat, and then throwing them into the audience.

For children, of course, the simple but rich pleasures and delights of *kathakali*'s easily accessible mimetic moments belie the years of arduous training it takes to reach a level of mastery in *kathakali*'s basic techniques and structures of performance, or the maturity of interpretation and subtlety of taste that an artist like Ramankutty Nayar brings to a role like Hanuman, which may be 'played to the gallery' by less mature actors. When I ask seasoned *kathakali* actors like Ramankutty Nayar 'What makes for the best acting?' they usually respond with one of two similar expressions – 'the actor becomes one with the character' (*natan kathapatravumayi tadatmyam prapikkanam*) or 'the actor becomes absorbed in the character' (*natan kathapatravum-ayi alinnu cerunnu*). In translation these statements sound quite similar to how some Stanislavskian-trained Western actors describe acting. In the analysis which follows I ask, 'What is the process of training and interiority which explains a *kathakali* actor's understanding of "becoming"?' I argue that the training, structure of performance, and assumptions about the body, bodymind, and character or role which inform what it means 'to become' reveal a process and set of assumptions with some similarities to, but also many differences from, that of most contemporary Western actors.

KATHAKALI ACTING: A GENERAL INTRODUCTION

It is generally agreed among both performers and connoisseurs that *kathakali* actors, with rare exception, do not reach 'maturity' until at least the age of forty. The path to becoming a 'mature' actor is long and arduous, and traditionally began at the age of seven or eight. Today's student may be ten or older when he begins training, but formal instruction in basic techniques and repertory still lasts six to ten years, and the years immediately following are spent playing smaller roles as apprentice, junior actors.

The anecdotal forty-year age of 'maturity' for the full-time male *kathakali* actor reflects the assumption that it takes a 'lifetime' to reach a level where one's technique has become second nature, and where one's artistry in playing important roles is recognized as one's own and is appreciated as such. To become a well-known *kathakali* actor whose performances are in demand means undergoing a gradual, long-term process of (re)shaping the bodymind, perfecting basic techniques of performance, growing and maturing as an individual, engaging in study and reflection, developing one's imagination, and integrating all the above into the shaping and playing of characters in the repertory each night of performance. This process is summarized (Figure 4.1) as a three-fold, including:

1 the pre-performance processes of formal training and informal enculturation prior to the day of a performance;
2 the actor's creative process as he approaches playing a role on any given night;
3 the performance *per se*.

The first phase of this process is the most obvious and includes both the formal process of lengthy training – the actor's initial onstage experience while a neophyte, his life-long study of India's epic and *puranic* literature in order to steep himself in the stories, mythology, and lore on which traditional plays are based – and the

gradual enculturation into the aesthetics, conventions, and social world of performance.

The second phase is the actor's creative process on the night of each performance. This creative process begins before or during the make-up process when the actor has time to reflect on the role he is to play. His process is a synthesis of training, reflection, study, maturity, and the engagement of the actor's individual imagination and creativity. Actors reflect on both the style and the nuances of past performances by great masters playing a particular role, on information and stories from the epics and *puranas* that give him a richer understanding of the character he is to play, or which provide him with new ideas and insights into how to perform imaginatively a particular interpolation.

Finally, there is the actual performance *per se* where the actor's relative 'success' depends on how well his own performance fits with the artistry and skill of the make-up artists and costumers, the musicians, the performances of his fellow actors, and the experience and knowledge an audience brings to the performance.

Kathakali training is a rigorous and arduous process of transmission of embodied performance knowledge achieved through constant, daily repetition of basic exercises which provide the psychophysiological foundation for developing both superb technique and individual artistic creativity when 'becoming a character.' At least in its initial stages, the process of transmission of performance knowledge in *kathakali* is more similar to dance or martial arts training than most Western actor training since, as *kathakali* actor M.P. Sankaran Namboodiri explains, 'First, perfection of the body is most important' (1978, interview). Perfection of the body is necessary to gain the flexibility, balance, control, and strength to shape the body to *kathakali*'s unique and difficult style of movement, and to acquire the ability to perform vigorous roles and dances for periods of up to two hours or more during all-night performances. Only when the fundamental techniques have been so well embedded into the neophyte's bodymind that such techniques are part of his performative body-consciousness, ready-at-hand to be used in the performative moment, can the maturing student eventually create characters, and be ready to give his individual artistic signature to a role.

Figure 4.1 *The* kathakali *actor's process: an overview*

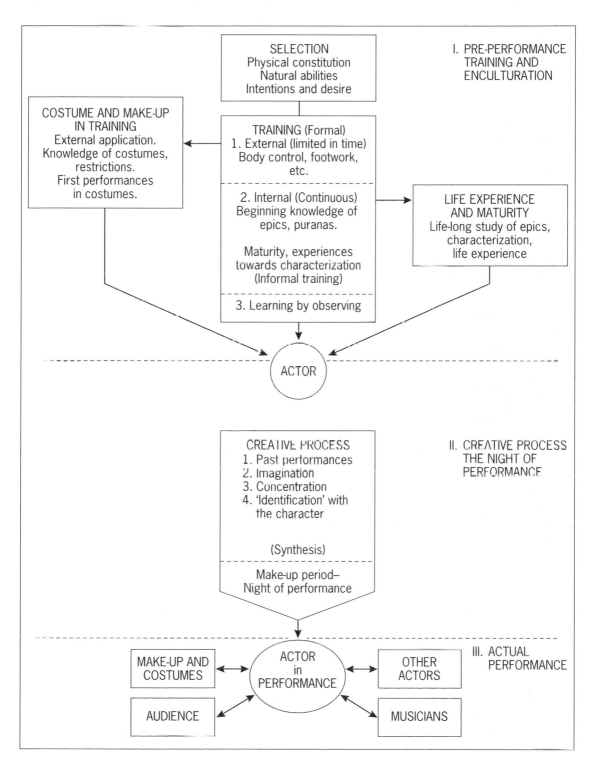

Without romanticizing the daily drudgery involved in repetition of basic exercises, it is assumed that only if a student follows the rigorous path of training before him can he eventually reshape his bodymind so that the actor can fully embody, interpret, and create characters with any degree of mastery. As *kathakali* actor Gopi Asan explains, 'only those who have thoroughly mastered the techniques for which a systematic and rigid training is available can successfully portray major roles . . . A kind of awareness of one's body, added to confidence, is gained through such training' (1993, interview).

Kathakali actors seek to actualize an 'ideal' characterization in each performance of a role. On the best night this ideal means that the actor has had sufficient time to prepare and reflect on the role, gives the role his full concentration, and is able to 'absorb' or 'become' the character. Achieving this ideal is a synthesis of the 'external,' psychophysiological score, and the 'internal' dimensions of playing a role. In terms drawn from the *Natyasastra*, the audience's experience is 'carried toward or forward' (*abhinaya*) through four elements:

1 *aharya* – the costumes, make-up, and properties;
2 *vacika* – the vocal element (carried primarily in *kathakali* by the onstage vocalists);
3 *sattvika* – the expressive, 'internal' element of acting;
4 *angika* – the embodied, 'expressive' element of acting.

The majority of the *kathakali* actor's time in formal training is spent in repetitiously learning the skills needed to perform the overtly expressive modes of creating and performing roles. The *sattvika* element is the subtler, more 'hidden' element of the actor's art.

Figure 4.2 is a summary of the *kathakali* actor's process synthesizing the 'external,' expressive/embodied process, with the more individual, 'internal' process.[1] *Kathakali*'s formalized external techniques – facial expression, hand-gestures, etc. – are used to create the nine basic 'enduring' states (*stayibhava*), eight of which were identified in the *Natyasastra*, including love, laughter, the heroic, sorrow, anger, fear, disgust, and astonishment. The ninth basic state in

kathakali, at-onement, was identified by the commentator Abhinavagupta in the twelfth century. There are also secondary or subordinate states of being/doing (*sancaribhava*), such as pride, which provide an even greater range of expression than the basic states. All of these states can be observed in everyday life, and the relatively stylized modes of codification which they assume in *kathakali* reflect the basic physiological signs through which these states are normally read; for example, when an individual is frightened, the eyes usually open wide. In *kathakali* such basic physiological traits have been codified, stylized, and taught as stereotypical expressions of these 'enduring states'; however, in performance of a specific character, the particular nuances of expression of each state are made specific to both the character type, and the dramatic circumstances.

In training, the complex modes of facial expression have been broken down into their most basic physiological/muscular components so that the actor independently exercises all the specific muscles needed to embody each state fully – his eyebrows, eyelids, lips, cheeks, etc. The meticulous and painstaking years of training in the independent use of each set of muscles, and each expressive state, eventually allows the actor to perform the codes intuitively as interpreted in the dramatic moment. It is to these fully embodied, psychophysiological states that the mature actor brings his individuality, his own life experience and maturity, and the subtler 'internal' elements of inhabiting these states with his mind/consciousness. It is the actor's full and dramatically 'appropriate' embodiment and actualization of these states that allow him to 'carry forward' his performance to the audience, and thereby makes available to the audience their experience of *rasa* – tasting aesthetic delight.

THE PROCESS AND STRUCTURE OF TRAINING

Embodied disciplines like *kathakali* were traditionally taught through the *gurukkula* system. A student, once accepted by a teacher, would reside in his teacher's home and, while undergoing training, serve the teacher. The intimacy, sharing, discipline, and embodiment of the teacher's unique artistic stamp are the ideal hallmarks of this model. It remains an ideal

Figure 4.2   *The* kathakali *actor's process: synthesizing the 'external' and the 'internal'*

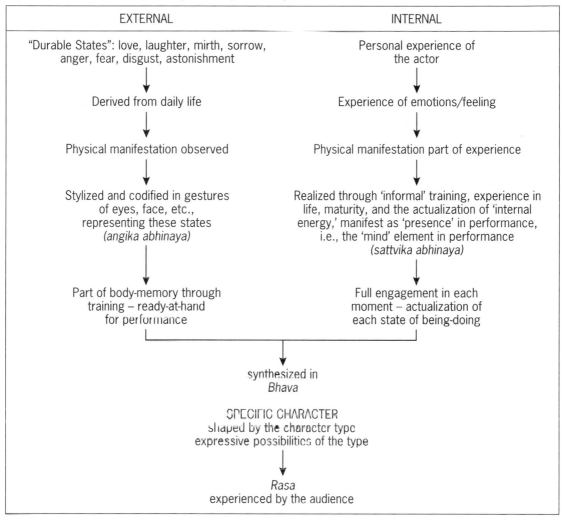

today, even in its increasing absence in the midst of modern institutional and political structures which make its realization increasingly difficult.

Since the founding of modern institutions, such as the Kerala Kalamandalam, full-time students usually live at the school where they are training, and receive a meagre subsistence stipend.[2] Conditions are spartan, but life generally is still lived quite simply for the majority of Malayalis. As I have previously pointed out, the spartan conditions of training should not be romanticized (Zarrilli 1977).

Admission to training at institutions is by a formal interview/audition process. Major criteria in selecting students include:

1   A boy's physical features. Is his body flexible and healthy? Has he had any previous injuries? What is the basic structure of his facial features, i.e., does his face lend itself to a basic type of character?
2   Sense of rhythm. Does the student have a basic 'natural' sense of rhythm? At an interview/audition prospective students may be asked to beat out basic rhythmic patterns to see if they are able to keep a basic rhythm.
3   Sincerity. Does the student have a sincere interest in *kathakali*, and would he be able to withstand the rigors of training?

Noted senior actor Gopi Asan explains how he was selected as a student at the Kalamandalam in 1951:

Every applicant in acting was asked to put on make-up and costume in order to know whether their physical features, especially the face, was suitable for an actor. In my case, it so happened that at first sight, Mahakavi Vallathol commented that this boy's physical features befitted an actor, and hence there was no need for me to audition!

(1993, interview)

Although the optimal age for beginning training is ten to twelve, since the young boy's body is still relatively flexible, an increasing number of students do not begin until the age of sixteen to eighteen. Admission to formal, full-time *kathakali* training today remains an exclusively male privilege and opportunity with the exception of foreign women, or their north Indian cosmopolitan counterparts. Malayali girls interested in *kathakali* train privately part-time, usually after school (see Pitkow 1998: 79; Zarrilli 1984a: 91–4). *Kathakali* actors, administrators, and connoisseurs alike share a common set of negative assumptions and arguments garnered against admitting (Malayali) girls to full-time *kathakali* training and performance. One actor explained,

> I don't think women will make good performers because they have some limitations age-wise and so on. If they reach a certain age they will not be able to concentrate on this, especially when they get married. They may do it all right before their marriage. The physical capabilities also differ from that of a man. In *kathakali* men can do all the difficult things, but not women.
>
> (1976, interview)

Women are generally perceived as not having a strong enough constitution to undergo the rigors of full-time *kathakali* training and performance with its vigorous, strong, and energetic (*tandava*) dance, its difficult body-exercise training and painful, deep full-body massage derived from Kerala martial tradition (*kalarippayattu*).[3] Marlene Pitkow relates the story about a member of the all-female 'traditional' *kathakali* troupe (Tripunithura Kathakali Kendra) who tried to gain admission to the Kerala Kalamandalam but

she was refused admission because she was a woman. The presence of Indian women

in the classroom would be too disruptive to the learning process, a member of the Kalamandalam's governing board told us. He also noted that because women would quit once they married, training them was not worth the investment.

(Pitkow 1998: 80)

Formal yearly training begins with the onset of the monsoon season in early June – the season considered suitable for vigorous exercise because it is relatively cool. A first-year student begins training by giving *dakshina* (offering/gifts) to his teacher, and then bowing at his master's feet as he receives the master's blessing. *Dakshina* traditionally consists of betel leaves, areca nut, and a few coins, symbolizing and actualizing the student's initiation into the rigorous training process. The master in turn gives the student his first *kacca* (loin cloth), which, as in martial training, is wrapped around the lower abdominal region to provide firm support for vigorous exercise.

In his explanation of his own rigorous training at the Kerala Kalamandalam between 1951 and 1957, master actor Gopi Asan describes all the basic elements of *kathakali* training:

> [At that time], there were only seven students in acting. The gurus were very particular about giving personal attention to the students. The first session began at 2.30 a.m. with an hour-long eye-practice. This was followed by various exercises and oil massage [given by the teacher's feet]. After a short break for morning bath and breakfast, the classes resumed from 8.30-11.30 a.m. During this session the preliminary dances (*todayam*, *purappatu*) and rehearsal of stories were done. Again, there was a break for lunch and a short rest. Acting students were not allowed to sleep while resting. This third session lasted from 3.30 to 5.30 p.m. This was also used for rehearsing stories (*colliyattam*). The fourth and final session started at 7.15 p.m. and lasted for an hour and fifteen minutes. Here we practised the nine basic facial expressions (*navarasas*), memorized texts, and learned appropriate hand-gestures. It was in this class that the guru gave lessons on character study, the meaning of the text, etc. Soon after dinner

Figure 4.3   Kathakali *training at the Kerala Kalamandalam: the overall pattern*

Year	Preliminary body preparation during monsoon season	Early morning class (non-monsoon period)	Morning class	Afternoon or evening class
First	Physical training: jumps body control exercises footwork patterns massage post-massage exercises Eye training (not always done today)	Eye exercises Footwork patterns Parts of sections of *kalasams* or pure dance patterns	(Continue learning physical exercises in first weeks of training) *Cuyippu*: body circles *Totayam*: pure dance *Purappatu*: pure dance *Ilakiyattam*: 8 ways of showing *mudras* with choreography for the first time Study of minor roles	*Mudras*: hand gestures *Rasabhinaya*: facial gesture Exercises for hands, wrists, and upper body; arm exercises *Tala*: rhythm patterns learned and repeated Learning *mudras* in story context Beginning study of texts
Second and third	As above	Eye exercises *Kalasams* Footwork patterns Pure dance sequences such as sari or women's dance	Repeat above for the first few months as review Learning minor roles (Music often added for first time here)	As above, but learning more texts, and more roles, with increasing complexity (By end of 3rd year should have learned all minor roles in the syllabus)
Advanced	As above	Eye exercises Pure dance sequences such as *keki* dance or choreography for battles	Story practice Minor and major roles rehearsed with musicians	Review morning mistakes *Mudras* learned for text in rehearsal Some discussion of stories, characters, sources, etc.

Plate 4.1   *One of the Southern-style kathakali jumps (*cattam*) learned as part of preliminary training to make the actor's body flexible and controlled*

at 9.00 p.m., all students went to bed, and were asleep before 10.00 p.m.

(1993, interview)

Although there is variability of the precise time for each element from school to school and teacher to teacher, the training process today covers all the basic elements that Gopi Asan describes, and is organized progressively according to the following overall pattern (Figure 4.3):

1 yearly body preparation and exercise;
2 basic training in techniques (first year of study);
3 intermediate training (second and third years);
4 advanced training (fourth through sixth years and beyond – 'post-graduate' training).

PRELIMINARY BODY PREPARATION AND EXERCISE[4]

With the onset of the cool monsoonal rains, all students, beginning to advanced, start their year of training by undergoing the same process of 'body preparation.' Based on Kerala's martial tradition, *kalarippayattu,* and assumptions about the body and bodymind relationship drawn from Ayurveda and yoga, the preliminary training is a rigorous physical regime of body-control exercises (*meyyarappatavu*) and oil massage (*uyiccil*) given with the teacher's feet which gradually renders the body flexible, balanced, controlled, and reshaped to suit *kathakali*'s aesthetic style and basic stance – grounded, wide stance, with splayed knees and full turn-out, arched back, use of the outsides of the feet, and the upturned big toe. After applying oil to his entire body, the student pays respects (*namaskaram*) with his body to Lord Ganesha – the elephant-headed incarnation of Lord Vishnu who is prayed to before any new undertaking – by prostrating himself on the floor, performing a series of jumps (*cattam*) and jumping steps (*ketticattam*), and then progressing through a series of body-control exercises (codified at the Kerala Kalamandalam as sixteen in number).

Early morning training also includes a series of gymnastic exercises performed either before or immediately following the massage – the splits (*suci,* literally, 'needles'), circling the body and

Figure 4.4 *Eye exercises* (kannusadhakam)

Students sit cross-legged on mats with a lengthened spine and gaze directed ahead. The instructor sits in front of the students. The student places the thumb of each hand gently on the lower lid, and the index finger lifts the upper lid. The teacher traces patterns with his index finger in nine patterns as the student keeps his focus on the teacher's finger. The geometrical designs include straight lines up and down and horizontal, circles, diagonals, and figure-eights. In making each pattern the student's eyes pass through the nine different points illustrated below. Point 5 represents neutral or center – eyes straight ahead. Circles are traced through points 2, 6, 8, and 4. Horizontals pass through 4, 5, 6, etc. Each pattern is taught in three speeds – slow, medium, and fast – to help develop the eyes' basic rhythmic patterns.

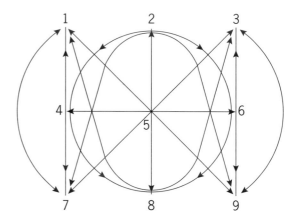

Illustrating position 2

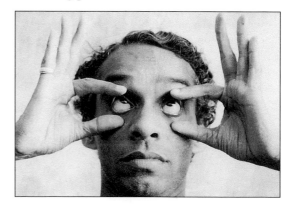

body flips, footwork patterns (*kalsadhakam*), and eye exercises (*kannusadhakam*) performed in nine different patterns each in three different speeds (Figure 4.4).

This part of the daily training takes place early each morning for two and a half to three months during the main south-west monsoon (June–August), and again at some schools in October–November during the shorter north-east monsoon. During these periods of intense exercise and massage, a special diet is prescribed which includes milk and ghee. The student must not sleep during the day nor stay awake at night, and takes a laxative during the course of massage to purge and cleanse his system.

The need for intensive exercise and massage was outlined as early as the *Natyasastra*. In the eleventh chapter, a 'method of exercise' is described which, in its overall plan and effect, is similar to *kathakali*:

> One should perform exercise . . . on the floor as well as (high up) in the air, and should have beforehand one's body massaged with the (seasamum) oil or with barley gruel. The floor is the proper place (lit. Mother) for exercise. Hence one should resort to the floor, and stretching oneself over it one should take exercise.
>
> (Ghosh 1967: 209)

In addition to vigorous exercise, the *Natyasastra* prescribes specific guidelines for maintaining health derived from Ayurveda, and reflected in *kathakali*'s regime as well:

> For strength of body one should take (proper) nasal medicine and get oneself purged . . . For, vitality is dependent on one's nourishment, and the exercise is dependent on vitality. Hence one should be careful about one's nourishment. When bowels are not cleansed and one is very very tired, hungry, thirsty, has drunk too much (water), eaten too much, one should not take exercise.
>
> (Ghosh 1967: 209)

Like the assumptions regarding healing and maintenance of health in Ayurveda and yoga, the actor's psychophysiological development is understood to be a long-term one. Change does not happen overnight, but 'in due course' both

his body and his bodymind relationship are ideally altered.

Basic training (first year)

During his first year of training the student concentrates on body-preparation and the rudiments of technique which provide the foundation for acting and dancing. After the early morning massage and body-preparation class, the remainder of his day is devoted to learning the basic exercises and techniques which constitute *kathakali*'s expressive vocabulary. Broken down from their composite forms into their most basic units for initial training, these techniques include the twenty-four basic hand-gestures (*mudra*), eight different ways of performing hand-gestures while acting, nine basic facial expressions (*navarasas*), rhythmic patterns, choreography and movement patterns, including preliminary dances (*totayam* and *purappatu*), circling patterns (*cuyippu*), which combine basic hand-gestures, rhythmic patterns, and specific focus of the eyes, and the dance patterns (*kalasam* and *iratti*), which punctuate delivery of the texts.

Since hand-gestures and facial expressions are the expressive means through which the actor conveys a character's states of being/doing (*bhava*) within the dramatic context of each story, the young actor must technically master each gesture and expression. This means exercising his fingers, wrists, hands, as well as each set of facial muscles (cheeks, lips, etc.) required to embody each expressive state fully.

Kathakali's language of gesture is part of its inheritance from the *Natyasastra* via *kutiyattam*. Both *kathakali* and *kutiyattam* base their gesture language with twenty-four root *mudras* (Plate 4.2) on a regional text, the *Hastalaksanadipika* – a catalogue of basic hand poses with lists of words which each pose represents (see Premakumar 1948; Venu 1984; Richmond 1999). While a common heritage and set of root *mudras* exist, many variations between the two have developed over the years.

Both *mudra* and *hasta* refer to the twenty-four root gestures performed with a single hand (*asamyukta*), combined hands (*samyukta*), or mixed hands (*misra*). Meanings are only created when the actor uses the basic alphabet to 'speak

Plate 4.2 *The twenty-four root hand-gestures (mudras)*

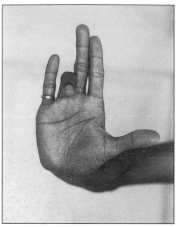

1 Pataka

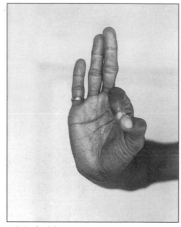

2 Mudrakhya

3 Kataka

4 Musti

5a Kartari mukha: (front)

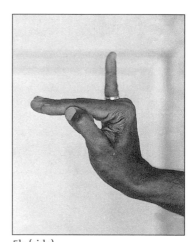

5b (side)

6 Sukatunda

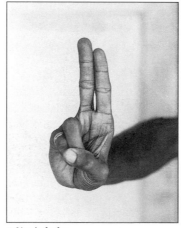

7 Kapitthaka

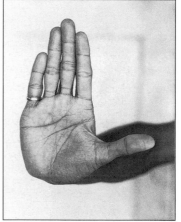

8 Hamsapaksa

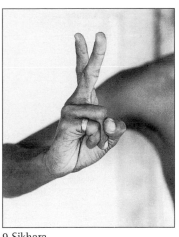

9 Sikhara

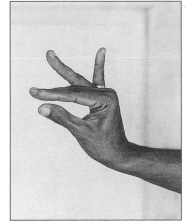

10 Hamsasya

11 Anjali

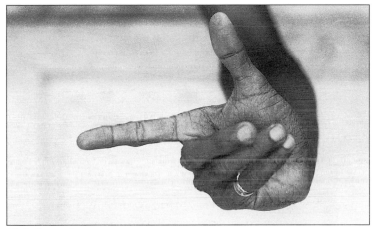

12 Ardhacandra

13 Mukura

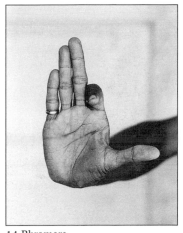

14 Bhramara

15 Sucimukha

16 Pallava

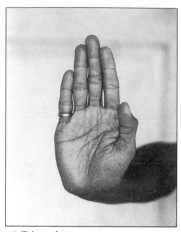

17 Tripataka

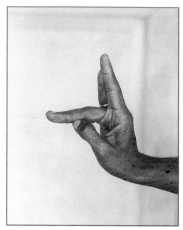

18 Mrgasirsa

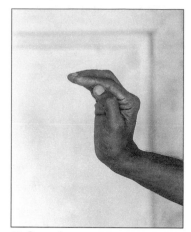

19 Sarpasiras

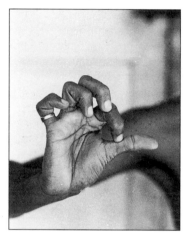

20 Vardhamanaka

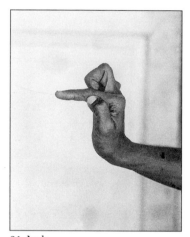

21 Arala

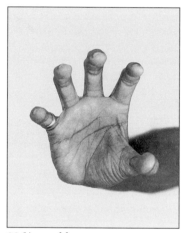

22 Urnanabha

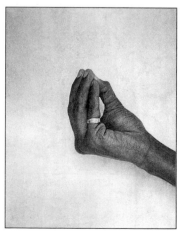

23 Mukula

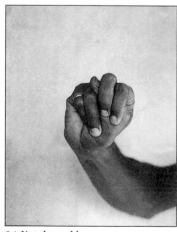

24 Katakamukha

with his hands' in a dramatic context. The student's training in hand-gestures begins by learning each of the twenty-four root gestures, and then quickly moving on to learning 'combined hands,' usually beginning with the names of various Hindu gods such as Vishnu:

> Beginning with both hands above the head in *anjali,* the hands move out at forehead level where they open into *hamsapaksa.* As the hands extend to elbow-length apart, each forms *kataka* (Plate 4.2: 11,8, 3).

In performance of hand-gestures, the eyes must follow the hands, i.e., they trace the same pattern as the hands.

Hand gestures serve a number of purposes. They are used to literally speak the text, and therefore in delivery follow the word order of Sanskritized Malayalam. When serving this purpose they range from literal, mimetic representation of an easily recognizable object, such as a 'deer' or 'lotus,' to signs for grammatical construction, tense, case ending, etc., such as the plural ending for a noun, or saying, 'etc.' When dancing, hand-gestures are often purely decorative, accentuate the beauty and quality of the movement in the dramatic context, and have no literal or symbolic meaning.

As the student learns the immense vocabulary of hand-gestures, he must also learn how to perform the gestures while playing a character. *Kathakali* training in central Kerala at the Kalamandalam has evolved eight basic ways of

performing hand-gestures which are adapted to the particular dramatic context of a scene. The categories and qualities of *mudras* clustered in each group include:

1   heroic gestures;
2   gestures for something or someone away from the body of the speaker such as 'chariot,' giving an order, refusing a request;
3   powerful gestures such as 'enemy,' 'destruction,' or 'obstruction';
4   gestures associated with the furious state such as 'demon,' 'cruel,' 'anger';
5   gestures for personal relationships such as 'brother,' 'sister,' 'elder brother';
6   gestures which describe the qualities of what is seen, such as 'mountain,' 'brightness,' 'black,' 'red,' 'clouds';
7   gestures performed in the neutral, stationary position such as 'lotus,' 'moon,' 'sun';
8   gestures associated with the erotic and pathos in which the hands move from the left to the right as the leg is closed such as 'beautiful lady,' 'face,' 'lips,' 'eyes.'

Some patterns, like descriptive *mudras,* involve considerable movement through space. The actor usually begins by taking two steps forward, then a 'slap' step to the side, and with large, sweeping movements of the hands and arms he delivers a *mudra* like 'mountain' while stepping backward. Although all hand-gestures have 'set' forms through which their meanings are conveyed, since actors do not vocalize their lines but speak

Plate 4.3   *The nine basic facial expressions* (navarasas) *plus one*

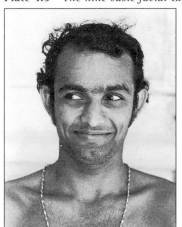
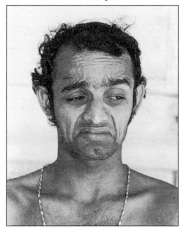
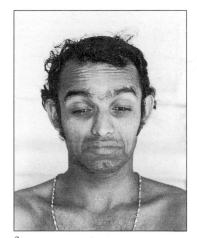

1   2   3

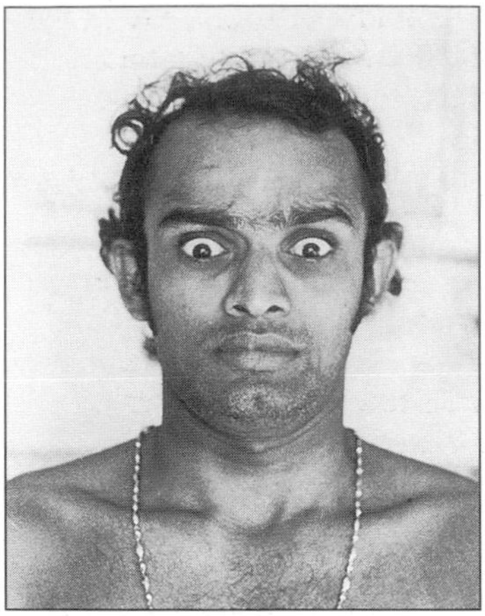
4

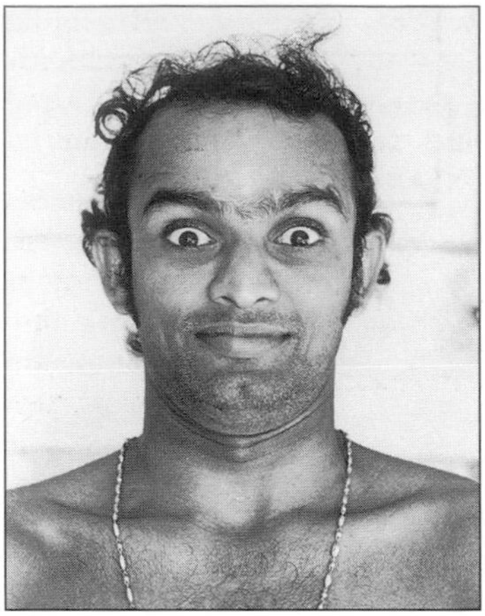
5

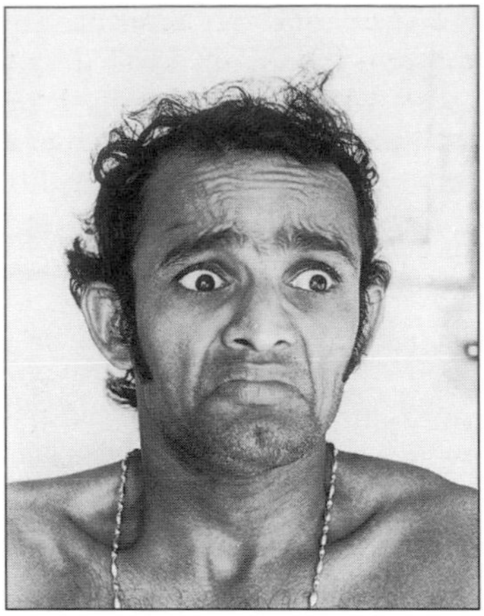
6

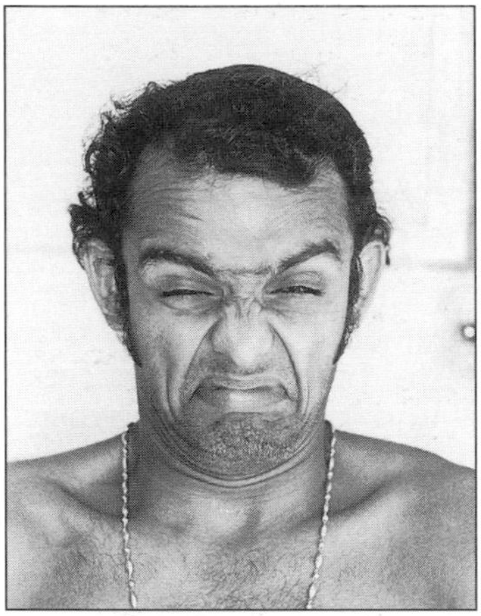
7

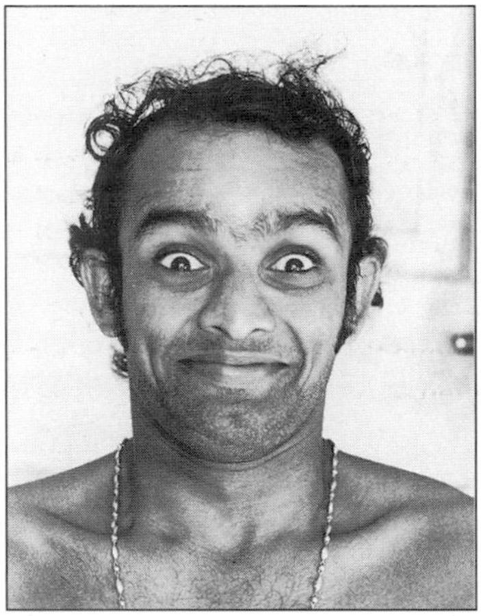
8

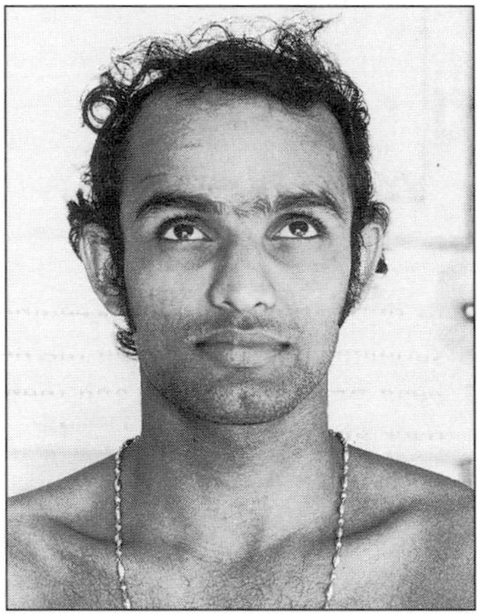
9

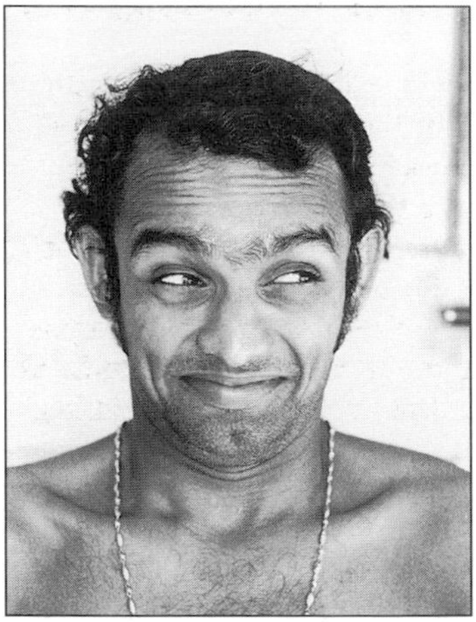
10

	Bhava	Corresponding *rasa*	Basic state
1	*rati bhava*	*srn gara rasa*	the erotic, love or pleasure
2	*hasa bhava*	*hasya rasa*	the comic, mirthful, or derision
3	*soka bhava*	*karuna rasa*	pathos, sadness
4	*krodha bhava*	*raudra rasa*	fury, anger, wrath
5	*utsaha bhava*	*vira rasa*	the heroic, vigorous
6	*bhaya bhava*	*bhayanaka rasa*	fear, the terrible
7	*jugupsa bhava*	*bibhatsa rasa*	repulsive, disgust
8	*vismaya bhava*	*adbhuta rasa*	wondrous, marvellous
9	*sama bhava*	*santa rasa*	peace, at-onement
10	*lajja* (one of three special female expressions)		shyness

with their hands, in performance each hand gesture is always interpreted by the actor as he adapts what he is saying to the specific state or mood appropriate to the character and scene.

In *kathakali* acting the face is a pliant vehicle for displaying the constantly shifting manifestations of the character's inner states of being/doing (*bhava*). The nine basic states (Plate 4.3) include: the erotic, love, or pleasure; the comic, mirthful, or derision; the pathetic/sadness; fury, anger, or wrath; the heroic/vigorous; the fearful or terrible; repulsive or disgust; the wondrous or marvellous; and peace or at-onement. At first, each expression is learned technically through continuous repetition and correction. Beginning instruction in how to assume the basic facial expression for the erotic, love, or pleasure (*rati bhava*; *srn gara rasa*) is usually very technical, much like the following:

Open the upper lids as wide as possible. Keep the lower lids slightly closed. With the lips make a soft, relaxed smile, but do not show the teeth. Keep the gaze focused straight ahead. Having assumed this position, begin to flutter the eyebrows. Keeping the shoulders still, and using the neck, move the head first to the right, and then the left – back and forth. While keeping the external focus fixed ahead on one point, move the head to a 45 degree angle to the right, continuing to flutter the eyebrows. Repeat to the left. [The focus sometimes moves to the right, and then the left.]

Similarly, instructions for assuming the comic or mirthful (*hasa bhava*; *hasya rasa*) are as follows:

Slightly raise the upper bridge of the nose between the eyebrows and slightly turn down the outsides of the eyebrows. Keep the eyelids slightly closed, and the lips drawn down on each side. Indent the upper lip muscles on the outsides.

In addition to the nine basic states, *kathakali* students also learn three other codified facial expressions associated with the playing of female roles, or for roles in which a male character imitates a woman, such as when Bhima impersonates Draupadi in *The Killing of Kichaka*. These include feminine shyness (*lajja*), and special forms of contempt and anger.

After initiating the students technically in the performance of each expression, instructors sometimes prompt the student to engage his imagination:

I ask the student to imagine something. Like for the heroic state, 'imagine an elephant.' For the erotic state, a 'lotus.' For the furious, imagine a 'lion.' For wonder, imagine a sudden action. I even do this with first-year students. I then ask them later in training if they are, for instance, performing wonder, 'imagine being in a big city.' Or 'imagine being in a forest, seeing elephants, snakes,' etc.

(K. Kannan Nayar 1976, interview)

Vasu Pisharody asks his students to 'show the feelings of an experience he can understand.' Vembayam Appukoothan Pillai explains the actor's expression of *bhava* as

how we feel toward a person or thing. For example, *srngara* is the emotion we feel towards a thing or a person we like. When we see this person or thing, our mind is enlarged. Similarly, for *hasya*, it is the feeling we get when we see a funny thing. Sorrow is the feeling we have when we experience difficulties, etc.

(1993 interview)

Gradually, over six to ten years of training, the student gains a 'fuller understanding of the states of expression' through reading and personal experience so that eventually he 'realizes what he had done at first by [technically] moving his facial muscles isn't enough' (Vasu Pisarody 1993, interview).

First-year students begin to apply their basic training in expressive states by learning some of the simpler minor roles in the repertory. As the student-actor learns more roles, he is gradually able to embody and manifest the nuances of each expressive state for different characters within different dramatic contexts. For example, 'pathos (*karuna*) may be expressed as a state of unfulfilled desire, loss over the death of a person, etc.' (ibid.). The student realizes that there are differences in how each character expresses the same basic state – the Brahmin's expression of pathos in *The Progeny of Krishna* is different from that of Dharmaputra. Panchali's sorrow is different from that of Damayanti. *Kathakali*'s, initially, technical and codified expressions are gradually individualized in playing particular characters.

Another important part of training today is providing students with the necessary linguistic tools to understand fully the nuances of *kathakali*'s highly Sanskritized poetic texts. Today some schools have followed the Kalamandalam's lead by teaching Sanskrit to first-year students in order to give them a working knowledge of grammar and vocabulary relevant to performance. In addition, students also read Malayalam versions of the major epics and *puranas* to provide them with background information necessary to bring a full knowledge of their characters to the creation of a role. Without such knowledge, as student actors mature they would be unable to bring a subtler understanding of the characters they play to the stage.

By the end of their first year of training, students usually perform one or both of *kathakali*'s preliminary dances (*purappatu* and *totayam*) on the stage in full costume and make-up. Since students do not rehearse in costume and make-up before their first performance, it is

both a rite of passage, as the student receives his teacher's blessing, and a 'trial by fire', where he hopes for little more than simply making it through the entire choreography without losing his balance, getting distracted and forgetting what comes next, having his crown fall to one side of his head, or having his facial make-up (especially the paper frame) tear loose or fall off!

Intermediate and advanced training: colliyattam – learning and rehearsing stories

During their six to ten years of training, students are expected to learn every role in each play taught from the official school syllabus. From an active repertory of around forty to fifty plays, the syllabus at the Kerala Kalamandalam consists of eighteen plays covered in the regular six-year course of study, with two plays included in the post-graduate course of training (Figure 4.5).[5] The plays in a school's syllabus are selected to ensure that students receive training in all role-

Plate 4.4 Colliyattam *of* The Killing of Lavanasura: *Lava and Kusa string their bows as they prepare to fight*

Figure 4.5   *Kerala Kalamandalam syllabus*

Regular six-year Acting Course	
Author	*Play(s)*
Kottayam Tampuran (c.1675–1725)	*Bakavadham (The Killing of Baka)* *Kirmiravadham (The Killing of Kirmira)* *Kalakeyavadham (The Killing of Kalakeya)* *Kalyanasaugandhikam (The Flower of Good Fortune)*
Irayimman Tampi (1783–1856)	*Kichakavadham (The Killing of Kichaka)* *Uttaraswayamvaram (The Marriage of Uttara)* *Daksayagam (Daksa's Sacrifice)*
Kottarakara Tampuram (c.1625–85)	*Balivadham (The Killing of Bali)*
Karthika Tirunal Rama Varma Maharaja (1724–98)	*Narakasuravadham (The Killing of Narakasura)*
Kallekkulangara Raghava Pisharody (1725–93)	*Ravanotbhavam (Ravana's 'State')*
Mandavappalli Ittiraricha Menon (1747–94)	*Santanagopalam (The Progeny of Krishna)** *Rugmamgadacaritam (King Rugmamgada's Law)**
Aswati Tirunal Rama Varma Tampuran (1756–94)	*Rukminiswayamvaram (The Marriage of Rukmini)* *Ambarishacaritam (Ambarisha's Law)*
Kalloor Namboodiripad (1774–1833)	*Balivijayan (Bali's Victory)*
Irrottakulangara Rama Variyar (1801–45)	*Kiratam (The Hunter)**
Vayaskara Aryan Narayanan Moosad (1841–1902)	*Duryodhanavadham (The Killing of Duryodhana)**
Manthredath Namboodiripad (1851–1906)	*Subhadraharanam*
TOTAL: 18 plays	

*Although part of the Kalamandalam official syllabus, these four plays are not taught as part of the regular training in the classroom.

Post-Graduate Course	
Unnayi Variyar (c.1675–1716)	*Nalacaritam (King Nala's Law:* selected portions of Parts I-IV)
Mandavappalli Ittiraricha Menon (c.1747–94)	*Rugmamgadacaritam (King Rugmamgada's Law:* advanced roles)

Plate 4.5 Colliyattam *of* The Killing of Lavanasura: *Hanuman. Note: The triangle illustrates the dynamic, oppositional triangulation created between the lower abdominal region and the floor, through the feet*

types and choreography so that by the end of his training, with additional study and preparation, a young actor would be able to play any role even if it has not been taught, or a new role in a new play.

During his second and third years, the student builds on the foundation laid during the first year. The first few months review and perfect the body-preparation exercises and basic performance techniques. At rehearsals, students learn to play somewhat more complex minor roles.

The process of rehearsing plays 'in the classroom' is known as *colliyattam*, literally meaning 'to recite' (*colli*) and 'to dance' (*attam*) the text. Since performers originally sang the text, *colliyattam* refers to the process of both vocalizing/learning the lines of the play and dancing/performing each role. Today it is the process by which the student rehearses the performance of each role of a text in all its specific details, and then 'sets' or fixes those details according to the performance tradition of his teacher(s). The first days of rehearsal of any particular role begin as mimetic, repetitious technical rehearsals where the teacher demonstrates for the students all the specific hand-gestures, expressive states, and choreography necessary to perform a role. Once students have learned the basic techniques for performing a role, the teacher simultaneously keeps the basic rhythmic pattern, beaten out by a stick with his right hand on top of a stool or table-top, sings the lines of each role, and corrects students in the proper performance of each hand-gesture and expressive state as they perform each line of the text.

By the end of the third year of training, students have learned all the minor roles of the syllabus, and in the fourth and fifth years of training students move on to roles of intermediate difficulty and length. The most difficult major roles in the regular syllabus are taught in the fifth and sixth years. This process of teaching roles based on size and degree of difficulty means that the students do not learn all the roles within a particular play at one time but, rather, learn them incrementally over several years. For the four scenes of *The Flower of Good Fortune* translated here (Chapter 5), students learn the role of Panchali during their first three years of training, the roles of Bhima and Dharmaputra (Scene 1) during their fourth year, and the major roles of Bhima and Hanuman during their fifth and sixth years. It is with such roles as Bhima in *The Killing of Baka* (see Chapter 2, p. 28), or Bhima and Hanuman in *The Flower of Good Fortune*, that students begin to learn the performance of interpolations in the original literary text – arguably the most creative and demanding parts of an actor's performance. Since the interpolations taught in the classroom have become relatively 'set' within lineages of actors and are not part of the original play text, when learned, students write out the text of each interpolation in their notebook, and take extensive notes on how they are to be performed. A student's notebook becomes his guidebook and reference when he prepares for a full performance of each role in the future.

For *The Killing of Kirmira* (Chapter 6) students learn the role of Panchali during their first three years, then the intermediate roles of

Lalita and Simhika during their fourth year, and the roles of Sahadeva and Kirmira during their fifth year. Like the roles of Bhima and Hanuman, the major roles of Sahadeva and Kirmira are taught last since they involve Kirmira's interpolation known as 'description of the sound' (*sabdavarnana*), and Sahadeva's complex, structured choreography known as 'preparing for battle' (*padapurappatu*).

Advanced classes become full rehearsals with a complete set of musicians present. Attending a *colliyattam* class for fifth- and sixth-year students at the Kerala Kalamandalam in 1976 when *The Killing of Kirmira* was being taught, I recorded the following description of the process:

This is the fourth day during which students have been working on this scene. The teacher of acting leading the rehearsal sits facing the students in his chair, stick in his right hand, and stool in front. The class begins with a long musical interlude played by two young drumming students, coached by their own teachers. Soon the master drummers take over as the performance of the text is about to begin. The four acting students in the class come forward and perform a salutation (*namaskaram*), paying respects to Lord Ganesha and to their teacher. They take their positions in pairs – two of the sixth-year students are rehearsing Lalita (Simhika in disguise), and two of the fifth-year students are rehearsing Draupadi (Panchali). The teacher leads the students through the rehearsal, showing a hand-gesture when necessary, following the patterns with his eyes. The students struggle to remember the gestures. Occasionally the teacher gets up to illustrate a particular dance pattern. A mistake is made, and the teacher shouts angrily.

For the first thirty-five minutes while the two sixth-year students perform the Lalita role without a break, the two fifth-year students playing Draupadi must stay perfectly still, remain 'in character,' and register occasional responses to what the Lalita says with their eyes. It is clear that the students are still somewhat unsure of

certain parts of their roles. There is as yet no attempt at interpretation – they constantly struggle to simply remember their lines, and what comes next.

Another bad mistake, and the teacher threatens to beat one of the students. The climax of the scene comes as Draupadi is carried away by the demoness.

It is the precise details of the complex performance score that teachers so severely correct, and 'fix' during *colliyattam* classes.

REPERTORY, TRAINING, AND RECEPTION

The plays in today's *kathakali* repertory can be described as falling along a continuum ranging from those which are narratively driven and focus on the events in the stories such as the original Ramayana plays, to the four plays authored by Kottayam Tampuran where virtuosic technique and structure are most important in elaborating narrative incidents, to those plays such as Unnayi Variyar's *King Nala's Law*, Mandavappalli Ittiraricha Menon's *King Rugmamgada's Law*, or the very recent play *Karna's Oath* (1967) by Mali Madhavan Nayar which provide the maximum opportunity for individual actors to explore an individual character's interior, mental state(s) of being. Of all these plays, the four plays authored by Kottayam Tampuran, including *The Flower of Good Fortune* and *The Killing of Kirmira*, are considered the most important in the training of the actor since correct performance of each role depends on mastery of *kathakali*'s basic techniques. When Kottayam Tampuran authored the plays, since he himself was also an actor, he specifically set the performance pattern of each element of a play. Each dialogue section (*padam*) of each play follows specific essential conventions (*cittapradanam*) to be precisely followed in performance. The singer is expected to sing the prescribed number of cycles of repetitions of the text, and each punctuating dance pattern (*kalasam*) must fit precisely into the performance score. Each hand-gesture is choreographed to have a specific relationship to time and space, especially when the text is set in a slow rhythm. Here, even the interpolations are specifically set. Therefore, all four of the

Kottayam plays allow the actor little if any 'freedom' from their structured, set scoring. Actors and connoisseurs alike describe the Kottayam plays as 'rigidly structured' (*cittapetta*), or having a structure in performance which is 'inviolable.' *Kathakali* actor Balasubramaniam described the plays as having a 'mathematical accuracy' which 'only allows the actor to do what has been taught in the classroom and nothing more. There is nothing to add to or subtract from [what has been taught]' (1993, interview). Vembayam Appukoothan Pillai described the structure of the plays as requiring the actor to 'make his performance fit within the music and rhythms' to which each section of a text is set (1993, interview). Gopi Asan explained how learning these rigidly structured plays allows the actor to 'understand the basic grammar of *kathakali* from its application in these stories' (1993, interview). So important are the Kottayam plays in training that some scenes from the four plays that are no longer typically performed at public performances are still taught in the classroom. By learning these rigidly structured plays 'correctly,' the *kathakali* actor is understood to be able 'to perform anything else' in the repertory (Vembayam Appukoothan Pillai 1993, interview), including plays with a much looser structure which are not taught in the formal syllabus.

In contrast to the four Kottayam plays, Unnayi Variyar's *King Nala's Law*, and the two plays by Mandavapalli Ittiraricha Menon translated here, *The Progeny of Krishna* and *King Rugmamgada's Law*, are much more loosely structured. Unlike the Kottayam plays, where even the major roles are 'set' within distinctive rhythmic patterns and choreographic structures, plays like these depend upon the histrionic abilities of the actor playing such major roles as Nala or Rugmamgada to achieve their aesthetic impact through creative interpretation of all aspects of the role, including its important interpolations.

As Gopi Asan explains, in the Kottayam plays, the dramatic conflict comes from the interplay between events within the stories, whereas in plays like *Nala's Law*, *King Rugmamgada's Law*, or *The Progeny of Krishna* 'the characters are more concerned with mental conflicts' of the major character. Given their quite different demands and the degree to which

the structure is or is not 'set,' both types of plays 'have theatrical impact, but in different ways' (1993, interview). The foremost pleasures afforded an audience of connoisseurs experiencing the more technically oriented Kottayam plays are virtuosic congruence of technique and score, and masterly interpretation within a relatively narrow range of variability. But at a performance of Rugmamgada in *King Rugmamgada's Law*, or the Brahmin in *The Progeny of Krishna*, the audience experiences a greater range of internal/mental state(s) more freely interpreted by the actor.[6]

Even though these less structured plays are in great demand at public performances and part of the official 'school syllabus,' since they are so dependent on the individual talent and interpretive abilities of the actor playing its major roles, they are not taught as part of the regular six-year syllabus of plays, but only in the post-graduate course of training.

To be more precise about the differences in structure and the demand for precision they place on the actor/dancer, I will focus on differences in rhythmic structures between 'set' plays like *The Flower of Good Fortune* and *The Killing of Kirmira* and more loosely structured plays like *King Rugmamgada's Law* and *The Progeny of Krishna*. Both of the latter are for the most part set in the simplest of *kathakali*'s rhythmic patterns (*tala*) – *cempata* and *tripata* (see Figure 3.9). Neither play makes use of the most difficult and complex rhythmic patterns such as *campa* or *atanta*. For example, in *cempata* the accented beats are always an unvariable three within the total of eight. When a dialogue passage (*padam*) is set in *cempata*, in performance it can always be performed somewhat more 'freely' because of the regularity of the three accented beats within eight, i.e., if the actor-dancer does not complete the performance of his hand-gestures in delivering a phrase within the usual number of cycles set for performance, he can easily extend his performance to 'fit' the regularity of *cempata*'s three accented beats.

In contrast, for a dialogue passage set in the much more complex *campa*, with its structure of four, two, and then one accented beats in a total of ten, there is much less allowance for variation because the structure is irregular. Consequently, when learning these much more difficult

Figure 4.6   Bhava *in performance: acting a line from* The Flower of Good Fortune

	[*danyasi* (raga); *cempata* (tala – 16 beats)]	
BHIMA:		
	caranam: O beautiful deer-eyed one, without hesitation I shall fetch the 　graceful Saugandhika flowers which 　you desire.　　　[K]+[I]	

Malayalam text:		
	man/cel　　　miyi/yale　　　ni/nnal	3 cycles
mudras:　deer　equal　eyed　one　　you　by 　　　　　　　　　　[addressive]		
bhava/rasa:*srngara* (erotic)		

vanchitannal/ayitunno/r/ancita/saugandhikannal	2 cycles
[the]　desired　[plural]　[connector][7]　beautiful　flower　[plural]	
srngara (erotic)	

anc/ate　　　　kontannituvan	2 cycles
[a little] delay without will bring	
(*hasya*) (mirthful) *vira* (heroic)	*kalasam/iratti*

	pallavi: O crown jewel among beautiful women with flickering eyes! (*slight increase in basic tempo*)	
caranam: 　Whether on top of a mountain, or in 　　Indra's heaven, 　with my prowess I will easily fulfill 　　your desire. [K]+[I]		

saila/mukal/il/　　　　　　ennalum	5 cycles
mountain　　top　　on　　whether　[or even if]	
vira (heroic)	

sakralokatt/ennakilum	2 cycles
heaven whether　[or even if]	
adbhuta (wonder) *vira* (heroic)	

velay/ illa tava hitam	3 cycles
difficulty/no　yours　　desire [or wish]	
karuna (pathos) *vira* (heroic) *srngara* (erotic)	

vikram/ena　　sadhippanum.	2 cycles
prowess　by　　will fulfill	
vira (heroic)	
	kalasam + *iratti*
	pallavi: O crown jewel among . . .

patterns, the student must be attentive to finding the beginning and conclusion of each phrase of the text, and each set of hand-gestures necessary to 'speak' the text as it is to be delivered within a typical number of rhythmic cycles. We should remember that hand-gestures are not simply gestures of the hands *per se*, but are also delivered with the entire body, and therefore the actor-dancer is taking a certain amount of time to move through space as he delivers each gesture. The creation of the appropriate state of being/doing (*bhava*) comes from the appropriate synchronization of the vocalist's repetition of the cycles of the text, the actor-dancer's delivery of the hand-gestures, and the drummers' accentuation and/or elaboration on the rhythmic cycle. The exact modes of synchronization are variable, depending on how passages of the text have historically been 'set.'

I will illustrate the performative demands of the 'set' structures of the Kottayam plays with several examples from *The Killing of Kirmira*. One unique performance structure is *Lalita*'s dialogue passage (*padam*) in Scene 9 (see p. 122). Set in *atanta tala* and in the slowest of slow tempos [*patinnakalam* at fifty-six beats], this is the only passage in the four Kottayam plays performed by a female character in the slowest of slow tempo. Learning this unique passage provides the foundation for a student's ability to perform similar passages set in *atanta tala*, and in the slowest tempo. It requires a great deal of precision on the actor's part.

A second example of unique structure is Lalita's *caranam* set in *cempata tala* in second speed with sixteen beats:

> Clusters of clouds and darkness contend with
> your long curly hair.
> O one with beautiful hair like the dark
> Valisneria, swarms of bees come here
> one after another to see your hair
> again and again.
> Alas! With grief they fly away!

In the first phrase of the Malayalam there are seven syllables, which take two rhythmic cycles (*tala*) to perform, set in sixteen beats. The much lengthier remainder of the passage is compressed so that it too is performed within two cycles of *tala*. The actor-dancer must ensure that he has learned this tricky and unusual shift in the number of syllables, and therefore in the number of hand-gestures he must perform within the set number of cycles in order to achieve the intended *dramatic* effect. This linguistic 'compression' gives the impression or feel of speeding up the tempo which 'fits' the swarming of the bees. When this passage is performed, what makes a *rasika* (connoisseur) a *rasika* is his intuitive knowledge of the 'correct' way to perform this passage, and strict expectation that the passage be performed within this set structure. Learning 'set' passages like these is crucial for the student's training since the performance structures are distinctive, complex, and serve as a 'model' for performance of complex passages in other plays.

A third example from *The Killing of Kirmira* is in the dialogue passage (*padam*) performed between Sahadeva and Simhika in Scene 11 (see p. 125). A common structure guides the actor-dancers performing both roles, beginning with Simhika's *caranam*. The first phrase of each *caranam* is followed by the performance of a punctuating dance-ending (*kalasam*). Immediately after the dance-ending, the vocalist repeats the original phrase. Then, at the conclusion of each *caranam*, the *pallavi* is repeated to accompany the dancing of a *tonkaram*. This rigidly 'set' pattern dramatically serves to underscore the mutual hurling of sarcastic insults typical of scenes which are the prelude to a fight-to-the-death. In this particular scene, Sahadeva hurls the initial insult in his *pallavi* as follows:

> Stop, demoness, stop!
> *Eti, eti, eti*, demoness!

Eti is the feminine addressive form of a common marketplace insult that is literally untranslatable. When punctuated by the percussive rhythm set in *cempata tala*, the insult is literally hurled with Sahadeva's entire body. Not to be outdone, Simhika scornfully retorts in her own *pallavi* with the male addressive, *eta,* returning the 'favor' in kind. As students learn this structure, they absorb a performance pattern typically found in the dynamic build-up of scenes ending in combat, and concluding with the 'killing' of demons like Kirmira.

These examples of the set structures of the Kottayam plays illustrate how the entire training of the *kathakali* actor might be thought of as a process of intuitive familiarization with enough of the unique synchronic structures of text, hand-gestures, and rhythmic patterns that will enable him to both co-produce those structures, and bring a virtuosic performative acumen and expressivity to them when a mature performer. It is the Kottayam plays which provide the actor with his initial performative experience of these 'external' structures and their rules.

THE 'INNER' ART OF KATHAKALI ACTING: TASK/ACTION, CHARACTER, AND ROLE

As should be evident from the earlier microanalysis of *kathakali*'s score in Chapter 3 as well as the discussion of the demands of the highly structured Kottayam plays, a *kathakali* performance constructs characters in part through a non-linear sequencing of 'actions'; indeed, what constitutes an 'action' (in the Western acting sense of the term) simply does not exist in *kathakali*. To analyse the specific tasks of the *kathakali* actor, I will examine the specific requirements for the performance of the states/moods for Bhima during a few lines of Scene 9 in *The Flower of Good Fortune* (Figure 4.6). In this example I provide the translation, a transliteration, a word-by-word translation (what the actor 'says' with his hand-gestures), the number of rhythmic cycles it normally takes for the actor-dancer to deliver the text in gesture language, and the state of being/doing (*bhava*) the actor embodies while delivering each phrase or word. Although the overall mood of the scene with Panchali is *srngara*, or the 'erotic' sentiment prompted by their pleasures in the garden, the *bhava* for each word or phrase must be appropriate to the meaning of the word or phrase as it is embodied in performance, and therefore it shifts appropriately.

Although the overall state of being/mood and that required in the first two parts of the first *caranam*, is the pleasurable sense of the erotic, it is clear from this brief example that the actor playing Bhima must shift his state of being/mood even within this *caranam*. In the final section of the *caranam* '[a little] delay without will bring,' the actor's *bhava* momentarily shifts from the erotic to the mirthful as the actor jokingly qualifies his statement of heroic prowess 'will bring without delay,' with the tongue-in-cheek

qualifier, 'a little' – as if he, the mighty Bhima, might ever encounter such difficulties! This shift to the heroic at the end of the first *caranam* is continued in the second. Here Bhima embodies and enacts this prowess, touting his ability to conquer whatever is in the way of achieving the fulfillment of Panchali's desire for the Saugandhika flowers. The heroic mood of this *caranam* is further elaborated as the actor playing Bhima enacts his 'wonder' when delivering the hand-gesture for Indra's 'heaven,' and the 'pathos' Panchali might feel if her desire were not fulfilled. The second *caranam* appropriately concludes with Bhima's heroic prowess and demeanor in full display since it is precisely Bhima's bursting pride that will be lanced in the scene to follow with Hanuman.

Although there is an overall dramatic arc to this elaboration of Bhima's interior state, the actor's task is first and foremost to embody completely each of the sequential hand-gestures in the enactment of each word of the text, and while embodying each gesture, to endow it psychophysiologically with the appropriate state of being/doing (*bhava*), i.e., 'seeing' a mountain is enacted *through time* with a certain quality of seeing. The actor's eyes/body/hands embody the psychophysiological act of seeing the mountain and Indra's heaven, and along with that comes the appropriate *bhava*, i.e., a certain degree of wonder or awe at Indra's heaven and/or the 'size' and immensity of the mountain. When the actor's task is to 'become' the image, there is often no *bhava* registered during that particular period of enactment of the character's *bhava per se*, i.e., the actor momentarily 'steps out' of the character, and is (becomes) what is being seen by the audience – the mountain.

The requirement that the *kathakali* actor 'step out' of his character is vividly exemplified in Bhima's well-known interpolation in Scene 9 of *The Flower of Good Fortune* (see pp. 106–7). This interpolation enacts the fight between an elephant, a python, and a lion that Bhima witnesses while traversing the forest on his way to find the Saugandhika flowers for Panchali. In enacting the interpolation Bhima narrates what he sees, and in quick succession plays the role of each animal he observes in the fight, embodying and playing in turn the elephant, python, and lion.[8]

When considered structurally, these examples suggest that the actor's performance score is two-fold: first are the task-specific set of embodied actions performed sequentially, in time, each task embodied on its own terms; and second is the overall dramatic arc of the character. When the mature *kathakali* actor says he 'becomes' or 'absorbs' the character, it is clear that he assumes that his act of 'becoming' operates at both these levels, and that there is a constant dialectic between them – of general 'identification' or absorption of the character-as-character, and in terms of 'becoming' embodied in each specific task of his score. The structure of the *kathakali* actor's set of tasks/actions is not an apparently 'seamless,' psychologically integrated set of behaviors as in much Western Stanislavskian-based realistic acting. The 'character' is always there but, simultaneously, can also be temporarily put in 'parentheses' in the sense that the character is 'set aside' from time to time. The shifts in state of being/mood are openly displayed and depend not just on the character's mood within the context of the drama *per se*, but also on the mood required to perform each image he embodies in delivering hand-gestures, or what is demanded by the structure of the score. The actor in this sense is not always simply playing what the character requires – he is also embodying and playing what the text-in-performance requires.

In this structural sense, a *kathakali* performance is not attempting to create the 'illusion of reality' happening in 'real time,' but rather creates opportunities for elaboration of states of mind/being/doing appropriate to the dramatic circumstances of a particular narrative, thereby making available a richly textured aesthetic experience for its audiences, especially connoisseurs. Because of this, the *kathakali* actor's relationship to time in structuring performance and character are quite different from performances of modern Western drama, whose performance structures are ultimately derived from an Aristotelian concept of mimesis.

My observations and analysis of the structure of the *kathakali* actor's tasks should not obscure the fundamental importance of 'character' to the actor's approach to any role on the *kathakali* stage.[9] Implicit in a *kathakali* actor's approach to acting is the assumption that he 'becomes one' with the role or character he plays, which thus guides each specific task or action he embodies in his score. Such statements are paralleled in the *Natyasastra*. In one passage the *Natyasastra* explains how

> In theatrical performance, after proper consideration of age and dress, he who has the suitable form should resemble the role in nature too. Just as a man's soul, discarding its nature along with the body, enters a different body with its different nature, in the same way, a wise man, exercising his mental faculties, makes other's nature his own, holding, 'I am he' and along with his dress, speech and body, follows his actions too.
>
> (Kale 1974: 58–9, translation of
> *Natyasastra* XXIV, 15–18)

The notion of the transmigration of a soul from one body to another is commonplace, paralleled in the assumption that it is even possible to attain a state of superior spiritual accomplishment (*siddha*) through which one might literally inhabit another body.[10]

Implicit in both the *Natyasastra* and *kathakali* actors' statements about 'becoming' the character is the assumption that it is possible to attain a non-dualistic state of actualization between the actor and the character. This understanding is reflected in discussions I have had over the years with many *kathakali* actors. Just beginning to reach the stride of his career at the age of 49 in 1993, Kalamandalam Vasu Pisharody explained to me his interpretation of *kathakali*'s roles:

> There are many 'green' (heroic) roles including Nala, Bhima, Bahuka, Pushkara, etc. Their movements are basically alike, but each character is different. We perceive each character from our reading and understanding, and then play that role according to our understanding and perception. For characters of this type, there is no single or special state of being/doing (*bhava*). Rather, it's better to think of them as 'unique in their differences and different in their uniqueness' . . . The core state (*stayibhava*) for Bhima is the heroic (*vira*), and for him the erotic (*rati*) is secondary. But for Nala his core state is the erotic, and the heroic is only secondary . . . Therefore, Bhima's expression of the erotic will be different from that of Nala . . . When Nala shows

the hand-gestures for 'lotus' it is different from Bhima. Likewise when Nala or Bhima speak to Panchali. In order to assimilate these differences, the actor has to absorb each character. The actor has to have his mind enculturated into this process. He creates [this state of mind] by his reading. After achieving [this state of mind], the audience will sense it.

(1993, interview)

The crucial notion is that the actor himself must both understand each character, and achieve a particular 'state of mind', thereby 'absorbing each character.'

Kalamandalam Bala Subramaniyan explains the subtle difference in playing two *pacca* characters, Dharmaputra and Nala, both of whom have suffered greatly in their lives. As eldest of the Pandavas, Dharmaputra carries the weight of responsibility for the fate of his brothers and their wife. As he appears in the Kottayam plays, Dharmaputra 'cannot act out his feelings as can Nala' (Balasubramaniyan 1993, interview). In the opening scene of *The Killing of Kirmira*, for example, when Dharmaputra expresses his great sympathy to Draupadi for their plight and the hardships they have suffered while in exile in the forest,

> the actor should feel [the suffering they have experienced] inside, and the audience should feel it by looking into his face; however, the actor playing Dharmaputra should not overtly show any *bhava* in his face. He should only use his eyes to reveal the *bhava*. The inhering (*stayi-*) expression is enough. No overt outside display of *bhava* is required.
>
> (Balasubramaniyan 1993, interview)

All senior *kathakali* actors stress how their own creativity is influenced by their study of the characters they play, and their constant reading of and reflection upon epic and *puranic* sources through which they can locate further insights into the character, and find potentially relevant passages from which an interpolation might be further elaborated. Gopi Asan, one of *kathakali*'s most distinguished and heralded actors today, explains his own process as he approaches each specific role he plays as follows:

I usually refresh my mind and my understanding of the character. Sometimes I make reference to resource books. Every time I view a performance as a challenge, and thus an experiment. But I am never satisfied even when an audience applauds and cheers my performance. I always think about the form and its structure, which is most important for a traditional art like *kathakali*. Sometimes I fix what will be improvised in advance. But often it happens spontaneously. In this context, I want to quote the following lines: 'A disciple gets one fourth [of what he learns] from his teacher; the second quarter from himself; the third part from his classmates; and the last quarter in the long run of one's life.' The maturity of an actor is expected only in the last stage.

(1993, interview)

Best known for his playing of roles like Nala and Rugmamgada, which are overtly 'dramatic' and less structured than many, Gopi Asan's emphasis on the mastery of form and structure reflects the fact that *kathakali*'s performance score, conventions, and technique always define the framework within which the actor exercises his creative imagination when creating a role.

In more (melo)dramatic, interior forms of acting used to enact *sloka* (see the example from *King Nala's Law* in Chapter 8, p. 167) or interpolations like those of Nala or Rugmamgada, the 'character' is literally and temporally 'more' present through time because the structure of performance allows for continuous focus on the internal states of the character. Margi Vijayakumar explained the nuances of interpretation he brings to playing the role of the demoness Putana in *Putanamoksham* – a character conflicted by the competing demands placed on her as the servant of Kamsa sent to kill the baby Krishna, and her maternal desire to feed and protect the child:

Within the demoness there is the woman's attraction to the baby. The pleasure and affection she feels come from feeding the child. Then there is the sense of duty to Kamsa who must kill even against her wishes.

(1993, interview)

But even the process of training toward the performance of such 'internal' moments is structured quite differently in *kathakali*. As we have seen this process begins not with the personal, the behavioral, or the motivational aspect of playing an action, but with the psychophysiological forms through which the 'emotional' is eventually expressed. The student actor's personal feelings are not the point of origin for the creation of a facial or hand-gesture. One's experience in life gradually informs the outer form as the student is asked to use his imagination as he enters the process of embodiment, becoming a lotus as he sees its beauty, and smells its fragrance. Through the actor's process of complete engagement in the act of embodying an expressive state, his imagination, perceiving consciousness, or 'mind' enters and 'fills out' the 'outer' form, as outlined in Figure 4.7.

The characters the *kathakali* actor creates are always shaped by what is considered 'appropriate to the action,' and the actor's engagement in this process is clearly one of acting. As one actor explained:

> It is not right to have real tears on stage: it does not fit our stylized type of theater. But the emotion of crying must be there and it will effect the audience. As an actor you must always use your emotions, knowing that you are onstage. There must be balance. After the long period of training, the gestures, the technique become automatic. You don't have to concentrate on them; then you can really fill in the role, add the emotion, and so on.

Enacting a *bhava* in *kathakali* is a fully physicalized and embodied psychophysiological task which ideally engages the actor's bodymind

completely. When Gopi Asan plays the role of Rugmamgada in *King Rugmamgada's Law*, and embodies his full surprise at Mohini's demand that he kills his son, at that moment of 'high (melo) drama' every sinew of the actor's bodymind is 'filled' with that *bhava*. Part of the difference between the subtle 'naturalistic' acting of the West and *kathakali* is that in *kathakali*, as in Japanese *kabuki*, this 'filling' of the body is openly displayed and indulged, while in naturalism it is usually hidden and not obvious. The act of physicalization of the state of being/feeling of the character is intentionally 'excessive' in the sense that the stage is the place to display openly the full or 'pure' emotion/*bhava*, i.e., nothing need be held back to inflect or nuance its expression. These are, after all, gods, epic heroes, heroines, and personalities at play on this cosmic stage, whose predicaments and responses to them are bound to be 'larger' than everyday life.

'WHERE THE HAND [IS] . . .': THE KATHAKALI PERFORMER'S IDEAL STATE OF BEING/DOING

One way of understanding the optimal state of actualization toward which the *kathakali* actor's years of training ideally leads him is to revisit the now often clichéd, and all too often quoted, statement (*sloka* 36) embedded in Nandikesvara's *Abhinayadarpanam* (usually dated between the tenth and thirteenth centuries), rightfully cited as an encapsulation of the *rasa*/*bhava* aesthetic.[11] The passage has been 'immortalized' in Coomaraswamy's translation, *The Mirror of Gesture*:

Figure 4.7   *Filling out the form*

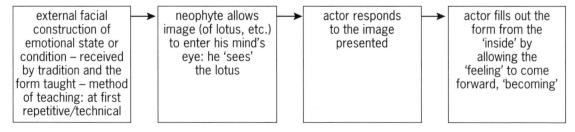

| external facial construction of emotional state or condition – received by tradition and the form taught – method of teaching: at first repetitive/technical | → | neophyte allows image (of lotus, etc.) to enter his mind's eye: he 'sees' the lotus | → | actor responds to the image presented | → | actor fills out the form from the 'inside' by allowing the 'feeling' to come forward, 'becoming' |

For wherever the hand moves, there the
glances flows; where the glances go, the
mind follows; where the mind goes, the
mood follows; where the mood goes, there
is the flavour.

(1957: 17)

Manomohan Ghosh provides a similar
translation:

Where the hand goes eyes also should go
there. Whither the mind goes Psychological
State (*bhava*) should turn thither, and
where there is the Psychological State,
there the Sentiment (*rasa*) arises.

(Ghosh 1975: 42)

Although constantly cited, the *sloka* has seldom
received commentary which analyzes the
assumptions that inform this optimal state-of-
being/actualization. It is my purpose here to
provide a re-reading and analysis, not from the
point of view of a Sanskrit expert, but rather
from the perspective of the
performer/performance scholar by giving an
alternative, more literal translation of the
passage, and then conducting an exegesis using
the specific example of the psychophysiological
process of the *kathakali* actor.

As Kapila Vatsyayan has indicated, the critical
texts on Indian aesthetics are primarily of two
quite distinct types: on the one hand are
discussions of the nature of the aesthetic
experience itself pursued by various schools of
philosophical thought; on the other are manuals
which focus on form and technique (1968a: 7).
While Nandikesvara's *Abhinayadarpanam* is of
the second type – primarily a technical manual
for the performer – this passage is important
because it links the technical treatise to
underlying philosophical assumptions which
inform performance *per se*.

Returning to the Coomaraswamy and Ghosh
translations of the passage above, the general
impression of both is that of sequential movement
– going from here to there. Implied is a stimulus
(wherever) and a response (follow). The primary
verb chosen in the two translations is the active 'to
go.' While it is certainly possible to read 'goes' –
and the succeeding verb 'follows' – as
simultaneous rather than sequential, the directional
indicators 'wherever,' 'there,' 'where,' 'whither,' and
'thither' certainly imply sequentiality.

But a literal word-by-word translation of this
passage would be:

> where hand there eye
> (*yato hasta tato drishtir*)
>
> where eye there mind
> (*Yato drishtistato manah*)
>
> where eye there *bhava*[12]
> (*yato mana tato bhavo*)
>
> where *bhava* there *rasa*[13]
> (*yato bhavastato rasah*) [*sloka* 36]

The Coomaraswamy and Ghosh translations
describe a process seen by outsiders. I wish to
consider the description from the inside – from
the point of view of the performer. I argue that
the fundamental psychophysiological process of
the performer and the assumed ideal of
simultaneous realization in the moment of
traditional Indian performances like *kathakali* fit
the literal meaning.

One of the major reasons why the *sloka* is so
important is that it makes use of the state-of-
being verb (*tato*) and is therefore a summary of
what in Indian theater is considered an optimal,
non-conditional state of accomplishment or
being/doing-in-performance for both spectators
and actors – the *bhava* of the actor and the *rasa*
of the audience are ideally non-conditional
states-of-being. I contend there is no suggestion
of sequentiality or conditionality in the original,
and to introduce even a hint of movement or
conditionality is to skew the meaning.
Coomaraswamy does introduce 'is' in the final
clause; however, the clear impression is that the
rasa is 'there' as the result of a sequential process
of movement. Certainly Ghosh's use of 'to be'
coupled with 'arises' in the final two clauses of
his translation is an improvement over
Coomaraswamy, however slight, since again a
conditional state is suggested by 'arises.' In sum,
the passage might simply and literally be
translated as:

> Where the hand [is], there [is] the eye;
> where the eye [is], there [is] the mind;
> where the mind [is], there [is] the *bhava*;
> where the *bhava* [is], there is the *rasa*.

Is the choice of the English verb in translation of
this passage important? It is. From the
performer's point of view, the non-conditional

state-of-being is possible only for an accomplished master, while the conditional is typical of the neophyte. An example from *kathakali* training will illustrate the difference.

As discussed earlier in this chapter, in the first stages of *kathakali* training the teacher supplies the initial stimulus as the student learns basic 'external' forms. For example, when training in basic eye exercises, the student sits in front of the teacher and is instructed to focus his eyes on the teacher's finger and follow the pattern it traces. Next he learns to focus his eyes where the hand moves, at first self-consciously tracking the movements of his hands. The eyes follow in response to the initial stimulus of directional hand movement. The beginner must also self-consciously trigger the mind to follow where the eyes have gone. The neophyte is easily distracted and must be deliberately re-minded to keep his mind on/in what he is doing.

Similarly, the student must master his facial musculature so that it can serve as a conduit for the embodiment of the various states of being/doing (*bhava*) demanded by the dramatic context. At first, the student is only able to perform sequential, conditional repetition and is reminded by his teacher to bring even a hint of *bhava* into his performance. In summary, then, sequentiality and conditionality are the conditions of the neophyte's earliest attempts at performance. Even when at the technical level, the eyes are going where the hands are moving, seldom is the student's mind yet 'there' nor has *bhava* yet filled out the forms learned through repetition.

My objection to the use of an active rather than state-of-being verb in translating this passage is that it implies the performance of neophyte rather than master. And clearly the *Abhinayadarpanam* is describing the optimal condition of a master. The *sloka* summarizes that state in which there is no sequential intentionality or conditionality. Only as the student moves toward mastery is he able to actualize that state. The master and his technique are ideally 'one' – he is what he does at each moment. The state-of-being verb establishes this condition as one in which four elements (hand, eye, mind, *bhava*) are simultaneously present within the performer. The fifth element, *rasa*, applies to the audience's state of engagement, and at an ideal performance is simultaneously present.

This describes the performer's accomplished state (*siddhi*) of being and mastery. The external 'forms' of training have been gradually encoded into the neophyte's bodymind through repetition and drill to a point where they become part of his performative 'body-consciousness' and as such are ready-at-hand to be used 'unthinkingly.' Just as the accomplished yogi attains a state of actualization where he is able to transcend habitualized in-body processes to attain higher stages of meditations (*dhyana*, etc.), likewise the master performer is eventually freed from the flux of the normative, everyday psychomental stream of consciousness for the performative moment. He is freed from 'consciousness about' for a state of 'concentratedness' in and for the task at hand – fully embodying and engaging himself in psychophysiological actions through which his character is created in time. While the neophyte moves toward, the master 'is.'

THE PSYCHOPHYSIOLOGY OF 'FORM': THE ASSUMPTIONS THAT INFORM 'BECOMING THE CHARACTER'

What is believed, but usually unarticulated, in disciplines of embodied practice like yoga, the martial arts, or performing arts like *kathakali* are the fundamental assumptions about the bodymind which inform the achievement of such an actualized state of being/doing. Continuing my exegesis of this passage, let me return to the literal translation and provide commentary on some of the performative assumptions about the bodymind relationship and the interior 'subtle' dimensions of embodiment which inform the four lines of the *sloka* from the perspective of *kathakali* actors today.

Where the hand [is], there [is] the eye . . .

The hands are central to most Indian genres of performance, and especially *kathakali* and *kutiyattam* where *mudra* are used for decorative effect as well as a complete grammar for delivery of the dramatic text. When learning hand-gestures the student moves from mimicry of externals to a state where he is psychophysiologically 'connected' to each *mudra* from the region of the navel (*nabhi*). Derived from assumptions about the body and bodymind relationship of both the traditional Indian system of health and medicine (Ayurveda, literally, the 'science of life'), and from the understanding of the 'subtle' body associated with yoga practice and philosophy, this connection is understood to be provided by the interior coursing of the breath, wind, or 'life force' (*prana-vayu*).[14] As *kathakali* actor M.P. Sankaran Namboodiri explained in an interview, 'the *vayu* is spread all over the body. It is how to control that that is [an implicit] part of the training.' Over time, the practice of vigorous psychophysiological exercises such as yoga postures (*asana*), martial arts (*kalarippayattu*), *kathakali*'s preliminary exercises derived from the martial arts, and/or undergoing vigorous massage is understood to control as well as stimulate the breath/life-force, and to clear the (often clogged) channels of the subtle body, thereby promoting good health and allowing ease of circulation of the vital-energy through both the physical and the subtle bodies.

In both *kalarippayattu* (martial arts) and *kathakali* training, students from the first day of training are instructed to breathe through the nose, and not the mouth – a simple instruction which, when adhered to in conjunction with correct spinal alignment while exercising, develops breathing which naturally originates at the 'root of the navel' (*nabhi mula*). Most important is the activation of this region (*nabhi mula*) to which and from which the breath/life-force is understood to circulate via the subtle body's channels (*nadi*) along the line of the spine and out through the limbs, as well as into the head/face. Correct instruction also comes from hands-on manipulation of the student's body by the teacher. As one teacher explained,

> Without a verbal word of instruction the teacher may, by pointing to or pressing certain parts of the body, make the student understand where the breath-energy should be held or released.

When taking *kathakali*'s basic position (Plate 4.5) with the feet parallel to each other and the toes 'gripping' the earth via a solid triangle of energy created between the soles of the feet and the region of the lower navel, the actor-dancer creates a dynamic set of oppositional forces with his internal energy – a force directed simultaneously up toward the navel and down into the earth. It is this 'gripping' which gives

kathakali, like its martial precursor, its strong, dynamic, (*tandava*) grounded quality of strength, as well as the literal force manifest when one's breath or 'energy' is directed in its most concentrated form along the outside of the dancer's foot as it hits the ground. Gradually the practitioner is able to control and manipulate his vital-energy as the 'enlivening' force which is circulated and directed to and from the navel region through his embodied practice so that, for the master as least, what could be 'empty' lifeless technique becomes 'enlivened' artistry.

This centered 'groundedness' is part of performing *kathakali*'s gesture language 'correctly.' Each articulation of the hands/arms is 'energized' from the region of the lower navel by the circulation of the breath through the hands. The breath/energy manifest in each gesture must of course be shaped by the qualitative dramatic and narrative context of the moment.

Intuitive release, circulation, and control of the breath and therefore of 'energy' through the entire body, including the face and eyes, is necessary for the accomplished realization of the 'emotional' dimension of *kathakali* performance – the full embodiment of the nine basic facial expressions. While in performance it is literally true that where the hands are there the eyes are, the eyes suggest much more than external focus. The eyes are a predominant medium for gaining 'knowledge' or affecting something or someone (Eck 1981: 6–7). When a devotee takes even a momentary glimpse (*darsan*) of a divine image, there is contact and an exchange, not a simple 'looking at.' The eyes are the window to one's internal condition. They are a conduit and zone of modulation between forces outside (such as the 'evil eye') or inside (using one's mental power, *manasakti*). When in a state of possession the ritual performer's eyes manifest the deity's power (*sakti*) and presence through the performer. In *kathakali* performance the eyes reveal the states of being/doing of the character through its more or less stylized, yet fully embodied form. The correct manipulation and control of the breath assumed when performing facial expressions and/or using the eyes is not taught systematically, but is developed through the pedagogical process of demonstration, imitation, and gradual correction by the teacher. For example, performing the erotic sentiment (*rati bhava*, Plate 4.3, 1) the external manipulation of the facial mask executes the following basic moves, which are closely coordinated with the breath as follows:

> Beginning with a long, slow and sustained in-breath, the eyebrows move slowly up and down. The eyelids are held open half-way on a quick catch breath, and when the object of pleasure or love is seen (a lotus flower; one's lover, etc.), the eyelids quickly open on an in-breath, as the corners of the mouth are pulled up and back, responding to the object of pleasure.

The breathing is deep, and connected to the region of the lower navel; it is never shallow chest breathing. The characteristic pattern associated with the erotic sentiment is slow, long, sustained in-breaths with which the object of love or pleasure is literally 'taken in,' i.e., breathing in the aroma, sight, etc. of the lotus, or the beloved.

For the furious sentiment (*krodha bhava*, Plate 4.3, 4), on seeing the object of fury

> the eyes are wide open, the nostrils flare and the internal wind is literally pushed from the root of the navel out into the lower eyelids, and through the nose, causing the nostrils to flare, and the lower lids to flutter, 'furiously.'

Occasionally, a teacher might tell a student to 'push the wind (*vayu*) from the navel into the face.' After gripping in the region of the navel, the breath/energy is literally pushed into the face, as the muscles of the diaphragm region contract. After holding the grip for a while, there may be a quick 'catch breath,' with a slight exhalation through the nose. In this act of internal psychophysiological actualization, the performer might be said to be 'seeing' (furiously) from within – from the navel. 'Where the eye [is]' is where there is simultaneously an outer and inner seeing.

G.S. Warrier tells the story of how Thottam Sankaran Namboodiri from Ambalapuzha was 'noted for his *raudra* ("furious") Bhima. There was no one to match him when he did this role. The terrible wrath on his face would be felt by the actors playing Dussassana so much that they could not even look at his face!' Warrier explained how and why Thottam Sankaran Namboodiri learned and achieved this effect:

In the *Natyasastra* they call this *sattvik* – you get the entire emotion on your face. Then you practise what is called 'concentrating the thought' there, and 'give it wind.' It's one of the great secrets of acting. The Ambalapuzha *kutiyattam cakyar* [who taught Thottam Sankaran Namboodiri] says you 'give *vayu* (wind/energy) like in *karate* – giving 'nervous' control [i.e., control via the channels of the subtle body]. So, Thottam Sankaran Namboodiri was able to 'push the wind' into this intense rage. Bhima here becomes a half-beast as Draupadi had predicted to avenge this dishonor. The great experts teach this!

(1993, interview)

The *kathakali* actor's score demands his engagement of a series of fully embodied states – realized as the actor focuses externally on specific points while delivering hand and facial gestures, and engages his 'inner eyes' (attention, or perceiving consciousness in the moment) as well as breath-energy in what he is doing. For the actor, his own 'concentration of thought' is the psychophysiological concentration of his breath and field of visual/mental focus in what he is doing in each moment of his score. In the example of *King Nala's Law* cited in Chapter 3 (pp. 44-5), as the actor moves his right hand to his chest and his external focus goes upward, he is not 'thinking about' or 'reflecting upon' either his own (actor's) state or condition of sorrow or that of the character; rather, 'sorrow' is his active engagement through time of his inner breath/energy in the embodied act of focusing his gaze and placing his hand. In this particular example, 'nervous control' is the virtuosic actor's ability to modulate his breath and focus through time so that the audience might have their own (aesthetic) experience of the character's 'emotional' state of sorrow.

. . . where the eye [is], there [is] the mind . . .

Implied in inner vision is engagement of the performer's entire bodymind. Movement of the master performer's hands or eyes is not simply physical movement separate from mental engagement. The inner psychophysiological coursing of the *prana-vayu* assumes cognitive/mental engagement. *Kathakali* actor

M.P. Sankaran Namboodiri explained to me how the student-actor must learn to 'take time to concentrate the mind in the hand-gestures,' i.e., gradually gain an intuitive ability to have his 'mind' focused in each gesture as it is performed. As June McDaniel explains, the Sanskrit

> *mana* means both mind and heart, as well as mood, feeling, mental state, memory, desire, attachment, interest, attention, devotion, and decision. These terms do not have a single referent in English, and must be understood through clusters of explicit and implicit meanings.
>
> (1995: 43)

The 'structuring of structure' is the actor's psychophysiological score, and the specificity of the *kathakali* actor's task of constantly directing his focus and breath reflects the engagement of the actor's mind/attention/heart in the act of performing each 'emotional' state in turn. In this sense, the actor trained through a corporeal discipline learns to 'direct' his 'passions' as he learns to control the breath/energy. This suggests an experience-rich cluster of associations involving the simultaneous engagement of intellect, understanding, perception, feeling in the act of performing. No Cartesian mind/body split is assumed. Rather, 'where the mind (*mana*) [is]' implies the engagement of the performer's entire being/bodymind in a state of psychophysiological connectedness and concentratedness through the internal coursing of the *prana-vayu*, and therefore engaging life itself (*jivan*).

> . . . where the mind [is], there [is] the *bhava* . . .

The dramatic context determines the external stylistic and interpretive forms which shape and channel the performer's bodymind. *Bhava* is optimally the enlivened and energized inner states of being/doing expressiveness (*sattvik abhinaya*) which fills out those exterior forms through the inner psychophysiological process described above. The actor ideally enters an embodied state, thereby 'becoming the character,'

> . . . where the *bhava* [is], there [is] the *rasa* . . .

Assuming an audience educated and prepared to 'taste,' the performer's embodied psychophysiological state-of-being (*bhava*) simultaneously establishes the possibility for the actualization of *rasa* – there is a 'tasting.' At least after Abhinavagupta's composition of his treatise on aesthetics, that state of tasting is often interpreted by connoisseurs like those at Margi as a further resonance – a glimpse, touching, and 'knowing' of a state of bliss itself (*ananda*).

Reflecting its psychophysiological/embodied roots in *kalarippayattu*, *kathakali*'s manipulation of breath and release of energy is manifest in the strength and facility of its footwork, use of gesture language, and facial expression. The 'drama' of *kathakali* performance is as much in the actor's psychophysiological engagement in each performative act of his score, and in the relationship between each specific task, its resonances and relationship to the shaping, form, and 'feeling tone' of the next moment. In each precise psychophysiological moment the 'character' is being created as an embodied and projected/energized/living form between actor and audience. In such moments of performance the actor becomes transparent, the medium for the 'carrying forward' of the states of being/doing of the character to the audience.

THE ACTOR'S CREATIVE PROCESS: DEVELOPING AND PERFORMING INTERPOLATIONS

The distinctive mark of the *kathakali* actor today is when connoisseurs take note of the mature actor's individual signature when playing particular roles, and especially in the actor's unique contributions to the relatively flexible interpolations in the performance score. Margi Vijayakumar explained his view of the creative process in the further elaboration of the role of Damayanti in *Nala's Law* for performances at Margi:

> The dominant state/mood (*stayi bhava*) in this role is sorrow, and all the other secondary modes of expressing elaborate sorrow. By extending this scene in performance to two hours, there is enough time to elaborate [both predominant and secondary] states fully . . . We can make the expression of each state perfect by adding interpolations and enacting what

we imagine happens to the character in this situation . . . [When enacting this role] it used to be that I simply performed what was written in the text. One incident happens after another. Typically, we show one hand-gesture after another, rushing through. But [when we elaborate], there is no rush; no time limitation. We have time to think.

(1993, interview)

To understand further the *kathakali* actor's creative process of developing a role and its interpolations, I will focus on how Nelliyode Vasudevan Namboodiri has developed and become widely noted for his acting of the role of Simhika in *The Killing of Kirmira*. An early graduate of the Kerala Kalamandalam now residing in Thiruvananthapuram where he recently inaugurated his own private training school, Nelliyode has become one of the most heralded and sought after senior actors of three types of roles: brahmin characters such the Brahmin in *The Progeny of Krishna*, 'red beard' roles, and forest dwelling 'black' female roles like Simhika. My description focuses on Nelliyode's performance of Simhika's lengthy two-part interpolation at the beginning of Chapter 8 in *The Killing of Kirmira* in which Simhika first elaborates her character's basic nature as a demoness, and then elaborates her anguished cry of 'Alas!' In performances edited to last approximately three hours, like the text translated in this volume (Chapter 6), this scene opens the performance.

Like most interpolations, the basic framework for performing this one is set by tradition (*citta*), and was taught to Nelliyode by his own teacher. Since beginning to perform the role about fifteen years ago, Nelliyode has gradually added his own interpretation and elaboration of specific moments.

The opening *sloka* of the scene describes Simhika's state of mind when she hears of her husband's death:

Hearing over and again about the killing of her dear one,
in her anger the demoness' eyes vomited blazing light like the flames of fire emitted by (the third eye) of Siva's forehead,
(and her) row of fangs emitted spiraling sparks –

this demoness, the infamous Simhika, (whose) speech has unbearably hard syllables, revealed herself.

The interpolation begins immediately after Simhika's curtain look as she begins to clean, adorn, and 'beautify' herself – this elaborates her basic nature as a demoness. Her process of 'beautification' mimetically copies, but comically parodies that of *kathakali*'s idealized female characters. As a demoness she embodies and represents the evil, hysterical, dark, untamed, uncivilized, sexually active, and ugly opposite of the idealized well-mannered, tame, fair, and beautiful heroine. Mimetic acts like cleaning and dressing her hair, placing a *tilaka* mark on her forehead, acting shyly and playing games to while away the time until her husband returns to her, all stylistically exaggerate and thereby comically subvert and invert the processes of beautification and behavior appropriate to 'proper' heroines. She 'fancies' herself beautiful as she 'walks proudly with her long hair,' believing that those watching her have become 'envious of her.' Once she has decorated herself, she decides 'I'll pretend I'm shy when he comes to embrace me,' i.e., she acts as if she's *not* the lustful, sexually active female that, as a demoness, she 'by nature' must be. Since she is 'naturally' 'black' (*kari*) and therefore 'dark' (*tamasa*), no matter how much she works at 'changing' her appearance or behavior by 'acting shy,' as a 'shape-changer' her substantive nature as 'dark' cannot be altered.

In creating his own version of Simhika's adornment, Nelliyode has taken into consideration the similar role of Nakratundi, the demoness servant of the demon-king Narakasura, who was sent to the abode of the gods to capture women for his enjoyment in *The Killing of Narakasura* by Kartika Tirunal (c.1724–98). Nakratundi also performs an interpolation in which she 'beautifies' herself; however, there is a major difference between their circumstances. Nelliyode explained in a 1993 interview that he has constructed his version of Simhika's adornment around the fact that she lives in the forest, and not at court like Nakratundi. Consequently, when she needs oil for cleaning her hair, rather than taking it from a bottle 'ready made' on a shelf, Nelliyode's Simhika looks around the forest for 'natural' oil. Seeing a tree laden with fruit, she goes to the tree, shakes it vigorously so that the fruit falls onto the ground, gathers the fruit, and proceeds to crush it, pressing out its oil. It is with *this* oil that she cleans her hair! Nelliyode's addition of the details of securing oil for her hair from her 'natural' environment in the forest is widely appreciated by connoisseurs since his choice has been read as appropriate to her fundamental nature as a forest-dwelling demoness, and because the vibrant accuracy of his detailed mime literalizes and magnifies her exaggerated process of beautification, thereby accentuating the comic parody which the first part of the interpolation elaborates.

Perhaps the most striking and dramatic of Nelliyode's additions to the traditional interpolation is at its abrupt conclusion where there is a sudden shift of mood from comic parody to her realization that the anguished cries she hears from someone about to die are those of her husband. At this moment of realization, Nelliyode's Simhika violently rips a chain (*tali*) from her neck, throws it away, and begins to hit her head and chest as she cries out in anger and sorrow, 'Who has done this!' The *tali* was traditionally given when a woman formed an arranged relationship with a man as approved by the eldest male of her household – signifying the traditional form of 'marriage.' In this state of sorrow and anger, Nelliyode's Simhika begins the performance of the first line of dialogue,

Alas! O my dear handsome husband!
Forsaking me, have you gone to the abode of death?

As V.R. Prabodhachandran Nayar noted in our discussion of Nelliyode's addition of this detail after a performance we both attended, the interpolation graphically answers the question,

'What does her cry of "Alas!" mean?' Simhika's dramatic response to the news of her husband's death elicits both her sorrow and anger, prompting all her ensuing actions against Panchali – the subject of the remainder of this part of the play. Nelliyode's interpolation captures the deep pathos of a woman's loss of her husband, and her reduction to a state of widowhood. It also provides a clear reason for her to seek revenge against Panchali. For all these reasons, Nelliyode's addition of this dramatic bit of stage business to his performance of Simhika's sorrow and rage over the loss of her husband has been widely praised for its appropriateness.

As a concluding note to this explanation of the actor's creative process, it is important to recognize the limitations within which the actor is working. We should remember that what is considered 'appropriate' in this scene, for this Simhika, is shaped entirely by male perceptions of the female. Nelliyode has developed this quite dramatic portrayal of a woman's rage and sorrow at the loss of her husband while playing a *Kari* demoness, and not in a refined (*minukku*) female role. Marlene Pitkow quotes noted *kathakali* actor Padmanabhan Nayar as saying that the 'heroine should show "full restraint of emotions and movement . . . and not be vulgar" . . . By definition, then, the *minukku* actor must be understated in his acting style, like the character he impersonates' (1998: 160). As the antithesis of the self-controlled *minukku*, and as a reflection of high-caste Nāyar/Namboodiri views of low caste Kerala women [and/or the black/dark indigenous Dravidian tribals 'scheduled castes'], who are loud, demonstrative, engage in overt displays of their emotions, and are anything but quiet and reserved, the *kari* ('black') is not just allowed, but expected to display openly such emotions.[15]

part ii

plays from the traditional repertory

the flower of good fortune[a] (kalyanasaugandhikam)

Kottayam Tampuran (c.1645–1716)

Translated by

V.R. PRABODHACHANDRAN NAYAR, M.P. SANKARAN NAMBOODIRI AND PHILLIP B. ZARRILLI

INTRODUCTION

Kottayam Tampuran is to *kathakali* what Zeami was to the Japanese *noh* theater – that multi-talented creative genius who as playwright, actor, and patron shaped the basic form and structure of the dance-drama. Although the seminal figure in the early history of *kathakali*, we know very little about this royal ruler. Whether legend or fact, what we do know has been summarized in Aymanam Krishnakaimal's brief notes on the author (1986: 349–62). As a young boy, growing up in the royal family at Kottayam, Kottayam Tampuran was considered a slow learner. On a visit to the ruler (Zamorin) of the nearby kingdom of Kozhikode in Northern Kerala he made a grammatical mistake when asking, 'What may I do for you?' Because of this embarrassment to his family, he was sent to undergo a test at a nearby waterfall where he was made to stand under the waterfall for a full day to see if he would survive. The premise of the test was that if he survived he would become great in some way; and if not, he would die from the test.

To his mother's wonder, he survived the test, and was therefore sent to the Mukambika Temple to undergo a year of intensive schooling. Thereafter, his mother brought a tutor, Govind

Dikshitar, back to court. Gradually, the young boy grew in his intellectual and literary abilities. Eventually, he composed the four *kathakali* plays which, as we have seen, remain central to both the training of the actor and the repertory. In order of authorship, his guru responded to each of the four plays as it was written:

> When he showed his teacher *The Killing of Baka*, he commented that it would be good for *kaikottakali* [central Kerala's folk dance performed as women sing poetic verses]. To his second play, *The Killing of Kirmira*, his teacher said that a commentary would be necessary to understand its difficult grammar. To his third play, *The Flower of Good Fortune*, his guru said that the author seemed to be one who likes to win the mind of women. And to his fourth and final play, *The Killing of Kalakeya*, his teacher commented that it was the best of the four and fit to be performed.
>
> (Krishnakaimal 1986: 351)

Whether legend or fact, this story reflects the increasing beauty and complexity of Kottayam Tampuran's language, polished and honed as he authored the four plays. By the time he completed *The Killing of Kalakeya* every word came to have a rich set of double meanings

---

[a] *Kalyanam* means fine, luck, happiness, or good fortune, and, therefore, marriage.

which could be applied either to each poetic image, and/or to the play's narrative.

As composed by Kottayam Tampuran, *The Flower of Good Fortune* has fourteen scenes. Today, however, the vast majority of performances only include two to five of the fourteen scenes. This translation includes the three scenes of *The Flower of Good Fortune* usually performed: Scenes 1, 9, and 10. Scene 1 between Dharmaputra (Yudhisthira) and Bhima is occasionally performed today, and remains extremely important in the training of actors.[1]

Synopsis of the play

While Arjuna was in the Himalayas in search of the divine arrow, his brothers and Panchali (Draupadi) spent their time visiting holy sites. Eventually they arrived in Kulinda, kingdom of Subahu in the Himalayas. There they visited and stayed in a beautiful forest known as Narayanasrama. In the first scene, when Arjuna leaves in search of the infamous Pasupata arrow, Bhima can no longer suppress his impatience with Dharmaputra's inaction. In Scenes 2–8 (not usually performed), the sage Romasa and Krishna arrive at the forest retreat. Bhima eventually intercepts the demon Jatasura and kills him.

In Scene 9, one day the wind brought a beautiful flower near Panchali. She was so enchanted by its fragrance that she asked Bhima to find some more of the same flower for her.

All that Bhima knew was that the flower came from the north since the wind had been blowing from that direction. Even though he had no idea of his ultimate destination, Bhima set off to find this special flower, the Saugandhika. Along the way in the forest he met many difficulties. Eventually (in Scene 10) he arrived at the place where his step-brother, Hanuman, was living. Hanuman, not knowing that his brother is coming, is disturbed in the midst of his meditations. He eventually recognizes that the one who is disturbing the forest as well as his meditations is his brother, Bhima. He wants to help him along his way, but decides that he must first be humbled; therefore, he transforms himself into a decrepit old monkey, and lies in Bhima's path. When Bhima discovers him along the way, he orders him to move. Hanuman toys with him, 'unable' to move, and requests that

Bhima move his tail if necessary. Bhima tries to move his tail, but is unable. He realizes this can be no ordinary monkey, and requests him to reveal his true nature. When Hanuman reveals his divine form and identity, Bhima is humbled and bows before him. After teasing Bhima for losing his club (mace), he assists Bhima in finding his way to the Kubera garden where he can collect the flowers and return with them to Panchali.

Following Scenes 9 and 10, Bhima approaches the Kubera garden. There he meets the demon Krodhavasa who is guarding the lake where the Saugandhika flowers grow. They fight, and Bhima kills the demon and collects the flowers. Scene 14 enacts Bhima's return to Panchali with the Saugandhika flowers, fulfilling her desire.

The Translated Text

This performance text/translation has been prepared from K.P.S. Menon's acting edition of *Kalyanasaugandhikam* in *Kathakali attaprakaram* (Menon 1979) and from a performance of Scenes 9 and 10 of the play on 13 May 1993 at Killimangalam, Trissur District, Kerala, India, commissioned by the Killimangalam Center for Documentation of the Performing Arts. The role of Bhima was played by Gopi Asan and the role of Hanuman by Ramankutty Nayar Asan. The interpolations (*ilakiyattam*) for Scenes 9 and 10 are from this performance, and those for Scene 1 are the basic interpolations taught at the Kerala Kalamandalam, and were provided by M.P. Sankaran Namboodiri.

Cast

DHARMAPUTRA (Yudhisthira): eldest of the Pandavas in *pacca* ('green') make-up
BHIMA: second of the Pandavas in *pacca*
PANCHALI: wife of the Pandavas in *minukku* ('radiant') make-up
HANUMAN: the wise and valorous chief of the monkeys in *vella tati* 'white beard' make-up

Note: As an aid for the reading of the four translations which follow, Figure 5.1 provides a convenient 'key' to the technical terms and annotations included in the translations.

Figure 5.1   *Key to textual and performance terms*

dandakam: narrative passages, usually composed in the third person, which serve the same function as the *sloka*, but are set in special rhythmic patterns and metrical feet each of which is longer than twenty-one syllables.
ilakiyattam: literally, 'having moved/dance,' are interpolations into the original text composed and created by actor-dancers and/or their patrons. When performed, the actors 'speak' the lines of the *ilakiyattam* only with hand-gestures, i.e., these lines are not sung by the vocalists.
iratti: dance compositions that come at the end of certain subrefrains (*anupallavi*) and *caranam* which are set in *cempata tala*. Although this choreography is like that of the *kalasam*, the singers accompany the dance by singing the refrain. Occasionally *iratti* are set in different *tala* in plays not included here, especially in *padam* performed at the slowest tempo. *Annotated in translations with an* (I).
kalasam: compositions that punctuate the stanzas of a *padam* and are danced according to the appropriate mood of the scene. The vocalists do not sing during the performance of *kalasams*. Depending on the dramatic context, sometimes *kalasam* are only performed by the percussionists, and the actor-dancer does not perform the set choreography. *Annotated in translations with a* (K).
nalamiratti: set in *ekatala* to a series of single beats, this is a fixed choreography used to connect or link an *ilakiyattam* to a scene, or to make an exit. (This is known as *etuttukalasam* in Southern Kerala.) *Annotated in translations with an* (N).
padam: verses composed specifically as dance music for interpretation by the actor-dancer; the dialogue or soliloquy portions of the text 'spoken' through gesture language. The structure of a typical *padam* includes three parts: *pallavi* (refrain), *anupallavi* (subrefrain), and *caranam* ('foot'). Only the initial *pallavi* is translated. When repeated after an *anupallavi* or *caranam*, only the first line of the *pallavi* appears here, followed by (. . .) to indicate repetition of the refrain.
purappatu: the preliminary pure dance usually performed by students.
raga: musical modes to which verses are set by the author/composer. Each accentuates a certain mood.
slokam: metrical verse composed in stanzas, usually in the third person, which indicate the context and tell what is going to happen in the ensuing dialogue portion of the play. Each foot should have only twenty-one syllables
lala: rhythmic patterns to which *padam* are set and within which dances and dramatic action are performed
tonkaram: a short dance choreography similar to an *iratti* in that it too is performed to a *pallavi*. *Annotated in translations with a* (T).

purappatu
[*sankarabharanam (raga); cempata (tala – 32 beats)*]

sloka:
When Arjuna left to obtain the Pasupata arrow[a]
  through the grace of Siva,
Dharmaputra – whose past is graceful like Rama;
  holding his bow; intent on killing their
  ferocious enemies;
  and continuously listening to devotional stories
  sweet to his ears as narrated by pious (bards) –
along with his brothers, rejoiced in the forest
  with (their) wife.

(*Behind the curtain and unseen by the audience, the actor playing Bhima performs a series of four salutations – three toward the curtain and one to the musicians. All four are set in a special rhythmic pattern, patinna kitatakadhimtam. The following* padam *with four* caranam *is sung to accompany the dancing of the* purappatu *which describes the current state of the hero.*)[2]

caranam:
Those (Pandavas) who are graceful jewels in the
  ocean of the moon's clan;
whose great fame from birth is like the white
  moonlight,

[a] The root of *pasupata* is *pasupati*, meaning protector. Siva is the protector of all beings. The Pasupata is an extremely powerful arrow blessed by Pasupati, or Siva.

caranam:
whose reputation gracefully deflects
 the accumulation of sins among those
 who simply think of them;

caranam:
who became forest ascetics because of the
 arrogant Duryodhana's
 misguided actions
when Arjuna went to worship Siva,

caranam:
Dharmaputra and the others threw off their
 lethargy and travelled to many places of
 pilgrimage.

(*The curtain is raised as the* purappatu *concludes.*)

Scene 1
[Dharmaputra and Bhima]

[*saramgam (raga)*; *campa (tala – 20 beats)*]
 sloka: [*After the initial singing of the* raga, *a*
 kalasam *is played with Bhima still behind the*
 curtain. Then the curtain is lowered to reveal
 Bhima as he enacts this sloka.]
When Arjuna left for the weapon,
mulling over Sakuni's deceitful action, Bhima –
 the one whose mind was heated (with anger)
 and sorrowful, with the fierce corners of
 his eyes focused on his mace as it
 rotated from his intense anger,
 and with that gluttonous heat directed
 against the vast array of (their) enemies
– said to Dharmaputra:

(*In the transition to the* padam, *Bhima dances*
a very short choreography known as
kitatakadhimtam.)

BHIMA:
            pallavi: O ocean of valor and justice,
            I bow with my hands at your feet, O
            respected one. [K]

anupallavi:
With (our) wife here, deprived of our valor,
 and assuming an ascetic lifestyle,

is it right for you to find comfort in
 this (way of life)? [K]

   caranam:
O son of Dharma with a pure mind,
 (please) look at the path of our Karma, O King –
Wrapped in bark like woodsmen,
 abandoning our duty and losing (our) bravery,
(we) wander aimlessly! [K][3]

   caranam:
Why have you sent Arjuna in vain
 for weapons now? [K] (*The speed doubles to 10*
 beats.)
(Please) realize, O bold one,
 right now I am able to swiftly vanquish
 all our enemies! [K]

   caranam: (*The speed returns to 20 beats.*)
Have no doubt that once our enemies
 are subjugated in battle
and with relief [K] (*The speed doubles to 10 beats.*)
 I have drunk over and again Dussassana's
 blood with the palm of my hand,
I will immediately decorate our wife's hair. [K]

   caranam: (*The speed returns to 20 beats.*)
Should you sympathize with (my point of view),
 then please order me to do this (i.e., to kill
 Dussassana)! [K] (*The speed doubles to 10*
 beats.)
Challenging (our enemies) with the sound of 'Hum!'
 and taking away their pride,
 please do not prevent me from
 giving them to Yama's attendant. [K] (*The speed*
 returns to 20 beats for the final part of the
 kalasam.)

            pallavi: O ocean of valor . . . [K][4]

   [*bhairavi (raga)*; *cempata (tala – 16 beats)*]

   sloka: (*The* sloka *is enacted.*)
The great hearted Dharmaputra –
 the one with unblemished heart,
 whose soft speech is principled by Dharma
 and good thought –
said with delight to his younger brother
 who was blind with anger:

---

[a] The period of exile in the forest.

DHARMAPUTRA:
> *pallavi*: O brother, son of Vayu,
> one with good qualities,
> please control your anger. [K]

anupallavi:
Do not take this path until the appointed
time is over.[a]
(Then) without delay you can achieve this. [K]+[I][5]

[*ilakiyattam*]

BHIMA:
Alas! Even though those rogues have done all
this,
your mind remains undisturbed.
Alas! Itself!
With just a single, small, kind command, all those
deceivers will be destroyed. Just one command!

DHARMAPUTRA:
Don't! You must be patient a little longer.

BHIMA:
Oh! Oh! It is written ('on the forehead'). As you
command.
(*Dharmaputra exits with Bhima, who
immediately turns and re-enters from upstage.*)

(*To their enemies.*) O deceivers! You only have a
short time to keep your pride! Later I shall
destroy all of you! You will see! [N]

(*Curtain.*)

Scene 9
[Bhima and Panchali]
[*sankarabharanam* (*raga*); *cempata* (*tala* – 32
beats)]

(*The two actors enter behind the hand-held
curtain as the* raga *is elaborated.*)

sloka:[6]
Later, when the season was felicitous for lovers,
as a breeze from Mount Malaya[a] lightly
jostled the jasmins,

the son of Vayu (Bhima), while walking in the
forest intent on love play,
said to his consort (Panchali),
who likewise was ripe for (amorous) games:

(*The curtain is lowered to reveal BHIMA and
PANCHALI in a special entrance known as
'patinna kitatakadhimtam'. The extraordinarily
slow rhythm helps to establish the erotic mood.*)
BHIMA:
> *pallavi*: O daughter of King
> Panchala! O lotus-eyed!
> O abode of Kama![b] [K]

anupallavi:
Do not feel anguish in your heart from our
relentless travels in the forest. [K]

Plate 5.1   *Bhima and Panchali embrace during
their lengthy entrance, establishing the erotic mood
for their love play in the forest*
Photo credit: Sharon Grady.

---

[a] These breezes are understood to carry the scent of the sandal trees that abound in this range.
[b] Kama, 'the five-arrowed one,' is the god of love.

caranam:
Having roamed among the graceful rivulets, and
  gently tasted the sweet smell of the flowers
  swinging with delight,
a graceful, pleasant breeze blows. [K]+[I]

caranam:[7]
O Devi,[a] prosperous parrot-voiced one,
please come to this flat rock for a little loveplay
  – an undisturbed spot where the good cuckoos
  sound '*pancama*,'[b]
and from which the beautiful deer have scattered,
  frightened by the sweetness exuded
  by your flickering eyes. [K]

[*mukhari* (*raga*); *cempata* (*tala* – 16 beats)]

sloka: (*This* sloka *is enacted as it is sung.
PANCHALI at first senses the flower's fragrance.
Seeing the bees attracted to the flower, she then
sees the Saugandhika flower. Picking it up, she
admires its beauty and fragrance.*)

Draupadi, gathering a supremely beautiful and
  divine flower borne to her by the wind as if out
  of affection,
and followed by swarms of bees due to its sweet
smell, approached Bhima, the son of Vayu, and
told him with delight:

PANCHALI:
            pallavi: My Lord, please see this
                        flower I possess. [K]

caranam:
If you feel sympathy (for me), certainly
  there will be occasion to obtain
  more of these graceful Saugandhika flowers.
  [K]+[I]

            pallavi: My Lord, please see . . .

caranam:
No one can imagine a place on this earth with
  such exceedingly beautiful flowers!
My delight overflows,
O lotus-petal-eyed! [K]+[I]

pallavi: My Lord, please see . . .

caranam:
Whatever it be, young women of excellent
  reputation never reveal their desires to anyone
  except their husbands. [K]+[I]

pallavi: My Lord, please see . . .

[*danyasi* (*raga*); *cempata* (*tala* – 16 beats)]
  BHIMA:
  caranam:
O beautiful deer-eyed one,
without hesitation I shall fetch the graceful
  Saugandhika flowers which you desire. [K]+[I]

            pallavi: O crown jewel among
                        beautiful women with
                        flickering eyes!

caranam:
Whether on top of a mountain, or in Indra's
  heaven,
with my prowess I will easily fulfill
  your desire. [K]+[I]

            pallavi: O crown jewel among . . .

[*ilakiyattam*]

BHIMA: So, should I go to get the flowers you desire?
PANCHALI: On your way, who will help you
vanquish your enemies?
BHIMA: The mace which I always keep in my hand!
PANCHALI: On your way, how will you quench
your thirst and hunger?
BHIMA: Your beautiful flickering glance itself is
  enough. Therefore, have a pleasant stay with my
  elder and younger brothers. I will return soon.
(*DRAUPADI exits. After seeing her offstage,
BHIMA turns and immediately re-enters. The
following section of the* ilakiyattam *is known as
the 'description of the forest.' Kodungallor
Koccunnittampuran composed the* sloka *that
forms the basis of this interpolation. What
follows is a selective summary of BHIMA's
thoughts and observations, spoken in gesture,
and his enactment of what he sees.*)

---

[a] As in many Sanskrit dramas, the hero calls his beloved queen 'Devi' – 'the Goddess.'
[b] '*Pancama*,' the fifth note of the Indian musical scale, is said to be produced by the cuckoo.

When Panchali expressed her wish, I immediately began my journey, not thinking about where and how to find the flower. It is the duty of a husband to fulfill his wife's desires. Who else would do this?

Anyway, my brother, the son of Vayu, will be kind enough to show the way.

Here is the mountain, Gandhamadana. I should approach it. On the top of the mountain, I see a lot of minerals. The clouds are like the smoke that emerges from the trees which have caught fire in the valley below.

Here is a thick forest. I hear a sound. What is it? Oh! Here is an elephant caught by a python. (*The actor enacts the struggle, taking first the part of the elephant and then the python.*) Oh, and here is a lion! (*The actor now enacts the lion's entry on the scene. The lion sees the elephant and python, then jumps onto the elephant's forehead. He claws the elephant's forehead and, holding it, sucks the elephant's blood through the wound.*) Unable to sustain the attack, the elephant falls down. The python gradually opens his mouth and swallows the elephant. What a remarkable incident!

Oh, here are two lion cubs about to attack me! (*He holds the two lions, smashes them together, and throws them aside.*)

Here I see grass, large rocks, big trees entangled with creepers. Because of its density, even the sunshine can't touch the ground. The forest is like solid darkness.

How should I proceed? Well, with my mace I shall cut a path through the forest. (*He enacts cutting his path through the forest.*) [N]

(*BHIMA exits. Curtain.*)

Scene 10
[*madhyamavati* (*raga*); *campa* (*tala* – 20 beats)]

(*The curtain remains raised during the singing of all three of the following verses.*)

sloka:
Thus, as requested by his consort, he whose lustre
  is undiminished and carries a mace,
jumped and alighted in the great mountain forest.

Because of his overwhelming strength and speed,
  when he landed everything was dispersed,
and a sound was emitted as if the mountain itself
  had cried out in fear.

sloka:
The son of Vayu, Bhima, who enjoys adventures,
  whose sole provision for the journey was the
  tremulous and gracefully falling glances of the
  slender-bellied Panchali,
reached the plantain forest where all its
  inhabitants were terrified by his forceful
  footsteps.

sloka:
Hanuman, in meditation on Rama and
  performing peaceful *tapas* there,[a]

Plate 5.2   *Ramankutty Nayar Asan in the role of Hanuman sits meditating in the forest, soon to be disturbed by the arrival of Bhima*
Photo credit: Sharon Grady.

---

[a] *Tapas* literally means 'warmth, ardor.' It refers to any ascetic technique such as fasting or special breath control exercises which warm or burn.

seeing Bhima effortlessly approaching with only the help of his most terrible mace, thought thus:

(*The curtain is lowered to reveal HANUMAN in meditation. A lengthy interpolation featuring the actor playing HANUMAN begins the scene. Behind the raised curtain, and therefore unseen by most of the audience, the actor playing Hanuman performs only the first part of the curtain look, which includes a series of choreographed steps. The second part of Hanuman's traditional curtain look is not performed in this play.*)

HANUMAN:
[*ilakiyattam*]

(*As the curtain is lowered, there is a short [N] performed on the drums. At the end of the [N], the drumming becomes very quiet as Hanuman is revealed in meditation. In the near-quiet the* centa *drum sounds with the first indication of a disturbance to Hanuman's meditation. Hanuman at first shows this disturbance only with his eyes, and not with hand-gestures or his body. He reflects. Again he returns to his meditation. The second disturbance is indicated more strongly by the drums. This time Hanuman looks around and with small hand-gestures speaks*):

Why is it that my meditation is being disturbed? I'll just focus my mind. (*He focuses on his meditation, but again he is disturbed.*) What is that ear-shattering sound? I should find out immediately. Is it the sound of the wings of mountains crashing together? No. Long ago Indra cut the mountains' wings and put them in different places. Therefore, it is not the sound of mountains.
 Then what? (*Thinking*) Fixing my mind at the feet of Sree Rama, the Lord of the Three Worlds, while meditating thus, why is my mind still disturbed? Long ago Sree Rama with Lakshmana and the monkeys like me crossed the ocean, reached Lanka, and annihilated all the demons. Then mounting the Pushpaka,[a] Sree Rama with Sita and Lakshmana reached Ayodhya. We also accompanied them. Sree Rama's coronation took place. We collected sacred water from various places and sprinkled the crown which he wore. Then he called us one by one and gave us gifts and blessings. The monkeys were overjoyed. Later, Sree Rama gave a golden garland to Sita and told her, 'O Devi, please give this to the one you consider most dear to you.' Sita called me, 'Hanuman, come.' (*He enacts bowing before her.*) She gave me the garland. I said, 'Of what use is a garland of golden pearls to a monkey? Well, I humbly accept.' I received the garland and put it around my neck. Then Lord called me, 'Hanuman, what is your wish?' I said, 'I have no wish except to remain focused in meditation at your feet.' Sree Rama said, 'Let it be so.' And he blessed me.
 Having accomplished such deep meditation at Sree Rama's feet, why is my mind shaken? (*He sees BHIMA coming.*) Here someone approaches hitting the trees with a big mace in his hand. Who is this? Well, I will think properly and find out. [N]

> *pallavi*: Who comes here? Is there no one in the forest to rival him with his ever-increasing pride? [K]

> *anupallavi*:
> It is as if the heroic *rasa* itself has suddenly assumed human form and come near! [K][8]

> *caranam*:
> The elephant herd, abandoning their mental peace, with trepidation helplessly run amok. [K]

> *caranam*:
> The lions, now afraid and sorrowful, hide inside a large cave. [K]

> *caranam*:
> Oh! In my mind, the feeling that he is my [brother] increases . . .[9]
> Vayu's son – he is my younger brother!

> *caranam*: (*The speed doubles to 10 beats, and a* kalasam *is danced in the middle of this* caranam.)

> I should affectionately allow him to display his strength, and then make him understand my truth. [K]

---

[a] The Pushpaka is an 'airplane' or conveyance for riding through the cosmos.

caranam: (*The speed returns to 20 beats.*)
Hail Rama! Hail Rama! Oh, one who is attractive
  to all, Hail!
Ravana's killer! Oh Rama, master of Sita! [K]+[N]

(*HANUMAN performs a lengthy mimetic process
of transformation as he literally becomes an old,
decrepit monkey lying helplessly on the ground in
BHIMA's path.*)

[*kamodari* (*raga*); *cempata* (*tala* – 8 beats)]

sloka:
Having thus decided, that steady-hearted one lay
  down, as if exhausted from old age, placing his
  tail in the path.
That Bhima, felling a grove of plantains by
  striking his mace and pushing forward,
said angrily to the one lying there comfortably:

(*BHIMA enters directly to the stage.*)

[*ilakiyattam*]
BHIMA: I should proceed along this path. Here are
the banana groves. See. Now I must enter and
continue my travels from here. (*Seeing
HANUMAN.*) Who is lying here obstructing the
path? I think it's a monkey. Well, I'll tell him to
get out of the way. [N]

> *pallavi*. Lowest among the monkeys,
> get off the path without
> delay! Get off the path
> without delay!

caranam:
If you don't go . . . [K]
  I will come after you ripe with anger, and with
  'compassion' grab you by the neck.
Tossing your obese body aside,
  I will have no obstacle to continuing my
  journey. [T]

> *pallavi*: Lowest among the
> monkeys . . .[10]

caranam:
'Please' note . . . [K]
Son of Vayu, I am the King born of the weighty
  moon's clan!
  Single-handed I can subjugate any enemy!
Oh, one with an evil mind, believe this now! [T]

> *pallavi*: Lowest among the
> monkeys . . .

caranam:
'Please' listen . . . [K]
I am foremost and best among kings!
  The one who has in mind only what
  Dharmaputra desires – his younger brother,
  Bhima, the wolf-bellied.
Also know that I am the strongest! [T]

> *pallavi*: Lowest among the
> monkeys . . .

caranam:
If without fear . . . [K]
you continue to lie there hesitating in my path –
  Oh, you overweight monkey, leader of fools –
quickly and skillfully I will pummel you into
dust. [T]

> *pallavi*: Lowest among the
> monkeys . . . [N]

[*nilambari* (*raga*); *atanta* (*tala* – 14 beats)]
  sloka: (*This sloka is acted.*)
With half-open eyes, that leader of monkeys
  looked at Bhima as he continued to torment
  him with his insults.
Without revealing himself, he trembled
  as if his strength was gone.
Although adroit, he spoke as if weak:

HANUMAN:
> *pallavi*: O King! Although I have not
> received you properly, please
> do not be angry! [K]

anupallavi:
Because of my age I am unable to walk.
Respected Sir, please know that I have been like
  this a long time. [K]

caranam:
O brave one! Please note that usually not even a
  single human passes this way.
The celestial beings will become irritated if you
  disturb things here.
O leader of kings, please return quickly to your
  own city. [K]

[*muriyatanta* (*tala* – 7 beats)]

BHIMA:
caranam:
Even if humankind and the gods . . . [K]
  join to attack me,
  I have no fear.
O monkey! Do not speak to me as if to a coward.
  Know that I am Vayu's son,
  the skillful one. [1/2K]

      pallavi: O evil-minded one! Get out
            of my way immediately,
            leader of monkeys! [K]

  [*atanta* (*tala* – 14 beats)]

  HANUMAN:
caranam:
You who are the strongest in this world,
  after stepping over me, please leave quickly.
Please know that because of this my mind will
  suffer no disturbance.
Please note that your clan duty is compassion for
  the disabled.[a] [K]

  [*muriyatanta* (*tala* – 7 beats)]

  BHIMA:
caranam:
O forest traveler! In your clan . . . [K]
  is Vayu's son, the leader of the monkey clan,
  Hanuman.
Thinking about this brother of mine, I hesitate to
  cross over you and depart. [1/2K]

      pallavi: O evil-minded one . . .

  [*bhairavi* (*raga*);[11] *muriyatanta* (*tala* – 14 beats)]

  HANUMAN:
caranam:
O bull among men, didn't you say there is a
  leader among the monkeys called Hanuman?
Oh, 'ocean of humility,' my interest increases.
Kindly tell me who he is. [K]

  [*nilambari* (*raga*); *muriyatanta* (*tala* – 7 beats)]

BHIMA:
caranam:[12]
Siva! O Siva! Is there a single person in the
entire world who does not know Hanuman,
Vayu's son?
That great-minded one who set fire to and
  burned down the palace of the ten-necked,
  Ravana, that thorn of the world. [1/2K]

      pallavi: O evil-minded one . . .

  HANUMAN:
caranam:[13]
Oh, ocean of great qualities and compassion,
  gently move aside my tail and go.
Leader of men, please consider that because of
  exhaustion from old age, I don't have the
  strength to move.

  [*ilakiyattam*]
  BHIMA: Don't keep repeating yourself. Move!
Even now your mind is filled with pride. Get rid
of it. (*To himself.*) There's no use telling him
again what to do. With my mace I'll lift and
move his tail and be on my way. [N]

[*nattakurunni* (*raga*); *cempata* (*tala* – 16 beats)]

  sloka: (*This* sloka *is acted.*)
Hearing these words, Bhima approached,
  but was unable to move even the tip of the
  monkey's mighty tail.
Sobered, exhausted, doubtful, bowed with shame,
  and having lost his daring,
he said to the monkey leader:

  BHIMA:
      pallavi: O bull among monkeys, most
            lustrous one, listen now to
            my respectful words. [K]

  caranam:
Please tell me if you are Varuna, the rope bearer,
  or Indra himself, O brave one!
I certainly know that you are not just a monkey
  leader. [K]+[I]

---

[a] Hanuman reminds Bhima that as a member of the warrior caste/clan (Ksatriya) his duty should be to protect and have compassion for all, especially the helpless.

pallavi: O bull among monkeys . . .

caranam:
Among all living beings, no one's strength
   equals yours.
So quickly now, please tell me the truth! [K]+[I]

pallavi: O bull among monkeys . . .

[*cempata* (*tala* – 8 beats)]

HANUMAN:
caranam: (*A* kalasam *begins this* caranam.)
I am Rama's messenger – the one who killed
Ravana. (*The speed changes to 16 beats.*)
I am your brother. My name is Hanuman. [K]+[I]

pallavi: O bull among men, please
         listen to my words.

caranam:
In order to see the lotus-eyed Janaka's daughter
   (Sita),
it is I who crossed the ocean, and
   it is I who completely destroyed Lanka with
   fire. [K]+[I]

pallavi: O bull among men . . .

[*panduvarati* (*raga*);[14] *cempata* (*tala* – 16 beats)]

BHIMA:
caranam:
Please do not be offended by the childish words I
   spoke.
I bow with my hands at your feet, O brother,
   ocean of compassion. [K]

caranam:
O elder brother, you crossed the ocean without
   difficulty.
My desire to see that form increases. [K]

[*nattakurunni* (*raga*); *cempata* (*tala* – 8 beats)]

HANUMAN:
caranam:
If that is your desire . . . [K]
   please see my body. (*The speed returns to 16
   beats.*)

I will reveal only the minimum so that you will
   not be overwhelmed. [K]

[*ilakiyattam*]

HANUMAN: Look. If you see that terrible form I
   assumed when I jumped across the ocean, won't
   you faint, become bewildered, and fall down?
BHIMA: Even if that happens, aren't you here with
me?
HANUMAN: Oh, yes, I will be here with you. Watch
carefully. [N]

[*sankarabharanam* (*raga*); *muriyatanta* (*tala* – 14
beats)]

sloka: (*The following* sloka *is acted.*)[15]
Hanuman, whose source is the tornado and who
   is the abode of justice,
saw Bhima, his younger brother, fallen out of
   fear at his feet.
Pleased, he assumed an agreeable form and then
   told Bhima:

HANUMAN:
         pallavi: Do not have even a little fear
               in your mind, Bhimasena![a] [K]

anupallavi:
Please listen to my words: have happiness in
   your mind,
O you who destroys the prosperity of enemies. [K][16]

caranam:
Now, without taking any more time,
   O Bhima, son of Vayu,
please obtain what your dear wife, the parrot-
   speeched one, desires. [K][17]

[*sriragam* (*raga*); *muriyatanta* (*tala* – 14 beats)]

BHIMA:
caranam:
Soon preparations begin for confronting the
   Kauravas in battle.
O brave one! On that day please come near us
   and destroy the leaders of our enemy. [K][18]

[*panduvarati* (*raga*);[19] *muriyatanta* (*tala* – 7 beats)]

---

[a] Bhima's full name, meaning one whose army is awe-inspiring.

Plate 5.3 *Hanuman exhibits his divine form for Bhima*
Photo credit: Sharon Grady.

HANUMAN:
  caranam: (*A* kalasam *begins this* caranam).
I will remain on the flagstaff of your respectable
  brother Arjuna, son of Indra, and
with awe-inspiring sound in battle I will bring to
  ruin our enemies. [K]

  [*ilakiyattam*][20]

HANUMAN: You've been saying one thing after
another. Now the time is getting late. Go soon to
secure and bring the Saugandhika flower that
Panchali desires. I will remain here and meditate
on Sree Rama.
BHIMA: As you say. (*He prostrates before
HANUMAN and receives his blessings. He is
about to leave, then turns back to HANUMAN.
He stands thinking.*)
HANUMAN: (*To himself.*) No, he won't leave just
like that. He'll return.
BHIMA: (*To himself.*) Where should I go? My mace
is still under his tail. How can I get it back? After
all, he's my elder brother. I will ask him. (*He
comes close to HANUMAN but, seeing him

uttering RAMA's name, does not want to disturb
him and steps back. But again he comes close,
touching his arm.*)
HANUMAN: (*Slapping at whatever might be
touching him.*) Oh, you didn't go. Why not?
BHIMA: I was on my way, but in order to defend
myself against my enemies, I had in my hand
one . . .
HANUMAN: What, you came empty-handed?
BHIMA: No, I had a mace in my hand.
HANUMAN: Oh, I have heard about that – that
Bhima used to carry a big mace in his hand.
Where is that mace now? Oh, I know. When
Panchali told you. . . (*Taking on the character of
PANCHALI . . .*) 'Only you can fulfill my desire.
Could you fetch me some Saugandhika flowers?
No one else could get this. Only you can.' (*He
steps out of the role of PANCHALI.*) When she
said that, you immediately set out. In the
confusion you must have forgotten the mace.
BHIMA: No, no. I didn't forget it.
HANUMAN: Then where is the mace?
BHIMA: When I came a while ago, you were lying
in the path having assumed the form of an old

monkey. Because of my ignorance, I angrily tried to throw your tail aside with my mace. Then I couldn't get the mace back. Forgive me.

HANUMAN: What, you left your mace under my tail? Oh, no. I didn't feel anything.

BHIMA: Please, kindly return my mace. It happened because of my ignorance.

HANUMAN: Are you sure you put it there?

BHIMA: Yes, I'm sure.

HANUMAN: Oh! Then maybe it was broken.

BHIMA: No! Don't say that. Kindly return it. After all, I'm your younger brother. Please forgive me.

HANUMAN: (*To himself and the audience.*) He has such a huge form, but his mind is so innocent. Well, he is my younger brother. I'll return the mace to him. (*Taking the mace.*) With this mace you have struck and crushed many enemies' heads. You left that club under an old monkey's tail and were unable to get it back. What a pity. From now on you should not do anything without first considering the consequences.

BHIMA: Nothing like this will happen again.

HANUMAN: (*Meditating, he hands over the mace. Once BHIMA receives it he rushes off toward his enemies angrily.*) Well, go quickly now. I will stay here meditating.

BHIMA: Where can I get the Saugandhika flowers?

HANUMAN: You know why I obstructed the path and lay in your way?

BHIMA: Why?

HANUMAN: Human beings are not allowed to pass this way. This is the abode of the devas. If the devas see a human being, they will curse him. Therefore, you should alter your path. That's why I closed my eyes and lay down. If you go this way, you will see Kubera's garden. After entering it, while walking you will see a pond where there are many Saugandhika flowers. You can collect as many as you want, and give them to Panchali.

BHIMA: As you command. Please shower me with your kindness always.

HANUMAN: Therefore, we are both blessed by Sree Rama. Always meditate on Sree Rama. (*Hugging him and blessing him, he sends him on his way.*) Now, taking Sree Rama in mind, I will fix my mind and continue my meditations. (*He assumes a posture of meditation.*)

(*Curtain.*)

COMMENTARY: DRAMATIZING THE AMBIGUITIES OF THE 'HEROIC'

Since the four plays translated here include one or more heroic characters (Bhima, Arjuna, Rugmamgada), in this and other commentaries I focus on the ambiguities of 'the heroic' as it is negotiated on the *kathakali* stage, and reflected in the socio-cultural milieu of historical Kerala. As discussed in Chapter 3, the *kathakali* epic hero can be read as an ideal figure who is a brave and/or valiant man (*viran*; *dhiran*), displaying his bravery (*virata*) and courage (*dhairyam*) as he upholds law and fulfills his duty (*dharma*). But this idealized concept of the heroic implicit in *kathakali* cannot be reduced to any single representation; rather, the heroic is negotiated between and among various heroic characters in a variety of dramatic texts. For example, among the five Pandavas the 'heroic' is negotiated between the three major brothers: Dharmaputra's carefully considered attention to matters of duty and rightful behavior; Arjuna's sage-like purity, acumen, and acquisition of awesome powers through meditation; and Bhima's explosive, impetuous demands for energetic action and use of his strength.

Although the hero always emerges victorious at the conclusion of a play, the path toward that glorious resolution is always fraught with severe trials and tribulations. The hero's putative powers, heroism, wisdom, and/or bravery are all put to the test and/or mocked by his enemies, or the gods themselves – a phenomenon which reveals an underlying ambiguity toward these all-powerful figures and what they symbolize, embody, and represent.

The anxieties and concerns of Kerala's historical 'heroes'

As discussed in Chapter 2, *kathakali* reflects the 'anxieties and concerns' of Kerala's 'royal political milieux' (Gitomer 1998: 34). The fractious, fragmentary, contestatory nature of Kerala's political landscape during the period of *kathakali*'s emergence and development is witnessed in the numerous petty principalities whose rulers engaged in almost constant warfare – a state of conflict made worse by the arrival of the Portuguese,

Dutch, French, and English colonial powers. The realities of living in small, segmented, and self-contained 'little kingdoms' can be inferred by reading between the lines of *kathakali* dramas, among other primary sources including European diaries and Kerala's folk ballads.

Soon after the arrival of Vasco da Gama at the close of the fifteenth century, outsiders began to comment upon the martial spirit and practices of Kerala's Nayars. Duarte Barbosa recorded the ideal pattern of martial service for Nayars to their local rulers:

> When these Nayres accept service with the King or with any other person by whom they are to be paid they bind themselves to die for him, and this rule is kept by most of them; some do not fulfil it, but it is a general obligation. Thus if in any way their Lord is killed and they are present, they do all they can even unto death; and if they are not at that place, even if they come from their homes they go in search of the slayer of the King who sent him forth to slay, and how many soever may be their enemies yet everyone of them does his utmost until they kill him.
>
> (Barbosa 1921, vol II: 48)

Fluent in Malayalam, Barbosa recorded how a *kalarippayattu*-trained Nayar underwent a special 'knighthood' ceremony which bound him to his master to death. In this ceremony,

> The King . . . asks him if he will maintain the customs and rules of the other Nayres, and he and his kinsmen respond 'Yes'. Then the King commands him to girt on his right side a sword with a red sheath, and when it is girt on he causes him to approach near to himself and lays his right hand on his head, saying therewith certain words which none may hear, seemingly a prayer, and then embraces him saying 'Paje Bugramarca', that is to say 'Protect cows and Brahmenes'.
>
> (ibid.: 45–7)

Barbosa concludes his account by noting that after the ceremony the 'knight' is able to 'serve the King, go to the wars, or challenge any man at his pleasure' (ibid.).

At a political level a Nayar's pledge theoretically circumscribed his right to exercise violence against anyone above him in the social/caste hierarchy, and only to use his martial skills at the behest of his ruler. However, as Barbosa's conclusion makes clear, his coming-into-manhood sanctioned his right to exercise violence virtually as he pleased by 'challenging' those equal to or lower than him in the hierarchy. Jonathan Duncan, who served more than once as Commissioner of Bengal and later as Governor of Bombay, visited Malabar in 1792–3 and described how a Nayar walked about

> holding up his naked sword with the same kind of unconcern as travellers in other countries carry in their hands a cane or walking staff. I have observed others of them have it fastened to their back, the hilt being stuck in their waist band, and the blade rising up and glittering between their shoulders.
>
> (Logan 1951: 139)

The sword he carried in public served as both symbol and icon of his 'right' to bear arms, and to exercise violence on behalf of his ruler. It also served as a marker of his ruler's participation in the sacrificial paradigm of divine kingship. The sword is therefore both symbolic and instrumental of the 'rights' and 'obligations' of the exercise of authority and power.

The lawful exercise of violence by those empowered with the right to carry 'the sword' (or other weapons) was a public affair ranging from interstate warfare, to a variety of forms of duel to the death. Interstate warfare erupted for a variety of reasons from caste differences (Menon 1967: 96), to pure and simple aggression, to challenges over ceremonial rights. Perhaps the most infamous example of the latter is the well-documented dispute between the Zamorin or Kozhikode and the Raja of Valluvanadu over which ruler was to serve as convenor and protector of the Mamakam festival. Held every twelve years, this 'great' festival celebrated the descent of the goddess Ganga into the Bharatpuzha river in Tirunavayi, north Malabar, which by her miraculous presence made the river as holy as the sacred Ganges itself. Until the thirteenth century, when the dispute probably arose, the ruler of Valluvanadu possessed the traditional right of inaugurating and conducting the festival. The Zamorin set out to usurp this right. After a protracted conflict, the Zamorin wrested power by killing two Vellatri princes. The event created a permanent schism between the kingdoms. At each subsequent festival, until its discontinuation in 1766 following the Mysorean invasion, some of the Valluvanadu fighters pledged to death-in-service to their royal house attended the Mamakam to avenge the honor of the fallen princes by fighting to the death against the Zamorins much superior, massed forces (Pallath 1976, *passim*; Ayyar 1928–32, *passim*). A few of these 'heroes' of the Valluvanadu kingdom continued to sacrifice themselves on behalf of their rulers' honor for years.

In this instance, the requirement that the ruler continuously attempt to 'expand' his kingdom was achieved for the Zamorin of Kozhikode. Since one's authority and ranking within the hierarchy was marked as much or more by the practices which one was entitled to perform, the Zamorin's 'power' was thus both symbolically and literally expanded by violently wresting control of the Mamakam festival. He 'expanded' his kingdom not literally through territorial expansion, but by expanding his 'rights and duties.'

Other forms of public violence where *kalarippayattu*-trained martial heroes exercised their valor were duels (*ankam*) which legally served as a means of last resort for solving disputes within higher-caste families, duels to resolve blood feuds, or duels intended to resolve interpersonal conflicts (Devi 1975, *passim*). The inherent instability of the socio-political order is evidenced not only in inter-state warfare, but also in stories of the infamous Nayar hero of the northern folk ballads, Tacholi Otenan. From a family said to have lost much of its previous wealth, Otenan's exercise of power should have been circumscribed by the authority of the local ruler in whose service his exercise of his martial skills would have been pledged. As revealed in these folk ballads, Tacholi Otenan's great powers and prowess are constantly negotiated and contested within specific contexts to very different ends. In some ballads he challenges and defeats a figure of traditional authority, as when he avenges the treatment of his younger brother, Kunjan, by the Ariarkovil Tampuran by beheading him. In another story Tacholi is deputed by a local ruler to collect three years' back rent from a land-holding family in the Kodumala area where the powerful young woman of the Kunki family was holding sway

and refusing to pay. Tacholi uses his expertise in attacking the body's vital spots to subdue her with a cattle prod, and sexually takes control of her as well. In this case, Tacholi tames and controls this malcontent ostensibly on behalf of the 'legitimate' local authority.

Tacholi's celebrated exercise of extraordinary power(s) is decidedly ambivalent in relation to the traditional local Kerala social and political hierarchy. When examined closely, he is something of a 'joker' in a supposedly ideal deck. But perhaps, on closer examination, even the great epic heroes as they appear in *kathakali* dance-dramas, whose power and character at first glance seem so absolute and ideal, are as ambivalent as Tacholi.

Time and again the epic heroes are represented on the *kathakali* stage as either possessing awesome strength, such as Bhima, or acquiring divine powers, such as Arjuna, in order to carry out their necessarily violent acts of blood-letting to rid the cosmos of the forces which have upset its balance. In the original version of *The Flower of Good Fortune* Bhima fulfills this necessary part of his heroic role by using his strength to kill two menacing demons, Jatasura and Krodhavasa. (This aspect of the operation of the heroic will be discussed further in the commentary on *The Killing of Kirmira* in Chapter 6.)

These same heroes repeatedly display an overweening pride which leads them continuously to test and overstep the boundaries of their authority, power, and/or rightful behavior. Similar to Tacholi, their energetic (*rajasa*) quality, so necessary in a South Asian understanding of the person for taking decisive action in the world, leads the hero constantly to overstep all these boundaries. Consequently, in plays like *The Flower of Good Fortune, The Progeny of Krishna*, and *Kiratam*, we find Bhima, and even the warrior-sage Arjuna, having their pride not only checked, but often mocked. In a discussion of *The Progeny of Krishna*, V.R. Prabodhachandran Nayar commented how in this play, 'self-pride is the vital spot (*marmmam*) of Arjuna!'[21] So ubiquitous is pride that, as Wendy O'Flaherty reminds us, it is not only the epic heroes, but occasionally even the gods themselves who are prone to a case of overweening pride (*abhimanam*) that must be humbled.[22] South Asian scholar Wendy

O'Flaherty relates the following story from the *Brahmavaivarta Purana* concerning Indra's pride:

> Once when Indra, the king of the gods, was puffed up with pride, he made Vishvakarman, the architect of the gods, build him a palace, to be the grandest palace ever built. But Vishvakarman humbled Indra by showing him a parade of ants and pointing out that every one of those ants had, in a former life, been an Indra.
>
> (1988: 66)

When Bhima first appears in Scene 1 of *The Flower of Good Fortune*, he clearly displays and represents the 'energetic' (*rajasic*) aspect of the heroic sentiment which calls for action again the Kauravas. The angry/furious (*raudra*) dimension 'necessary' to act is embodied and displayed, if not yet unleashed, by Bhima. The construction of the heroic here takes place between Bhima's demands for immediate action and Dharmaputra's voice of principled reason and patience in the working out of their duty.

In Scene 9, Bhima appears as the dutiful husband, and idealized lover with his 'undiminished lustre' when, 'as requested by his consort,' he sets out to seek the 'flowers of good fortune.' So powerful is Bhima that when he jumps and alights in the 'great mountain forest' the strength and speed of his steps cause a sound so great that it is as if 'the mountain itself had cried out in fear!' Indeed, Bhima is so powerful that his 'forceful footsteps' terrify all the inhabitants of the forest, and disrupt Hanuman's meditation on Rama. When Hanuman eventually discovers the source of disruption to his meditation, he exclaims, 'it is as if the heroic *rasa* itself has suddenly assumed human form and come near!'

Represented thus far as an ideal embodiment of the heroic, in Scene 10 Bhima 'fails' miserably. Given the requirement that warrior princes protect the innocent and uphold the social order, Bhima neglects to show proper respect to the elderly monkey who blocks his way when he angrily tries to remove the monkey by force. Finally, with great self-aggrandizement he touts his own great strength, and goes so far as to mock the decrepit old monkey sarcastically! Bhima's pride is accentuated when he addresses this 'old monkey' with great sarcasm – 'If you don't go . . . I will come after you ripe

with anger, and with "compassion" grab you by the neck. Tossing your obese body aside, I will have no obstacle to continuing my journey.' Using the self-referential 'I,' he continues to tout his 'great' powers falsely:

Even if humankind and the gods . . .
  join to attack me,
  I have no fear.
O monkey! Do not speak to me as if to a coward.
  Know that I am Vayu's son,
  the skillful one.

Further accentuating this aspect of Bhima's pride, he sarcastically address Hanuman with such 'respectful' titles as 'leader of the monkeys.' Even when the actor dances Bhima's *kalasams*, they punctuate this section of the text with his impetuous, explosive impatience and disdain for the old monkey. Having built up the bubble of Bhima's self-pride, the remainder of the scene enacts the humbling of this pride as Bhima's supposedly 'great' powers are rendered paltry in comparison to those of the Hanuman – the simple, pious, egoless devotee of Rama.

Humor and the pleasures of *The Flower of Good Fortune*

An element of humor (*hasya*) is nearly always part of playing scenes in which an epic hero is humiliated. The degree and type of humor varies according to the character and situation. In *The Flower of Good Fortune*, Hanuman at first playfully toys with Bhima when he retorts, 'O "ocean of humility," my interest increases.' By the end of their encounter, when the tables are turned and Hanuman has revealed his identity, Bhima is completely humiliated. So much is the humor emphasized and enjoyed that in today's performances the actor playing Hanuman rubs extra salt into Bhima's wounded pride in the final interpolation when he taunts Bhima over the 'loss' of his great mace – the symbol and icon of his supposedly great strength which he uses to 'vanquish his enemies.' It is of course with this mace that he does eventually crush Dussassana's thighs, thereby rectifying the dishonor done to their wife, Panchali.[23]

Scenes like this, in which the hero's pride is lanced, always involve some degree of a hero's self-examination of his own faults and/or shortcomings, and/or at least an acknowledgment of the 'greatness' of the (higher) power which has defeated him. In keeping with the quite different temperaments of each of the epic heroes, Arjuna's self-examination in *The Progeny of Krishna* (Chapter 7) is very different from Bhima's in *The Flower of Good Fortune.* In keeping with Arjuna's sage-like single-mindedness of purpose and moral duty, the agony over his failure to protect the Brahmin, his wife, and their son is profound and deep, and results in his attempt to throw himself, as pledged, into a fire! In contrast, Hanuman's test of the almost child-like Bhima in *The Flower of Good Fortune* results in a simple act of contrition – Bhima merely 'bows with my hands at your feet, O brother, ocean of compassion.' Having sought and won his brother's forgiveness, Bhima immediately expresses his desire to see his divine, super-human form. With child-like simplicity, he wants to experience the awe of Hanuman's full countenance.

The Flower of Good Fortune remains a favorite for both connoisseurs, and general audiences. Children delight in Hanuman's playful antics, especially when he first enters the stage and is disturbed from his meditations. In one of our many discussions, Vasudevan Namboodiripad explained to me the pleasures he has found in watching performances of Scenes 9 and 10 of *The Flower of Good Fortune* over the years:

During the opening (love) scene [between Bhima and Draupadi], I feel the beauty of the slow *patina padam.* It's very complex – the listening. Since I have seen the scene many times, I have a model in mind.

I particularly enjoy performances which feature the dignity of particular characters. I like to watch those actors who are restrained, and therefore more controlled. Therefore, I always liked seeing Kunju Nayar playing Bhima, and Raman Kutty Nayar playing Hanuman in *The Flower of Good Fortune.* Even though *kathakali* is not 'natural,' you feel like it is natural. After Hanuman meets Bhima, he's really 'acting,' i.e., concealing his identity and playing another role [the old monkey]. He's motivated by his brotherly love and affection, and the result is his playful acting. Here he's a 'monkey.' Even though he's not presenting himself as Hanuman, the internal [*stayi*] understanding of Hanuman must be there. During the final interpolation of the play between Bhima and Hanuman, you feel the fraternal bonds between them. That's very captivating to me.

I have a preconceived concept of how these characters should be, and their mode of acting. There's enjoyment of the whole, and enjoyment of the specific sections. For example, when Raman Kutty Nayar plays Hanuman, although he's conscious of the audience, he doesn't play to the audience. But restraint is a word which can't be applied to every character in the same way.

(1993, interview)

ॐॐॐ **6**

the killing of kirmira (kirmiravadham)

Kottayam Tampuran (c.1645–1716)

Translated by

V.R. PRABODHACHANDRAN NAYAR, M.P. SANKARAN NAMBOODIRI AND PHILLIP B. ZARRILLI

INTRODUCTION:

Along with *The Flower of Good Fortune, The Killing of Kirmira* is one of the most important plays in the training of the *kathakali* actor. The play falls into three major parts: the opening scenes where the focus is on the major role of Dharmaputra and Panchali and the dramatic focus is on the dilemma of the Pandavas in exile; the middle scenes where the focus is on Panchali's relationship with Krishna and the visit of the sage Durvasa to their forest home; and the final scenes where the focus shifts to the Pandavas' encounter with the demon Sardula, his wife Simhika, and her brother Kirmira. Unlike *The Flower of Good Fortune, King Rugmamgada's Law,* and *The Progeny of Krishna* for which entire acts are often not performed today, most of *The Killing of Kirmira* is still performed; however, it is seldom performed in one all-night performance. More often the first one or two parts of the play focusing on Dharmaputra, Panchali, and Krishna are performed (Scenes 1–6), or the later part of the play (Scenes 7–14).

When the final part of the play is enacted, the performance usually begins with Scene 8 in which the demoness Simhika makes her entrance. (Scene 7 enacting the encounter between Arjuna and Sardula, culminating in Sardula's death, is seldom enacted; and Scene 12 between the Pandavas and Panchali has not been enacted

within memory of many performers and audience members today.)

SYNOPSIS OF THE PLAY

After losing the game of dice, the Pandavas and their common wife, Panchali (Draupadi), have been living in exile in the forest for twelve years.

(Scenes 1–6, not included in this translation): The opening scene between Dharmaputra and Panchali is set in a very slow tempo to accentuate the pathos (*karuna*) of their situation in exile. Dharmaputra is concerned not with his suffering or that of his brothers, but rather with Panchali's suffering. And Panchali is not so much concerned with her own plight, but rather with the suffering of the 88,000 brahmins and 10,000 sanyasins who have followed them from their court into exile in the forest. They are all exhausted, weak, and hungry, and Panchali feels responsibility for providing them with the same hospitality and food they received at the court. Dharmaputra sympathizes with her plight and concerns.

To find relief from their difficulties, the sage Dhaumya suggests that Dharmaputra worship the sun god, Surya. Surya appears and gives Dharmaputra a magic vessel which will provide a continuous supply of food until Panchali herself (who takes her own meal after everyone else has finished) has eaten.

Krishna comes to visit the Pandavas in their forest home. Dharmaputra asks, 'Aren't you ashamed to see us in such a state?' Remembering how the Kauravas tricked the Pandavas, Krishna becomes angry, and calls forth his divine weapon, Sudarsana Cakra, to punish Duryodhana.[a] Dharmaputra is terrified that the Cakra, which is capable of destroying the entire world, will be unleashed, and pacifies Krishna, pleading with him to send away the terrible weapon, and thereby saving the Kauravas from certain destruction.

Prompted by Duryodhana, the sage Durvasa, widely known for his quick and angry temper, travels to the forest with his disciples.[b] Dharmaputra welcomes them; however, they have arrived at a most inopportune moment. Everyone, including Panchali, has already eaten. Indeed, Panchali has already washed the magic pot and set it out to dry. There is nothing left to feed the guests. Distraught that she cannot provide the required hospitality necessary to welcome an honored guest, Panchali prays to Krishna for assistance. Krishna appears and pretends that he too is very hungry. He asks Panchali to bring the magic vessel so that he can eat. Panchali brings the vessel to convince Krishna that it is empty, but he finds a small left-over piece of leaf in it and asks her to give him a spoonful of water. When Krishna eats this bit of leaf he is fully satisfied. He immediately turns and exits, knowing the result of his own eating. Miraculously, the sage Durvasa and his disciples, who have been purifying themselves by bathing in the nearby river, also feel satisfied, as if they have eaten a full meal. Durvasa explains to Dharmaputra that although he and his 10,000 disciples asked for food, they suddenly feel full, and cannot eat. He and his disciples bless Dharmaputra and Panchali, and leave satisfied and happy.

(Scenes 8–14, translated): When Arjuna is attacked by the demon Sardula he kills him. Sardula's wife, Simhika, tries to abduct Draupadi. Sahadeva, the youngest of the Pandavas, intercepts Simhika, gains Panchali's release, is momentarily captured by Simhika, and finally

disfigures the demoness by cutting off her nose and breasts. Simhika's brother, Kirmira, is infuriated. He challenges the Pandavas, and is killed in the encounter with Bhima.

The translation is based on the Menon and Redyar texts. The *ilakiyattam* are translated from a performance on 1 August 1996 at Tirthapada Mandapam, Thiruvananthapuram, sponsored by Dryshyavedi, the Kerala Studies Program of the University of Kerala, and the University of Wisconsin-Madison Kerala Summer Performing Arts Program. The cast included Nelliyode Vasudevan Namboodiripad as Simhika, Margi Vijayakumar as the Lalita, Margi Sukumaran as Panchali, Ettumanur Kannan as Sahadeva, Ramachandran Pilla as Kirmira, and Ettumanur Kannan as Bhima. The interpolations translated are from this performance.

CAST (Scenes 8–14)
SIMHIKA: a demoness – the wife of Sardula, and sister to the demon Kirmira, in *kari* ('black') female make-up.
LALITA: Simhika in disguise as a beautiful young woman, in *minukku* ('radiant') make-up.
SAHADEVA: fifth and youngest of the Pandavas, in *pacca* ('green') make-up.

[DHARMAPUTRA, BHIMA, ARJUNA, NAKULA: the other four Pandavas, in *pacca* make-up – usually do not appear on stage today in Scene 12.]

KIRMIRA: A demon, and brother of Simhika, in *katti* ('knife') make-up.
BHIMA: SECOND of the Pandavas, in *pacca* make-up.
BRAHMINS: in *minukku* ('radiant') make-up – usually do not appear today.

Scene 8[1]
[Simhika]
[*saurashtram* (*raga*); *atanta* (*tala* – 7 beats)]
(*The curtain is raised.*)

sloka:
Hearing over and again about the killing of her dear one,
in her anger the demoness's eyes vomited blazing

[a] In personified form, the Sudarsana Cakra appears on stage in 'red beard' make-up (indicating the power and terror of the weapon) with a superimposed six-cornered double-triangle motif.
[b] Duryodhana had hoped that the visit of the ill-tempered Durvasa would be a disaster, and incur his wrath and a curse. Krishna's intercession foils Duryodhana's plan.

light like the flames of fire emitted by (the third eye) of Siva's forehead,[a]
(and her) row of fangs emitted spiraling sparks – this demoness, the infamous Simhika, (whose) speech has unbearably hard syllables, revealed herself.

ilakiyattam
(*Simhika performs her curtain look. After her curtain look, she begins to play with the branches of trees in the forest as she dances.*[b] *Examining her body, she says to herself:*)

SIMHIKA: It's not pleasant. It's been a long time since I even washed my face. I should look better than this.
(*Taking part of her hair, she smells it, and reacts. It's become very matted. She looks around for a tree with fruit. Seeing one, she goes to it, shakes it, and collects the fruit which have fallen to the ground. She puts the fruit on a stool, prevents them from falling off, and crushes them. Soaking her palm in the oil of the fruit, she puts it on her hair. She does the same to the other half of her hair. She removes all the loose hair she finds, rolls it into a small ball, and tucks it into the waist of her costume. She ties the tip of the right half of her hair, and puts it back, and then does the same with the left side. She acts as if others are watching her, and becoming envious of her hair. She walks proudly with her long hair. She decides to put a* tilaka *mark on her forehead. She looks in one of the mirrors at her costume. After putting the mark for the first time, she's not satisfied, so she does it again. She decides to make a paste to blacken her eyebrows. She begins by making a small fire. She takes some soot on her index fingers and draws the outline of her eyebrows. One*

Plate 6.1   *Simhika's (Vembayam Appukoothan Pillai) curtain look during which she reveals her inner-nature as a dark forest-dweller*

[a] Literally, 'Kama's killer.'
[b] The actor uses actual tree branches for her curtain entrance, literally emphasizing the demoness's association with the forest and nature; however, in the interpolation which follows, the forest, fruit, soot, etc. are all mimed.

is irritated. *She reacts. Afterward, she admires her eyes, and becomes very happy with herself. She wants to decorate her forehead with another paste. She knows she needs water. Where can she find some? She tries to draw milk from her breasts, but then she realizes she can't draw milk because her children are too old. She makes the mark of Vishnu on her forehead. Now she places ornaments on her ears. She shakes the branch of a tree to get the flowers, and then makes garlands, adorning her earrings. She covers her breast modestly, and ties her cloth to her waist.*

Now I've decorated myself. I look beautiful. Whoever sees me will be pleased. My husband will come home and be happy with me. I'll pretend I'm shy, and he's come to embrace me. To while away the time, I'll play some games. Let me see if anyone in this forest wants to play. *(She walks around looking for someone with whom to play, and calls out:)*

Shall we play? Oh! You're not ready to play? Then go away.

(Simhika begins to play by herself, clapping her hands, and then picking up a ball. After playing ball, she dances kaikottakali.[a] Seeing someone else, she asks if she wants to play too.)

Oh, you're not ready to play? I know how to play by myself, but don't dare stare at me!

(Simhika sits down on the ground, holding sticks in her hands, and begins to play kumi. She gets up and sits on a stool, tired, and wipes away the perspiration from her play.)

I want a drink of water. What shall I do? I'll see if I can find my husband.

(She begins to look for her husband, but he's not to be seen. Her right shoulder begins to shiver, and her right eye twitches.[b])

What harm could ever come to me? So, how can this be? Well, I'll just search for him.

(Simhika gets up from the stool and begins looking for her husband's footsteps, and following them. Eventually they disappear. She begins to hear wailing to one side, and then on the other.)

Who's crying out? Someone is being killed. Is this my husband I hear? Yes! Yes!

(Hitting her head and chest with her hands, she immediately tears the tali from around her neck and throws it away.[c] Again she hits her head and chest, crying out:)

Who has done this!

(Then with sorrow and anger she says:) [N]

SIMHIKA:

> *pallavi*: Alas! O my dear handsome husband! Forsaking me, have you gone to the abode of Death?[2]

anupallavi:

What a pity! Immersed in overwhelming grief in this forest, what am I living for?

caranam:

That weakling Bhima killed Hidimba, [K][J] leader of the demons.[d]

This shows that at times even the weak become strong.

caranam:

When they (the Pandavas) lived in Ekacakra [K] begging for their daily bread, Bhima single-handedly killed the demon, Baka.[e]

---

[a] Kerala's traditional women's hand-clapping folk dance.
[b] Both are bad omens.
[c] The *tali* was a chain tied around a woman's neck when an official alliance was formed with a man. This traditional form of 'marriage' was known as a *sambandam* alliance.
[d] The story of Hidimba and Hidimbi is enacted as part of *The Killing of Baka* (*Bakavadham*), also by Kottayam Tampuran. The demon Hidimba tells his sister, Hidimbi, that he smells human flesh. He sends her to find the man he smells for his breakfast. Hidimbi promises to fulfill his wish and departs; however, as soon as she sees the Pandavas she immediately falls in love with Bhima. To entice him, she transforms herself into a beautiful maiden (Lalita). When the beautiful maiden approaches Bhima and declares her love, he explains that he cannot marry until his eldest brother is married, and sends her away. Meanwhile, Hidimba is upset that his sister is taking so long. When he finds her enamored of Bhima, he becomes furious and attacks Bhima, who kills him. On the advice of the sage Vyasa, Bhima accepts Hidimbi so that she can bear his son, Ghatolkacha. After receiving his father's blessings, Ghatolkacha and his mother, Hidimbi, leave.
[e] The story of the killing of the demon Baka is the second part of *The Killing of Baka*. In this part of the play, according to an agreement between the villagers of Ekacakra and the demon Baka, Baka agrees not to wipe out the entire village if he

The more I see such unseemly acts, the more the
  grief in my heart increases.

  caranam:
And with that wicked (Bhima) who killed her
brother, [K]
  Hidimbi goes on enjoying herself daily!
Surprisingly, nowhere in all the three worlds
  have I ever seen such a shameless woman!

  caranam:
All five men responsible for my husband's death
  [K] live in this forest. I do not have enough
  strength to retaliate [against them all] immediately.

  caranam:
However, I hear that there is only one woman
  who is the dear wife of all five. [K]
I shall quickly deceive them by luring her into
  the interior of the forest.

  caranam:
Then I shall give her as a gift [K]
  to my brother, the brave Kirmira.
She will be the cause of their going to the abode
  of death!

  ilakiyattam
(*Taking branches from some of the trees in the
forest again, Simhika walks about, reflecting.*)

SIMHIKA: If I just go like this . . . They have gone
to the riverside along with their teacher. Before
they come back, I'll capture her. I know how to
deceive them. I'll transform myself into a
charming woman. I'll approach her, and start a
conversation. While her husbands are gone, I
must capture her and escape.

(*She chants a mantra, changes her shape, and
after performing an N is transformed into the
form of a beautiful woman (Lalita), and exits.*)

(*Curtain*)

Scene 9
[Lalita and Panchali]

  [*navarasam* (*raga*); *atanta* (*tala*) (*patinnakalam*
  – 56 beats)]

(*The curtain remains up during the singing of the
following* sloka.)

  sloka:
Having determined when the Pandavas would be
  gone, the demoness waited;
transforming herself into a beautiful-bodied one,
  the one who intended to kill, approached
  Panchali – separated from her husbands – and
  said:

(*Panchali sits on the left as the Lalita enters to a
kitatakadimtam from upstage. She ties her cloth
to her waist, wondering whether she's been seen.*[f]
*She comes close to Panchali. They see each other,
and react with affection.*)

  LALITA:
              pallavi: O garland adorning the hair
                          of beautiful women! Please
                          listen to my good words: [K]

  anupallavi:
O one with graceful hair, resembling darkness!
On finding you near me my sorrow has vanished.
[K]
  (*The speed changes to 14 beats.*)
  caranam:
O one with a face like the moon,
  whose eyes resemble the petal of the red lotus,
with your lotus-feet please do not walk
needlessly in this unfit forest inhabited by lions.
[K]

  caranam:[4]
O one whose gait excels that of elephants,
  please know that I am one of those women who
  roam the skies.

is fed regularly. When the Pandavas arrive there disguised as brahmins, a brahmin and his wife are bemoaning their fate
since their only son must be sacrificed to feed the demon. Kunti, the mother of the Pandavas, consoles him and promises
that her son, Bhima, will go in place of his son. Bhima takes a cart full of food and toddy intended to satisfy Baka. As
Bhima awaits Baka on the sacrificial grounds in the forest where the brahmins are supposed to leave their offerings to
him, he gets voraciously hungry and starts consuming everything intended for Baka. When Baka arrives and sees Bhima
eating what was intended for him, he becomes outraged. Baka declares that by consuming Bhima he will get to eat both
the food offerings and Bhima himself. In the fight that follows Bhima kills Baka.
[f]Tying her cloth indicates that she is concealing her identity from Panchali.

Seeing you in the forest, I have come here.
  My own name is Ganika. [K]

  caranam:
O innocent lass, my friend, one with admirable
  qualities!
Dearest and most pure one, don't think [I ask out
  of] jealousy, but out of affection:
please tell (me), what is your name, and which is
  your clan? [K]

  [*erikkilakkamodari* (*raga*); *atanta* (*tala*)
(*etavattam* – 14 beats)]

  PANCHALI:
            pallavi: Please know that I am King
                Drupada's daughter – the
                one in whom he delights.[5]

  anupallavi:
O lovely woman, because of my many sins I am
  living in this inaccessible forest.

  caranam:
[With me] here are five distinguished princes.
Please know that I am happy serving as their
consort.[6]
  caranam:
Having gone to the Ganges to perform evening

prayers with their Guru, they will return here
shortly. [K]

  [*bhairavi* (*raga*); *muriatanta* (*tala* – 14 beats)][7]

  LALITA:
  caranam:
A thicket of trees and a shrine of the goddess
  Durga are nearby.
O lotus-eyed damsel, let us go see them.
Many women have worshipped (there) in the
  proper manner, and even from olden times have
  obtained the boons they desired. [K]

  [*kamodari* (*raga*); *cembata* (*tala* – 16 beats)]
  sloka: (*This* sloka *is acted*.)
Thus, having tempted Panchali with her (sweet)
  words, holding her hand with pleasure,
together they reached the interior forest anxious
  to take *darsan* of Durga,
and (there the Lalita) said to her:

  LALITA:
            pallavi: Seeing this forest, pleasure
                comes. Have you seen it? [K]

  caranam:
Clusters of clouds and darkness contend with
  your long, curly hair.

Plate 6.2   *Simhika in disguise as a Lalita (Margi Vijayakumar) entices Panchali to go with her to the nearby Durga temple*

O one with beautiful hair like the dark
  Valisneria,[a] swarms of bees come here one after
  another to see your hair again and again.[b]
Alas! With grief they fly away.

  pallavi: Seeing . . . [K] + [I][8]

  caranam:
Lo, the bamboo plays (like) the flute in
  synchrony with the music of the cuckoo.
(Like) actresses, some creepers take their place
  here, and show their pleasure,
gesticulating with their fingers which are tender
  leaves, moved by the wind.[c]

  pallavi: Seeing . . . [K] + [I]

  caranam:
Lo, from the rows of the (red) amaranth trees,
  flowers fall on the locks of your hair.
O one with eyes like petals of the blue water-lily,
  it appears as if this (forest) is about to receive
  you.

  pallavi: Seeing . . . [K] + [I]

  [*erikkilakkamodari* (*raga*); *cempata* (*tala* – 16
  beats)]

  PANCHALI:[9]
  caranam:
Here, the cricket's sound resonates intensely, and
  my creeper-like body repeatedly shivers.
Friend, aren't we going to return immediately?
  (*At this point the Lalita holds Panchali's
  hand. Panchali tries to release her hand, but
  Lalita won't let go. Even though the actor's hand
  playing Panchali is 'free' so that he can perform
  the mudras, it is assumed that the Lalita is still
  holding her hand and will not let her go.*)
Leave! Leave me! O one with unsteady eyes!
  You have been deceiving me! Telling me lies,
  haven't you! [1/2 K]

  [*cempata* (*tala* – 8 beats)]

Plate 6.3 *Smearing her face with black and
putting her loosened hair in her mouth, Simhika
reveals her 'true' form as she rushes forward,
screaming and threatening Panchali*

  LALITA:
  caranam:
[Do you think] I will let you leave quickly [K]
  and simply release you to rejoice with your
  dear ones?
By the power of fate, I have captured you, and
  shall consume your flesh to my full satisfaction.

  pallavi: Seeing my body, terror
      comes! Have you seen it? [T]

(*When Lalita completes the enacting of the
pallavi and T, she turns upstage and puts* kari
[*black*] *on her face, showing her real shape, and
exits. Immediately Simhika enters in black* kari
*make-up, running in, and dancing a piece of
choreography known as* addiddikkana. *When she
concludes, she takes Panchali away.*)

(*Curtain*)[10]

---

[a] A water plant which is blue-green in color.
[b] The actor elaborates the visit of the swarms of bees as the singers repeat the line over and over.
[c] The actor elaborates this image at length while the singers repeat the phrase.

Scene 10
[Simhika, Panchali]
[*dvijavanti* (*raga*); *muriatanta* (*tala* – 14 beats)][11]

   sloka:
In Simhika's control,[a] Panchali –
   whose heart, completely attached to her
   husband's, was completely distraught –
wailed like a heron fallen into Rohu's mother's
   mouth.[b]

(*After the* sloka *is sung and the curtain is
removed, standing on a stool, Panchali cries out.
Simhika dances with one foot while the other
remains on the stool, giving the impression that
she holds Panchali on her shoulder. The more
Draupadi cries, the happier Simhika becomes.*)

PANCHALI:
                pallavi: Oh god, how could this happen!
                How could this happen! [K][c]

   caranam:
O my lords! Hearing my cries, will you come
   before the demoness swallows me? [K]

   caranam:
O son of Dharma (Yudhisthira) –
   one concerned with *dharma*, pure-bodied one –
have you forsaken me, allowing this demoness to
   abduct me without any obstacle?[17] [K]

   caranam:
Before (I) am devoured by the demoness's cave-
   like mouth,
O son of Madri, brave Sahadeva,
   please protect me quickly! [K]

(*Curtain*)[13]

Scene 11
[Simhika, Panchali, Sahadeva]
[*kedaragaudam* (*raga*);[14] *cempata* (*tala* – 8 beats)]
(*The curtain remains raised as the following
sloka is sung.*)

   sloka:
Arjuna's younger brother, whose valor is equal to
   Narasimha, after gathering his weapons,
   obstructed (the path)
with his sharp arrows, and said to Simhika, that
   cruel demoness who sounds like a lion:

   ilakiyattam
(*Simhika and Panchali stand left. Sahadeva enters
with a sword on the right side to an* etuttukalasam.)

SAHADEVA: I hear the wailing of our wife. I
must find out why.
(*After performing a K, he sees Simhika and
orders her to release Panchali. When Simhika
sees Sahadeva, she examines him from head to
foot and mockingly says:*)

SIMHIKA: Such a tiny fellow has come to quarrel
with me!
SAHADEVA: She's our wife. Release her immediately!
SIMHIKA: Do you think I will ever do this?
(*When she does not obey, Sahadeva forcibly releases
Panchali. He blesses her, and she exits to an N.*)
SIMHIKA: For me, he'll do [instead of her]. He'll be
equally good to eat!

SAHADEVA:
                pallavi: Stop, demoness, stop!
                Eti, eti, eti, demoness![d] [K]

   caranam:
O you who are precious to demons,
   one who desires human flesh,
my sturdy, strong, and very sharp scimitar is
   about to fall on your breasts.

                pallavi: Stop . . . [T][15]

SIMHIKA:
caranam:
Even the strong, [K]
   proud elephants positioned in the cardinal
   directions quickly run away
since they can't stand the blows of my hands!

---

[a] The phrase literally reads, 'Having fallen into Simhika's mouth' – a colloquial expression indicating that you are under somone's control.
[b] Rohu and Ketu are two serpents who swallowed the sun and the moon. Our translation is only one of a number of possibilities. Another would be, 'who was forced to remain in the interior forest (filled) with lionesses.'
[c] With Panchali on the stool, this and the following *kalasams* are played by the percussionists but not danced.
[d] *Eti* is the feminine addressive form of a common, marketplace insult that is untranslatable.

Plate 6.4   *Sahadeva intercepts Simhika as she attempts to take Panchali away*

pallavi: Stop, 'man,' stop!
Eta, eta, eta, 'man'![a] [T]

SAHADEVA:
caranam:
Since my reputed wife, [K]
 was so skillfully abducted by you,
 I will kill you.

pallavi: Stop, demoness . . . [T]

SIMHIKA:
caranam:
O petty enemy! [K]
 Proud one! Leader of fools!
 Can you even stand before me?

pallavi: Stop, man . . . [T]

SAHADEVA:
caranam:
Women who act indecently [K]
 deserve to be killed like Rama's example.[b]

pallavi: Stop, demoness . . . [T]

SIMHIKA:
caranam:
O you uncontrolled, [K]
 ill-tempered, despicable mortal! I have done
 this for my own satisfaction
to retaliate for the killing of my husband.

pallavi: Stop, man . . . [T]

SAHADEVA:
caranam:
Jumping like Khalgi,[c] [K]
 I will swiftly cut off both your hard breasts![16]

[a] She matches his insult in kind using the male form (*eta*), and by taunting him as a mere 'man.'
[b] A reference to Rama's killing of the demoness Thadaka near the sage Viswamitra's hermitage. This is enacted as part of the *kathakali* play *Sita Swayamvara* by Kottarkara Tampuran (c.1555–1605).
[c] The tenth incarnation of Vishnu always shown with a sword.

pallavi: Stop, demoness . . . [T]

ilakiyattam
(*As in the case of other battle* padams, *it is typical for the actors to exchange positions after each* caranam. *After the* padam, *during the fight, Simhika is about to capture Sahadeva when he cuts her with his sword. Simhika runs away crying, 'ayyayyo.'*[a] *Sahadeva cleans his sword.*)

SAHADEVA: The demoness has run away with blood streaming from her nose and breasts, crying aloud. That's as it should be.
(*Sahadeva exits with an N.*)

(*Curtain*)[17]

Scene 13[18]
[Kirmira, Simhika]
[*ghantharam* (raga); *muriatanta* (tala – 14 beats)]
  (*The curtain remains up as the following* sloka *is sung.*)

sloka:
Simhika, whose breasts and nose had been sliced,
  soiled with freely flowing blood,
racing here and there (as) her cries echoed
  through the four quarters (of the world),
spoke without a single nasal sound[b] to (her)
  brother who possessed all strength and was
  surrounded
by fellow demons.

ilakiyattam[c]
(*Kirmira performs his curtain look, and then says:*)
  KIRMIRA:
I am very pleased. Why? Oh, I know why. No one is as strong and brave as me. That's why I am so pleased. (*Thinking to himself.*) Now what

shall I do? It's time for my daily worship of Siva.[d] If Siva is pleased I will be able to subdue the *devas*. (*Kirmira goes to the Siva shrine. Ringing the bell, he opens the door to the sanctum sanctorum. He removes the previous day's decorations and offerings, cleaning the idol. Sitting on a stool, he performs the ritual of bathing the Siva lingam three times. He puts sandal paste on the idol. He performs* puspanjali (*worship with flowers*), *does* arati (*waving a lit flame before the deity*) *while ringing a bell with his left hand. Again he offers more flowers, and then* arati *with both hands. He meditates, chanting the names of Siva while counting on his fingers each repetition. Suddenly, he hears a sound.*) Oh, it's nothing. (*He returns to his meditation. Again he hears the sound, slightly louder.*) What is that sound? Someone is crying out, but I should complete this *puja*. (*He returns to his meditation. A third time he hears the sound – much louder this time.*) This can't be ignored. (*He closes the sanctum, moves upstage indicating that he has left the shrine. He rushes downstage performing a piece of set choreography known as* addhiddhikkana. *Looking around, he says:*)[e] Oh, the ocean has been churned up, and its waves are huge. All the eight directions reverberate with this sound that pierces all ears. (*Climbing onto the stool, and looking ahead he asks:*) What is it that's coming? Someone is coming in this direction. A woman whose nose and breasts have been sliced and are smeared with blood is coming. Who is she? (*He climbs down from the stool and rushes downstage, looking.*) It's my sister! (*Recognizing who it is.*) Come to me! Come to me! (*One of Simhika's assistants rushes to the stage cupping a handful of blood which he shows to Kirmira.*[f] Simhika with ninam *make-up appears making her entrance through the audience, and approaches Kirmira face-to-face, crying out as*

[a] '*Ayyo*' is a commonplace expression used to express a variety of emotions from surprise or wonder, to anguish, to pain.
[b] Among all languages, Malayalam perhaps possesses the largest number (six) of nasal sounds that are significant or phonemic. Kottayam Tampuran has managed to compose the following *padam* for Simhika without using a single nasal sound. Given her noseless condition, she naturally cannot pronounce a single nasal sound.
[c] Like Simhika's opening interpolation, the following detailed interpolation is completely mimed.
[d] Demons and demonesses are worshippers of Siva. Through worship of Siva and the practice of austerities, they gain many of their great powers.
[e] At this time additional drummers will come onstage if the Simhika scene is to be played with blood (*ninam*). (See the commentary below for an explanation.)
[f] This gesture indicates that a great calamity has taken place.

Plate 6.5 *Supported by two attendants covered, like her, in blood, Simhika (Nelliyode Vasudevan Namboodiripad) enters howling in pain through the audience*

she moves forward with faltering steps.)[a]
(*Kirmira turns around and moves to the left corner of the stage, returning to center stage several times. He beckons her with his hand, once again running toward her, saying:*) I'm coming! (*Finally, Simhika enters the stage and falls at his feet. He examines her carefully.*)
   Alas! Who has done this? Tell me immediately!

SIMHIKA:
         pallavi: Alas! Alas, brave demon.
                  Look!
                  Alas! Alas! My body has
                  been disfigured.

anupallavi:
Alas! Alas! The pain is unbearable. O god!
Alas! Alas, brave brother, protect (me).[19]

caranam:[20]
Alas! Then and there, Sahadeva's weapon cut my
   breasts and disfigured (me). [K]

   [*pantuvarali* (*raga*); *cempata* (*tala* – 8 beats)]

KIRMIRA:
         pallavi: Dear, why this useless
                  wailing!
                  My sister, don't worry. [K][21]

   caranam:
Alas, disfiguring you, [K]
   who on earth can live in peace?
Who is there from Meru to Lanka [in the whole
   universe] who can resist the strength of my
   hands?[22]

   ilakiyattam

[a] There are two ways of enacting this scene. One is popularly known as '*ninam*' ('blood') since it uses copious amounts of stage blood made by boiling and dyeing a large quantity of rice, areca nut flowers, and other ingredients literally to create the texture of cut flesh that is graphic and gruesome. When played 'with blood,' sometimes the actor playing the role of Simhika also appears as the bloodied Simhika, and on other occasions a different, second actor plays this part.
The second method of staging is a form of mono-acting in which Simhika never appears, but is played by the actor playing Kirmira. See the commentary below for further discussion.

KIRMIRA:

Alright. Do not worry at all. Cutting his throat, I will give you his blood to drink. (*He enacts the wiping of the blade of his sword, and taking the final drops of blood from the sword to pour into her wide-open mouth*). Is that enough? (*Seeing that she is satisfied.*) If so, then go without delay. (*He blesses her, and she exits through the audience if the performance is with* ninam. *Kirmira returns downstage. He enacts the preparations for battle known as* patappurappatu.) Quickly, I will go and call him to fight. (*Looking from right to left, he sees the messenger.*) O, Messenger, bring the chariot immediately. (*He asks the messenger on his left to bring his weapons. He examines the chariot when it arrives. Then he receives the weapons one by one, and places them in the chariot. From his waist he removes his sword from its sheath, wipes it clean, returns it to the scabbard, and ties it to his waist. Dancing* tripata vattam thatti, *he puts on his armor, instructs his army to move ahead, and asks the charioteer to drive. He climbs onto the stool, sees that his warriors are beginning to move, and says, 'Move ahead!' Then he descends from the stool.*) I too must start immediately. (*At the end of the N, he jumps on the chariot and proceeds to the battle.*) (*Curtain*)[23]

Scene 15

[Kirmira, Bhima]
[*saramgam (raga*); *cempata (tala* – 8 beats)]
(*The curtain remains up as the following* sloka *is sung.*)

sloka:
Simhika fell down, soaked in flowing blood,
 and rose again, beating her breasts forcefully
 with her long arms;
she looked like an enormous mountain-slope
 from which many red springs spouted.
Consoling her again, Kirmira went to fight, and
 angrily called out to Bhima:

ilakiyattam
KIRMIRA:

(*Standing on the stool, Kirmira brings down the curtain and sees the forest.*) Where are (our) enemies in this forest? Let me see. (*Jumping down from the stool, he turns around and looks:*)

They are not to be found. (*Smelling the air, he catches Bhima's scent:*) The wind has carried his scent. They are in this direction, I will call them, and then fight. [N]

caranam:
With an army which wages battles against the ocean, I will skillfully smash the trees of this forest creating a noisy cacophony! [K][24]

 pallavi: Fool! Watch my technique!
 You, come here! [T][25]

caranam:
Cruelty to women [K]
 is the only skill your hand possesses, you rogue!
You worm, I am weaving about to shatter your body with my expert blows. [K]

 pallavi: Fool . . . [T]

caranam:
Like a lofty mountain hit by Indra's Vajra, [K]
 your body, pierced by my very sharp arrows
 will fall here now.

 pallavi: Fool . . . [T]

caranam:
Moving mountains [K]
 and oceans with my cacophonous army, I will fight you now. [K]

 pallavi: Fool . . . [T]

[*porvakalyam (raga)*;[26] *cempata (tala* – 8 beats)][27]

ilakiyattam
BHIMA: (*Entering:*) I hear someone calling me to fight. I'll go see who challenges me. (*He sees Kirmira. Bhima dances an* edutthukalasam, *and says:*) Is it you who challenges me to fight?
KIRMIRA: Yes.
BHIMA: If so, then I will show you! [N]

BHIMA:

 pallavi: Resist this mass of weapons,
 meanest of demons![a]
 Resist these weapons!

---

[a] According to traditional battle etiquette fighters would challenge their opponents to defend against a particular blow before it is delivered.

caranam:
Vilest demon, [K]
  your body will be chopped into pieces before
  the 'auspicious' time for you to go to
Yama's good residence. [K]

>   _pallavi_: Resist . . . [T]

KIRMIRA:
caranam:
You who committed such an act against good
women! [K]
My weapons are enough to retaliate against you,
  lowest of humans, indisciplined one!ª [K]

>   _pallavi_: Resist this mass of weapons,
>   meanest of humans!
>   Resist these weapons! [T]

BHIMA:
caranam:
In a shower of strong, cruel arrows [K]
  I will annihilate you here,
O wicked and obese one! [K]

>   _pallavi_: Resist . . . [T]

KIRMIRA:
caranam:
O shameless, paltry human, [K]
  right now (my) weapons will dance on the stage
  of your wide chest! [K]

>   _pallavi_: Resist . . . [T]²⁸

ilakiyattam
(_In the fight, Kirmira is killed by Bhima. Bhima
then turns around and says:_)
Now, without delay, I will go and report to my
elder brother. [N]
(_Bhima then performs the closing dance_ [Dhanasi.])

(_Curtain_)²⁹

COMMENTARY: THE SACRIFICIAL PARADIGM,
AND CONTESTATION OVER ITS BLOODY
REPRESENTATION

In 1996 when the version of _The Killing of
Kirmira_ translated here was staged at the
Tirthapada Mandapam in Thiruvananthapuram,
Kerala, the performance played to an enthusiastic,
standing-room only audience. The overflow
crowd was drawn to the performance for two
reasons. It was the first time in approximately
thirty years that the play had been staged 'with
blood' in the capital city, and the major role of
Simhika was being played by Nelliyode
Vasudevan Namboodiripad, who is well-known
for his playing of demons and demonesses.

Given the centrality of blood-letting in _The
Killing of Kirmira_ and many other _kathakali_
dramas, I continue in this commentary to explore
the significance of the act of killing and the
sacrificial paradigm implicit in _kathakali_'s
representations of kingship and the heroic.³⁰ I also
examine current debates over the use or non-use of
stage blood in Scene 13 of _The Killing of Kirmira_ to
illustrate the tendency toward 'pacification,'
'aestheticization,' and 'Brahmanization' of _kathakali_
by some of its connoisseurs.

The heroic, the furious, and the significance of the bloody act of 'killing'

In the original, full-length version of _The Killing
of Kirmira_ after Bhima kills Kirmira there is a
short concluding scene seldom performed today
(see endnote 29). In this scene one or more of the
ascetics living in the forest where the Pandavas
are residing in exile enter to bless Bhima. This
act of blessing, after Bhima's killing of Kirmira,
accentuates the ideal model of _kshatriya_
behavior which requires that Bhima kills Kirmira.
As a warrior ('King'), Bhima's 'most important
duty' is to 'protect the pious' so that they can
'live in this forest without fear,' and 'perform the
fire sacrifice with pleasure,' thereby maintaining
the cosmic order.

The idealized relationship between the
kshatriya's duty to protect brahmins and
maintain the order of the cosmos is spelled out
specifically in Kerala in the legendary Kerala
brahmin chronicle, _Keralopathi_, as well as in
Duarte Barbosa's detailed account of the
'knighthood' ritual of initiation of Nayars into
service to their ruler as described previously.
Under the obligation to 'expand' their kingdoms

ª According to Kirmira's logic, as Sahadeva's elder brother, Bhima deserves the same punishment as his brother for his violation of Simhika.

through acts of 'sacrificial destruction' (Fuller 1992: 124–5), engaging in warfare was a necessity, as was the inevitably bloody act of killing which is the 'harvest of war' (Freeman 1991: 289). *Kathakali*'s enactments of blood-letting, most graphically represented in scenes 'with blood' like the disfigurement of Simhika or the disembowelment of Dussassana, are one of many Kerala cultural performances and/or rituals which clearly establish blood as 'the central metaphor for the essential fertilizing fluid of life' by means of which 'the health and fertility of the kingdom' is promoted (Freeman 1991: 289).

The significance of this fundamental sacrificial paradigm in Kerala is underscored by the central importance of the goddess to Nayar life and ritual, and of animal sacrifices traditionally part of the offerings enjoyed by the goddess (among many other Kerala deities). In the play itself the Lalita lures Panchali to Durga's shrine where 'many women have obtained the boons they desired.' The goddess takes various forms and her names (Bhagavati, Bhadrakali, Chamundi or Durga) are virtually interchangeable. She is best known as Bhagavati. As Bhagavati she encompasses 'a wide range of divine personalities ranging from the benign to the ferocious . . . (and is) associated with both the Sanskritic goddesses of the greater pan-Indian Hindu tradition, and with local village goddesses associated with fever diseases' (Caldwell 1995: 17). Bhagavati is 'conceived of as primarily benevolent and powerful, simultaneously a chaste virgin and a care-giving mother' (ibid). She is central to all aspects of Nayar life. She assumes 'paramount importance among household deities' where it is typical for her to be installed in a room on the western side of a Nayar house or a niche where household deities are maintained (Moore 1983: 242).

When propitiated by Kurup ritual specialists, she is conceived in elaborate multi-colored floor drawings as 'an even more intense form of the *urga* class of fierce deities' notable for her 'energized eyes,' and with an expression evoking the '*rasa* of *vira* or valour, supported by *raudra* or fury' (Jones 1981: 73). Given these associations, not surprisingly, Bhagavati is the primary form of the guardian deity of all *kalari* where the traditional martial art, *kalarippayattu*, is taught, and in which the goddess is propitiated daily (Zarrilli 1998: Chapter 3).

Bhadrakali is her violent form. She is the goddess of war and weapons and is popularly known as that form of Kali which possesses boundless powers of destruction. Bhadrakali is depicted in popular religious art as holding a sword representing her destructive power. As Bhadrakali she is the goddess 'of the hot months' (Meenam) who in Kerala 'never marries, is never tamed,' and remains 'independent and unfulfilled' and whose 'sexual desire can be quenched only by violence and . . . by incestuous union with her father, Siva' (Caldwell 1995: 328). In her form as Bhadrakali, the 'fierce virgin' is the heroine of *mudiyettu*, the most likely one of *kathakali*'s most important precursors. *Mudiyettu* is a ritual possession performance in which the legend of the 'killing of Darika' is performed in Bhagavati temples during the annual temple festival (see Caldwell 1995: *passim*).

Bhagavati also played a central role in realizing the aspirations to kingship of each of the local rulers of medieval Kerala. As Caldwell notes:

> each king had his own local installation of the goddess, who was considered to be a tutelary matrilineal ancestor and protectress of his family's personal political interests . . . Propitiation of one's own local Bhagavati ensured the power and success of the kingdom and its dependants.
> (1995: 34)

For the goddess, as well as other deities, 'the most significant insignia of the god's power, and the essential prop . . . of all forms of worship in this region, are weapons' (Freeman 1991: 242). Weapons do not simply represent or symbolize a deity's power, they are invested with and animate the deity's power since the weapons themselves are often installed, propitiated and then utilized for the literal transfer of the deity's power to his medium – at Bhagavati temples the oracle is known as a *veliccappatu* (see Caldwell 1995: 19ff; Freeman 1991: 244–6). Weapons in general, and the sword in particular, are the vehicle through which divine power is manifest in the human spatio-temporal domain. Royal power is invested in rulers and royal lineages symbolized by the sword. That power is literally actualized through the martial-warrior whose hands wield power through their swords and other weapons (Zarrilli 1998: Chapter 4).

Freeman notes that ritual weapons are indexical icons:

> ritual weapons, through being icons of those used in battle [killing], are believed to actually index that charismatically divine capacity to kill; in other words, the capacity and drive to kill are perceived as instantiated in the symbols that signify them.
>
> (1991: 299)

In traditional Kerala ritual performances such as *mudiyettu*, *teyyam*, or Ayappan *tiyatta* the deity's sword is the literal vehicle through which the power of the deity passes directly into the oracular vehicle whose state of possession, dance, etc. is a manifestation of the visitation of the god. The literal use of the sword to let blood is part of the *veliccappatu*'s process of serving as an oracle for the deity when he cuts his forehead with her sword, as well as part of those ritual performances in which cocks were traditionally sacrificed to propitiate many of Kerala's 'heated' deities, including some forms of the goddess. As we shall see in the commentary in Chapter 8, the presence and 'visitation' of the deity is also reflected in the hero's 'transformative' state of fury – a state necessary for undertaking his sacrificial acts. When the sword is wielded by the ritual specialist to draw blood by sacrificing cocks or by cutting his forehead, or by the martial practitioner to slay his 'enemy', each 'sacrificial' act of blood-letting is indexical and iconic of the deity's power and presence.

The central significance of blood is witnessed in the presence and meanings associated with the color red. Red is associated with the goddess in her 'heated' or 'furious' form, and with *sakti* – the dangerous, unstable feminine energy which inspires terror. As Caldwell notes, 'the color worn by Bhadrakali in *mudiyettu* is brilliant red, which generally symbolizes feminine energy in south Indian ritual' (1995: 324). The associations are clearly reflected in the blood associated with animal sacrifices for the goddess, the sacrifice of war, and the color worn by traditional martial practitioners when they tied the *kacca* (a long cloth wrapped around their hips to support their 'vital energy' in combat).

When Simhika's 'round breasts' are 'cut off by the scimitar's tip and showered with blood' (Scene 12, *sloka* 1), and when her 'breasts and nose' have been 'sliced and soiled with freely flowing blood,' she participates in the iconic and indexical construction of this fundamental sacrificial paradigm. Besides, it makes very compelling theater.

The contestation over bloody representation in *The Killing of Kirmira*: Lokadharmi versus Natyadharmi aesthetics

As indicated in Footnote 27 in this chapter, there are two very different ways of enacting Simhika's 'appearance' before her brother in Scene 13 after her nose and breasts have been cut by Sahadeva's sword. One is popularly known as 'with blood' (*ninam*) since it makes copious use of stage blood, rice, areca nut flowers, etc. to re-create the texture of cut flesh that should be graphic and gruesome. This literal method of representing Simhika's disfigurement is not new, and originated in the staging of similar scenes in the *kutiyattam* repertory.

A second method is also employed to enact this scene. It is known as *pakarnnattam*, or 'transformed acting.' In this method of enactment, the actor playing the role of Kirmira appears alone onstage. First, he mimetically enacts Simhika's pathetic condition, and then he enacts his response to her condition. Pacifying his sister, Kirmira vows to banish the Pandavas. When this method of acting the scene is used, Simhika's sections of dialogue are simply omitted.

This second method of enacting the scene is used to shorten the time of the performance, and to focus the audience's attention on the actor playing the role of Kirmira. It is a form of mono-acting drawn from *kutiyattam* as well. Modelled on the *nirvahana* section of a performance, a single actor in a single role performs a complete story in which, for several days in a row, s/he performs a complete story in which s/he takes all the roles in turn. In this scene the actor playing Kirmira only performs his role, and that of the (absent) Simhika. For the past thirty years, until the 1996 performance in Thiruvananthapuram 'with blood,' Scene 13 had been performed with only the actor playing Kirmira onstage.

In one of our many lengthy discussions, *kathakali* connoisseur Ganesha Iyer explained why he and other aficionados prefer mono-acting for this scene:

> when Simhika appears in all her bloody appearance it spoils the interpolation which follows in which Kirmira prepares for battle. If an audience [of connoisseurs] wants to see 'blood,' they usually ask for *The Killing of Narakasura* since that *ninam* is best known.

Ganesha Iyer's preference for mono-acting reflects an increasing preference on behalf of some connoisseurs to provide more opportunities for senior actors to display the subtler talents of what they often call the 'ideational' (*natyadharmi*).

Natyadharmi is a Sanskrit term which, along with its counterpart, *lokadharmi* ('ordinary' or 'concrete'), has come into increasing use among both *kathakali* patron/connoisseurs and actors during the past thirty to forty years. Their use as one among several discursive constructs such as a 'sense of appropriateness' (*aucitya bodham*) for evaluation of performances is part of a tendency to use terms drawn from the *Natyasastra* and/or other Sanskrit texts in critiquing performances, and in shaping aesthetic and performance choices such as the staging of Scene 13 'with blood' or without.

Following the detailed etymological and historical study of Vidya Niwas Misra and Prem Lata Sharma, *lokadharmi* might best be translated as the 'ordinary' or 'concrete.' *Lokadharmi* is that from which the 'extraordinary' or 'ideational' (*natyadharmi*) is elaborated, abstracted, transformed, and/or distilled:

> The evolution of *natyadharmi* itself is based on what is happening in this *loka*. Any abstraction for that matter presupposes something concrete. Moreover a *natyadharmi* (an ideational presentation) is aimed at giving the essence of what one finds at the concrete level and is necessitated by the impossibility of presenting the whole activity of all times and spaces in a physically bound time and space . . . [The] mutual interaction of these two has to be ensured, so that the performance continues to be a process, rather than to be a dead end, and still it has to be ideational in order to be able to communicate, to people of all time and space.
>
> (1992: 145–6)

Since these two terms appeared as early as the *Natyasastra* with reference to drama, they have received considerable attention among scholars of Sanskrit drama and Indian performing arts. Focusing more specifically on the terms as used in the *Natyasastra*, scholars such as Kapila Vatsyayan translate *dharmi* as 'modes' or 'conventions' and *lokadharmi* and *natyadharmi* as 'realistic . . . or suggestive' conventions (1968a: 8–9, 24). *Natyadharmi* then is usually translated as the 'stylized' mode of enacting drama, and *lokadharmi* is the 'realistic' (ibid: p. 24). Similarly V. Raghavan translates the terms as 'realism' and 'idealism' (1993: *passim*).

Misra and Sharma take account of these more specific uses, but manage to keep their account of the terms open-ended. They conclude their study by asserting that

> *loka* is a generalised concept of space filled up primarily with activity of various kinds now and here, but secondarily of possible transformations at a higher or lower level. It can neither be equated with the world nor with common people, nor with the sphere of direct perceptions or the manifest, nor the folk or rustic as against the elite; nor the oral unformed tradition as against the codified written tradition nor the real as against the ideal. And yet it covers all these ranges of meaning interrelated to each other. Unfortunately, the term *loka* has been devalued during the last 150 years in India as folk, and has come to mean a subterranean flow of collective consciousness forgotten and rediscovered.
>
> (1992: 155)

When performances of *The Killing of Kirmira* are held 'with blood,' the '*ninam aharya*' or 'bloody costume/accoutrements' are perceived as relatively 'realistic' or *lokadharmi*. Because there is no nuance of expression in the acting, and the bloody figure of Simhika dominates the scene between her and her brother Kirmira, spectators have little to watch other than the bloody spectacle *per se*. Performances 'with blood' are perceived by some connoisseurs as playing to 'the gallery' or the 'lowest common denominator.'

In contrast, when Scene 13 is enacted through mono-acting it is interpreted as *natyadharmi* –

the much more restrained, refined, and 'ideational' mode of performance which fits the 'aesthetic of the mind' described in Chapter 2. As increasingly Sanskritized modes of appreciation have come to shape *kathakali* performance in recent years, the 'choice' to present a scene like Simhika's disfigurement through mono-acting is gradually naturalized as aesthetically superior – both hiding the construction of this mode of staging as a choice, and displacing the paradigmatic set of meanings regarding sacrificial kingship which are assumed in its literally 'bloody' staging. The paradigm of kingship and sacrifice implicit in the articulation of the literal letting of blood in indexical/iconic acts of sacrifice, whether on the field of battle or in the ritual field of the deity's manifestation of power, and *kathakali*'s enactments 'with blood' of scenes like the disfigurement of Simhika recede into the background as this aestheticized version comes into the foreground. Historically the growth of the preference for performances without blood parallels the official government ban of animal sacrifices in traditional ritual performances, and the substitution of 'stage blood' for animal blood in sacrificial rituals such as *teyyam*. Both reflect the colonial/Victorian 'cleansing' of representational practices like these in Kerala associated with the rediscovery of the *Natyasastra* and the increasing use of Sanskrit tropes of aestheticization such as concepts like *natyadharmi* to justify changes in stage practices as well as aesthetic taste.

When the 'everyday' becomes the extra-daily: the 'pleasures' of mimetic exactitude

Although 'the everyday' or 'the realistic' are often critiqued by today's connoisseurs, they also take great pleasure precisely in one aspect of *kathakali* which draws directly on another aspect of 'the everyday' – its mimetic exactitude in representing and embodying the performance of everyday tasks. One of the most important pleasures that connoisseurs take in 'good' performances of *The Killing of Kirmira* is the pleasure of seeing daily tasks performed with mimetic attention to the details of the everyday. Such tasks abound in *The Killing of Kirmira* from Simhika's satiric rendering of a woman's process of making-up, to her playing of games like *kumi* and dancing *kaikottakali*, to Kirmira's interpolation which abounds with the details of performing daily worship (*puja*) to Siva, from the ringing of the bell, to the opening of the door to the *sanctum sanctorum*, to the cleaning of the idol, etc. This is also evident in the detailed playing of Kirmira's 'preparations for battle' (*patappurappatu*). When performed with mimetic precision and attention to each detail of these daily tasks, the sense of appreciation and pleasure in an audience can be palpable. It is precisely the disruption of this pleasure with the intrusion of Simhika's literal stage blood that causes connoisseurs like Ganesha Iyer to prefer Kirmira's mono-acting of the scene.

the progeny of krishna (santanagopalam)ᵃ

Mandavappalli Ittiraricha Menon (c.1747–94)

Translated by V.R. PRABODHACHANDRAN NAYAR, M.P. SANKARAN NAMBOODIRI AND PHILLIP B. ZARRILLI

INTRODUCTION

Mandavappalli Ittiraricha Menon was one of the poets in the court of Kartikatirunal Maharaja of Travancore, southern Kerala. His exact dates are disputed. K.P.S. Menon suggests 1747–94, and Krishnakaimal 1745–1805 (1986: 282). Krishnakaimal's brief biographical note on the poet tells us that he was born in Ambalapura (Travancore District) to a poor family, nevertheless knowledgeable in Sanskrit (ibid.). He came to the Travancore Raja's attention in 1763 when he presented a verse (*sloka*) which included the line, 'I have nothing to say except my poetry.' It was while a poet in residence at court that he composed the two plays translated here. He was awarded the *virashramkala* – a gold bracelet considered the highest award one can receive from a ruler.

As Krishnakaimal notes, 'even though there are no red or black beard characters which make *kathakali* so effective, these stories gained popularity because of their devotional content' (ibid.). Both plays were probably first performed either at court or as part of the *kathakali* performances given annually as part of the temple festival at Sri Padmanabhaswamy Temple, Thiruvananthapuram. Given the integral relationship between the Maharaja of Travancore and the Padmanabhaswamy Temple, both plays center around devotion to Lord Vishnu. In *King Rugmamgada's Law* this takes the severe form of the testing of a king's devotion, while in *The Progeny of Krishna* the devotion of a simple brahmin is tested.

Mandavappalli Ittiraricha Menon adapted *The Progeny of Krishna* from a story in the *Bhagavata Purana* (X.89.22–66),[1] Like other stories in the *Bhagavata Purana*, it was originally told to illustrate how Vishnu is 'the greatest [deity] of them all' (Raghuthan, 1976: 503), especially in his incarnation as Krishna. There are twelve scenes in the original text, but five scenes (6, 7, 9, 10, and 11) are not usually performed today. Some actors and connoisseurs in Thiruvananthapuram, where the play has always been popular, still remember performances fifteen to twenty years ago when the play was performed in its entirety.

SYNOPSIS OF THE PLAY

After the great battle of Kurukshetra, Arjuna visits Krishna. One day a Brahmin, carrying the

---

ᵃ *Santana* means child, issue, or progeny, as well as the celestial tree that grants a boon – usually wealth, longevity, and children. *Gopala* (cow herder) is one of the many names for Lord Krishna; therefore, the title can be translated as 'The Progeny of Krishna,' 'The Children and Krishna,' or 'Krishna the Celestial Tree.'

body of his ninth dead son, comes to the gate of Krishna's Council Hall and pours out his misfortune to the court. Each of nine sons born to his wife have died at birth. Krishna turns a deaf ear to the Brahmin's tale, and walks out of the Council Hall. Arjuna, moved by the Brahmin's sorrow, offers to help him. He promises that the next child to be born will be saved. To convince the skeptical Brahmin, he vows that he will immolate himself if anything happens to the child.

The Brahmin's wife is soon pregnant again. The Brahmin rushes to tell Arjuna, who builds a house of arrows to protect the child. The Midwife and Brahmin's Wife enter the delivery house. Arjuna guards the entrance as the Brahmin paces nervously outside. The wife delivers a new son, but immediately there is no trace of the child. It has vanished! The Brahmin is furious at Arjuna, and mocks him as a 'fool.'

At this point in the original dramatic narrative (Scenes 6 and 7) Arjuna travels to Yama's (the god of death, also known as Kala) abode where he angrily confronts Yama and Chitragupta, the keeper of his registry of the dead, at his side.[2] He accuses Yama of having deceitfully stolen the Brahmin's last son from his tent of arrows. Yama replies that he himself does not have the 'power to accomplish this,' and suggests that 'if your dear friend (Krishna) searches, all the Brahmin's ten sons will appear!' Arjuna now travels to Indra's heavenly world where he angrily requests Indra to return the sons of the 'great Brahmin' who have been taken away. Indra pleads ignorance of their whereabouts, and concludes by telling Arjuna:

It is impossible for anyone to imagine the
  extraordinary illusions (created by) Krishna,
  Lord of the worlds.
O brave Arjuna, go to Krishna and you will
  find the Brahmin's sons.

As Scene 8 opens, Arjuna is determined to complete his vow and throw himself into the fire. Just as Arjuna is about to immolate himself, Krishna stops him. Having humbled his pride, he invites Arjuna to travel with him in his chariot to find the Brahmin's sons.

During Scenes 9–11, which are no longer performed today, Krishna and Arjuna travel first 'to the west along the sky path' where they encounter Chakra (Sudarsanam), the

personification of the wheel or discus of Vishnu.[3] Finally, they reach Vaikuntha, the heavenly abode of Mahavishnu – Vishnu's supreme form. As they enter his kingdom they are overcome by what they encounter there, including Vishnu in the form of Padmanabha, 'the embodiment of supreme knowledge, the one who reclines on the graceful couch of the Serpent-king, (whose) sides are beautified by the goddess of Earth and Lakshmi.' Mahavishnu is very pleased to see Krishna and Arjuna. Mahavishnu tells them how it was 'only to make you come here' that he brought 'that best among Brahmins' children here with delight.' He then presents the children to them 'arranged in the order of their death.' When Krishna and Arjuna beckon the children to go with them and return to their parents who await their return, they 'don't have the slightest desire' to to leave Vishnu's abode. Vishnu intercedes, and tells the children that they must return 'to earth with Krishna, and after living there patiently and with great pleasure and comfort, you can then return to my side and live with delight.'

In Scene 12, which immediately follows Scene 8 today, they return the boys to the Brahmin and his wife – a scene of joy and devotion to Krishna. The couple and their children bless Arjuna and Krishna.

There are many reasons that Scenes 6–7, and 9–11 are no longer performed. Except for occasional glimpses of excellence, the poetry is relatively mundane. More practically, these five scenes require Yama, Chitragupta, Chakra, Indra, and probably also the goddesses Bhumi Devi and Lakshmi. Without these characters the play only requires four actors, plus the children. Perhaps, more significantly, all the cut scenes focus on the play (*lila*) of the gods, while the scenes still performed focus on the human plight of the Brahmin and his suffering. In addition, during the past thirty years, the Brahmin has gradually become a popular role for star performers, and the edited version of the play keeps the focus on the Brahmin. Divorced from the scenes which contextualize the Brahmin's suffering within the larger play of the gods, the emphasis is decidedly on the human domain, and while devotion ultimately triumphs, other than the celebration at the conclusion of the play, the dramatic focus is on the individual characters rather than the play of the gods.

The translation which follows includes only those scenes usually performed today (Scenes 1–5, 8, and 12). This performance text and translation has been prepared from two published versions of *The Progeny of Krishna* – K.P.S. Menon's acting edition, and the S.T. Redyar edition – and from a performance of the play on 16 May 1993 at Killimangalam, Trissur District, Kerala, India, commissioned by the Killimangalam Centre for Documentation of the Performing Arts. The role of the Brahmin was played by M.P. Sankaran Namboodiri and the role of Arjuna by Kalamandalam Balasubramanian. The interpolations translated are from the 16 May 1993 performance.

CAST

KRISHNA: born in the Yadava dynasty as the son of Vasudeva and Devaki, Krishna was the ninth of the ten incarnations of Vishnu. Also known as Hari and Narayana[a] in *pacca* with a special crown (*muti*) used for Krishna.[b]

ARJUNA: third of the Pandava brothers, son of Kunti (Prtha) (impregnated by Indra after Kunti's repetition of a sacred *mantra*), also known as Nara in a previous birth,[c] as Vijaya (secret name given to Arjuna by Dharmaputra when they had to remain anonymous), and as Phalguna (reference to his birth in the Uttaraphalguni constellation) in *pacca*.

BRAHMIN: a male householder, in *minukku* ('radiant').

BRAHMIN'S WIFE: in *minukku*.

VRIDDHA: the midwife, an old woman with special, somewhat comic make-up.

VISHNU: the preserver and embodiment of mercy and goodness who appeared in ten incarnations and is the object of great devotion, in *pacca*.

CHILDREN: of the Brahmin and his wife, in simple *minukku*.

Preliminaries

purappatu
(*When the opening pure dance is performed, the following verse is sung to accompany the dance.*)[4]

sankarabharanam (*raga*)

(*Before singing of other* slokas, *the vocalists may improvise a preliminary composition within the structure of the* raga. *Once their improvisation and the ensuing K are complete, they begin the* sloka *in the same* raga, *followed by a short K.*)

sloka:
Hari (Vishnu/Krishna),
whose mind is full of dense, supreme pleasure;
the one who is gracious toward his devotees;
the pious one who took incarnation as the son of
Devaki to protect the worlds;
he – the singular Lord of all the worlds;
who along with Balabhadra[d] killed Kamsa[e] with
the wrestlers,
and who lived with pleasure accompanied by
numerous wives in the very prosperous city of
Dvaravati.[f]

[*saveri* (*raga*); *campa* (*tala* – 16 beats)]
sloka:
When the Supreme Lord was living in the city of
the Yadus,
having protected the full expanse of the earth,
Pritha's son, Arjuna, possessing greater might of

[a] In keeping with the conventions of Sanskrit poetry and drama, *kathakali* playwrights make extensive use of epithets. Their selection often depends on the internal demands of poetic conventions and structure. But as David L. Gitomer explains, 'these names also bear resonances in mythological identities, references to character traits, reminders of past exploits, and perhaps most important, placement in . . . multigenerational narrative' (1998: 46). The most often used epithets for Krishna and Arjuna are included here.

[b] This special crown is also used for Rama before his coronation, as well as his sons Lava, and Kusa.

[c] Arjuna and Krishna together are sometimes referred to as Naranarayanas – a reference to the two sages (*rsis*) Nara and Narayana, who lived together inseparably. The estrangement and eventual reuniting of Arjuna and Krishna in *The Progeny of Krishna* might be read as a return to the inseparable union of Nara and Narayana.

[d] Balabhadra (also known as Balarama) is the elder brother of Krishna and eighth incarnation of Vishnu.

[e] Son of Ugrasena, King of Mathura, and an incarnation of an Asura called Kalanemi. Vishnu took incarnation as Krishna in Mathura as the son of Devaki and Vasudeva, all of whose children had been killed by Kamsa. In the *kathakali* version of this story, written by Kilimanoor Ravi Varma Tampuran (1782–1854), Krishna's birth, childhood, and eventual killing of Kamsa are featured.

[f] Sri Krishna's capital is also known as Dvaraka.

hands and wanting to see the lotus-eyed one
(Krishna),
arrived with great pleasure (at Krishna's court).

Scene 1
[Krishna and Arjuna]

[*saveri* (*raga*); *cempata* (*tala* – 16 beats)]

(*The curtain is lowered. Krishna is seated on the
right; Arjuna stands to his left, and enters
dancing a* kitatakadhimtam.)

KRISHNA:

pallavi: O seat of all auspiciousness,
friend, Vijaya, intelligent
one, foundation of all good
qualities, are you happy,
o handsome one? [K]

anupallavi:
Upon seeing your lotus face
before which the moon that attracts the three
  worlds bows,
this day is now one filled with great pleasure!
[K]+[I]

pallavi: Oh seat of all
auspiciousness . . .

caranam
O Leader of the Kurus,
are not Dharmaputra,[a] the valorous one, jewel
  among the fortunate,
foundation of diplomacy and humility, the most
generous one,
and the brave (wolf bellied) Bhima living happily
along with (your) other brothers, (my) sister and
  your wife who is great with many inborn
  qualities? [K]+[I]

pallavi: Oh seat of all
auspiciousness . . .

[*devagandharam* (*raga*); *cempata* (*tala* – 16 beats)]

ARJUNA:
caranam
O, Lord, for those of us who are servants
at your feet, can there ever be any sorrow?[b]
All of us live without doubts, and with pleasure.[c]
O, red lotus-eyed one, the ambrosia of your
  compassion protects those who seek refuge. [K]+[I]

(*Sung to accompany the* iratti:)
O you who are fit to be saluted
by the leader of all the gods (Indra), Siva, etc.,
  at your lotus feet, I always bow. [K]

KRISHNA:
caranam
O glittering jewel in the Kuru's crown,
stay here for a while enjoying (life) with me.
Life is like a shining water drop
in the middle of the moving lotus leaf,
(and) sublime pleasure is remaining
in the company of good friends.[d] [K]+[I]

pallavi: Oh seat of all
auspiciousness . . .

(*ilakiyattam*: Krishna and Arjuna)[5]

ARJUNA:
For a long time I have wanted to see you, but my
wish was not fulfilled until now. I am fortunate
today because I have seen you.

KRISHNA:
For a long time I too wished to see you. Stay
here with me for a few days.

ARJUNA: As you wish.

(*Arjuna salutes Krishna and goes upstage
standing behind him.*)

[*Curtain*]

---

[a] 'Dharmaputra' is another name for Yudhisthira, eldest of the Pandavas.
[b] *Badha* means the result of being affected. Given the context, the actor shows the *mudra* for 'sorrow,' literally showing the
effect that any affliction, difficulty, or obstacle might have on devotees.
[c] Arjuna's assertion that they are living 'without doubts' reflects the ideal state of the martial hero – that doubtless (*vita
sankam*, Sanskrit) state reflected in the *Bhagavad Gita*.
[d] The implication here is that like the beauty of the water drop which falls when the wind blows and evaporates quickly, so
all the pleasures in life are also too fleeting.

Scene 2
[Krishna, Arjuna, and Brahmin]
[*ghantaram* (*raga*) – *cempata* (*tala* – 20 beats)]

sloka: (*Sung while the curtain is raised.*)
Along with his dear Arjuna, Krishna lived
  comfortably in his capital city.
There, death came to a pious Brahmin's eight
  sons in eight years.
On the death of his ninth son, that Brahmin,
  holding the child's body in his arms, began to
  wail uncontrollably, and reached Krishna's
  court crying out with grief:
(*The curtain is lowered. Krishna is sitting stage
right. The Brahmin enters from upstage left.*)

Plate 7.1 *With Arjuna watching in the background
and the body of his eighth son lying before him, the
Brahmin (M.P. Sankaran Namboodiri) pours out his
tale of woe at Krishna's court.*

ilakiyattam
(*This short opening interpolation is set to a special
percussion composition for dramatic effect. Known
as* patinna kitatakadhimtam, *the composition is in
five different parts at five different speeds. The
first part is the most complex, and is played in the
slowest speed. The second part is less complex,
and played in a faster speed. This second part is
then repeated three more times, each in a faster
rhythm, building to a climax.*)

BRAHMIN:
(*1st cycle/slowest speed*)
O god, I haven't sinned with mind, words, or
  deeds, but even so, this has happened to me!

(*2nd cycle*) To whom can I express my sorrow?

(*3rd cycle*) How can I see Krishna again?

(*4th cycle*) Anyway, I will go to the Yadava court,
  leave this dead body before Krishna, and return.

(*5th cycle/fastest speed. He sees Krishna, and
places the body before him.*)

[*ghantaram* (*raga*); *campa* (*tala* – 20 beats)]

BRAHMIN:
  pallavi: Alas, what am I to do here,
           O god! Alas, in whom can I
           find refuge? [K]

  anupallavi:
Surely in all the other worlds there is no comfort
  for a man without a son. Alas, Siva, Siva![6] [K]

  caranam:
O brave Yadavas, listen closely:
  this grief is unbearable.
I have done nothing forbidden to Brahmins.
(So why) has this happened? O son! Siva! Siva! [K]

  caranam:
Alas, what you see here is my dear child
lying with his eyes turned up.
Thus eight boys are lost and gone because of this
  arrogant king![a]
O, Siva! Siva! [K]

[a] Beginning with 'Thus eight boys' the Brahmin counts on his fingers to dramatize his loss. The tempo momentarily
doubles to 10 beats, and then returns by the end of this *caranam* to the slower 20 beats. The doubling of the tempo
emphatically underscores the accusation of arrogance.

caranam: (*The speed doubles to 10 beats.*)
For (Krishna), the one whose enemy was Madhu,
  the weight of responsibility of knowing what is
  best for more than 16,000 wives and their
  children,
and for protecting them all, is always increasing.[a]
Does he have time to protect this Brahmin? [K]

[*sankarabharanam* (*raga*); *cempata* (*tala* – 16
beats)]

sloka:
Thus, having heard this good Brahmin's wailing
over and again, (Krishna) the enemy of demons,
the one who assiduously protects the world, the
divine Balabhadra who bears the hoe, as well as
Pradyumna[b] and all the other Yadavas, said
nothing. (*Krishna exits.*)[c] Then Arjuna came
before the Brahmin and said the following:

ilakiyattam
(*A short* ilakiyattam *set within a rhythmic
phrase,* kitatakadhimtam, *is enacted as Arjuna
rushes forward to address the Brahmin.*)

ARJUNA: Oh, noble Brahmin. Listen well to what I
say.[d]

   pallavi: O, simple hearted Brahmin,
     enough wailing, enough! [K]

anupallavi:
I will protect and give you your next-born son.
[K]+[I]

pallavi: O, simple hearted Brahmin . . .
 caranam:
A Kshatriya's duty is to do away with the grief of
  the Brahmin clan and protect them forever.
You should forget past sorrows.
Hereafter if a son is born to you, Arjuna (son of
  Prtha) will protect him and deliver him to you!
  [K]+[I]

   pallavi: O, simple hearted Brahmin . . .

BRAHMIN:[e]
 caranam:
When Vishnu, the master of the worlds and
  protector of the good, heard of my sorrow,
He did not move.
But, surprisingly, without even thinking a little
  why this was so,
you, Fool![f] have ventured into this! [K]+[I]

   pallavi: Alas, certainly you are
     indiscriminate, Arjuna,
     you treasure of bravery.[g]

ARJUNA:
 caranam:[h]
Alas! You are blind from the weight of your
  grief.
Therefore, I am not offended by what you have
  said.
Do not doubt that if a son is born to you, and
I do not protect and deliver him to you, then I
  am not Indra's son! [K]+[I]

---

[a] Madhu was a demon who, along with his brother Kaitabha, was born of the right ear of Mahavishnu. After acquiring boons they stole the Vedas. Brahma called on Mahavishnu to confront them. He did so and eventually was able to kill them.

[b] Krishna's son by Rukmini.

[c] Throughout this scene Krishna's attitude toward the Brahmin is passive – a response which makes the Brahmin even more agitated. Whenever the Brahmin looks at Krishna, he turns away, showing no interest in the Brahmin's entreaties. Part of the 'message' implicit here is about fate. Even Krishna, the great protector, may not always protect.

[d] The Brahmin's response to Arjuna is to assume a mockingly humorous tone. Although his primary state (*sthayi bhava*) remains sorrow or pathos (*karuna*), due to the circumstances his secondary state (*sanchari bhava*) is a mocking form of humor (*hasya*). When Arjuna first comes forward, the Brahmin lies on the ground in despair and sorrow. As he hears Arjuna's words, the mocking sarcasm increases until Arjuna completes performing this *padam*. Then he gradually looks with mocking sarcasm at Arjuna out of the corner of his eyes.

[e] Although set in the same *tala* and *raga*, the tempo is increased to a faster speed to emphasize the Brahmin's mocking tone.

[f] The Malayalam word for 'fool,' *pottan*, is a very derogatory colloquial expression which emphasizes the fact that only a complete fool would do what Arjuna has done.

[g] The poet chooses to use a term of respect for Arjuna, but does so to mock him. In addition, calling Arjuna

pallavi: O, simple hearted Brahmin . . .

BRAHMIN:

caranam:[i]

Krishna who is affectionate to his devotees, and
the enemy of demons, as well as the mighty
Balabhadra and others,

did not move since no one thought it possible (to
protect my son).

I no longer desire to see the face of a son. [K]+[I]

pallavi: Alas, certainly you are . . .

[*vekata* (*raga*); *muri atanta* (*tala* – 28 beats)]

ARJUNA:

pallavi: O you of virtuous character!
O best among the Brahmins!
Take pleasure in what I say.
[K]

anupallavi:

Don't you know and haven't you heard of
Phalguna (Arjuna) – the one who distributes
well-being even to the residents of the
heavens? [K]

caranam:

You know I am neither Krishna nor Balabhadra.
I am not even one one of the Vrisni heroes;[j]
rather,
I am the ever-victorious who bears divine
weapons –
Indra's son, the lustrous, principled,
compassionate.[k] [K]

caranam:[7]

Can there be even the slightest fear of Death in a
tent of arrows (made by) Indra's son who in
battle defeats even Lord Siva – he who brings
death to death itself?[l]

Could even Indra, Lord of the gods and ruler of
heaven, steal the boy? [K][8]

caranam: (*The speed doubles.*)

Hereafter if the son born (to you) has not been
protected and delivered to you without
incident,

I will immediately jump into a well of fire,
immolating myself.

I promise you, I shall do so! [K][9]

ilakiyattam[10]

(*After a long pause, Arjuna 'speaks'.*)

ARJUNA:

You still don't believe me? (*Pause.*) What . . . are
you continuing to think like this?

BRAHMIN:

No, no. O Arjuna, your boasting is absolutely
wonderful! What did you say? 'I am not Krishna!
I am not Balabhadra! I am not one of the Yadava
heroes!' (*Pause.*) Could I just say one more thing?
How brave you are to humiliate your good
friend, Krishna, like this!

ARJUNA:

When I heard your sorrow, my mental balance
was disturbed. That's all.

'indiscriminate' emphasizes the fact that he can no longer appropriately differentiate between what is possible and what is
not possible. He has done something completely inappropriate to the context. A *pallavi*, which according to poetic
structure usually comes first, is here placed last to give this scene a greater sense of drama.

[h] Sung in medium speed, the *caranam* emphasizes that Arjuna is trying to appease the Brahmin's anger. Although insulted,
he keeps his sense of dignified heroism.

[i] The speed quickens to a very fast *tala* to emphasize the strength of the Brahmin's retort, and the despair he feels.
Although there is still a sense of mocking humor, the object of his mockery is no longer Arjuna, but is turned more inward
to his own fate. Therefore, he gradually becomes more and more dejected and sorrowful, feeling that all hope has been
lost.

[j] A well-known king of the Yadu dynasty. Krishna was born in the Vrisni line.

[k] Arjuna's pride comes out of his supreme self-confidence in his powers. By meditating and getting all the powers at his
disposal, he has full confidence in his abilities. He believes he can accomplish this act of protection without any help. The
actor playing the role must be careful not to overact Arjuna's sense of pride.

[l] This is Arjuna's interpretation of how he supposedly defeated Siva when disguised as a hunter. Actually, it was Siva who
humbled Arjuna and before whom Arjuna prostrated himself after his defeat by Siva. This story is enacted in the *kathakali*
play *Kiratam*, which also explores Arjuna's sometimes overweening pride.

BRAHMIN:

Oh! Only that! You know all about Krishna's greatness – he is so affectionate to his devotees. (*Thinking to himself.*) But in my case, I made so many offerings and meditated on him, yet he did nothing. (*To Arjuna.*) Did you ever hear how, long ago, Krishna gave life to his guru's son – the one who had fallen into a river and died, and then placed his (revived) body before his guru while bowing before him?

ARJUNA:

Yes, I have heard (about that).

BRAHMIN:

A little while ago Krishna gave life to the six sons killed by Kamsa and brought them to their mother. How can I believe you when you stand in front of me and forget Krishna's miracles, and only boast loudly about yourself? I can't believe you!

ARJUNA:

I will tell you one story to settle your mind. Long ago, one brahmin who had no sons meditated on Siva. Lord Siva appeared and said, 'I will give you a boon of either a highly intelligent boy who will only live sixteen years, or, I will give a child whose entire lifetime will be lived by acting mischievously and foolishly.' The brahmin accepted saying that having a child for sixteen years would be enough. So, a child was born to that brahmin. The child was properly cared for and raised. The sixteen years were almost over. The last day had come. When the child was eating, his mother and father began to cry. The child, without knowing anything, looked into their faces and asked, 'why are you crying?' (The boy saw) Kalan[a] with a rope in one hand, mounted on a buffalo coming toward him. Seeing this the child ran in fear and hid. He went to Vishnu and asked for his protection. Kalan stood with the rope in hand ready (to capture him). Vishnu quickly sent the child to Siva. The child saw a great Siva lingam, ran to it, hugged it, and began to cry. Kalan tried to tie his rope (around the child), but couldn't. Siva became very angry, and with his trident stabbed Kalan, who died. So, the child escaped.

Haven't you heard this story before? (Just like this) I shall protect your child and give him to you. Please don't worry!

(*Pause. The Brahmin does not respond.*)

What? Do you still have a doubt?

BRAHMIN:

Alright. Are you sure you can protect my child?

ARJUNA:

Yes! I am sure.

BRAHMIN:

If so, wait. Let me ask just one more thing. Because of the sadness in my mind, I must ask one more thing. Could you take a vow?

ARJUNA:

I will take a vow.

BRAHMIN:

If so, I will feel confident. Please take a vow on the feet of your elder brother, Dharmaputra, who is among the most revered and truthful people in the world. Will you do this?

ARJUNA:

I will. Oh best among brahmins, I vow on my elder brother, Dharmaputra's feet – if I do not protect your new born son, I will jump into the fire pit and destroy myself!

BRAHMIN:

(Your words) are like water poured on the fire of my sorrow. I feel relieved.

ARJUNA:

Then I feel fortunate. Now you can depart happily. Share this news with your wife.

BRAHMIN:

Shall I go? Shall I go with relief?

(*The Brahmin picks up the body of his dead son, and is about to go, but then pauses to ask himself.*) Oh no! Arjuna cannot do anything

---

[a] Another name for Yama, the god of death.

without Krishna's help. So, I must also make him vow on Krishna's name.

ARJUNA:
Why haven't you gone yet?

BRAHMIN:
My mind is still not fully relieved.

ARJUNA: (*Mockingly.*) Then recite *namam.*[a]

BRAHMIN:
Even if I recite many times, my mind still won't be steady and unshaken. What can I do. Always Krishna, and only Krishna comes (into my mind). If you won't get angry, let me ask one more thing.

ARJUNA:
Me become angry? I don't have any enmity toward you.

BRAHMIN:
I know all the many heroic deeds you have accomplished. Siva, Siva! But one thing. What have you gained without the help of Krishna?

ARJUNA:
Krishna is in my soul.

BRAHMIN:
Wait! When you were preparing to begin the dreadful part of the Bharata-War, Krishna got into the chariot and drove it to the battlefield. Do you remember that? At that time, while holding your bow and arrow in your hands, when you saw the (enemy's) army spread before you like an ocean, all your courage left you and you fell to the floor of the chariot.

ARJUNA:
I didn't lose my mental courage. In my inner mind, it was still there. Anyway, I feel confident now that I can protect and hand over your child.

BRAHMIN:
Alas! It is only because of Krishna's help that

you can stand in front of me and say all these boastful words. Therefore, make one more vow at Krishna's feet. (*To himself.*) Is it because I am not feeling confident that I am asking all this?

ARJUNA: (*To himself.*)
Isn't this characteristic of brahmins? I can't ignore him even if this is typical. (*Thinking.*) What? Should I take another vow at Krishna's feet? (*To the Brahmin.*) Let me tell you one more thing. When your eight sons died, you came here and pleaded, 'please protect me.' But the whole time Krishna was silent. If only my ungenerous vow to that ungenerous Krishna will appease you, I can't do that![b]

BRAHMIN:
Well, then I shall leave since I am sure you can't do anything without Krishna's help!

ARJUNA:
I am certain I cannot take another vow.

BRAHMIN:
No? Alas! This great man has rekindled my hopes. I will accept my fate and leave. (*The Brahmin takes his child's body in his arms and is about to leave when Arjuna rushes to him and brings him back.*) Give me your hand and take the vow!

ARJUNA:
Don't go! (*To himself.*) Oh, the Brahmin has become angry. (*To the Brahmin.*) I will take (the vow). Come! Hereafter, I will protect (this Brahmin's) next born child. If I am unable to do this, with my bow I will jump into the fire pit and destroy myself. Because of my devotion to Krishna, I surrender all my abilities to him and vow at his feet.

BRAHMIN: (*The Brahmin embraces Arjuna.*)
I am relieved. Now, let me go.

ARJUNA:
Please go happily.

---

[a] Recitation of the names of the deity is supposed to give mental strength.

[b] A number of people in the audience at the performance where this *ilakiyattam* was enacted reacted negatively to the actor's use of the adjective 'ungenerous' for Krishna. For them it was unfitting for a character like Arjuna to call Krishna 'ungenerous.' They felt this interpretation took his pride beyond the bounds of what they considered appropriate to the character.

BRAHMIN: (*Hesitating.*)
Is there anything else to do? (*Pause.*) You will remain here?

ARJUNA: Yes, I will stay here. (*The Brahmin exits.*)

(*Curtain*)

Scene 3
[Brahmin and his Wife]
[*kamodari* (*raga*); *campa* (*tala* – 10 beats)]
(*The curtain remains up as the following* sloka *is sung.*)

   sloka:
Hearing Arjuna's vow, the Brahmin regained his
   strength of mind and said:
'When my dear wife's pregnancy is at full term, I
   shall come.'
Reaching his house and consoling his chaste wife
   who was tired from her great grief, he spoke
   with words sweeter than flowing honey:

(*The curtain is lowered. The Wife is seated stage right. The Brahmin enters, and moves to stage right.*)[a]

BRAHMIN:
   caranam:
O beautiful lotus faced, listen to my words.
My dear young one, no more crying. [K]

   caranam:
This grief will pass. In the future it will become
   the source of (our) happiness.
O wife, what we desire will be realized. [K]

   caranam:
Bearing the body of (our) dead son,
when I reached the Yadava's court wailing with
   grief,
I heard words which can wash away (our) grief.
   Please listen. [K]

   caranam:
Arjuna, supreme hero of the world, brother-in-
   law of Krishna who is the ruler of the world,
   came forward

and promised that he would duly protect (our)
   son whom you will deliver.
O wife, having stepped forward, he promised
   (this). [K]

[*saveeri* (*raga*); *muri atanta* (*tala* – 14 beats)][11]

WIFE:
         pallavi: Is it possible for even those
              who are accomplished to
              turn away fate?[b] [K]

   anupallavi:
Can anyone turn away fate?
All that we have experienced has brought us (to
   a place) beyond grief or pleasure.
Inwardly undisturbed, we must experience
   whatever comes. [K]

   caranam:
Other than this, can anyone change fate?
Like grass (consumed) by the five fires,
   have not more than five or six boys been
   reduced to the five basic elements by devious
   actions of an
unhesitating Brahma?
Can anything obstruct Brahma's decisions? [K]

[*kamodari* (*raga*); *campa* (*tala* – 10 beats)]

   BRAHMIN:
   caranam:
Wife! Will Krishna forsake Arjuna who has
   vowed thus:
'I will quickly die by leaping into the fire pit on
   the same day if I do not take away this
   sorrow?'[12] [K]

   ilakiyattam
BRAHMIN:
Soon, we will be fortunate enough to see the
footprints of a child in this house. With that in
mind, let us meditate on Krishna.

WIFE:
As you wish.

(*Curtain*)

---

[a] The right side is considered the honorable side.
[b] Arjuna represents 'the' quintessential Kshatriya who has become 'accomplished' in his practice of the martial arts. The
pallavi points to the fact that even the most accomplished human hero cannot overcome what is 'written on the forehead,'
i.e., one's fate.

Scene 4
[Brahmin and his Wife]
[*kanakkurinni* (*raga*); *cempata* (*tala* – 16 beats)]
(*The curtain remains raised as the following*
sloka *is sung.*)

sloka:
Thus, speaking about obtaining a son in the future
and consoling his wife, with a mind given solely
to god in prayer, the Brahmin remained at home.

Soon that Brahmin woman became pregnant.
As her pregnancy drew to a close, with delight
she, whose charming face resembled the moon,
said to her husband:
(*As the curtain is lowered the Brahmin and his
Wife are seated.*)

WIFE:
caranam:
O, leader of my life,
I bow at your feet.
Please listen carefully to my words and (give
  your) undivided attention. [K]

caranam:
(My) pregnancy is complete. The time for
delivery is near – I think within three days. [K]

caranam:
O, ocean of all good actions, go without delay
  and bring that enemy of Karna, Arjuna, whose
  bow is the
  Gandiva.[13] [K]

[*saveeri* (*raga*); *muri atanta* (*tala* – 7 beats)][14]

BRAHMIN:
caranam:
O, abode of all that is auspicious, do not worry
  even a little.
O, one with lotus like eyes, don't make me worry
  either!
O wife, I go without delay to bring that expert
  bowman, Arjuna. [K]

                    pallavi:[15] Oh dear one, whose behavior
                              is always appropriate, let us
                              have strength.

   ilakiyattam
BRAHMIN: (*Calling the midwife.*)

Plate 7.2   *The Brahmin's Wife (Margi Vijayakumar),
in pain as the time for her delivery draws near, is
helped by the village Midwife (Margi Suresh)*

Care for her properly. I will come soon.
(*The Brahmin exits.*)

(*Curtain*)

Scene 5
[Arjuna and Brahmin]
[*madhyamavati* (*raga*); *cempata* (*tala* – 16 beats)]
(*The curtain remains raised as the following*
sloka *is sung.*)

sloka:
Thus, that Brahmin, having consoled her whose
  eyes were weak from the weight of tiredness,
quickly reached Krishna's residence and spoke to
  Arjuna, the brave one.

(*The curtain is lowered. The Brahmin enters to a*
kitatakadhimtam.)

BRAHMIN:

> *pallavi*: Oh Pandu's son, bravest of
> the brave and diamond
> among the valiant, come
> with me to my house
> immediately. [K]

anupallavi:

O one whose fame is as white as an abundance
of milk,

O one whose body is as handsome as Kamadeva.[a]

O one who has kept away the griefs created by
enemies, and is the auspicious fame of the Puru
clan. [K]+[I]

> *pallavi*: Oh Pandu's son, bravest . . .

caranam:

O handsome one, don't you remember, it was
here that we met earlier?

O one of good conduct, my wife is pregnant
again,

and since the time for delivery is near, we are
very excited! [K]+[I]

> *pallavi*: Oh Pandu's son, bravest . . .

caranam:

O one of wondrous valor, please don't delay!

I do not have the strength of mind to wait!

Salute (Krishna) the embodiment of supreme
knowledge, and bow before the Lord of the
heavens.[b]

Take your bow with its ever-increasing power,
and let us proceed! [K]+[I]

> *pallavi*: Oh Pandu's son, bravest . . .

[*athana* (*raga*); *cempata* (*tala* – 16 beats)]

ARJUNA:

caranam:

O best among Brahmins, I am coming with you
to provide protection for the son your wife will
deliver.

See, this is the bow which will help to protect
your son.

Now, is it possible for Yama or anyone else to
overcome my will? [K]

> *pallavi*:[16] Oh crown among Brahmins,
> please do not allow
> anything to upset you. Let
> us go without delay.

ilakiyattam

(*The Brahmin and Arjuna are about to exit.*)

ARJUNA: So, shall we leave now?

BRAHMIN: Oh! (*Doubtful.*) Should we mention
something to Krishna? If you wish, you can.

ARJUNA: Isn't it enough to show him the child
after the delivery?

(*Both exit. The curtain is brought upstage to
represent the house. They re-enter around the
curtain, indicating they have entered the
Brahmin's house.*)

BRAHMIN: Here the amenities are meagre.

ARJUNA: That's alright. Now I will make a house
of arrows.

BRAHMIN: (*Looking for an appropriate place.*) Here
is a very open space.

ARJUNA: Alright. I will quickly construct the
house of arrows. Please sit there.

(*Arjuna begins to build the house of arrows.
He ties the bowstring, and pulls the string,
testing it.*)

BRAHMIN: Alas! A sound like thunder!

ARJUNA: That's not the sound of thunder. It was
only the bowstring being pulled. Don't be afraid.

(*He continues to mime building the house of
arrows. When it is complete he says:*) This is
enough. Alright. (*To the Brahmin.*) The
construction is finished. Come! Come!

BRAHMIN: (*Eyeing and examining the house
carefully.*) I think there might be one hole. Look
there!

ARJUNA: Rub your eyes and look again.

BRAHMIN: (*Rubbing his eyes.*) No, there is a hole.

ARJUNA: No, no. It's because of all the tears you
cried. There's no hole.

BRAHMIN: Yes, my mind must have been confused.[17]

ARJUNA: Please bring your wife now.

BRAHMIN: (*Bringing his wife to the house of
arrows, the Wife and Midwife cross upstage
behind the curtain.*) Walk slowly, slowly, not
quickly. (*To Arjuna.*) Are you brave enough?

ARJUNA: Surely. Sit peacefully. (*Looking
around.*) I will display my valor for the
celestial beings.

---

[a] The god of love.

[b] Indra, Arjuna's father.

[*punagavarali* (*raga*); *muri atanta* (*tala* – 28 beats)]

(*The following* sloka *and the Wife's* padam *are sung with the curtain up, i.e., she and the Midwife are 'inside' the house of arrows. The Brahmin and Arjuna remain in front of the curtain, 'outside' the house, waiting, watching, and guarding. While the following* sloka *is sung, Arjuna and Krishna improvise their waiting and watching.*)

sloka:
That Brahmin's young wife, with moon-like
  charming face, upright conduct, and vina-like
  speech,
quickly and joyously gave birth.
Her friend was happily about to hold the child in
  her hands when suddenly, unable to see her son
  and exhausted from sorrow
that chaste woman cried out:[a]

(*Simultaneously, while the text (in the left column below) is being sung and is assumed to be happening in the birth house behind the curtain, the Brahmin and Arjuna interact in an* ilakiyattam *(in the right column below).*)

ilakiyattam

WIFE:	BRAHMIN: (*Showing his reaction to a bad omen.*)
	Why is my left side shaking?
caranam:	
O Krishna, ocean of compassion,	
have you deceived even Nara?[b]	ARJUNA: It's nothing. Just sit there quietly!
O supreme one,	
because of us who	
are without any refuge,	
do you relish	
the fact that your young	
sister[c] will suffer the	
terrible sorrow of widowhood?	

caranam:
The child shone with lustre at birth
  and before he could even touch the earth,
  fate took him away.
Even his dead body could not be found.

Arjuna's plan did not bear fruit.
Is it possible for what is written
on the forehead to be reversed?

caranam: (*The speed doubles.*)
Friends, please go quickly and tell
  these events to my dear one who stands
  at the door of the house exhausted from
  great worries and meditating at the feet
  of Krishna,
and also to Indra's son.

[*balahari* (*raga*); *muri atanta* (*tala* – 7 beats)]
  sloka: (*This* sloka *is acted.*)
When unexpectedly, from inside the delivery
  house the Brahmin heard his wife's words,
  distorted from her weeping, with great sorrow
  he fainted and fell down.
Suddenly, like a fire flamed by the wind, he became
  blind with fury and, forsaking all affection,
he cruelly admonished Indra's son: [N]

BRAHMIN:
      pallavi: Fool! What happened to your
                highly accomplished skill? [K]

  anupallavi:
O best among dunces, what is the use of this tent
  of arrows with all its 'pomp and circumstance?'
  [1/2K]

      pallavi: Fool! What happened . . . [K]

  caranam:
Earlier I politely but repeatedly told you that all
  this was unnecessary and one should not have
  bad intentions.
But what I said so emphatically then did not
  enter your heart at that time because of your
  deep rooted and ever increasing pride.
Now best among dullards, because of your
  'power' I have not even seen my recently born
  son's dead body! [1/2K]

      pallavi: Fool! What happened . . . [K][18]

(*The actor playing Arjuna puts his hands on his belly.*)

---

[a] Since the cry of the Brahmin's wife described in the *sloka* is not enacted, the focus is on the reactions of the Brahmin and Arjuna.

[b] Nara and Narayana are considered mutually complementary; therefore, without Arjuna (Nara), Krishna cannot be complete.

[c] If Arjuna commits suicide then Krishna's younger sister, Subhadra, will be a widow.

caranam:
Why rub your belly and look around helplessly?
Even if you jump into the fire, will it save my child?
O hard-hearted son of Indra, having given up
  helping us, leave quickly.
Enter Krishna's mansion, eat until your heart's
  content, and go on living,
O chief among dunces! [1/2K]

pallavi: Fool! What happened . . . [K]

ilakiyattam
BRAHMIN: Hereafter you should not stand before
me for even a single second! Get out! Go! So . . .
look out! (*He performs a choreography, but
Arjuna still stands there. So he commands him:*)
Go! Go! Go! (*Arjuna exits.*)

(*Curtain*)

Scene 8
[Arjuna and Krishna]
[*mukhari* (*raga*); *camba* (*tala* – 10 beats)]
(*The curtain remains raised during the singing of
the following* sloka.)

sloka:
Having heard Indra's words, Arjuna set out from
the heavens and searched all the worlds without
  finding the Brahmin's children.
Then he realized this must have been Krishna's
  test.
Resolving his indecision, that great one tried to
  jump into the fire.
(*The curtain is lowered to reveal Arjuna.*)

ARJUNA:[19]
(*To himself:*)
pallavi: Excellent! Wonderful! This is
  the play of Fate. [K]

caranam:
The boys' deaths took place without Yama
  knowing about it.
The present time is not good for Arjuna.
My duty is singular – I will immerse myself in
  the fire and be blessed. O Krishna, protect me!
[K]

ilakiyattam
ARJUNA: O, Krishna! Assuming that you are
always ready to help me, I decided to fulfill that
Brahmin's wish. Now, have you abandoned me,
or refused to help me?
Anyway, I will light the fire, and jump into it.

O, Agni![a] Long ago you assumed the form of a
brahmin and came to me, and I fulfilled your
wish. Then you gave me your divine weapon, the
Gandhiva bow. Now, to fulfill another brahmin's
wish, I am returning this Gandhiva to you. Now I
will jump into the fire itself. [N]

[*mohanam* (*raga*); *muri atanta* (*tala* – 7 beats)]
(*As the following* sloka *is enacted, Krishna comes
and stops Arjuna from jumping into the fire.*)

sloka
Having dug a large fire pit, Arjuna kindled the
  flame with his arrows.
As he was leaping into the fire holding (his) bow,
  Krishna, whose mind flows with the
rising waves of compassion, reached (there),
stopped Arjuna with his hand, held him, and
  said:[20]

[*kamodari* (*raga*); *muriyatanta* (*tala* – 28 beats)]

KRISHNA:
caranam:
Do not act rashly! Do not act rashly![21]
I, Madhava – am I not here?
For you there are no obstacles to anything.
  Isn't this known throughout the world? [K]

caranam:
Alas, O blessed one, have you forgotten all the
  beneficial things I have done?
Oh friend, what did I do for you to forget me? [K]

ARJUNA:
caranam:
Enough! You have said enough!
Enough dishonor has come to me.
Having called upon your name, I vainly strutted
  about. Enough of that also.
I am determined.[22] [K]

---

[a] The god of fire.

caranam:

Unable to bear the grief of the loss of his sons,
  how severely one Brahmin reviled you!
But in response not even one person raised their
  voice.
Just imagine how belittling this was. [K]

caranam:

Consider this: you watched as I took a vow with
  your blessings. You watched unmoved.
So why do you assume an air of friendship now?
  [K]²³

KRISHNA:
  caranam:
O Partha, my friend, please don't be angry.
  Why should you die?
Whatever is in your mind, I will accomplish it for
  you. [K]²⁴

caranam:

No need to be listless. Those virtuous boys are
  living in a place without unhappiness.
Let us go and find them. [K]²⁵

*ilakiyattam*²⁶

ARJUNA: Forgive me! Seeing the Brahmin's
sorrow, I could not remain quiet. Whatever you
feel in your mind about what has happened,
please forgive me.
KRISHNA: Whatever my devotees do, don't I
forgive them?
ARJUNA: You give sorrow to your devotees, and then
take it away. Isn't that so? What shall I do now?
KRISHNA: Shall we go to Vishnu's abode?
ARJUNA: (Shall I go) with you?
KRISHNA: There the children are playing.
ARJUNA: As you wish.
(*They exit the stage in the chariot.*)

(*Curtain*)

Plate 7.3   *With his seventh son on his shoulders, the Brahmin dances with joy at his return*

Scene 12
[Arjuna, Krishna, Brahmin, Brahmin's Wife,
Children]
[*puranira* (*raga*); *cempata* (*tala* – 16 beats)]
(*The curtain remains raised as the following
sloka is sung.*)

  sloka
Having held the Brahmin's children, then having
  bowed before Vishnu, that ocean of compassion,
Arjuna, with a gratified mind, boarded the
  chariot with Krishna, the enemy of Mura.
Having returned to the earth and reached the
  abode of that best among Brahmins, having
  given him his sons, thus (the one who has been)
  disciplined
said with folded hands:
(*The curtain is lowered to reveal Krishna and
Arjuna with the Children beside them, and with
the Brahmin and his Wife on the opposite side of
the stage.*)

ARJUNA:

  pallavi: Salutations to you, crown
           among Brahmins! (Please)
           forgive my fault. By the
           compassion of the Lord, all
           of your sons have been
           obtained! [K]

  caranam:
0 one who was weak from sadness over (the loss
  of) your sons, when my vital spots[a] (were)
  pierced by the arrows of your words,
I quickly searched through Yama's abode and the
  heavens, but did not see your sons. [K]+[I]

           pallavi: Salutations to you . . .

  caranam:
Unable to obtain the boys anywhere in the three
  worlds, I started to jump fearlessly into the fire
  pit to be consumed.
Then that deceitful one, Krishna, kindly came to
  me and together we quickly reached Vishnu's
  abode. [K]+[I]

           pallavi: Salutations to you . . .

  caranam:
With delight we received the boys who were
  befittingly near that Supreme One on his
  serpent-bed, and quickly came here.
0 one who has accumulated such exceedingly
  good deeds, along with your better half, to your
  great delight, please see (them). [K]+[I]

           pallavi: Salutations to you . . .

  caranam:
This (is) the first boy, and (here is) the second.
The third one is of virtuous qualities.
The fourth is without any impurity, (and) here is
  the fifth boy.
0 ocean of good luck, setting aside all confusion,
  please receive all your ten sons I return to you.
[K]+[I]
           pallavi: Salutations to you . . .

[*bhupalam* (*raga*); *cempata* (*tala* – 16 beats)]

BRAHMIN:
  caranam:
Hail to thee, Krishna.
Hail to thee, brave Arjuna!
Do not imagine in your heart of hearts that I
  intended anything (negative) when I scolded
  you there in my overwhelming grief.
0 one whose strength of arms is unimpeded,
0 ocean of supreme good fortune, those who
  take your name in mind will enjoy immense
  prosperity from the pleasure of Krishna!
[K]

  ilakiyattam
BRAHMIN: Alas! Earlier I humiliated you very
much. Please don't take it to heart. Then I was
immersed in an ocean of sorrow. Now you have
saved me and pushed me into the ocean of
happiness. That's all. So, what did you do after
that?
ARJUNA:[b] I lit the fire, and was about to jump
when (someone) grabbed my hand.

BRAHMIN: (*To his Wife:*) Do you know (who held
his hand)?

---

[a] *Marmmam*, the 'vital spots' of the body which, when pierced in combat, could lead to instant death.
[b] The actor playing Arjuna often includes some information about his travels to Yama and Indra's abode as he searched for
the boys.

(*Humorously.*) Oh, you don't know anything. (*As if whispering to her.*) Krishna did that.

ARJUNA: Later I went to the abode of Vishnu and found the children there. According to Vishnu's command, we have brought the children back.

BRAHMIN: They all stayed with Vishnu? That's most fortunate!

ARJUNA: (*Pointing to one of the boys.*) This boy played with the serpent, Ananta's tail. And this boy suckled at Lakshmi Devi's breast!

BRAHMIN: Alas! This boy is most fortunate to have suckled at Lakshmi's breast. What can I say now? Why don't both of you stay here happily for a few days, and only after that leave.

ARJUNA: We will visit later.

KRISHNA: For now, we will leave, but later we will return.

ARJUNA: We will come for the boys' *upanayana*.[a]

BRAHMIN: Ah! Alright, as you wish. O Arjuna, may all auspicious things happen to you. May much fame come to you.

(*Krishna dances the concluding dance* [danasi].)

(*Curtain*)

COMMENTARY: THEODICY, HUMAN SUFFERING, AND DIVINE PLAY IN *THE PROGENY OF KRISHNA*

The *Progeny of Krishna* in performance

As discussed in Chapter 1, in addition to its heralded pleasures as a 'classical' performance for connoisseurs, *The Progeny of Krishna* in performance today is a very accessible play which creates multiple pleasures for its audiences. Performances elicit everything from interest in the story as a drama, to empathy for the main character of the Brahmin, to raucous laughter, to animated commentary and discussion, to a sense of devotion (*bhakti*) for Krishna, to subtler responses among connoisseurs to the more virtuosic elements of an actor's performance of a role. In this commentary, I pay particular attention to the elements of story, characterization, and theme that invite everyone to the 'ocean of possibilities' that makes a play like this so accessible and popular.

It was the *kathakali* actor Margi Vijayan who told me that he thought *The Progeny of Krishna* was accessible and popular not only because its language was relatively uncomplicated but also because it was 'a very simple play.' G.S. Warrier, a connoisseur of *kathakali*, echoed Vijayan's opinion when he said that the play 'has an everyday (*lokadharmi*) aspect.' Both were referring to the enactment in *The Progeny of Krishna* of the very human dilemma faced by a simple Brahmin householder and his wife who are suffering a tremendous loss: nine sons have been born to them, and all nine have died at birth.

As originally written, *The Progeny of Krishna* emphasizes and elaborates the overarching point of view of the original story in the *Bhagavata Purana* – that Vishnu is 'the greatest' of all the gods whose own inscrutable, capricious divine play (*lila*) is manifest not only in his incarnation in Lord Krishna but also in his own 'play,' and that he has actually brought the Brahmin's children to Vaikuntha in order to necessitate a visit by Krishna and Arjuna. As described by Krishna in Scene 10 of the original unedited play, these scenes reveal the wonder and glory of Vishnu's abode, elaborated by Krishna and Arjuna as they witness, and describe these wonders with awe where their 'eyes begin to swim and play in the immense waves of this ocean of ambrosia.' This view of Vishnu's abode provides a dramatic theological and cosmological framework within which the Brahmin's, and thereby the audience's, own day-to-day human sufferings are subsumed.

The Progeny of Krishna's importance as an accessible play emphasizing devotionalism is witnessed by its regular performance at certain temples, especially in southern Kerala. Similar to commissioning a *Krishnattam* performance at Guruvayur Temple, at Panavalli Temple near Alleppey, as well as at the Kollam Asrama and Tiruvalla temples, *The Progeny of Krishna* is at least occasionally if not regularly performed as an offering to the deity of the temple. At the Tiruvalla temple, if a *kathakali* play other than

---

[a] Ritual for investiture of the sacred thread.

The Progeny of Krishna is performed as an offering, the final scene of *The Progeny of Krishna* is performed beginning about 4.30 a.m. in order to conclude with the auspicious return of the children to the Brahmin. And it was at the Panavalli temple that the great *kathakali* actor Kunju Nayar Asan, who popularized the role of the Brahmin, used to perform the role as a personal offering, accepting in this case only expense money, and taking no fee.[27]

At the Sri Padmanabhaswamy Temple in Thiruvananthapuram, performances of *The Progeny of Krishna* are compulsory on the tenth and final day of the great ten-day temple festival during Meenam (March/April), which features all-night *kathakali* performances on each of the ten nights. Ganesha Iyer explained that the performance of *The Progeny of Krishna* in the *natya sala* ('drama house'), just inside the east temple gate, is held on the tenth and final day to close the festival 'because it returns the dead children and ensures growth in the family.' Since children are literally and symbolically the 'prosperity' of a family, gaining progeny is the future.

Until approximately forty years ago *The Progeny of Krishna* was still performed in its entirety, at least at the temple festivals at Varkala and Thiruvananthapuram. But as Krishnan Nayar popularized the role of the Brahmin, and enacted some of his now infamous *ilakiyattam* focusing on the dilemma of the Brahmin, it gradually became standard to cut scenes 6, 7, 9, 10, and 11. With these scenes cut, the dramatic narrative is focused more specifically on the Brahmin's dilemma, Arjuna's prideful attempt to resolve that dilemma, and the joy and devotion (*bhakti*) which comes with Krishna's gracious return of the children.[28] The simplicity and 'everydayness' of the story lies in the fact that it focuses so closely on the Brahmin's human dilemma.

Within the seven scenes normally performed redundancies have been eliminated so that the pace of the play is decidedly up-tempo – in keeping with the Brahmin's sense of urgency about his situation. *The Progeny of Krishna* is also unusual in that there is little emphasis on solo acting, and the only interpolations of any length are interactive – those between Arjuna and the Brahmin in Scene 2 and Scene 5.[29] These interactive interpolations serve to push forward and elaborate on these two characters and their relationship *within the story at hand*. For

example, the long *attam* in Scene 2 elaborates the presumptuousness of Arjuna's pride which makes him declare that he can accomplish what no one else, including Krishna, has been able to do – protect the Brahmin's children – and it also emphasizes the Brahmin's total trust in and devotion to Krishna.[30]

Thus, unlike many *kathakali* plays in performance whose narratives temporarily 'stand still' while the focus remains on a single senior actor performing a virtuosic elaboration, in this shortened version particularly *The Progeny of Krishna* plays as a drama in which mostly two-character scenes push the narrative along toward its joyous conclusion with the return of the children.

The Progeny of Krishna's everyday concerns: the importance of [male] progeny and raising the question, 'Why do the pious suffer?'

> In Indian mythology, the greatest loss one can suffer is to lose a child.
> (Vasu Pisharodi, *Kathakali* actor)

The dilemma of childlessness, and, in particular, lack of male progeny, which bursts upon the stage with the Brahmin's dramatic entrance in Scene 2 of *The Progeny of Krishna*, is perhaps the worst case scenario that a traditional Hindu male, and especially a brahmin, can face in life. As South Asian scholar Wendy Doniger O'Flaherty explains:

> Children in India represent the only form of physical permanence. They are the links of the eternal chain of rebirths in an infinity of bodies (*samsara*), in contrast with (and often at the sacrifice of) the setting free or release (*moksa*) of the eternal soul. We see our physical selves preserved in the bodies of our children; and we see our mythical selves preserved in their memories. For many – all but those who claim to have achieved release – this is the only eternity there is. As the Hindu lawbook put it, 'You beget children, and that's your immortality, O mortal.'
> (1988: 73)

The point of view assumed in *The Progeny of Krishna* is that of the Dharma Sastras, which collectively 'set forth a model of how society *ought* to be organized and not a sociological description of existing society' (Hopkins 1971: 84). According to this Brahminical religious ideal, the [male] brahmin passes through at least the first two of the four 'stages of life' (*asrama*) open to him: student, householder, forest dwelling hermit, and renunciant (*sannyasin*). In *The Progeny of Krishna*, the Brahmin is attempting to fulfill the two most essential duties of the brahmin householder through which society itself would be preserved, i.e., offering sacrifices and raising sons.[31] Although release from the cycle of rebirths is the ultimate goal,

> for most people, householder life was the limit of their present existence: they married, raised a family, carried out their social duties, performed their prescribed rituals, and ended life as householders, hoping that they had prepared the way for a better future birth.
>
> (ibid.: 81)

According to the 'majority view' expressed by *Manu*, the 'householder life is the most important' of the four stages since 'it alone leads to the production of offspring and the support of society'; however, it could only be successfully completed when one produces 'male offspring to the second generation' and provides 'for the continuing support of one's family.'

> Every Brahmin was said to be born with a triple indebtedness: to the sages, to the gods, and to his ancestors. He became free of these only when he had satisfied the sages with celibacy, the gods with sacrifices, and his ancestors with a son.
>
> (ibid.: 82, 77).

Not only are sons necessary for the future continuation and prosperity of the family, but it is also the eldest son's duty to perform his father's funeral rites (*sra ddha*).[32] From the point of view of the Dharma Sastras, to remain son-less is to be unable to fulfill one's obligations as a householder, and to lack a son to perform one's funeral rites.

The emphasis throughout *The Progeny of Krishna* on the birth of a male child places the woman (Brahmin's wife) in the traditional role as having responsibility for fulfilling her role of bearing (male) children. As anthropologist Margaret Trawick Egnor explains, the indigenous Ayurvedic medical perspective assumes that

> physical conception and birth is roughly parallel to . . . cosmic conception and birth . . . Just as the body exists for the purpose of the soul only . . . woman is treated as existing for the sole purpose of producing a (male) child only, and the female body is discussed only in connection with pregnancy.
>
> (1983: 936).

For the Brahmin and his Wife the everyday concern for (male) progeny is not only tragically multiplied, but also exacerbated by the 'injustice' of their suffering in a situation over which they have no control and for which they have no blame.[33] Quite simply, the Brahmin and his Wife are faultless. As *kathakali* actor Nelliyode Vasudevan Namboodiripad explains, this Brahmin 'leads a mundane and pious life.' Throughout the play the Brahmin is addressed and/or described as 'pious,' 'noble,' 'good,' or that 'crown' and/or 'best among brahmins.' *The Progeny of Krishna* dramatically raises the question that confronts all families – why the pious and innocent suffer.

In his study of local interpretations of popular Hindu religious concepts in a northern Kerala community, sociologist of religion A.M. Abraham Ayrookuzhiel (1983) discusses how Malayalis understand and interpret a situation like that faced by the Brahmin in *The Progeny of Krishna* – why would a good, pious person suffer? Three Chirakkal village residents shared the following thoughts which echo the Brahmin's Wife's attribution of their suffering to what has been divinely ordained, i.e., their fate (*vidhi*):

> Sometimes really good people suffer, as in the case of Harischandra. Harischandra suffered not because of his *dushkarma* (evil deeds) but because of *vidhi* (fate) . . .
> What is to happen will happen. One cannot prevent it. It is called *vidhi* . . .
> *Vidhi* means the happenings in life which are beyond one's control, e.g., the sudden death of a young person . . . This can only be *vidhi*.
>
> (Ayrookuzhiel 1983: 123, 126, 127)

Pious, upright individuals like the Brahmin and his Wife in *The Progeny of Krishna* are clearly suffering, not from some sin committed in the past, but from a present fate (*vidhi*) over which they 'have no control' – 'innocent people also suffer. It cannot be that they have done something wrong. It may be (what is written on their foreheads)' (1983: 129).[34]

It is the very everydayness of these concerns with progeny and the question of suffering that gives *The Progeny of Krishna* its strong thematic appeal to *kathakali*'s most broad-based audiences. Although *The Progeny of Krishna* is played out between heaven and earth, especially in the shortened version performed today, the thematic appeal of these everyday, human concerns is reflected in the characters in *The Progeny of Krishna*, especially the Brahmin, his Wife, the Midwife, and the children.

The Brahmin and the Midwife: 'everyday' characters of *The Progeny of Krishna*

Along with the Brahmin character in *Kuchela Vrttam* by Muringoor Sankara Potti (1851–1914), of the major roles in the *kathakali* repertory, the Brahmin in *The Progeny of Krishna* is, as G.S. Warrier explained, 'more everyday' than most major characters. Part of the 'everydayness' which characterizes these two roles is the fact that both are brahmins, and therefore appear in the *minukku* (literally, 'radiant') costume and make-up (*vesam*). In contrast to the other categories, their make-up and costuming are relatively close to the appearance of brahmins in everyday life with a non-stylized grey beard, simple wrapped lower cloth, upper body cloth draped over his left arm, sacred thread, and beads.

The Brahmin's everydayness also comes from his familiarity – those inhering characteristics of personality and behavior which are understood by *kathakali* actors to characterize brahmins as an identifiable social type, and which form the basis of acting the role of a brahmin on the *kathakali* stage.[35] *Kathakali* actor Vasu Pisharodi, who often plays the role of the Brahmin in *The Progeny of Krishna*, explains that

> This Brahmin is a typical brahmin character. He is very very innocent.

Because of his innocence, he lashes out, terribly angry, against the ruler and loses control.

> (interview)

His innocence derives from his inborn qualities at birth, i.e., his substantive purity (*satvika gunam*), as well as from purity of mind (*guddhan*) which leaves him uncorrupted.[36] As M.P. Sankaran Namboodiri explains, 'whatever comes to his mind/heart comes out. He's like a vessel.' When he first enters he is filled with the anguish of sorrow (*karuna*) over the loss of his eighth son. But his sorrow (the dominant emotional state) is tinged with anger (*raudra*, or *kopam*) over the death of yet another son.[37] He moves back and forth between expressing his pathos, and his anger/outrage. But immediately after becoming angry, he regrets it. As M.P. Sankaran Namboodiri explains, even when the Brahmin does become angry, he remains innocent, 'because there is no malice or evil in it. It's a result of his circumstances.'

Nelliyode Vasudevan Namboodiripad explains how this innocence is manifest in his behavior:

> Since the Brahmin is so innocent, he shows everything in the extreme. If he is happy, he will be extremely happy. His mind is very innocent, and this innocence is the common characteristic of a brahmin . . . If he gets angry he won't consider the consequences or the position of the person. When he is angry, he won't think first, 'Who is Krishna?' He won't consider whether he is a god or not . . . A mature man controls his emotions, but the Brahmin doesn't.
> . . . So at last, when he sees all his children together, he is very happy and he can't control his happiness! It's like a person winning the lottery! Some people die when they hear this. They don't have the mental power to withstand such news!

> (interview)

The Kunju Nayar tradition of playing the role of the Brahmin involves an important element of endearing humor. Ideally it is a humor born out of the actor's ability to sustain the Brahmin's purity and innocence – so extreme are his reactions to his situation *in extremis* that his over-distraught behavior, when played with specific actions, takes on this element of endearing humor. *Kathakali* actor Vasu Pisharodi explains how

> Sometimes people laugh when I show some minute details of the Brahmin's character. For example, when he goes with Arjuna, he's so totally frustrated and upset that his shoulder cloth falls off! Whenever this episode is performed, women in the audience will laugh. Their laughter is part of the sympathy they have for the character.
>
> (interview)

When Pisharodi's Brahmin reacts to the thunderous sound of Arjuna's first arrow shot, he shouts that his 'ears are broken!' Improvising, he goes on to add, 'I'm only familiar with the sounds of worship (*puja*) – the ringing of the bell.' Again, it is the innocence of this response, which shows the Brahmin's piety, that becomes humorous.

The dramatic effectiveness of the juxtaposition of the wide range of emotions, and the endearing humor which it can produce, is also apparent in the scenes leading up to the birth of the ninth son. The Brahmin pacifies his wife's fears in Scene 3 and convinces her that Arjuna would indeed protect their next son, and Scene 4 then takes place nine months later. When the Brahmin's Wife announces her pregnancy, the Brahmin's primary *bhava* is happiness, but it is mixed with anxiety about her condition. The Brahmin 'takes control' of the situation when he announces:

> Oh, abode of all that is auspicious, do not have even a little worry.

But immediately the overly anxious, over-concerned, and over protective potential father says,

> Oh, one with lotus like eyes, you should also not make me worry!

This mixture of joy with anxious concern makes the Brahmin into the stereotypically anxious husband who is over-protective of his pregnant wife. Occasionally actors playing the Brahmin add a short interpolation in which he tells his wife

> Don't sweep! Don't grind!
> And don't climb any steps!
> Just take rest!

The humor of this scene plays as a counterbalance to the impending pathos of the loss of yet another child.

The Brahmin passes through this phenomenally wide-ranging and quickly changing sea of emotions in the course of *The Progeny of Krishna*. It is precisely this uncensored innocence of the Brahmin which allows both the role and the play to have such a broad appeal. As G.S. Warrier explains, 'Part of the enjoyment of a really good performance of *The Progeny of Krishna* is seeing the wide gamut of emotions through which a character like this passes. This wide gamut of emotions is what makes the play unusual. It is also what makes the play popular.' All this, but especially the Brahmin's innocence, helps the audience develop, in Pisharodi's words, a 'sympathetic love' toward the Brahmin.

Although the Brahmin is a familiar character who possesses this sense of the 'everyday' and must be played broadly, by no means is he a caricature. In G.S. Warrier's explanation of *The Progeny of Krishna* as having a strong 'everyday' (*lokadharmi*) aspect, he qualified this description by adding, 'but it should not be acted that way. Too often the acting descends to *lokadharmi*. It should not.' Used in this negative sense, *lokadharmi* might best be translated 'pedestrian,' i.e., the type of acting in which one 'plays to the gallery' and the role of the Brahmin becomes a caricature. M.P. Sankaran Namboodiri explains how playing the Brahmin requires the actor to keep within the bounds of 'what is appropriate' (*aucityam-bodham*) to the type:

> Playing the Brahmin requires a more 'realistic' form of acting than many other roles.[38] But even though he is more 'realistically' played, it shouldn't be that realistic. The ideal Brahmin, even though there are of course vast differences among brahmins, is that one should keep up the dignity and reputation of one's family line. It is called *taravatittam*, i.e., what is due the *taravatu*,[39] keeping up the family name. The opposite is *capalyam* or when one behaves without respect for one's family, i.e., behaving with disrespect for tradition and for the family's reputation. Behaving with reserve, dignity and within the limits that should guide a person of this caste.
>
> (interview)

What is particularly difficult about playing the role of the Brahmin is keeping the delicate balance between playing the role fully and broadly, but keeping the innocence, especially when playing moments that are humorous. As M.P. Sankaran Namboodiri explains

> A poor actor might break the bounds [of what is appropriate] by trying to play humor. That's a problem. He can't play at humor, but only at being angry at Krishna for ignoring him! It's the extremity of his condition and situation that brings this on.
> (interview)

So, the Brahmin must be played with broad and extreme emotions, but he must do so as specific responses to an ever-changing dramatic context.

If the mature actor playing the Brahmin must be careful not to overplay the role so that it becomes a caricature, the young actor who takes the role of the Midwife should play this small role specifically as a caricature, i.e., the most everyday or *lokadharmi* types of roles in the repertory. The Midwife is among the group of 'special' caricatures which spice the *kathakali* repertory. Like other caricatures, *kathakali*'s are created by the careful copying of the easily identifiable stereotypical behaviors of particular groups of people within the society at large. In *The Progeny of Krishna* the Midwife is usually played as a buck-toothed, hunchbacked old woman from the village. It never fails to elicit a good humored response from the audience.[40]

Responding to *The Progeny of Krishna* today: from cupped hands to the cooking pot

Wendy O'Flaherty astutely observes that 'It is the particular talent of mythology to bridge the gap between the affective and cognitive aspects of religion – to fill the heart' (1976: 15). In the concluding section of this chapter, I turn my attention to the way in which *kathakali*'s performance of mythology, especially a play like *The Progeny of Krishna*, provides an aesthetic experience which fills the 'hearts' *and/or* 'minds' of its diverse audiences, from those whose hands are cupped to those who bring cooking pots.

In one of our discussions, Vasu Pisharoti

recollected how, at the age of thirteen or fourteen, 'tears fell unconsciously from [my] eyes' during a performance of *The Progeny of Krishna*. Although he had seen *The Progeny of Krishna* before and knew the story, on this particular night, responding to the pathos and innocence of the Brahmin, Kunju Nayar Asan's performance 'touched and pierced my heart/mind. It is a special feeling . . . I cried and so did many other people in the audience.' Such an overtly empathetic response may be occasioned either by the Brahmin's moments of pathos, and/or by the occasion of overwhelming joy which concludes a good performance – a moment when joy, wonder, grace, and devotion are melded as parents and children are united and the Brahmin's suffering is ended.

Unlike other small roles in the *kathakali* repertory, such as the Midwife, the roles of the Brahmin's eight oldest children in *The Progeny of Krishna* are not taken by younger, relatively inexperienced *kathakali* students, but rather by children from the community where the performance is being held. (The ninth and final son is the stage property infant wrapped in a cloth.) Ideally, the organizers of the performance gather eight 'volunteer' children (male or female) from families attending the performance to play the eight sons. If possible, the eight children should be of different heights, ranging from four- or five-year-olds up to fourteen- or fifteen-year-olds, so that they can be arranged onstage from oldest/tallest to youngest/smallest. This ideal casting reflects the fact that Vishnu had taken all of the children to his heavenly abode where they had been living fully and joyfully with their heavenly father (Vishnu) and mothers (Lakshmi and Bhumi Devi) until they were taken by Arjuna and Krishna to rejoin their parents of birth.

Naturally, the spectator/actor relationship is altered with village children on stage. The audience is usually abuzz with conversation and commentary throughout the opening of the final scene as Krishna serves as onstage stage manager for the children, arranging them according to height from the tallest to the shortest, prompting the children about how to hold their hands to pay proper respects to their parents, when to go forward to Arjuna to be given to their parents, etc. Much of this is impromptu, and the actors playing Arjuna and the Brahmin often take full advantage to improvise. Since the predominant mood, once the children are brought forward, is the Brahmin's exploding abundance of joy, the good humored improvisations are often uproariously funny. At the performance at Killimangalam in 1993, the son of the actor (M.P. Sankaran Namboodiri) playing the Brahmin was one of the eight children. Sankaran Namboodiri took full advantage of the audience's knowledge of this fact to humorously ask why this child (his son) did not look like him, but rather his wife! When a young girl with long hair was introduced, it led to improvised comments on how he got such long hair!

By bringing village children onto the stage, in more than most *kathakali* plays the context is put *into the performance text* (see Blackburn 1992), i.e., Krishna's grace is not an abstract theological/cosmological construct, but instantiated in the village's progeny here and now. In *The Progeny of Krishna* the 'everyday' (*lokadharmi*) has the potential to take on the sense of being *this* particular day for these particular people.

Among connoisseurs the same performative moments that brought tears to Pisharoti's then young eyes are often experienced and interpreted as a subtler internal resonation or 'vibration' 'within the mind' – signs of the actualization of the *rasa* aesthetic. That *kathakali* is an 'ocean of possibilities' for its audiences should by now be self evident. What is often not self-evident is that most narratives about *kathakali* privilege the educated point of view of the connoisseur, and his 'theater of the mind.' When *kathakali* is discussed as a 'classical' art (most often by Westerners), it suggests that *kathakali* is an art of the elite to the exclusion of the everyday and the mundane, i.e., that it could have no interest or meaning for non-connoisseurs. When *kathakali* is discussed as a 'theater of the mind,' among some connoisseurs this 'higher' aesthetic sensibility is used to disparage implicitly and/or explicitly the 'lower,' 'sensual,' 'worldly,' or 'everyday' appreciation of the 'un'-educated – a sense of disparagement that has the potential to make *kathakali* into an art for an exclusive elite which might no longer be an 'ocean' welcoming all.

As an outsider to Kerala and to *kathakali*, and therefore as little more than a child at *kathakali* performances, it is reassuring for me to know that, even with water falling between the gaps in a child's uneducated, awkwardly cupped hands, there is much to be taken away from a *kathakali* play like *The Progeny of Krishna*.

Theodicy, god's 'play,' and historical shifts in meaning

Thematically and dramatically *The Progeny of Krishna* enacts one of popular Hinduism's most important ways of addressing the problem of theodicy – if there is an all-powerful force of divine creation, how and why would such a force allow human suffering. The fact that *The Progeny of Krishna*, as performed today in its edited version, focuses the audience's attention and response on the 'human face' of the Brahmin's predicament and suffering, and therefore creates and even 'encourages' the possibility of a sentimental response, is not at all surprising. What we need to keep in mind are the historical factors that have contributed to emphasizing this response. First is the development of an acting style which has increasingly emphasized playing roles like the Brahmin with increasing attention to their human predicament, especially in the development of the interpolations where these states of mind/being/doing are theatrically elaborated. Certainly the 'play' of the gods remains fundamental to this edited version of the play in-performance, however, editing Scenes 6–7 and 9–11 considerably de-emphasizes Mahavishnu's *lila*, and the wonders of his grace. These missing scenes enact the futility of Arjuna's pride-filled frantic search for the children, and the 'culprit' who ostensibly caused their death. They emphasize and culminate, not so much in the final return of the children to their human parents, but in Scenes 10–11 with Krishna and Arjuna's arrival at Vishnu's heavenly abode where they (and the audience) encounter the divine. Leaving behind their chariot, Krishna and Arjuna describe their almost blinding encounter with the wonders of Vaikuntha where their eyes 'swim and play in the immense waves of this ocean of ambrosia.'

> (Finally), the two of them reached Vishnu's
>   abode and saw Padmanabha, the
>   embodiment of supreme knowledge,
> the one who reclines on the graceful couch of
>   the Serpent-king,

(whose) sides are beautified by the goddesses of Earth and Lakshmi.

His wonder-inspiring abode is suffused with pure grace since it is the residence of immortal souls.

Scene 11 opens as the curtain is lowered to reveal Mahavishnu in tableau, perhaps reclining as described above with Bhumi Devi and Lakshmi at his sides, and surrounded by the missing children. As Krishna and Arjuna bow before him they speak for devotees of Vishnu gathered in the audience when they repeat over and again in their *pallavi*:

O one who is the embodiment of bliss, we bow (to you).

Certainly, having seen your visage (*darsan*), this birth has become fruitful.

Like the audience before them, by taking *darsan* of Mahavishnu in this tableau they have encountered the divine. Mahavishnu himself explains that it was 'Only to make you come here, did I bring that best among Brahmin's children here with delight,' i.e., Vishnu's inscrutable divine play has once again been at work! From this encounter with the divine, Krishna and Arjuna conclude, 'Is it possible for there to be grief in the minds of those who are devotees at your feet?'

There can be no doubt that this earlier version of the play-in-performance elaborates popular Hinduism's answer to the problem of suffering as the divine 'play' of the gods:

The idea is that God's creation of the world is motivated not by any desire or lack, since these would be incompatible with his or her self-fulfilled and complete nature, but rather by a free and spontaneous creativity. Later commentators explain this passage through the metaphor of a great king who plays at sports in order to amuse himself, or a healthy man who, upon awakening from a sound sleep, dances from sheer exuberance.
(Sax 1995: 4)

Especially relevant to *The Progeny of Krishna* is Norvein Hein's comment on how the concept of *lila* as 'divine sportiveness' is commonly used

to domesticate the tragedies of life by reflecting that wealth and poverty, health and sickness, and even death itself are apportioned to creatures of God in his mysterious play. The reasons for such fateful intervention are beyond human comprehension, but devotees who understand their fortunes to be the sport of God will know that it is not blind fate that controls their lot, and hence they will accept their condition as providential.
(in Sax 1995: 15)

Certainly, this drama, especially as originally authored and performed until approximately forty to fifty years ago, reflects Mahavishnu at play with the fate of the Brahmin and his sons. The very fact of his faultless character serves to underscore the inscrutability of the divine's 'mysterious play.'

king rugmamgada's law (rugmamgada caritam)

Mandavappalli Ittiraricha Menon (c.1747–94)

Translated by V.R. PRABODHACHANDRAN NAYAR, M.P. SANKARAN NAMBOODIRI AND PHILLIP B. ZARRILLI

INTRODUCTION

The full text of *King Rugmamgada's Law* has ten scenes. Today, only the final three scenes (8–10) are performed. The play is based on Chapter 21 of the *Padma Purana*. It focuses on how *ekadasi* became such an important day of devotion to Vishnu. *Ekadasi* is the eleventh day of every fortnight in a lunar month, sacred to Vishnu. On *ekadasi* devotees are supposed to fast and meditate. *Ekadasi* is also the subject of another *kathakali* play, *Ambarishacaritam* by Aswati Tirunal Tampuran (c.1756–94), a contemporary of Mandavappalli Ittiraricha Menon.

Marking the importance of *ekadasi*, *Ambarishacaritam* is performed each *ekadasi* day during the ten-day temple festival in Meenam (March–April) at the Thiruvananthapuram Sri Padmanabhaswamy Temple every year. Similarly, at the Varkala temple, it was traditional to perform *King Rugmamgada's Law* in its entirety on *ekadasi* day.

SYNOPSIS OF THE PLAY:[1]

One day when King Rugmamgada and his wife, Sandhyavali, were enjoying the pleasures of their garden, they noticed that some of the beautiful flowers were missing. Rugmamgada wanted to know why. During the night, he hid himself to observe the garden. Some celestial nymphs came to the garden riding in their airborne chariot. They began to pluck the flowers, and loaded their chariot. When they were about to leave, Rugmamgada came forward and touched their chariot, freezing it to the ground. The nymphs became angry, and cursed Rugmamgada. Afraid of their curses, he pleaded for their forgiveness. He asked how the chariot might be freed so they could leave. They said that if he could locate one individual in his kingdom who had observed *ekadasi* rites and taken absolutely no food that day, that individual would be able to free the chariot simply by touching it.

King Rugmamgada sent his servants throughout the kingdom in search of someone who had observed these rites and fasted. Eventually they found one poor, old woman who, although she had not been officially observing the rites, had nevertheless not eaten all day since she was so poor. They brought her to Rugmamgada. He ordered her to touch the chariot, and when she did it was freed. Rugmamgada was amazed at her power, and asked the nymphs to explain how someone might obtain such powers. They instructed him on how to observe the *ekadasi* rites correctly through fasting and meditation. Rugmamgada describes the observance of these rites at length.

Once Rugmamgada and all his subjects began to perform the *ekadasi* rites, it affected the entire world. Everyone in Rugmamgada's kingdom went to Vaikuntha, Vishnu's heavenly abode. Since no one was going to hell where the lord of death presided, Yama became concerned and asked Sage Narada what was happening. When Narada explained the effect of *ekadasi* observances on Rugmamgada's kingdom, Yama sent his agents into the world to find a single *chandala* to take to hell.[a] Vishnu's attendants interceded, and Yama's agents returned empty-handed. Yama angrily announced that he would go into the world himself to bring back not only a *chandala*, but Vishnu's attendants as well! Yama's assistant Chitragupta intercedes, asking Yama whether it might not be better for him to approach Lord Brahma than to go to the world himself.

Yama pleads his case before Brahma. He explains that with everyone observing *ekadasi* so faithfully, no one is coming to his kingdom, and therefore he has no work. Brahma tells Yama not to worry, and that he will try another way of dissuading Rugmamgada from being so vigilant in his observances of *ekadasi*.

The three scenes (8–10) performed today and translated here begin at this point in the dramatic narrative. Brahma sends the enchantress Mohini to obstruct Rugmamgada's observances by testing his devotion. When Rugmamgada encounters Mohini, not knowing that she has been sent by Brahma to test him, he immediately falls in love with her, and he invites her to live with him as his consort. She agrees on condition that he will never deny her anything she desires. He agrees by taking an oath.

Two brahmins discuss King Rugmamgada's relationship with Mohini, but note that even in the midst of this new love, he has not neglected his duties.

On *ekadasi* day, after undergoing the necessary purificatory rites, King Rugmamgada begins meditating on Vishnu. Mohini enters in an amorous mood. Rugmamgada tries to dissuade her, explaining that as a devotee of Vishnu he must remain pure the entire day and can only fast and meditate. Mohini then reminds him of the vow he has taken never to deny her what she desires – and at this moment she desires him. She challenges him – she will allow him to continue his fasting and meditation, but on condition that

he behead his only son, Dharmamgada, while lying in his mother's lap. Rugmamgada becomes angry with her, and then begs her to relent from her demand, but she refuses.

Dharmamgada himself comes forward and reminds his father that for members of their clan (ksatriyas) a vow must always be honored. Rugmamgada undergoes the emotional torment of the contradictory demands of his situation, but finally knows that he must sacrifice his son. Just as he raises his sword to strike, Vishnu appears and, after blessing Rugmamgada, takes him to Vaikuntha, the heavenly abode, and installs his son as king.

The translation of Scenes 8–10 has been prepared from the K.P.S. Menon and Redyar versions of the text, and from a performance of the play on 28 August 1993 at Killimangalam, Trissur District, Kerala, India, commissioned by the Killimangalam Centre for Documentation of the Performing Arts. The role of King Rugmamgada was played by Kalamandalam Gopi Asan, and the role of Mohini by Margi Vijayakumar. The interpolations are from this performance.

CAST
RUGMAMGADA: the great king of the Sun clan, in *pacca* ('green') make-up.
MOHINI: the enchantress, in *minukku* ('radiant') make-up.
TWO BRAHMINS: in *minukku* make-up.
DHARMAMGADA: son of Rugmamgada, in *pacca* make-up.
SANDHYAVALI: Rugmamgada's wife and mother of Dharmamgada, in *minukku* make-up.
VISHNU: in *pacca* make-up.

[*sankarabharanam* (*raga*)]

sloka:[2]
Long ago was born in the prosperous Sun clan, a King named Rugmamgada.
Graceful and handsome,
  his only delight was serving Lord Vishnu,
  whose mark is the distinctive Valsa.[b]
(Rugmamgada) the strong one (was) counted
  foremost of the brave – the one with good
  conduct and status;

---

[a] A *chandala* is of such low birth that anyone of this caste is not supposed to perform such sacred rites.
[b] Valsa is the mark of the foot of the sage Bhrigu on the chest of Lord Vishnu.

the one who had garnered the greatest
reputation;
and who was praised by even the gods.
To the darkness of pride filled enemies, he was
the Sun with its scorching rays.

Scene 8[3]

[Rugmamgada and Mohini]

[*erikkilakkamodari* (*raga*); *cempa* (*tala* – 16 beats)]

  sloka:
After sending the Sun's son, Yama, back to his
city, with delight Brahma created the
enchantress, Mohini[a] – a woman whose face
resembled the perfect and graceful moon.
Following Brahma's directions,
she reached the forest near the city of Ayodhya
and lived there.
Rugmamgada, the best among kings, arrived
there to hunt.

(*The curtain is lowered to reveal Mohini with
Rugmamgada seated stage right.*)

  [*sari dance*][b]
  padam:
Mohini the enchantress had a lovely body –
brilliant and delightful, and of excellent
qualities. [K]
The five-arrowed (Kama) admits the superiority
of her smile;
the farthest corners of her eyes were tremulous
and graceful;
she was possessed of amorous delight; [K]
her hair was long, dark, and curly;
for her breasts (even) Kama felt constant
desire; [K]
her entire form was like flashes of lightning.
Standing before him, seeing her form,
the King (too) was enamored of her. [K]

(*Rugmamgada gets up and dances a*
kitatakadhimtam. *Sometimes a short* ilakiyattam
is also enacted here.)

[*kamodari* (*raga*); *cempata* (*tala* – 16 beats)]

RUGMAMGADA:
        pallavi: O one whose face is so sweet
                and graceful!
                O one whose gait resembles
                the elephant in rut! [K]

  anupallavi:
One with speech like honey,
why do you live alone in this forest? [K]+[I]

  caranam:
O one whose hair is (black) like the bees!
Seeing you (I am) overwhelmed with desire.
O young woman, surprisingly Kama has become
increasingly quarrelsome with me. [K]+[I]

  caranam:
(Please) understand that from now on
if (I am) separated from you it will cause grief
greater than death.
(Therefore, please) remain together with me.
I will serve at your lotus-feet. [K]+[I]

[*erikkilakkamodari* (*raga*); *muriatanta* (*tala* – 16
beats)]

MOHINI:
        pallavi: O moon-faced one, one with
                (such a) handsome form,
                please listen closely. [K]

  anupallavi:
O one more charming than (even) Kama,
seeing you, my love increases. [K]

  caranam:
If you will take (the following) small vow,
I will become your most beloved and stay
(with you):
'I shall never do anything either unaffectionate
to you or against your desire.'

[*dhanyasi* (*raga*); *atanta* (*tala* – 14 beats)]

---

[a] Mohini literally means 'enchantress'. Mohini was created when Vishnu transformed himself into a beautiful woman in
order to enchant Siva. The result of their union was the birth of Ayyappa – a popular deity throughout Kerala.
[b] The *sari* dance is a set piece of choreography used for the entrance of female characters such as Mohini, Lalitas,
Damayanti, etc. which describes the beauty of the female character and/or praises various deities and sages. The lengthy
padam which follows is sung while the *sari* dance is performed.

RUGMAMGADA:
  caranam:
I hereby take this oath and offer (it to you):
  'I will never commit even the smallest
  unaffectionate act toward you.' [K]

[*erikkilakkamodari* (*raga*); *muriatanta* (*tala* – 14
beats)]

MOHINI:
  caranam:
Joyfully I will join you and come to your
  house. [K]

  [*ilakiyattam*][4]

RUGMAMGADA: I'm extremely lucky to have you.
MOHINI: I am also fortunate.
RUGMAMGADA: Look! This tree's branches are full
of flowers. These full blossoms are shining and
swaying in the breeze, as if they are enjoying our
union. Should we stay awhile at the foot of this
tree, and then go?
MOHINI: Yes!
RUGMAMGADA: Here is an elephant with a slow
gait approaching you. It thinks you are a friend
and is coming near. But it quickly runs away. Do
you know why?
MOHINI: Why?
RUGMAMGADA: It thought your waist was that of a
lion, and it ran away . . . There is a Cakravaka
bird! Seeing your breasts it happily flies nearby.
But the Cakravaka has quickly flown away. Do
you know why?
MOHINI: Why?
RUGMAMGADA: Well, seeing your moon-like face, it
hesitated, and then flew away.[a]

(*Looking elsewhere.*) Look! Seeing the hairs of
your navel, a serpent is slithering toward you,
but it leaves quickly. Do you know why? Well, it
thought your hairs were the feathers of a
peacock. It was afraid and left.[b]

(*Looking elsewhere.*) Here, the sound of the
cuckoo can be heard. They come flying. Seeing
your pearl bracelets, they think they are the eyes
of a cat. They've become afraid, and leave.

All creatures in this forest have been attracted by
your beauty. Brahma created you with his hands.
It's extremely wonderful!

MOHINI: Brahma didn't create me with his hands.
RUGMAMGADA: He didn't touch you with his hands?
MOHINI: No, I was born from his mind.
RUGMAMGADA: Oh, that's why your body is
without blemish. Well, it's a gift given to me by
Brahma because of my devotion to Vishnu.
Brahma thought, 'I should give this king an
appropriate gift.' Because of my devotion, he
meditated and created you for me.
MOHINI: Oh, are you a devotee of Vishnu?
RUGMAMGADA: For a very long time I have been
Vishnu's devotee.
MOHINI: What benefit do you derive from your
devotion to Vishnu?
RUGMAMGADA: O Siva, Siva! I have only had
benefits and no problems. Every person in this
country is happy. There's isn't even a touch of
sadness in anyone's mind.
MOHINI: Why do you meditate on Vishnu?
RUGMAMGADA: Long ago celestial nymphs used to
come to my garden at night and pluck the
flowers. The guards could not see them. One
night I hid myself and watched. The celestial
nymphs came in an airborne chariot and
descended, plucked the flowers, ascended, and
were about to leave. Before it rose from the
earth, I touched the chariot. It stayed on the
ground. Then the nymphs began to curse me. I
asked them not to curse me. Please excuse me,
but on that day if anyone who had taken food or
water touched the chariot, it would not rise;
therefore, I had to find someone (appropriate). I
sent messengers everywhere. Finally they found
an old woman who had not taken food or water
that day. They brought her on their shoulders.
She touched the chariot and it rose.
MOHINI: Why was that?
RUGMAMGADA: I asked the same question of the
nymphs. They said, 'O King, today is the
auspicious *ekadasi* day. Those who perform that
vow will attain union with the divine with no
hindrance at all; therefore, you too should
observe *ekadasi*. I have always performed these
austerities. Not only me, but everyone in my

---

[a] By poetic conceit in Sanskrit literature, Cakravaka birds always must leave their spouses when the moon rises.
[b] Another typical poetic conceit is that the serpent and peacock are deadly enemies.

kingdom. Therefore, our wealth and fame have increased. That's how I became a devotee of Vishnu. Haven't you heard this before?

MOHINI: Well, I have heard of your fame.

RUGMAMGADA: Do the gods speak badly about me?

MOHINI: No, no! They only praise you. In the dancing hall, nymphs used to dance and sing, playing the veena. The songs sing of your fame.

RUGMAMGADA: Having heard these songs of praise, you came to see me? Do you really love me?

MOHINI: Surely.

RUGMAMGADA: Then why do you want me to take a vow?

MOHINI: Well, after all, you are a king. You have many wives. If they see me coming with you, they may tell me to leave and you may abandon me.

RUGMAMGADA: No. I have one wife who is devoted to me. She is a jewel among the devoted. When she sees you, she will treat you as her sister. Remember that. I have a boy too. Not a youth, but a boy. He too will treat you like his mother. So why do you have any doubts? Well, let us start to the palace.

MOHINI: Surely.

RUGMAMGADA: Wait. Let me get my chariot. Oh, Charioteer! Bring my chariot. (*To his army.*) Oh! Get ready to return to the palace. Inform the queen and the prince that I am bringing a beautiful lady with me. Inform everyone with the beat of the drums. (*Checking the chariot.*) Let us start. (*To Mohini.*) If you are afraid of getting into the chariot, please hold onto me. (*To the Charioteer.*) Drive the chariot slowly to the palace. [N]

(*Curtain*)

Scene 9
[Two Brahmins]
[*sahana* (raga); *atanta* (tala – 7 beats)]

sloka:
Under Kama's spell, mutual love developed between that best of kings and the lotus-faced, passionate Mohini.
After entering his palace with the slender-bodied lady,

he made love to his heart's content and delightfully stayed there.
Then some brahmins secretly spoke among themselves (these) good words:

(*The curtain is lowered as the two Brahmins enter dancing a* kitatakadhimtam.)

FIRST BRAHMIN:
   caranam:
Haven't you heard, Brahmins!
Once when the King went to the forest hunting, what he obtained was an excellent woman. [K]

SECOND BRAHMIN:
   caranam:
I (too) heard that, O Brahmin.
It is said that her name is the good Mohini.
It is also said that she is an extremely attractive woman. [K]

FIRST BRAHMIN:
   caranam:
Day and night the King is so engaged in amorous games that (he has) no other interests. [K]

SECOND BRAHMIN:
   caranam:
It is praiseworthy that even after joining with Mohini the King has not neglected to observe the *ekadasi* rites.

FIRST BRAHMIN:
   caranam:
O Brahmin, let us go immediately.
It is time to place the leaves in the King's mansion for the Dvadasi feast.[a] [K]

SECOND BRAHMIN:
   caranam:
Oh! I will come along, Brahmin.
The King will happily grant many gifts and cloths to all brahmins (present)![b] [K]

(*Dancing a* kitatakshimtam, *the two Brahmins move upstage as the curtain is raised.*)

---

[a] Dvadasivrata is the twelfth lunar feast day immediately following *ekadasi* on which brahmins are fed. For traditional Kerala meals, food is served on a banana leaf placed on the floor.
[b] Special ritual occasions are often marked by the gifting of cloth. The traditional lower garment worn by men is the *muntu*.

Scene 10
[Rugmamgada and Mohini]
[*anandabhairavi* (*raga*); *muriatanta* (*tala* – 14 beats)]

(*The curtain remains raised during the singing of the following* sloka.)

sloka:
Having united quickly and joyously with the
  King of Ayodhya,
Mohini stayed there forgetting (even) her
  instructions from the Lord of the Worlds
  (Brahma).[a]
Then, on the morning of the highly auspicious
  ekadasi day in the month of Vriscika,[b]
she told her dearest king who was anxious to
  complete the ritual:

(*The curtain is lowered as Mohini dances a*
kitatakadhimtam *while King Rugmamgada is
seated, meditating, stage right.*)

MOHINI:
  caranam:
O my lover,
  one whose body is as handsome as Kama,
  (and) one as deep as the ocean;
  one who resembles Kama in (your) amorous
  games,
please come to me with delight! [K]

  caranam:
I haven't yet had the slightest gratification
  from love play.
O good decorative mark of the Ksatriya clan,
  O kind one, please listen.[5] [K]

[*surutti* (*raga*); *cempata* (*tala* – 16 beats)]

RUGMAMGADA:
  caranam:
O young lady,
I will do everything you desire,
  (but) today is the auspicious *ekadasi* day. [K]

  caranam:

All Kama's sports are prohibited,
O young lady, my life-blood, my life-blood. [K]+[I]

  caranam:
O auspicious one,
  (today one) must avoid rich foods,
  oiling the body, and other pleasures.
(One) should only meditate on Vishnu. [K]+[I]

[*anandabhairavi* (*raga*); *muriatanta* (*tala* – 14 beats)]

MOHINI:
  caranam:
Lo! Anyone loses their strength if they are
  starved.
Love play pleases and is the essence of
  happiness. [K]

  caranam:
Listen. I say for sure that I will not observe
  (this rite).
Not only that, but you too will not observe it
  today!
Let us have our love play in abundance, now! [K]

[*surutti* (*raga*); *cempata* (*tala* – 16 beats)]

RUGMAMGADA:
  caranam:
I will give up (the city of) Ayodhya, and all else.
(But please), permit (me) to observe (my) *ekadasi*
  rites without delay. [K]+[I]

  [*nilambari* (*raga*); *cempata* (*tala* – 16 beats)]

MOHINI:
  caranam:
O King! Is it proper to break a vow like this?
Your reputation for upholding the truth
  reverberates throughout the world. [K]

  caranam:
Have you suddenly forgotten the vow that you
  took with delight:
'My dear, I will do nothing displeasing to you or
  without love.' [K]

---

[a] Since Mohini has been sent by Brahma, she experiences conflict between her anxiety over completing the task for which she has been sent, and her desire for pleasure in the world.
[b] Vriscika is the fourth month of the Malayalam calendar corresponding to the second half of November and the first half of December.

[*surutti* (*raga*); *cempata* (*tala* – 16 beats)]

RUGMAMGADA:
  caranam:
You know I am neither displeased nor in
  disagreement with you.
(But please), permit me to observe the Lord's rites,
O crown among women! O lady! Mohini!
  Beloved wife! [K]+[I]

[*nilambari* (*raga*); *cempata* (*tala* – 16 beats)]

MOHINI:
  caranam:
You may observe this great rite if (you meet one
  condition):[6]
Place your son, Dharmamgada, on his mother's
  lap and gracefully cut (his neck) with your
  sword. [K]

[*dvijavanti* (*raga*); *cempata* (*tala* – 16 beats)]

RUGMAMGADA:
  caranam:
Alas! O wicked one! How can you make such
  hideous demands?
Give up such cruelty and state what you want. [K]

[*nilambari* (*raga*); *cempata* (*tala* – 16 beats)]

MOHINI:
  caranam:
If both father and mother freely do (as I have
  asked) without shedding a single tear,
then you may observe (the rites) without
  hindrance. [K]

[*toti* (*raga*); *cempata* (*tala* – 16 beats)]

RUGMAMGADA:
  caranam:
O Lord! How is it that events turn out like this?
  Why is Mohini angry with me?
O one full of pleasure from love's ambrosia!
  O attractive one!
(Please) do not deceive (us)! [K]

[*nilambari* (*raga*); *cempata* (*tala* – 16 beats)]

MOHINI:
  caranam:
O King, do (you) understand that if you observe
  this rite today without killing your son,
you will break your vow? [K]

[*mukhari* (*raga*); *cempata* (*tala* – 16 beats)]

  sloka: (*This* sloka *is acted.*)
When Mohini's cruel words suddenly fell on the
  King's ears,
he became delirious from the weight of his grief,
  and fell to the ground, fainting.
Soon after, when his delirium ended,
  extremely distressed, he cried out:
'O one who always protects your devotees,[7]
  O Supreme One! Sri Padmanabha!
Please protect me, the tormented one!'

RUGMAMGADA:
  caranam:
O Lord! Janardana![a]
  O one full of kindness for all, and of the
  pleasure of knowledge.
O Hari!
With a clear conscience, how am I to sacrifice
  my son without shedding a single tear?
O evil minded Mohini!
Alas! Your words are unkind, wicked, and most
  horrible.
Why has (your) anger arisen against my dear
  child who is so pleasing to the eyes? [K][8]

[*bilahari* (*raga*); *cempata* (*tala* – 16 beats)]

sloka: (*This* sloka *is acted. Sandhyavali and
Dharmamgada enter the stage directly dancing a*
kitatakadhimtam *as the* sloka *is sung.*)
While the King, filled with undiminished
  devotion to Brahmins,
and abode of the constancy of duty, said this,
Rugmamgada's son, and his mother, arrived
  before (the King) and said:

DHARMAMGADA:
              pallavi: O Father, I respectfully
                  bow at your feet. [K]

---

[a] An epithet of Vishnu.

Plate 8.1
*Rugmamgada in a state
of disbelief over what
has been asked of him*

caranam:
My birth has become fruitful because of (my step
  mother's) demand.
For those born in the world what is important is
  to achieve their parents' desires by whatever
  means. [K]+[I]

caranam:
Great sons will be born to you in the future.
O one of praiseworthy conduct, if a vow is
  broken, the effect of such an evil act will not
  end for the clan. [K]+[I]

caranam:
Father, such grief is not appropriate.
  Here is (your) sword – please take it.
O protector of the people, please fulfill this vow.
  With (mental) calm, gracefully complete this
  rite (*vratam*). [K]+[I]

caranam:
O mother, I also bow at your feet.
  O one whose conduct is pleasing!
With goodness please sit here calmly.
  I will lay on your lap without regret. [K]+[I]

[*ilakiyattam*][9]

DHARMAMGADA: O father, protect the truth to
increase the fame of our dynasty!

RUGMAMGADA: Alas! (How has) such a fate[a]
happened to me? All this time I have never
knowingly committed any sin. Yet this has
happened to me. Why? O seat of affection, your
father, this sinner, doesn't know what to do. I am
immersed in the ocean of sorrow. Since my mind
is not firm and brave, I acted like this.

DHARMAMGADA: Don't have any sorrow. Please
maintain the truth.

RUGMAMGADA: (*To Mohini.*) Alas! Mohini, you
knew the importance of this great day. So why
have you said all these foolish things?

MOHINI: Go ahead and perform your rite. Don't
kill your son, but . . .

RUGMAMGADA: O demoness! You are not a celestial
nymph! You are a demoness who assumed the

---

[a] Literally, 'head writing.'

form of a beautiful lady. You have brought a bad name to this dynasty, and you've pushed me into the pit of destruction. Why?

MOHINI: Quickly, kill your son!

RUGMAMGADA: (*Referring to his wife, Sandhyavali.*) After I married my wife, we waited a long time to see this child's face. We performed many auspicious rites. As a result, god gave us this boy. We were happy to see him growing day by day. Now, with this hand, I have to cut off his neck? A sinner like me has not been born on this earth before! (*To Sandhyavali.*) O dear one, devotee of your husband, without consulting you, long ago in the forest I married this woman thinking she was a celestial being. But she is a demoness! A messenger of the god of death. Please forgive me, sinner that I am!

SANDHYAVALI: Do not be sorry. Protect the truth.

RUGMAMGADA: A jewel among women like her cannot be found anywhere. How great is her mind. Having born ten months of pregnancy, having delivered and raised this boy, and now thinking only of the good fame of our dynasty, she advises me to protect the truth! (*To Mohini.*) Are you a woman? There's no way you can understand her. You don't deserve (the right) to ever deliver a child.

(*Dharmamgada takes the sword and hands it to his father. Looking at the sword, he says:*) This sword has drunk the blood of many of my enemies. Will you cut this boy's neck and lick his blood? No! I have no fear. (*He gradually gains the power to cut off his son's head.*) I will sacrifice the boy and maintain the good fame of our dynasty. (*He raises the sword and is about to cut, but while looking at his son, he drops the sword, and falls to the ground in a faint. He revives, and then embraces his son.*)

(*Turning to Mohini.*) O Mohini! Look at his innocent face! Where did you get the courage to tell me to cut his neck? Alas! No! I won't break my vow, or take any food, and I will never cut his neck. I won't break my vow!

MOHINI: (But) don't you remember the vow you took long ago? Remember, if you break *that* vow it will ruin your reputation.

RUGMAMGADA: This woman may bring about my destruction, but because of me, my dynasty will not suffer bad fame.

O Lord of the World, Vishnu! If you don't show kindness toward your devotees, who will worship you? From time to time, assuming different forms, you have killed those who are cruel, and protected the good. At first you took the form of

Plate 8.2 *Rugmamgada is about to cut off Dharmamgada's head when, seeing his beloved son at his feet, he freezes, unable to complete the 'sacrifice.' In the next moment he collapses in a faint to the ground*

a fish, tortoise, boar, half-man half-lion – you incarnated in all these (forms). And you protected Prahlada! Now why can't you protect this boy? (*Taking the sword again.*) O, Vishnu! Please give me the courage to sacrifice my son, thereby protecting the truth, and in order to maintain the good fame of our dynasty. Please be kind. I sacrifice the boy to protect the truth!

(*He looks at the sword, then at Mohini, and finally at his son. This series of three actions is repeated as Rugmamgada literally enacts the three conflicting demands placed on him.*) O, Lord of the World, please protect me. I have no fear. What you see with your naked eye is perishable. The truth is the only thing that is imperishable. Therefore, now what should I do? Cut the boy's neck and protect the truth itself!

(*Looking at Mohini.*) Watch what I do!

(*To Sandhyavali.*) You should not cry! Let all auspicious things come to you. (*He raises his hand to bless Dharmamgada. Rugmamgada then performs a N, raises his sword, and is about to cut his son's neck when Vishnu appears and stops him as the curtain is partially lowered.*)

[*mohanam* (*raga*); *cempata* (*tala* – 16 beats)]

VISHNU: (*To Rugmamgada*)
  caranam:
Don't kill the boy,
  O one with a shining and graceful reputation.
O King, you have attained final release,[a]
  as well as fame in this world!
O one who collects virtuous acts,
  (please) understand:
Brahma instructed Mohini to come and obstruct
  your intensive observances of this rite.
Allow her to leave as she pleases.
She will receive one-sixth of the fruits of the
  rites of those who sleep during the daylight
  hours of Dvadasi.[b] [K]

(*Mohini exits.*)

[*sriragam* (*raga*); *cempa* (*tala* – 10 beats)]

(*To Dharmamgada*)
  caranam:
Hello, dear Dharmamgada!
  Come to me with delight.
No one on the earth can be as gratified as you.
You will live in this world with great comfort for
  a long time.

Plate 8.3 *Loosening his hair, Rugmamgada enters a transformative state of 'fury' in which he will be able to sacrifice his son as required*

[a] According to traditional Hindu belief, *mukti* or *moksa* is the ultimate release from worldly ties and is the final destination for all souls.
[b] No one is supposed to sleep when observing Dvadasi rites; therefore, for those who do sleep, the fruits of their observances are given to Mohini in return for her service to Vishnu.

In the final days, you too will achieve oneness
  with me. [K]

[*mohanam* (*raga*); *cempata* (*tala* – 16 beats)]

(*To Rugmamgada*)
  caranam:
O ocean of good fortune,
  complete his coronation immediately and
  crown him ruler.
Having attained oneness with me,
  along with your wife, continue to live near me
  with great comfort. [K][10]

(*There usually follows a short* ilakiyattam *in
which the coronation of Dharmamgada is
enacted. Rugmamgada and his wife move to the
other side of the curtain to be with Vishnu. They
all then bless Dharmamgada who prostrates
himself before them. The* dhanasi *or closing
dance is normally performed by Dharmamgada.*)

(*Curtain*)

COMMENTARY: THE 'FAILURE' AND
EXERCISE OF 'POWER' IN *KING
RUGMAMGADA'S LAW*

As discussed in the commentaries in Chapters 5
and 6, *kathakali* dance-dramas clearly reflect the
symbiotic historical relationship between
kingship, the maintenance of the cosmos, and
the 'sacrifice' of battle required of rulers to
protect this order as historically configured in
Kerala. While *The Killing of Kirmira* literally
dramatizes the bloody acts of sacrifice required
of ksatriyas as they uphold their idealized duty
of protecting brahmin ascetics and their
sacrificial rites by cleansing the world of the
'evil' archetypically embodied and symbolized by
demonesses and demon-kings, *King
Rugmamgada's Law* both underscores how
fundamental this sacrificial paradigm is to Kerala
notions of kingship and duty, and provides
detailed insight into the existential state of
mind/being/doing required of the martial
practitioner when attempting to carry out his
duty to kill. The 'archive' of the 'annals of a
cultural imagination' (Comaroff and Comaroff
1992: xi) through which a historical ethnography

of *kathakali* can be understood is an intertextual
reading between the representations and
enactments of power/sacrifice/kingship required
of *kathakali*'s idealized, but always flawed, epic
heroes, and the discourses and practices in the
ethnographic present of Kerala's *kalarippayattu*
practitioners – those local martial 'heroes'
trained to actualize similar powers. My interest
in this commentary is in precisely how this act of
sacrifice is enacted, i.e., in the state of
mind/being of the martial/princely sacrificer in
the act of bloody sacrifice.

In this commentary I read between
representations and enactments of 'heroic' power,
sacrifice, and kingship in *King Rugmamgada's
Law* and some of the commonplace ethnosemantic
representations of heroic power in the
ethnographic present in order to gain a better
understanding of 'power' as a complex, nuanced,
contextually, and historically specific set of
discourses, practices, and behaviors. I focus in
particular on the state of mind/being of the
martial practitioner at the moment he wields his
sword to kill – that existential moment when he
should ideally be 'doubtless,' have 'mental
courage,' possess 'mental power,' i.e., that moment
when his 'body is all eyes' and he attains a state
of transformative 'fury.' These commonplace
expressions represent that idealized state or
condition of selfhood to which martial artists
aspire as they practise their bodily based
techniques in order to 'transform themselves in
order to attain a certain state' (Foucault 1988: 18).

The divine tests his devotee

Like the Abraham/Isaac story, *King Rugmamgada's
Law* (melo)dramatically elaborates a divine test of
an avid devotee – here Brahma/Vishnu tests King
Rugmamgada. I focus my commentary on that
aspect of edited performances today of most
interest to connoisseurs – the performative
elaboration of Rugmamgada's inner state of
mind/being/doing in Scene 10.

In the course of the scene, when the great
king is reduced to pleading with Mohini, 'not [to]
deceive (us)!' she counters by reminding him of
the solemn oath he has taken, and of the weight
of this obligation. Like Arjuna's vow in *The
Progeny of Krishna*, to break any vow, even this
one, would be a transgression of keeping one's

word – a word which, for the ksatriya/ruler must never be broken. In the *sloka* which follows, the effect which Mohini's unexpected demand makes on Rugmamgada's state of mind is enacted as

> the king became greatly delirious because of the weight of (his) grief, and (he) fell, fainting, to the ground.

As a celebrated king, an heroic 'royal sage' and *viran*, even in the face of the extreme and unexpected demand Mohini makes of him, Rugmamgada ideally should have been able to 'control his senses,' maintain an inner equilibrium, and fulfill his duty by sacrificing his son. Recovering from his faint, but still in a state of distress and imbalance, Rugmamgada prays to the reclining form of Vishnu, Sri Padmanabha, to protect him, 'the tormented one.'[11] But Vishnu does not come to his aid.

When Rugmamgada's son, Dharmamgada (literally, 'the mace of duty') comes to the stage, he literally embodies sacred law or duty (*dharma*), as well as the continuation of divine rule within Rugmamgada's kingdom. After bowing respectfully at his father's feet and dutifully reciting the reasons a son is born into this world, Dharmamgada stands before his father as the icon and index, as well as voice and embodiment of heroic duty and behavior expected of the ksatriya clan. Therefore, he reminds his father that 'grief does not become you.' With Rugmamgada's honor and sword on trial, Dharmamgada picks up the sword – itself an indexical icon and the vehicle of divine, royal, and martial power – and tells his father to 'preserve your vow,' thereby upholding duty (*dharma*). With the sword now in his father's right hand, Dharmamgada calmly presents himself as this 'graceful rite (*vratam*) [of sacrifice] with delight.'

The performative interpolation (*ilakiyattam*) which follows between Rugmamgada, Mohini, and Dharmamgada elaborates the complex set of competing demands which Rugmamgada faces: that he exercise the power of his sword as a ksatriya to uphold the truth of his vow and maintain the sanctity and legitimacy of their rule, and that he do so by engaging in an act of transgression by killing/sacrificing his son. When Dharmamgada tells his father to 'protect the truth (*satyam*) to increase the fame of our own

dynasty' by going ahead with his sacrifice, Rugmamgada responds by reflecting on his mental state, concluding that it was 'because my mind is not firm and brave I acted like this.'

Had Rugmamgada kept his mind 'firm and brave,' he would not have fainted or experienced disequilibrium, but maintained the optimal state of 'doubtlessness' (*vita sankam*) reflected in the *Bhagavad Gita*, and been able to bring himself to sacrifice his son. In the *Bhagavad Gita* the ideal

> is that one should not be perturbed by feelings and emotions and lose one's balance . . . the mature person is one in whom desires enter without upsetting him. The analogy of the sea is given. Though rivers discharge their water continuously into the sea, the sea is ever motionless. In the same way the mature person experiences continually feelings and emotions, but he does not allow himself to be overpowered by them or to be swayed by them.
>
> (Kuppuswamy 1993: 26, II.70)

Rugmamgada is literally suffering the somatic effects of mental distress which affects his ability to maintain a heroic (*utsaha bhava*) demeanor, and carry out his duty. When even a single 'doubt' or 'emotion' creates a ripple in one's consciousness, it is understood to lead potentially to that individual's ruin. In the *Bhagavad Gita*, when Arjuna's mind was 'distressed with grief,' (I, 47. Zaehner 1969: 117) he too displays somatic effects like those of Rugmamgada:

> My limbs give way, my mouth dries up, trembling seizes upon my body, and my [body's] hairs stand in dread. [My bow,] Gandiva slips from my hand, my very skin is all ablaze; I cannot stand and my mind seems to wander.
>
> (I, 29–30. ibid.: 117)

Since 'the natural state of the mind/body is regarded in Hindu philosophy as basically flawed,' one practises exercise, dietary, and meditational techniques to compensate for 'natural irregularities' (Alter 1992: 95). Only when one achieves self-realization is perfect health and balance achieved – a state in which 'a person is not plagued by emotions of any sort' (ibid.). But even for epic and puranic heroes like Arjuna and Rugmamgada, the road to becoming a self-actualized royal sage is not easy, and one falters along the way. *King Rugmamgada's Law* dramatizes Rugmamgada's 'flawed' moment of weakness, emotional imbalance, and all too human 'doubt' along the road to actualization and release.

The dramatic and performative focus throughout this interpolation remains on Rugmamgada's mental state, allowing the senior actor playing the role to elaborate further the excruciating emotional roller-coaster ride that Rugmamgada takes as he attempts over and again to eradicate his 'fears,' overcome the overwhelming pathos caused by the demand that he kill his son, make his mind 'firm' or controlled, and therefore regain his optimal state of 'bravery' and heroic demeanor so that he can fulfill his duty. After Dharmamgada gives his father his sword, he talks to it as a personified being which 'has drunk the blood of many of my enemies.' He asks the sword, 'Will you cut this boy's neck and lick his blood?' Rugmamgada implicitly answers the question when he tells himself, 'No, I [can] have no fear.' By erasing his personal 'fear' and anguish in this situation he attempts to regain mental equilibrium, and thereby the 'mental power,' necessary to sacrifice his son.

But just as he raises the sword and is about to 'cut the boy's neck and maintain the good fame of our dynasty,' as soon as he sees his son before him, he loses his inner resolve, drops the sword, and falls to the ground in a faint. Desperate, Rugmamgada turns once again to Lord Vishnu, and after performatively embodying and enacting Vishnu's ten major manifestations (*avatars*), demands the same protection from him that he provided Prahlada, another of his great devotees. He prays not that Vishnu allow him to forgo killing his son, but rather for the 'courage to sacrifice my son, thus protecting the truth, in order to maintain the good fame of our dynasty.' But, once again, having called on Vishnu and taking him in mind, Rugmamgada fails to enter into a state which allows him to transcend the limitations of his feelings. He is still unable to sacrifice his son as he knows he must.

As the performative interpolation continues, Rugmamgada (melo)dramatically enacts his inner turmoil as he looks at the sword exhibiting the 'heroic' demands of the moment, at Mohini embodying 'anger' at her demands on him, and at his son enacting the pathos of his impending loss. For *kathakali* connoisseurs, this particular moment in the performance is the highlight when the actor sequentially enacts in quick succession the three conflicting states which have produced Rugmamgada's mental confusion and inability to act. But then, in a moment of internal realization of what is demanded of him in the moment to fulfill his overriding duty, Rugmamgada leans forward, loosening his hair, and draws its long strands to either side of his head. As he raises himself up, Rugmamgada's eyes are wide open, revealing the fact that he has now entered a state of 'fury' (*raudra*). It is now, and only now, that he can definitely announce, 'I have no fear. What you see with your naked eye is perishable. The truth is the only thing that is imperishable.' In this transformed state he can now, and only now, 'Cut the boy's neck and protect the truth itself.' Therefore, he tells Mohini to 'Watch what I do!'

After Rugmamgada blesses Dharmamgada before his sacrificial beheading, he dances a final 'heroic' pure dance, raises his sword and is about to complete the act of killing when Vishnu appears to stop him, much as Krishna appeared to stop Arjuna jumping into the fire in *The Progeny of Krishna*. The auspicious conch shell is blown, flower petals rain down on Rugmamgada who is taken to Vishnu's abode having attained a state of accomplishment and release through his transformative ability to carry out such a sacrifice.

Achieving an idealized state of being/doing

What this *kathakali* performance dramatically enacts is Rugmamgada's progression from the very familiar human condition of mental disequilibrium, lack of focus, and loss of mental power 'caused' by our normative human frailties, to a transformative state of *raudra* ('fury') beyond all such potential distractions, and in which he is finally able to fulfill the 'heroic' demands of *dharma* by completing the ultimate act of transgressive blood sacrifice of his son. It is a state of concentrated awareness characterized by single point focus and concentration (*ekagrata*) in which all doubts, emotional upset, and consciousness itself are transcended. It is an activated state (*rajasa*) of single-minded doing. At least temporarily entering into this transcendent state of *raudra* is necessary for the hero to be able ultimately to fulfill his duty by killing.[12]

Rugmamgada's entry into this state is clearly marked performatively when, unable to fulfill his vow after calling on Lord Vishnu, he leans forward to loosen his hair. In other *kathakali* performances, transformations into this state of 'fury' are marked by the loosening of the hair, as when beautiful women-in-disguise (*lalitas*) are transformed into demonesses (*Puthana Moksha* or *The Killing of Kirmira*), or when Bhima appears in his 'furious' (*raudra*) form when he is about to kill Dussassana by tearing out his entrails in *The Killing of Duryodhana*.[13] As discussed in Chapter 3, and exemplified in the translation of *The Killing of Kirmira*, the furious state is 'normative' for demonic characters whose fundamental nature (*gunam*) is to be shape changers (*tamasa*) who engage in transgressive acts. It is also the normative state of the goddess Bhagavati (Bhadrakali, Kali) in her 'terrifying' form' (Caldwell 1995) when she appears with her fierce, 'energized eyes,' whose total visual effect is to assume an expression that equally evokes *vira* (the heroic) *rasa* and *raudra* or fury – her inexorably conquering/victorious form as she defeats the demon Daruka (Jones 1981: 73). Iconographically, with his wide-open eyes, Rugmamgada's state combining *vira* and *raudra* clearly articulates with that of the violent/conquering Bhagavati.

But for heroic (*pacca*) characters like Bhima and Rugmamgada who are required to engage in sacrificially transgressive acts of slaughter/sacrifice to fulfill their duty (*dharma*), and for whom blood-letting is not 'natural,' they can only do so when this state is appropriately marked as 'altered.' For Raudra Bhima it is literally marked by the fact that this special role is played by a separate actor from the one playing Bhima in the remainder of the play who appears in a special form of 'furious' make-up.[14]

In this state of single-mindedness, the royal sage Rugmamgada has overcome his emotional imbalance, doubts, and sorrows, and stands without 'fear.' This state is marked by the signs of *raudra* in *kathakali* performance and is distinct from the state of anger common to 'ordinary' experience. If it were not, it would be a state in which the practitioner were so absorbed in

reacting *with* anger that he would not be in 'control,' focused, or have 'mental power.' Rather, like Rugmamgada at first, he would be overcome by one or more emotion, and therefore be unable to fight with 'detachment.' The *raudra* state is a state of actualization quite different from a 'normative' state of consciousness. It is similar to that described in the 'Dhanur Veda' (Science of War/Bow) chapters of *Agni Purana* as one in which the martial practitioner 'conquers even Yama (the god of death)' (Dasgupta 1993), i.e., conquers his 'fears' and 'emotions' and therefore is ready to die in battle. As represented in *kathakali*, it is a state of heightened acuity in which the 'heroic' becomes realizable through one's actions in battle. For Rugmamgada, or Bhima, or the traditional *kalarippayattu* practitioner, everything is erased except the act of the 'sword.'

This is a state to which Mohini, hitherto in command and control, now responds with fear and distress. Seeing Rugmamgada before her in his transformed state, she is 'terrified.' She sees that he *will* complete this bloody sacrifice before her eyes. In this sense, when a hero embodies a state of '*raudra*,' it refers not to Rugmamgada's state of mind, but to the witness's experience of what happens when one *enters* this transformative state. In this state of sacrificial activation, the hero is as 'terrifying' as a demon, or the goddess when she appears in her terrifying forms as Kali or Bhadrakali. Just as the *kathakali* actor 'becomes' the character, so the martial artist 'becomes' a vehicle of the goddess's fury. The terror is in the eye of the beholder because of the 'terrible' things that happen when the divinely instantiated power (*sakti*) concentrated in this state is unleashed. Mohini is 'terrified' of what Rugmamgada will do,[15] just as villagers are 'terrified' of what the goddess might do. And the most appropriate iconic index of this terrifying power is the sword where divine, royal, and martial are manifest.

Sarah Caldwell asserts that in Kerala, sexuality and war are both understood to 'release potentially uncontrollable passions leading to both life and death of sorts. Only heroic beings of great power can properly control these forces once they are unleashed' (1995: 308). When heroes engage in battle, a fight, or an act of sacrifice like Rugmamgada, their predominant heroic state (*utsaha bhava*) must be complemented by moments of entering a furious state (*raudra*) when they must kill. It is the ability to enter this transformative state that allows the hero to 'properly control' the divine power and forces 'unleashed' by his practice which raise and actualize his 'powers.' When *kathakali*'s princes and kings enter this state of 'transformative fury' which allows them to 'act,' they can become the 'heroes' they ideally aspire to be.

Transformative 'fury,' 'doubtlessness,' and 'mental courage' in the ethnographic present

It may seem a long way from the late eighteenth-century *kathakali* stage to the late twentieth-century *kalari* where Kerala's martial art is still practised, but I think it no coincidence that the commonplace vocabulary used by today's martial masters to discuss the optimal state of actualization of the *kalarippayattu* practitioner are terms describing the state that *kathakali*'s heroic characters like Rugmamgada had to achieve – a state where the practitioner is single-minded, 'doubtless,' has 'mental courage,' or attains 'mental power.' In the remainder of this commentary I briefly explore these traditional discourses of practice in order to understand how this play reflects some of the existential concerns of Kerala's traditional martial practitioners.

Through the practice of the martial art, one attains congruence of the three humors as understood in Ayurveda, as well as to 'naturally' begin to develop a calm and stable mental state. Gurukkal Govindankutty Nayar explained in a discussion that '*kalarippayattu* is eighty percent mental and only the remainder is physical.' The eighty percent mental is developed not only through the psychophysiological martial exercises where single-point focus is first raised, but also by following a strict routine of observances like Rugmamgada's observance of *ekadasi*.

If you perform the exercises correctly and have the proper grip, then you begin to 'enjoy' practice. By doing this the whole body finds enjoyment. The mind won't be wandering here and there. You can do it with full confidence and courage. Your

mind won't be in a flurry (*sambhramam*). Sometimes, in combat, one might become flustered. If an opponent is powerful, one might become nervous; so, slowly you must develop this ability to be calm, to have mental peace.

What is most gratifying for an individual is when the mind is in a calm and stable state. What is ungratifying is when the mind is unstable and easily distracted.

This state is said to give the practitioner 'mental courage' (*manodhiryam*), i.e., the 'power to face anything that is dangerous to my health or mind. If I am confident of my art and health, then only can I have mental power (*manasakti*).'

Mental equilibrium is said to be 'read' on a person's face. 'If one faces an attack, relaxation of the face reflects mental equilibrium.' Ideally, this increased mental calm is not something esoteric, but of great practical use. Like the ideal epic hero, the ideal practitioner gains control of his emotions, achieves mental calm and courage, and becomes 'concentrated with a strong will' – a state of decidedness and singular focus on one's duty similar to the 'heroic' demeanor of the *kathakali* hero.

The common Malayalam folk expression, 'the body becomes all eyes' (*meyyu kannakuka*) encapsulates the martial practitioner's idealized state of actualization where the bodymind is in such a concentrated state of acuity and awareness that, like Brahma, the 'thousand-eyed,' the practitioner can 'see' everything around him, intuitively sensing and responding with his accomplished 'powers' to any/everything in the immediate environment. For the traditional martial practitioner, this state of superior actualization developed in tandem with a notion of power (*sakti*) which, as we have seen, is not absolute, but highly ambiguous, contingent, and context specific (see Zarrilli 1998). Having awakened and raised 'serpent power' (*kundalini sakti*) within from the psychophysiological practice of exercises, this 'power' was traditionally understood to take on the furious, wrathful (*raudra*), or destructive aspect of the goddess either alone or in combination with Siva as the fearful (*kala-bhairava*). Through practice itself and/or realizing special sacred syllables (*mantram*) one might, as P.K. Balan described it, attain 'this special power of fury,' i.e., reach an embodied state where 'fury' is concentrated and actualized.

I want to argue that this 'special power of fury' is comparable to the state of single-minded 'transformative fury' represented by Rugmamgada – a state similar to that described by J. Richardson Freeman regarding Kerala's *teyyam* ritual performers. Freeman has observed that their bodymind state in performance 'entails no loss of consciousness, or "dissociation" in psychological terms, but rather a *heightened* sense of consciousness' in which 'one's consciousness has not travelled somewhere else, shaman-like, but that instead, one's own body and mind are taken over and animated by a higher and more powerful [and I would add more concentrated] form of consciousness' (1991: 131). Some masters point out that the combination of self-confidence, doubtless heroism and internal fury manifest in the raising of the 'serpent power' (*kundalini sakti*) does not lead to emotional upset or anger, but rather to a state of intense concentration of energy (*aveshakaram*), 'the power generated from concentration.' In *teyyam* this heightened sense of consciousness takes the shape of 'performative acuity with regard to the rituals' (1991: 131). For the martial practitioner, like Rugmamgada, it is a single-minded performative acuity with regard to wielding the weapon.

This ideal state of 'transformative fury' where the 'body is all eyes' and one possesses 'mental power' is a discursive field of the possibilities for the exercise of power. But that power can only be manifest when exercised on a particular body in a context since 'power' only comes into being as it is practised.

Kathakali's traditional representations and enactments of the state of being/doing, through which its idealized epic heroes go forth to 'sacrifice' themselves in the 'glorious' harvest of war on the battlefield of death, reflects the traditional concerns, trials, and tribulations of Kerala's Nayars – those charged with maintaining and upholding *dharma* of the kings to whom they had pledged themselves to death on their battlefields. Of course today in Kerala, with rare exception, the practice of *kalarippayattu* is becoming more about actualizing and harnessing one's bodymind and powers for use in daily life than on a traditional battlefield.

part iii

৬৹৬৹৬৹

contested narratives: new plays, discourses and contexts

9

for whom *is* the king a king?

Issues of Intercultural Production, Perception,

and Reception in a *Kathakali King Lear*

As noted in Chapter 1, *kathakali* is constantly being (re)created and (re)positioned by and/or for its many different participants as well as audiences. Thus far I have focused on changes 'within the tradition,' and on some of the meanings the traditional repertory makes available to Malayali audiences, especially its connoisseurs, who judge innovation in terms of what they consider more or less 'appropriate' to the context. In Chapters 9 and 10 I provide a description and analysis of a variety of recent *kathakali* plays-in-performance which have 'fashioned novel performances' by 'manipulating' *kathakali* 'in innovative ways' both 'within' and 'outside' the tradition (Bauman 1977: 34–5). I give most attention to three very different experiments, each of which adapts *kathakali* techniques and/or content in very different contexts and for very different audiences:

1   Bengali playwright Asif Currimbhoy's little discussed 1960s English language modern drama, *The Dumb Dancer*, in which *kathakali* literally and metaphorically plays a central role.
2   The intercultural production of *Kathakali King Lear*, created and performed primarily for today's international, cosmopolitan, festival-going performing arts audiences.
3   *People's Victory*, created and performed exclusively within Kerala for local consumption by left-front political audiences within Kerala.

These chapters serve two purposes. First, in all the criticism and debate surrounding contemporary 'non-traditional' experiments in general and *Kathakali King Lear* and *People's Victory* in particular, other than my own history of *kathakali* through the early 1980s (Zarrilli 1984a: 263–352) there has been little if any historical analysis of such experiments; therefore, I begin this chapter with a historical overview of *kathakali* experimentation, and of the constantly shifting discourses used to justify, evaluate, and/or decry such experiments.

Second, these chapters provide a diverse set of specific examples of experimentation with and through *kathakali*. In contrast to the *Kathakali King Lear* project with its appeal to international/intercultural audiences, *People's Victory* is a decidedly 'local' production, growing out of Kerala's particular political history.

SETTING THE STAGE: *KATHAKALI* ENTERS THE TRANSNATIONAL, GLOBAL STAGE OF 'PUBLIC CULTURE'

As discussed in Chapter 2, in 1930 when Vallathol founded the Kerala Kalamandalam, *kathakali* was a regional form of performance known primarily to Malayalis. It was only with Vallathol's effort to bring *kathakali* to a larger public that it began to emerge from its relatively isolated status toward its present status as an 'internationally' known form of 'classical' Indian performance. As *kathakali* encountered these newer publics both at home, through tourism, and abroad (whether within a wider India or on foreign soil), it inevitably led to a series of transnational encounters, adaptations, and translations, which can be summarized as including:

1 writing and staging new plays based on non-traditional sources such as current events in productions like *The Killing of Hitler*, *Gandhi's Victory*, or *People's Victory*;
2 adapting non-Hindu myths, stories, plays, and poems for *kathakali*-style productions including Mary Magdalene, the Buddha, Faust, *The Iliad*, *King Lear*, *Hamlet*, *Snow White*, Shelly's 'La Sensitive,' etc.;
3 shaping and marketing *kathakali* for tourist audiences whether in Kerala, New Delhi, or abroad;
4 transforming *kathakali*'s basic techniques and choreography into modern 'ballet' dance or dance-drama, such as the work of innovators like Guru Gopinath who, following the early lead of Uday Shankar, institutionalized such changes at his Thiruvananthapuram school (the Viswa Kala Kendra) (Zarrilli 1984a: 311–15).

Simultaneously, a variety of experiments were taking place more 'within' the *kathakali* tradition – experiments with content, character, narrative form, etc.

Kathakali performances today reach many non-traditional audiences in Kerala, as well as in other parts of India and abroad either under government, institutional, or private sponsorship. Performances of *kathakali* in Kerala especially designed and adapted for foreign tourists have been taking place at least since 1969 when the Gurukulam Kathakali Yogam created a ninety-minute evening lecture-demonstration and performance intended for tourists in the port cities of Kochi/Ernakulam. Tourist performances today run the gamut from competent attempts to present a foreign audience with an 'authentic' experience of traditional *kathakali*, albeit in a shorter, edited version, to highly romantic/orientalist repackagings which emphasize *kathakali* as a 'thousand year old ritual' drama full of 'mysteries' and therefore part of the 'wisdom of the east' (Zarrilli 1977), to inept

performances by third-rate, ill-trained performers which capitalize on the naivete of foreign tourists willing to pay for just about anything that seems 'indigenous' while on a two-week sun, surf, and sand holiday at the Kovalam beach resort.

Since the 1930s kathakali programs have been regularly organized for national and/or international tours outside of Kerala, such as the five-night 1993 'Kathakali Mahotsavam' festival organized by the Indian central government's Sangeet Natak Akademi in New Delhi, the 1995 US tour of the Kerala Kalamandalam company, or the privately sponsored 1995 and 1997 tours of the UK organized by the Kala Chethena Kathakali Company and Centre Ocean Stream Theater Company in Southampton, UK. Some of these more recent tours have included performances of non-traditional plays such as the 1989–90 production of *Kathakali King Lear* co-produced by the Kerala Kalamandalam and Association Keli (Paris), and performed throughout Europe and at the August 1990 Edinburgh festival; French Canadian Richard Tremblay's adaptation (Iyyemgode Sridharan's translation) of Homer's *The Iliad* first performed in Bombay in 1990, in Trissur in 1993, and again in 1996; Annette LeDay's 1993 experimental choreography of Shelly's poem, *La Sensitive*, which young *kathakali* actor-dancers performed in London; Kala Chethena Kathakali Company's 1995 adaptation and UK tour of his version of 'Snow White' entitled *Oppression of the Innocent*; and most recently in 1996–97 an International Centre for Kathakali production of *Othello* at two sites in New Delhi (Jisha Menon 1998), and a very recent *kathakali Cinderella* adapted and staged by Paris-based choreographer Annette LeDay.

Reflecting *kathakali*'s flexibility, each specific adaptation, translation, or transformation has to varying degrees shaped *kathakali*'s content, techniques, etc. to suit the expectations of particular, and sometimes 'new' audiences. In addition, each 'experiment' more or less reflects and contributes to the formation of socio-political realities. Some adaptations, such as the creation of short tourist performances in the port cities of Cochin-Ernakulam, have been responses to the complex contemporary socio-political and economic realities of Kerala today (Zarrilli 1977).

Although no attempt has yet been made to document every *kathakali* experiment with non-traditional, non-epic content and characters, as early as World War II there was a precedent-setting production of *The Killing of Hitler* which the poet Vallathol helped create and whose characters were the major 'real life' leaders in the theater of war.[1] Hitler appeared in red-beard make-up as the evil demon-king who had set out to conquer the world. Opposing him were a variety of virtuous, heroic ('green' make-up) opponents, including Chiang Kai-Shek, Stalin, and Roosevelt. According to one-time secretary of the Kalamandalam P.C. Namboodiripad, the heroic characters 'went about asking support and people came to support them. [Culminating the production] there was a fight and ultimately Hitler was killed' (quoted in Hanna 1983: 160). Not long after, a second experimental *kathakali* was performed in which 'living people' entered the *kathakali* stage – *Gandhi's Victory*. These early productions were only performed once and were probably something of a historical anomaly at the time since it is not until the 1960s that non-epic characters began to appear more regularly on some *kathakali* stages.

A number of the experiments during the 1960s took place in New Delhi under the sponsorship of the International Centre for Kathakali, which was founded in 1960 in order to 'lift Kerala's Kathakali from its regional character, and to impart to it a new dimension by making this unique art known to audiences drawn from not only the various other States of India, but also from other countries' (International Centre for Kathakali, New Delhi, program, 1968). *Mary Magdelene*, the 1965 adaptation of the poet Vallathol's poem *Maddalana Mariyam* by T.M.B. Nedungadi, was the first of a series of experiments intended to 'adapt Kathakali to the modern stage' and attract new audiences. Other experimental productions during the 1960s included stagings of *David and Goliath*, *Buddha Caritam*, *Salome*, and adaptations of Tagore's plays *Chandalika* and *Visarjan* (*Sacrifice*).[2] Although both the content and characters in these productions were not from traditional epic sources, the Centre represented itself as attempting to preserve the 'authentic traditions of Kathakali' by re-elaborating each of these new narratives using traditional *kathakali* techniques and bringing 'eminent artists from Kerala' to ensure authenticity. Among them was one of the most

respected actors of the 1950s and 1960s, Vazkenkata Kunchu Nair, who was Chief Instructor at the P.S.V. Natyasangham (Kottakkal), and Principal of the Kerala Kalamandalam from 1960. The anonymous author of a review of Kunchu Nair's career on the occasion of his sixtieth birthday called him

> a traditionalist. But traditionalism in his case puts no inhibitions on his creativeness. Among his own productions are *Buddha Caritam* and *Chitrangada,* two new *kathakali* stories.
>
> (Anon 1969: 5)

Other experiments followed during the 1970s. In 1977 the cultural organization 'Kaliyarang' in Kottayam adapted and produced Aymanam Krishna Kaimal's version of Goethe's *Faust, Faust's Release* (*Faust Moksham*). In his enthusiastic *Indian Express* review, K. Thulaseedharan praised the production for the 'appropriateness' of the adaptation of theme, characters, and musical modes, and for 'giving the spectators as much delight as they would have derived had they been witnessing a story from our ancient scriptures' (1977: 5). For K. Thulaseedharan the production 'proved, beyond doubt, that purely western themes can form suitable material for a classical art like *kathakali*' (ibid.). As discussed in Chapters 3 and 4, the concepts of 'appropriateness' and 'aesthetic delight' (*rasa*) are the primary interpretive categories through which *kathakali* performances are evaluated by its connoisseurs today. Thulaseedharan draws upon both concepts not to evaluate the acting or interpolations in this specific performance, but to assess the production's non-traditional content and characters.

Written in 1966, C.G.R. Kurup's essay, '*Kathakali* on the Modern Stage,' exemplifies the predominant attitude toward experimentation and change evident between the founding of the Kalamandalam in 1930, and the mid-1980s – an attitude of reasonable engagement between tradition and contemporary innovations and concerns, whether in lighting, staging, or content. Although Kurup argues that as 'a distinct, evolved classical tradition . . . any change [in *kathakali*] . . . should be effected from within the tradition' (1966–67: 25), he also recommends that through 'study, research and experimentation' *kathakali* can be a 'progressive theater' (1966–67: 31). Among his many recommendations, Kurup argues for the expansion of the repertory through the restaging of neglected plays from the past, the writing of new plays based on puranic sources, and the composition of plays from non-puranic sources including 'history, Buddhist lore, the Bible, Tagore's dramas, Vikramaditya tales, and so on' (ibid.). Kurup even suggests that as long as *kathakali* keeps its 'classical form' (i.e., techniques) intact, in a democratic era *kathakali* should be flexible enough to 'respond to new social urges' by bringing 'contemporary life and aspirations' to the *kathakali* stage (ibid.). As we shall see, by the 1980s this 'reasonable' attitude among *kathakali* critics and connoisseurs had changed considerably.

EXPERIMENTS FROM 'WITHIN' THE TRADITION

The writing of new *kathakali* plays based on traditional epic and puranic stories has continued since *kathakali*'s birth; however, only occasionally do new plays sufficiently capture and hold the attention of *kathakali*'s highly critical audience of connoisseurs to enter the regular performance repertory for more than one or two performances. Some innovations, such as the Kottakkal P.S.V. Natyasangham's introduction of *Lord Ayappa's Law* (*Ayappa Caritam*) (1967), based on the life of the popular Kerala deity, Lord Ayappan, as well as its version of '*The Complete Ramayana*' (*Sampoorna Ramayana*) are an attempt to please popular Kerala temple-festival audiences and continue to attract numerous bookings for its performing company.

Arguably the most successful and controversial play based on traditional epic sources is V. Madhavan Nair's 1967 play, *Karna's Oath* (*Karnasapadham*). After its first performance under the sponsorship of the Thiruvananthapuram Kathakali Club, it rose in popularity to a point where during the 1980s it became one of the most performed plays in the active repertory. As K.K. Gopalakrishnan observed, 'the sign of *Karna's Oath*'s success is that among those in the *kathakali* audience who are "mad" about the Kottayam stories, they are

willing to spend sleepless nights watching not only *King Nala's Law*, but also *Karna's Oath*' (1993).

What makes *Karna's Oath* equally as successful as controversial is its almost exclusive focus on the pathos (*karuna rasa*) of the title character, Karna, in his quest to search out the truth of his parentage. *Karna's Oath* is structured to 'increase the intensity of emotion (*bhava*)' (Gopalakrishnan 1993). It follows Karna's personal quest at the high moment of (melo)drama just before the battle of Kurukshetra, taking Karna on a journey that surprises and horrifies him with each new personal discovery of his previously unknown past. Popularized by the well-known actor Kalamandalam Gopi Asan, the role of Karna is most similar to the title roles of Nala and Rugmamgada since they too focus much more than most other plays in the *kathakali* repertory on the character's personal dilemma and suffering. Because the role of Karna depends almost exclusively on the histrionic virtuosity of the actor playing the title role, and not so much on the choreographic structure of the play-in-performance as a whole, it has aroused considerable controversy. *Kathakali* actor Vasu Pisharody explains that

> *Karna's Oath* can be easily understood and appreciated by an audience not familiar with *kathakali*'s traditional form and structure. It's like the difference between popular vocal music and classical music. When reading a play by Rabindranath Tagore, we might get a feeling much like that from seeing a performance of *Karna's Oath*. Its story is accessible and popular, and when shown in *kathakali* has gained popularity. But the structure of *Karna's Oath* is entirely different [from the four Kottayam plays]. It cannot be performed in the *kathakali* structure very easily . . . The author thought that by foregrounding a situation of such emotional intensity, the play would attract an audience and gain popularity. But in fact, this is not fit for the *kathakali* stage. Only a very talented actor can make *Karna's Oath* work within the *kathakali* style and structure. If the artist absorbs the character and performs it within the framework of *kathakali*, the

performance may have a sense of the overall structure *kathakali*; but seeing *Karna's Oath* is not like seeing the Kottayam plays. Successful performances of *Karna's Oath* in particular depend on the contribution of the artist's personality. Moreover, unlike other *kathakali* plays which do not depend so much on music, performances of *Karna's Oath* will fail if the primary vocalist is not absolutely perfect.

(1993, interview)

As one Namboodiri connoisseur commented:

one can only see it no more than twice since it doesn't have all the features of a traditional *kathakali*. It's missing all the essentials. It's more like a one-act play. For example, there's not the full use of the curtain a number of times throughout the play. Once the curtain comes down, the play and all its entrances and exits just go on one after the other.

Critic K.K. Gopalakrishnan's description of the content of the play as 'heart touching' encapsulates the sentimentality of the play-in-performance.

One of a number of more recent experiments with epic and puranic source materials is the 1995 Trissur Kathakali Club production of L.S. Rajagopal's adaptation of the Tamil language *Ramanatakam* (*The Play of Rama*). *Ramanatakam* is the well-known work of the great Tamil poet Arunachalam Kavirayar whose devotional songs (*bhajans*) are well-known and loved by Malayalis as well as Tamils. The first *kathakali* play to be performed in a language other than Malayalam, the Tamil-language adaptation enacts several scenes from the Ramayana, focusing in particular on Viswamithra's request that the young Rama protect his forthcoming sacrifice (*yaga*), and culminating with the killing of the demoness Thadaka. G.S. Paul praised the production as successful for its 'total simplicity,' the ingenuity of the choreography, and 'as a major breakthrough . . . in popularising *kathakali* among Tamil audience' (1995: 26). Similarly, 'Scorpio,' writing for the *Indian Express*, praised the 'experimental' production for its ability to initiate a 'novice-[Tamil speaking] audience to the nuances of *kathakali*' (1995).

Continuing its sponsorship of a series of experimental productions, in 1996 the Trissur Kathakali Club also premiered *kathakali* actor Kalamandalam Balasubramanian's new play, *Markande yacaritam*. The play elaborates on an incident often performed as an interpolation in *The Progeny of Krishna* – the story of the Sage Mrukandu and his wife, Mayavati, who are granted their request by Siva for a child.

Whether based on traditional epic and puranic stories, such as *Ramanatakam*, or non-indigenous sources like *Hamlet* and *King Lear*, all these 'new' productions require playwrights, musical composers, and director/choreographers to write the texts, develop the choreography, and set them to music. Public discussions of these new productions comment on the language of the poetry, the musical settings, as well as the choreography/direction. Critics like G.S. Paul are expanding the critical and creative vocabulary in the *kathakali* lexicon by regularly commenting on the choreography. Paul wrote of *Ramanatakam* that 'the ingenuity of the choreographers [Kalamandalam M.P.S. Namboodiri and Kalamandalam Vasu Pisharody] could be felt on many occasions' (1995: 26). From the perspective of a number of today's *kathakali* actor-dancers who sense an increasing lethargy and indifference among many of their traditional audiences at temple performances, there is a growing desire both to grow in their art through such experiments and to take *kathakali* to new audiences.

The controversies and contestations over 'experimentation' are in part constructed around issues of what is or is not viewed as legitimized authority. In Chapter 2 we saw that Margi was engaged in three modes of 'experimentation': restoring 'lost' scenes to plays-in-performance, restaging plays no longer in the active repertory, and 'elaborating' ever longer interpolations into the performance of scenes in the repertory. However, their experiments are usually not thought of as 'experiments' *per se* since the elaborations and reconstructions are easily legitimized by citation of authoritative sources within the tradition. The further experiments move away from what is perceived as legitimized by an authoritative source, or to 'what is appropriate' to the tradition, the greater the possibility and likelihood of challenge and controversy.

KATHAKALI ON THE 1960S EXPERIMENTAL
STAGE: ASIF CURRIMBHOY'S *THE DUMB
DANCER*

One experiment which is clearly outside the
tradition, but which illustrates the historical
desire among modern dramatists throughout
India to return to their 'roots' and indigenous
traditions, is Bengali Asif Currimbhoy's 1961
drama, *The Dumb Dancer*. This is the first
experimental modern drama to make use of
kathakali thematically as well as in performance,
and deserves discussion as a model of the non-
traditional use and influence of *kathakali* within
modern Indian drama – a subject seldom if ever
discussed among those 'within' the *kathakali*
community of interest. Educated at the University
of California-Berkeley and a member of the
Calcutta Writer's Workshop, Currimbhoy wrote
approximately thirty plays in English between
1959 and 1989. Along with *The Hungry Ones*, *The
Dumb Dancer* was produced and performed at
Ellen Stewart's La Mama Theater in New York
during the 1960s. *The Dumb Dancer*, *The Refugee*,
and *The Hungry Ones* were subsequently
translated into Malayalam by well-known
Malayali scholar K.M. George so that he could
introduce 'this talented Indian playwright to the
Malayalam reading public' (George n.d.: 10).

Making use of *kathakali*, and more specifically
of an episode from *The Killing of Duryodhana* as
a 'dance play within the play,' Currimbhoy's *The
Dumb Dancer* moves fluidly between the past and
present, 'reality' and 'madness.' Not unlike other
experimental plays of the 1960s, *The Dumb
Dancer* explores that liminal, loosely 'Jungian'
netherworld where the 'madness' of the insane
asylum becomes a site for exploring the allure of
a heightened 'real' – the ambiguous 'dark' side of
self, passion, myth, madness that 'acting,' through
its transformative process of 'becoming,' is often
represented as signifying. In this case, *kathakali*
is the appropriately 'exotic' style of acting that
Currimbhoy chooses for this 'mad' journey, and
the bloody scene of the epic hero, Bhima's
disembowelment of Dussassana from *The Killing
of Duryodhana*, becomes the highly theatrical
vehicle for the 'existential' blurring of these lines
between 'reality' and 'madness.'

The main character, Bhima, is a student of
kathakali dance-drama. In Act II, which is a
flashback scene set during Bhima's rigorous
training, we discover that through relentless
practise he is attempting to please his teacher and
become the 'greatest' *kathakali* artist/actor
possible. During a rehearsal of the climactic scene
of *The Killing of Duryodhana*, Bhima is playing
the role of his namesake, the epic hero, Bhima,
while the blind musician/singer Madhu sings the
text for him as he acts. At the conclusion of the
rehearsal, Bhima asks his teacher, 'I was greater
than he [Madhu], was I not? Was I not? [*Guru
does not reply.*] Well . . . was I not?' When his
guru responds, 'No,' Bhima becomes angry, and
presses his guru to demonstrate how and why
Madhu is 'greater.' When the guru suggests that
he 'cannot teach' Bhima the kind of artistic
sensitivity that Madhu possesses, he also suggests
that perhaps Madhu's genius is due to his
blindness since 'Those that lack one of the senses
develop an unerring accuracy in another. That is
part of the explanation. The rest . . . is his own
creation' (Currimbhoy 1961: 45). The guru tells
Bhima to 'Get back to work' since 'there can be
no greatness . . . without sacrifice. Speech
interferes for you . . . Practise being the dumb
dancer' (ibid.).

Immediately, Bhima cuts out his tongue,
throwing it '*at the feet of his Guru.*' Through his
'dumbness' he compulsively wants to match the
blind singer Madhu's depth and subtlety of
sensory awareness, and therefore further plumb
the 'depths' and subtleties of his art. Having
crossed this transgressive line, we find out later
that Bhima believes that he has actually become
his namesake, and in playing the *kathakali* play
The Killing of Duryodhana thinks he has actually
killed Dussassana and disembowelled him.

Act I opens with Bhima in full *kathakali* style
costume and make-up playing the role of Bhima
in the climactic scene of Bhima's
disembowelment of Dussassana.[3] However, it is
soon revealed that this scene is taking place in
an unusual setting – it is a performance arranged
in a surgical Operational Theater by Prema, a
young female psychiatrist who is the
Superintendent of a mental asylum. In addition
to the omniscient audience, two other 'audiences'
are also watching the *kathakali* performance, but
oblivious to each other – the inmates of the
asylum on the right, and a group of well-dressed
interns and doctors who politely witness the
performance as a 'social occasion' (ibid.: 12) on

the left. The performance has been organized by Prema, who has become both romantically and professionally obsessed with the handsome young actor-dancer, and desires to cure him at any cost. Since Bhima 'is likely to lapse into a state of permanent insanity,' she chooses to attempt a 'drastic turn-around' by having Bhima replay the scene that caused his illness – the bloody scene of the killing of Dussassana which culminates with Bhima washing the hair of the violated Draupadi in Dussassana's blood. When the scene is first 'therapeutically' played out in Act I, the other actors are *kathakali* actors from outside the asylum; therefore, in Prema's opinion, for Bhima it was 'not real enough . . . graphic enough . . . to make him live through it again' (ibid.: 22–3).

The obsessive/compulsive Prema can be read as both Currimbhoy's (male) fantasy as well as a reflection of the Western/cosmopolitan 1960s counter-cultural view of the allure of 'madness' – a kind of South Asian 'Marat/Sade.' Currimbhoy translates the *kathakali* play's title as *Duryodhana's Slaughter*, emphasizing the killing, not as a sacrificial rite linked to traditional notions of kingship and duty central to *ksatriya* identity discussed earlier, but as part of a quasi-Jungian reading of the attraction of the bloody 'gore' representing the 'dark side' of our experience and persona to be explored fully in order to understand more deeply one's inner/existential dark side or 'reality.' While doing her 'man's job,' Prema deliberately rejects the advances of her male surgeon/colleague Dilip and personalizes her involvement and investment in Bhima's 'cure.' Since 'he cannot speak, the study must go deeper . . . on a personalized basis . . . until it becomes a living experience for doctor and patient' (ibid.: 56). Prema represents the allure of the 1960s flirtation with 'danger' – Bhima is the forbidden 'mad' male, and as such his mad world is 'the inner depth of an ocean' where 'a vertigo' beckons her (ibid.: 23). For her, Bhima is a 'thing of beauty.' She reacts with jealousy when the Guru and his daughter, Shakuntala, come to visit Bhima, and Shakuntala reveals that in their innocent childhood he created her as his Draupadi in their play. Prema's desire/passion for Bhima is literally played out in Act III, Scene 1 in Prema's office when, noticing that he is sweating after exercising, she begins to rub him down with oil – '*her movements becoming more passionate, more irregular between its restraint and desire*' (ibid.: 53). Eventually it is Prema who in the final scene of the play 'enters' the world of Bhima's 'madness' by becoming Draupadi in the last playing of *The Killing of Duryodhana*. Prema falls victim to the dark 'vertigo . . . the vortex . . . I found myself slipping into the terrifying abyss of darkness . . . slipping, slipping without being able to hold myself back' (ibid.: 74). Prema ultimately enters this world completely, slaughtering her young female rival, Shakuntala, so that she can provide Bhima with the 'real' blood to wash *her* hair as she herself fully enters the role of Draupadi in her attempt to 'bring about . . . a drastic turn-around' for Bhima (ibid.: 56).

As an educated, cosmopolitan Bengali Muslim writing in English, Currimbhoy's understanding, appreciation, and use of *kathakali* is that of an artistic and even cultural 'outsider.' Writing during the 1960s, and very much a part of the period, he selected those aspects and interpretations of *kathakali* which to 'outsiders' most exemplify its exotic difference from a 'modern,' cosmopolitan sensibility – its 'dark' blood letting, and the 'dumbness' of the actors – a term that had been used pejoratively by English-educated commentators earlier in this century. His experimental use of *kathakali* obviously was never intended to serve *kathakali* or its typical aesthetic proclivities and indulgences, but rather his own ends as a modern playwright intrigued by the fine line between madness and reality. This is the territory of Carl Jung's (limited) vision and understanding of *kathakali*, and of a 1960s Western acting psychology – a psychology which assumes that gaining a sense of one's 'full' self involves erasing the personal distinctions between the 'roles' one plays and one's (darker/hidden) inner self, or complete 'identification.' Eventually it is Prema that represents the desire to cross that line to the other side of the forbidden.

The Dumb Dancer is a form of experimentation in which *kathakali* serves literally, metaphorically, and theatrically as a source for creating an experiment in which *kathakali* represents 'itself' as an identifiable genre and tradition of performing traditional epic stories, but in which the epic heroes and story, and traditional techniques cannot be contained by their traditional references.

Although experiments like *The Dumb Dancer* are rare, a similar premise served as the basis for an extraordinary collaborative experimental film *Marattam* between Malayali theater director K.M. Panikkar, and internationally known film-maker Aravindan. Only screened a few times, and never for more than restricted 'art' audiences, *Marattam* is filmed in one seemingly unending take as it too explores the line between 'reality' onstage and off through a *kathakali* performance of *The Killing of Kichaka*.

KATHAKALI KING LEAR

I turn now to a second, quite different, and more recent experiment – this time with non-traditional content. On 28 July 1989 I attended the inaugural performance of a *kathakali* version of Shakespeare's *King Lear* (*Kathakali King Lear*) on the proscenium stage of the Victorian-styled V.J.T. Hall, Trivandrum, Kerala, India.[4] The European premiere took place on 2 September 1989 at the Festival of Rovereto, Italy, followed by two and a half months of performances in the Netherlands, France, and Spain. A second international touring production appeared in Singapore as part of its 25th Independence Day celebrations and at the Edinburgh Theater Festival in August 1990.[5] Australian playwright/director David McRuvie and French actor-dancer Annette LeDay originally conceived *Kathakali King Lear*, and the first production was co-produced by their Association Keli (Paris) with the Kerala State Arts Academy (Kerala Kalamandalam, Cheruthuruthy, Kerala, India). Scripted by McRuvie in English and originally translated by Iyyamgode Sridharan (poet and at that time Secretary of the Kerala Kalamandalam) into Malayalam, *Kathakali King Lear* was choreographed and rehearsed collaboratively at the Kalamandalam by McRuvie, LeDay (who also played Cordelia), and a group of highly regarded senior *kathakali* artists (K. Kumaran Nayar (King Lear), C. Padmanabhan Nayar (King Lear), Kalamandalam Gopi (France), K.P. Krishnankutty Poduval (percussion), T.K. Appukutty Poduval (percussion), Madambi Subramaniam Namboodiri (vocalist)) whose approval for undertaking the project was secured well in advance of rehearsals.

With its Western content, its highly conventionalized *kathakali mise-en-scène* and techniques, its collaborative process of conceptualization and realization, and its performances in continental Europe, Edinburgh, Singapore, and Kerala, *Kathakali King Lear* was certainly 'intercultural' in both production and reception. The production prompted considerable critical response and/or debate in a number of locations:

1   within Kerala among connoisseurs and journalists writing in both the Malayalam and English language presses about the 'limits' of the *kathakali* tradition and the value of such experiments with non-traditional roles and content;

2   in the European press where discussions and responses focused on *kathakali*'s attractions as a dance in response to the continental tour;

3   in the UK press where responses focused on the Edinburgh festival production as a specific interpretation of Shakespeare's *Lear*;

4   in academic circles where the production has been analysed, applauded, and/or vilified as an example of intercultural performance (Zarrilli 1991; Awasthi 1993; Bennett 1996).

From its inception, the producers of *Kathakali King Lear* intended the production to be more than a superficial dressing up of Shakespeare's *Lear* in colorful *kathakali* costumes as an exotic novelty for Western audiences. Rather, it was to serve as an intercultural experiment in production and reception, opening in Kerala for Malayali audiences and then touring continental Europe. For Malayalis the production was intended to provide a *kathakali* experience of one of Shakespeare's great plays and roles. Assuming that many European and especially UK audiences would know Shakespeare's play, the production was intended as an accessible way of experiencing *kathakali* and the aesthetic delight of *rasa*. For LeDay and McRuvie, *kathakali*'s 'rich means of expression and its intensity of effect' seemed an appropriate performative means through which to 'find a theatrical expression for the larger-than-life dimension and explosive power of the play' (LeDay and McRuvie 1989: 1).

Following theater semiotician Patrice Pavis, the lengthy process of adaptation and translation which created *Kathakali King Lear* might best be described as a series of *re-elaborations* of text, gesture, and choreography into a new frame (ibid.: 50). The process began with McRuvie's re-elaboration of the *King Lear* text to conform with *kathakali*'s theatrical criteria in length, action, and number of characters – a process which radically transformed the original. The typed English adaptation ran barely twenty pages for the two-hour plus performance. The action focused exclusively on Lear and his three daughters. The Gloucester subplot was completely cut, as were Kent, Cornwall, and Albany. Only eight characters appeared including Lear, his three daughters (Cordelia, Goneril, and Regan), the King of France (in a somewhat expanded role), the Fool, mad Tom, and a soldier. Each of nine scenes – (1) King Lear Divides His Kingdom; (2) The Departure of Cordelia and France; (3) At Goneril's Palace; (4) At Regan's Palace; (5) The Storm; (6) The Return of Cordelia and France; (7) The Reconciliation of Lear and Cordelia; (8) The Battle; (9) the Death of Lear – was organized around one or two major dramatic actions. For example, the first scene enacted the division of the kingdom and banishment of Cordelia. The second scene dramatized the wedding and departure of Cordelia and France in which Cordelia expresses her sorrow at leaving her father, and pledges herself to her husband.

McRuvie rendered his English adaptation into a somewhat simplified version of the three major components of a traditional *kathakali* performance script: narrative passages (*sloka*) in third person describing the context of the action, dialogue passages (*padam*) sung by the onstage vocalists and spoken by the actors through hand-gestures, and passages (*attam*) delivered in gesture language and mimetic dance by the actors but not sung by the onstage vocalists. The *sloka* and *padam* were then translated into Malayalam and set in the appropriate musical mode for the vocalists and/or rhythm for the percussionists.

The production ensemble also carried out a series of specific spatial, gestural, choreographic, and musical re-elaborations of McRuvie's translated text to fit *kathakali*'s theatrical conventions – a process which required reinterpretation of a number of *kathakali* conventions as well as the creation of one new role (*vesam*). Since the *vesam*, literally 'dress, mask, disguise' which is the 'whole outward appearance, shape' (Gundert 1872: 995), determines not only the external contours but also the basic nature of each character an actor

plays, the decision on each *vesam* was the actor's beginning place in trying to create roles for which there was no tradition to follow. A few roles were obvious and easy to select: the heroic King France, who marries Cordelia, defeats her evil sisters, and attempts to return Lear to his throne, had to be played as a *pacca* – the primarily green-colored, ideal, heroic, kingly type of character; Cordelia, the devoted, loving, chaste daughter had to be played as a female 'radiant' type; Mad Tom could be played as a 'special' type (*teppu*) close to animal in nature, and therefore with a smeared black-face.

The selection of *vesam* for the other major characters, including Goneril, Regan, the Fool, and Lear, generated considerable controversy in Kerala. For Lear the 'knife' (*katti*) *vesam* was selected since its mixture of green and red symbolized his combination of kingly and turbulent attributes. For the first production, and in keeping with *kathakali* convention, the role of Lear was split into two parts, each to be played by a senior *kathakali* actor: the fully costumed Lear who appears at the opening of the play in court through the moment in the storm scene when he removes his crown and ornaments to become like mad Tom; and the partially costumed mad Lear on the heath. For Goneril and Regan the *kari vesam*, typically used for demoness roles, was selected and each was costumed in black and blue respectively, symbolizing their primitive nature. Finally, for the Fool, no *kathakali vesam* existed; however,

Plate 9.1 Kathakali King Lear. *Goneril (right) bows before her father as Cordelia (left) asks herself, 'What shall Cordelia speak? Love, and be silent'*
Photo credit: Annette LeDay and David McRuvie.

the brahmin clown (*vidusaka*) who serves as the king's court fool in the *kutiyattam* Sanskrit drama tradition, provided the closest model adapted for the production.

Appropriate ways of enacting each role and scene were developed in the collaborative rehearsal process. Beginning with the basic *vesam* in which each role was to be played, the spatial, choreographic, gestural, and musical elements were carefully re-elaborated to fit the non-indigenous narrative and the peculiarities of the story's characters. Vasudevan Namboodiripad, former Superintendent of the Kerala Kalamandalam who served as an advisor for the production, explained that LeDay and McRuvie made sure that the production was more than a superficial appropriation of *kathakali* conventions and techniques:

> Thought had to be given to not only the outer structure of *kathakali*, but also to the inner structure and nuance. For example, for King Lear's initial entrance with his 'curtain look' (*tiranokku*), you retain the visible structure of the look but you may change the inner structure of the nuance of expression in the look. The ultimate purpose of the curtain look is kept, but these subtle changes are made. Otherwise, it is just a copy of the same scene from any

other curtain look of any other play in the repertory. To accomplish this, you must have people like Padmanabhan Asan [playing Lear] who have the capacity to analyse the character's inner state or condition (*bhava*). From this analysis every phrase must be worked out in detail.

(interview, 1989)

This sensitivity to the nuance of expressive interpretation was one reason for the decision that LeDay would play Cordelia. McRuvie explained his view of the centrality of the Cordelia role to me: 'What makes *King Lear* great is a great king, which is rare. Second in making the king is the Fool. But the one thing that can ruin it is Cordelia' (interview, 1989). To McRuvie's decidedly Western eye, potential disaster threatened if one of the young male actors specializing in female roles (*strivesam*) were to act the 'delicate role of Cordelia' in what McRuvie correctly characterized as 'their boyish quality . . . that becomes kind of campy.'[6]

The lengthy process of re-elaboration created a completely new performance text that would provide both Malayali and European audiences with a new performance experience – a *kathakali*-style production of Shakespeare.

*[handwritten margin note: * 'campy' – qualities similar to pantomime]*

Plate 9.2 *In the midst of the storm mad Tom is discovered by Lear and the Fool. Lear: 'Unaccommodated man is not more but such a poor, bare, forked animal as thou art'*
Photo credit: Annette LeDay and David McRuvie.

PRODUCTION, PERCEPTION, AND RECEPTION

Although *Kathakali King Lear* was originally re-elaborated for continental European and Malayali audiences, in fact, it played for audiences in four quite different cultural locations on its first two tours: not only Kerala and continental Europe, but also at the Singapore and Edinburgh international festivals. Both between and within each set of cultural boundaries there are 'different viewing publics' (Bennett 1990: 101), each of which brought to the production not only their own 'native' cultural assumptions but also an increasingly global flow of ideas, images, and information all of which affected their expectations about what they would experience, their perceptions and categories for understanding that experience, and therefore how they received and responded to *Kathakali King Lear*. How are we to understand reception of *Kathakali King Lear* among such diverse audiences?

Phenomenologist Maurice Natanson explains that our perceptions are shaped by a consciousness that posits horizons of probabilities which constitute expectations (1973: *passim*). In performance, expectations are created in four interdependent ways:

1 The daily experiences and cultural assumptions that inform the experience that each spectator brings to the performance.
2 Performance experiences similar to or different from the one that each is having now.
3 Expectations created by publicity, word of mouth, etc.
4 What happens within the frame of the performance one is attending.

In the fourth mode, a set of expectations is created as the performance is enacted.

The way in which *kathakali* structures an audience's experience creates the possibility for a particular range of meaning very different from other genres of performance whether that is American psychological realism or Japanese *noh*. Likewise, the way in which a Shakespeare play and its characters create the possibility for a particular range of meaning is very different from other types of dramas such as any of the *kathakali* plays translated here, or such diverse genres as melodrama or a contemporary American musical.

As theater semiotician Marco De Marinis, following Umberto Eco, asserts, 'Production and reception are strictly linked even though they obviously do not altogether coincide . . . [and that] a [performance] text postulates its own receiver as an indispensible condition not only of its own, concrete communicative ability, but also its own potential for meaning' (1987: 102). We have seen how *kathakali*, as a genre of performance, postulates both a general audience and one of connoisseurs educated to receive a range of cultural meanings implicit in the conventions used to enact its stories. Each specific *kathakali* play-in-performance articulates a specific set of meanings for both these generic audiences and its particular audiences. Like other adaptations of *kathakali*, such as P.K. Devan's one-hour performances for tourists in Ernakulam, Kerala, *Kathakali King Lear* postulated its own receiver in the process of re-elaboration described above, and possesses its own potential for meaning different from other *kathakali*.

When *kathakali* performances of Indian epic stories are held for Kerala audiences, it may often be said with reception theorist Anne Ubersfeld that the

> signs refer to what corresponds to them in the experience of the spectator. The fictional universe set before him [sic] summons up the referential universe of the spectator, that of his personal as well as his cultural experience.
>
> (1982: 131)

In intercultural performance, however, codes and conventions easily read by those within one culture may be opaque to those outside. Those working interculturally have evolved a number of different production strategies for dealing with this fundamental problem. Peter Brook's recent production of India's great epic, *The Mahabharata*, demonstrates one strategy. For Brook 'art means extracting the essence from every detail so that the detail can reveal itself as a meaningful part of an inseparable whole' (Carriere 1987: xiv). Brook problematically assumes that if one can erase all the cultural codes in the way of reaching a hypothetically universal 'reality of zero' common to all humanity, then 'geography and history cease to exist' (Schechner 1986: 55). Brook works with an international acting company whose style attempts to reach this zero state of communication by removing any cultural marks which might require of the audience the ability to read any special cultural codes. Consequently, 'to tell [the Mahabharata] we had to avoid evoking India too strongly so as to not lead us away from human identification, but also we had to nevertheless tell it as a story rooted in Indian earth' (ibid.: 68).[7]

If Brook erases distinctive cultural codes in his attempt to be universal, LeDay and McRuvie chose to challenge their European audiences by maintaining as much of *kathakali*'s structure and technique as possible.[8] Given the fact that *Kathakali King Lear* was originally re-elaborated for two quite different audiences, played in four quite different geographical/cultural contexts, and has conventions or content that are non-indigenous to one or more of its audiences,[9] I want to ask the following questions: Who was the receiver postulated by the production? What potential meanings and/or experiences were implicit in the production? What meanings were read into the production? Specifically how was the production received?

European reception: from 'curiosity' to 'bewitching ritual' to a 'moving performance'

For anyone watching something from outside one's own 'culture' for the first time there is bound to be some degree of difference in assimilation and understanding of what is being seen and heard between an indigenous and non-indigenous audience. Moreover, as Anne Ubersfeld explains,

> when he is faced with signs which he does not understand to which he cannot give a name (objects, gestures, discourse), which do not refer to anything in his experience, or, more simply, which pose a problem for him, the spectator's own inventiveness is stimulated: it is up to him to manufacture the relationship between the sign and its intelligibility, or its relationship to the world.
>
> (1982: 133)

The West has a long and continuing history of manufacturing a variety of meanings for non-indigenous customs, persons, or cultural artifacts/performances it could not (or did not wish to) understand. Historically, the West took this experience of difference, and encapsulated it in a series of discourses on the cultural Other.[10] In the Western-initiated colonial drama of subjugation and domination, India was cast in several key roles. Most importantly, as South Asian historian Ronald Inden relates, for empiricists and rationalists that role was 'THE unchangeable' and/or 'THE *absolutely* different' (and therefore inscrutable and dominatable), and for romantics, the 'SPIRITUAL or IDEAL' Other (1986: 402–46). As the period of colonial expansion reached its final climax at the turn of the nineteenth century, this drama of subjugation and domination was played out symbolically rather than literally at the 'World's' Fairs (Benedict 1983; Rydell 1984) and even at Coney Island and other amusement parks where exotic Indian nautch dancers were featured in the Durbar of Delhi. Our abilities to read, understand,

assimilate, and even participate in Indian performance have been shaped by these discourses of Otherness which feed both our imagination of Otherness and the way we describe it.[11]

Kathakali King Lear generated all these responses and more. On continental Europe, the original production was received with great and near universal acclaim by French dance critics who filled their columns with information on *kathakali* interspersed with comments which ranged from F.C.'s vacuous but appreciative 'a splendidly colorful show' (1989), to Pichot's more adamant expression of appreciation – 'a dazzling marriage' of *kathakali* and Shakespeare filled with 'intensity, energy, and extravaganza' (1989). Not surprisingly, in Shakespeare's home, responses focused on the production as a specific interpretation of Shakespeare's *Lear* rather than on *kathakali per se*. The colorfully opinionated British theater press greeted the Edinburgh Festival performances with less than universal praise where it reaped everything from Michael Billington's cynical scorn ('Empty gestures of a frustrating Lear') (1990), to Charles Spencer's appreciative evocation of the production as both exotic and mysterious ('Hypnotic power of an Indian Lear') (1990), to Randall Stevenson's grudging appreciation ('Beat of a different drum') which marvelled that even if 'Shakespeare transformed into the traditional, colorful, highly stylised dance drama of Kerala . . . doesn't sound entirely promising . . . [It is] one of the most enthralling performances of the Festival' (1990). The one near-universal point of agreement among most of the British press was that *Kathakali King Lear* had, as Tom Morris put it, 'little to do with Shakespeare' (1990).

Beyond the general praise and blame, there were those like the reviewer from the *Cannes-Matin/Nice-Matin* who found the production inscrutable and difficult to decode: 'we do not have all of the keys to this code, which allows us only sporadically to decipher them' ('L'histoire du roi Lear' 1989). For the writer from *La Presse de la Manche* the only pleasure of the production was the spectacle of the costumes:

> The costumes are the main attraction of the show at least for the western audience, incapable of understanding the complex language of the hand and face gestures,

somewhere between mime and a sign language conversation.

('Le Roi Lear version Kathakali' 1989)

For Sergio Trombetta from *La Danse* this inscrutability made the spectacle fascinating: 'The interplay of the dance, the facial expressions and the hands remain impenetrable and fascinating' (1989).

Some like Grandmontagne writing for *Le Telegramme* responded to the difficulties of reading the production by inventing *kathakali* as a romantic, timeless, Jungian dream-like world:

> Without any training, you can appreciate this theater by allowing yourself to be invaded by the music, by the rhythms; by marvelling at the splendid, glittering, colorful costumes, the make-up that completely re-sculpts the actors' faces and make them timeless even while accentuating the expression of each individual character . . .
> You can, without any training, be subjugated, letting the music intoxicate you.
>
> (1989)

Pierre Gilles responded similarly, finding in the production a realization of a universal Artaudian reverie in which

> the drama of the aging King Lear . . . [was] promoted to the ranks of the sacred, rendered to the 'primitive destination' of theater – which Artaud sought – and, therefore, to the universal.
>
> (1989)

The most extreme problem with response is when either too many demands are made on the spectator so that she withdraws her participation (Ubersfeld 1982: 133), or an audience member is unwilling to make any attempt to respond to the performance and therefore withdraws his participation. It appears that the latter may have been the case for John Percival of *The Times*, who in a remarkably snide, nothing short of racist, tongue-in-cheek commentary entitled 'Lear's heath at half blast' ungenerously wrote of the vocalists as 'two fellows with skirts, bare chests and cymbals,' of Tom as a 'dirty little chap,' of the adaptation as 'crippling,' and the production as a 'curiosity' (1990).

If, for some, *Kathakali King Lear* was inscrutable, or all spectacle, for others the production communicated at more than a level of surface exoticism. I think it an oversimplification to assume with Bennett that 'audiences are at best "fascinated" with performances that do not fall into their cultural experience, performances that resist or deny the usual channels of decoding' (1990: 103). Randall Stevenson provides a balanced and sensible account of his fascination with *kathakali*'s spectacle, his simple enjoyment of its exciting moments of obvious and colorful action, as well as the subtler way in which the performance affected him.

> From the opening moment, when the screen brought on to signal scene changes drops to reveal magnificently poised and costumed performers, Kathakali offered spectacle and simple excitement. The two onstage percussionists add a mesmeric heartbeat to every move and turn onstage – creating a devastating prelude to the storm, for example – while the singers who chant the narrative fill in tone and color for every scene. More subtly, what seems 'simple' spectacle quickly communicates a great deal of emotion. Stylized movement, minute repeated hand-gestures, progressively indicate Lear's poised withdrawal, even before Goneril's ecstatic devil dance steals a vision of insanity and the stresses which create it.
>
> (1990)

The argument I want to make regarding the kind of reception of *Kathakali King Lear* represented by Stevenson's review depends upon a prior understanding of the Malayali reception.

Malayali reception: from 'bouquets to brickbats'

Although *Kathakali King Lear* was originally co-produced by the Kerala State government arts school, featured some of the most distinguished performers of the *kathakali* stage, played well over thirty performances on its contental tour and at Edinburgh, and, with the important exceptions noted above in the British press, was generally appreciated and praised on tour, *Indian*

Express journalist Paul Jacob recalled one year after the original production that it opened in Kerala to 'no great critical or popular acclaim' (1990). As early as the January 1989 experimental staging of four scenes at the Kerala Kalamandalam, the production aroused considerable controversy in Kerala – a situation reflected in the *Hindu* staff writer's report that 'comments from the spectators . . . came out in the form of a mixed bag of bouquets and brickbats' ('"*King Lear*" in Kathakali,' 1989).

In Kerala during the final months of rehearsal before the production opened, I read and heard the artistic and aesthetic 'brickbats' thrown at the production. Debated both within rehearsals and in the public and press, the controversy swirled around the following five issues all having to do with the 'sense of appropriateness' (*aucityam bodham*) in *kathakali*:

1   Were non-Indian, non-epic, non-mythic stories like *Lear* appropriate for the *kathakali* stage?
2   To what degree was the title character of Lear kingly?
3   Was the selection of the 'knife' make-up (*katti vesam*) appropriate for Lear, or should the heroic 'green' (*pacca*) have been selected?
4   During the storm scene was it appropriate to have Lear 'realistically' remove part or all of his kingly accoutrements and typifying make-up, or should his relative 'nakedness' have been imagined by the audience?
5   Was it appropriate to borrow the clown's (*vidusaka*) make-up and costume directly from *kutiyattam*?

As is evident in all five of these issues, and as discussed in Chapters 3 and 4, the paradigmatic past is present for the *kathakali* actor each time he approaches any important role on the stage, and his performance will be judged on the degree of appropriateness of each choice he makes during a performance. Although *Kathakali King Lear* was a new production for which no precedents had been set for particular roles, there was very real pressure felt by some of the actors that they would be severely criticized for transgressing the boundaries of appropriateness. This was especially true of Balasubramaniam who, just reaching the age of maturity as a performer, originated the role of the Fool in a costume/make-up (*vesham*) over which

controversy raged to and past the official opening production.

All five issues are part of a continuing 'internal cultural debate' (Parkin 1978: *passim*) within the *kathakali* cultural community over the limits of experimentation within the tradition. As there are wide differences of opinion on these issues, my task here is to represent several parties to the debate, situate each point of view so that the terms of argument informing each is clear, and discuss how this internal debate shaped perception and reception of *Kathakali King Lear*.

I will explore Malayali response to the production primarily through the eyes of one of the most visible and certainly the most outspoken champions of a radically conservative interpretation of the *kathakali* tradition,

Plate 9.3   *Lear is revealed after he has removed his ornaments and crown to be like Mad Tom at the Kerala Kalamandalam dress rehearsal. A great deal of controversy was raised when Kumaran Asan appeared as depicted here bareheaded and virtually without makeup*

Photo credit: Kunju Vasudevan Namboodiripad.

Plate 9.4 *For the Thiruvananthapuram performances and subsequent tour, more of the original costume and make-up were kept for Kumaran Asan's mad Lear. The trial scene in which Lear says, 'Anatomize Regan; see what breeds about her heart.'*

Photo credit: Annette LeDay and David McRuvie.

Appakoothan Nayar, one of the founders of the Margi Kathakali School in the capital city, Thiruvananthapuram. An engineer by training who holds a graduate degree from the University of Michigan, Appakoothan Nayar is the architect who designed the Kerala Kalamandalam Kuttambalam Theater discussed in Chapter 2. Not surprisingly, his response to *Kathakali King Lear* was straightforward and blunt: 'I could not stand it . . . Even though there are thirty performances abroad, after five years, nobody here will remember it. It will die a natural death' (interview, 1989). To understand Appakoothan Nayar's negative response to *Kathakali King Lear*, it is necessary to recall his discussion of a 'nonworldly' 'aesthetic of the mind' in Chapter 2.

Appakoothan Nayar differentiates between two levels of aesthetic realization. The first and 'lower' aesthetic he calls 'sensual' or 'worldly' because it limits reception to the feelings of the five senses. Such reception is a simplistic and immediate sensual response, i.e., 'when you see [touch, taste, feel, etc.] a thing you like it, but it

doesn't go to the mind.' An example is the appearance of an everyday character like the elephant mahoot in *Kamsavadham*, or the Midwife in *The Progeny of Krishna*, where the spectator's simple recognition of the character could be characterized as sensual, immediate, and based on what one sees in daily life.

In contrast, the second aesthetic is what Appakoothan Nayar calls an 'aesthetics of the mind,' i.e., an act of reception which resonates long beyond the immediate apprehension of the five senses. It is an aesthetic built on the cultivation of the aesthetic sensibilities of the connoisseur's tasting and savoring of *rasa*, as discussed earlier. This interpretation of *kathakali*'s aesthetic as 'of the mind' is derived from *kutiyattam* and the classical Sanskrit drama tradition. Sanskrit scholar Barbara Stoller Miller calls the aesthetic of the most celebrated Sanskrit poet Kalidasa an 'aesthetic of memory' and identifies Sanskrit theater as a 'theater of memory' (1984: *passim*). In many Sanskrit dramas such as Kalidasa's *Sakuntala* and Bhasa's *The Vision of Vasavadatta*, the act of remembering is both a literal mode of reconciling and relating love-in-separation and love-in-union and remembrance of a 'deeper metaphysical kind' (Stoller Miller 1984: 40).

> Indian epistemologists hold that whatever we perceive by means of the sense organs leaves an impression on the mind. Memory occurs when a latent impression is awakened. Indian literary theorists define memory as a recollection of a condition of happiness or misery, whether it was conceived in the mind or actually occurred. In what is considered one of the key passages of Sanskrit aesthetics, the tenth-century Kashmiri philosopher Abhinavagupta explains what Kalidasa means by 'memory.' It is not discursive recollection of past events, but rather an intuitive insight into the past that transcends personal experience, into the imaginative universe that beauty evokes.
>
> (ibid.: 40)

This aesthetic of mind is accomplished through extended narrative and performative elaboration of the basic story and playtext. The poetic conceits imbedded in a *padam*, such as Nala's description of Damayanti (see pp. 44–5, Chapter

3), provide opportunities for the actor to embody each image through gesture language, thereby serving as the vehicle for the creation of an image of Damayanti not only in Nala's mind, but also in the mind of the spectator.

From Appakoothan Nayar's point of view, it is precisely these moments of superb 'interior acting' which epitomize an aesthetic of the mind and inform his critique of *Kathakali King Lear*. The two major problems with *Kathakali King Lear* are its all too brief two hour running time, and its non-epic characters. In contrast to *King Lear* where everything 'has been cut short,' Appakoothan Nayar is proud of the fact that the recent Margi production of Variyar's *Nalacaritam* expanded its running time to thirty hours to allow more elaboration. Appakoothan Nayar told me how one friend commented,

> 'If you go on like this it will come to 365 days!' and I said, 'it will go on to one thousand days!' And this is precisely why I don't like *Kathakali King Lear*. The potential for elaboration *must* be there. In most [new] *kathakali* they simply translate the text into gestures and say, 'that's *kathakali*.' But that is *not kathakali*! You must take the text and see how much scope there is for expansion and decoration.

From Appakoothan Nayar's perspective, it is impossible to elaborate non-epic stories because the characters are 'not fit for *kathakali*.' Unlike epic characters who 'never existed' and therefore must be created in the imagination of the spectator, Appakoothan Nayar reasons that Lear, like Jesus, Karl Marx, or Franklin Roosevelt is an historical figure who at one time existed and therefore for whom one has a set of associations.

> Although one has images of epic characters, the image is not supported by any visual comparison because the characters never existed. Ravana is supposed to have ten heads and twenty hands – can he ever have existed in any stage of human evolution?[12] Lear's features you know because he was a human being. But in the case of Ravana, he is the concretization of a concept . . . The concretization of the abstract is there [in ritual and theatrical arts] in order to reach the abstract.[13]

For Appakoothan Nayar, *kathakali* is a metaphysical theater of the imagination where the spectator 'creates [each character] in his mind,' and for Appakoothan Nayar-the-spectator his ability to imagine freely or 'take in his mind' a Lear was disrupted 'because I have that [previous] image [of Lear] in mind.'

On the one hand, Appakoothan Nayar's argument against *Kathakali King Lear* is constructed from an aesthetic paradigm of the past – the *rasa* aesthetic – and his institution is an attempt to insure that this aesthetic remains central to *kathakali*'s creativity in the future. It is a paradigm written for and from the privileged position of the traditional patron/connoisseur for whose pleasure *kathakali* was originally created. While his is an inventive form of intercultural discourse in its use of the Western intellectual icons of history and evolution as part of its argument against experimentation, it is a reactionary one which stakes exclusive claim to interpreting what is or is not appropriate within the tradition and what qualifies as a legitimate form of experimentation. Appakoothan Nayar's critique implies a denial of the validity of experiments attempting to reach audiences other than connoisseurs. Such experiments range from *Kathakali King Lear*, to populist adaptations with little elaboration for Malayali mass audiences at annual temple festivals, to the 1987 production of *People's Victory*, discussed in Chapter 10.

AESTHETIC CONGRUENCE AND KINGLY DISSONANCE

Although *Kathakali King Lear* evoked little aesthetic delight in Appakoothan Nayar and some other *kathakali* connoisseurs, for at least some among the European and Malayali audiences the subtlety of *kathakali*'s interior acting was communicated and experienced. I refer especially to the penultimate and ultimate moments of pathos in the production – the seventh and ninth scenes of the production in which Lear is first reunited with Cordelia, and then dies from grief over her loss.

[His crown having been placed beside him by the Fool. Lear slowly wakes. Cordelia stands back, but the Fool urges her to present herself to Lear. Lears sits up.]

LEAR: I do not know whether I am alive or
dead. I do not remember these clothes.
CORDELIA: Sir, do you know me?
LEAR: I fear I am not in my right mind, but I
think you are my child.
CORDELIA: Yes! I am, I am your child!
LEAR: You have cause to hate me.
CORDELIA: No cause, no cause.
LEAR: Forgive me, I am old and foolish.

They embrace. The Soldier appears. He claims
Cordelia and the Fool as prisoners. [After their
departure] *Lear picks up his* kiritam *[crown].*
(McRuvie 1989: mss.)

In the battle which ensues during the eighth
scene, Regan orders her Soldier to kill his
prisoners, Cordelia and the Fool. The order sends
France into a wild fury, played out in *kathakali*'s
typical stylized battle choreography as he slays
both Regan and Goneril. As the final scene
opens, the vocalists create a transition from the
cacophony of battle with its loud-sounding
drums to the pathos of loss and death as they
sing the opening *sloka* in a slow rhythm,
reporting what has happened, and telling what
will happen:

The young Queen and the King's Fool have
been brutally murdered. The old King finds
his beloved daughter dead. He dies from
grief and so ends his terrible suffering.

Even though the Western audience cannot
understand what the vocalists are singing, the
pathos carried by the music alone sets the
appropriate mood. The hand-held curtain is
lowered to reveal Cordelia's body.

Lear enters in full katti vesam. *He walks*
slowly but stands very straight. Lear
approaches Cordelia. He turns her head and
recognizes her. He screams with grief. He falls
down beside his daughter.

LEAR: I know when someone is alive or dead.
My child is as dead as earth.

In spite of reservations about certain aspects of
the production, reviewers of the Edinburgh
performances in particular focused much of their
positive commentary on Lear's pathos over the

loss of Cordelia. Although Tom Morris, writing in
the *Times Literary Supplement*, responded to
most of the production with 'remote fascination,'
it was different with the closing scene – 'at Lear's
cry over the dead Cordelia, magical and spot-lit,
there is a frightening and uninterrupted moment
of agonized theatrical communication' (1990).
For Randall Stevenson who responded positively
to the shape, contours, and variety of the entire
production, the closing scene in which Lear dies
of grief was also a profoundly moving moment:

Lear's concluding, rhythmic keening over
Cordelia, picked up by the percussion,
provides almost the first remotely human
sound from performers rather than the
accompanying singers.
It both wrings the heart and moves the
performance forward into another
dimension: towards the awesome,
elemental world from which Shakespeare's
original vision was compounded.
(1990)

Plate 9.5 *Lear: 'She's gone forever'*
Photo credit: Annette LeDay and David McRuvie.

Among Malayalis who responded at least in part favorably, V. Kaldharan acknowledged that both Kumaran Nayar and Padmanabhan Nayar were 'successful in portraying the full depth of King Lear's sorrow (*karuna rasa*)' (1989).

I would suggest that the emotive resonance that Stevenson describes was a moment of aesthetic congruence where at least some among the Edinburgh audience experienced the resonance of aesthetic delight similar to if not the same as a Malayali connoisseur's arousal of *rasa*. As steeped in Shakespeare as a Kerala audience in the Mahabharata and Nala stories, at least some in the Edinburgh audience share a common knowledge of Lear's mental state equal to that of the actors playing the roles. The knowledgeable audience 'knows' that Lear's mental state moves from his deranged, wandering, forgetfulness and impromptu ravings to one of the dawn of remembrance when he awakes from his sleep.

In contrast to Appakoothan Nayar's judgement that there is not sufficient time for elaboration in *Kathakali King Lear*, I want to argue that at least during Scene 7 McRuvie's sparse text allows the *kathakali* performer the time necessary to embody through internal acting the appropriate *bhavas* – *cinta bhava*, 'reflection' or 'remembrance.' Lear, in a dream-like state of forgetfulness, awakens to Cordelia and the Fool. In the process of remembering he gradually remembers Cordelia, his loss of her, his foolishness in rejecting her, and the mental agony of their separation. Although the tone and specific dramatic context and circumstances are quite different, Lear's act of 'reflection' or remembrance is similar to that of Nala. The scene is that moment of classic Western recognition where Lear realizes his loss. It makes possible the Western audience's experience of Lear as a 'tragic' character.

As staged at Edinburgh, the entire final scene could be characterized as Lear's grieving cry over the loss of his beloved daughter. When Lear returns in the final scene to discover the dead Cordelia, he is resplendent in his full costume and make-up. With only one line 'spoken' during the entire scene, Padmanabhan Nayar was free to elaborate through interior acting *soka bhava*, the pathos of his loss, and the moment-by-moment search for any signs that she might still be alive. Since he was playing Lear as a 'knife' (*katti*)

character considered less refined than the idealized kingly *pacca* roles, he was permitted by convention to utter sounds. In his brilliant elaboration of this long dramatic moment, Padmanabhan Nayar chose to make full use of the psychophysical means of embodiment in the *kathakali* repertory, subtly uttering whimpers through the control of his breath, and manifesting other signs of the grief of loss such as trembling. The sounds and signs of Lear's grief gradually draw out of him his own life force (*prana-vayu*), so that he collapses beside his daughter, dead of grief.

The narrative and mimetic simplicity of these scenes meant that it was unnecessary for the Western audience to be able to read *kathakali*'s codified gesture language in order to follow or appreciate the action. Given the familiar trajectory of both the Lear story and the narrative of pathos, at least some in the Edinburgh and European audiences savored *karuna rasa* (pathos) – the closest emotional tone in Indian theater to Western tragedy.

Kathakali King Lear's success at communicating pathos is not unproblematic. The positive reception of Padmanabhan Nayar's empathic cry of loss over Cordelia unquestionably assumes a modernist paradigm of the main character's emotional state as the essence of the pleasure of dramatic reception. It was also a problem for some in the Malayali audience – how could one appreciate a play in which the predominant *rasa* or flavor of aesthetic delight is pathos and in which the King does not act like a (South Asian) KING? Understating the case somewhat, Malayali reviewer Vinita noted, 'It is unusual to conclude a *kathakali* on a tragic note' (1989).[14] But even more problematic was Lear's behavior. *Kathakali* actor Nelliyode Vasudevan Namboodiripad, who played the role of the Fool in the original experimental staging of the storm scene and Goneril on the second tour, described his problems with understanding Lear:

> When Lear's older daughters tell him they love him so much, and Cordelia says she can only give half her love, he believes all these things. It is difficult to believe that Lear, at 80 years of age, with all his life experience, would respond this way to his daughters!
>
> (interview, 1989)

V. Kaladharan raised the same problem in his *Mathrabhumi* article, noting that even master percussionist Krishnankutty Poduval, who helped conceive the production, was puzzled by the fact that Lear would 'forgo his daughter who is prepared to share her love between her father and her husband' (1989). Given the fact that social convention dictates that a daughter will naturally give her love to her husband, and that tragedy and the individual human weaknesses that prompt Lear's downfall have little resonance in Kerala culture where kingship was historically idealized and related to maintenance of the cosmic order, to some Malayalis Lear's behavior toward Cordelia appeared naive, and even silly.

Even with the emergence of a secular national government in the post-Independence period, the ideal model of royal kingship as at the center of the universe discussed in Chapter 8 and exemplified by characters like Rugmamgada, Nala, Rama, etc., continues to shape conceptions of kingship. As Kaladharan concluded, for those in the audience for whom Lear could *not* be perceived as a king, 'the theme which is important for a Western audience becomes totally awkward for an Indian audience' (1989).

Although *Kathakali King Lear* was conceived ideally by its producers as an inter-cultural project to be performed for Kerala and European audiences, the commercial realities (over thirty performances abroad and two in Kerala), the Western Lear narrative, and McRuvie's directorial eye naturally shaped the production for a cosmopolitan, international, and primarily Western theater-going public. In doing so it may not have been as well received by Malayali audiences as Western audiences, but it brought to its Western audiences one type of integrity of process difficult to find in some other intercultural experiments. Unlike Peter Brook's naturalized Mahabharata which 'flattened' (Pavis 1989) the Indianness of the epic's cultural markers and suppressed any use of India's

codified performance techniques, LeDay and McRuvie's project intentionally kept an active tension between a simplified Western narrative played in a fully codified theatrical and choreographic re-elaboration of that narrative.

As Daryl Chin argues, in the increasingly intercultural world in which we live

> the interconnections of the geopolitical structure are so intricate and so intertwined that there is no way out of the dilemma of [inter]dependence. And that dependence . . . means that diplomacy must be vigilant . . . Interculturalism can so easily accommodate an agenda of cultural imperialism. This is what happens when Lee Breuer tosses disparate elements together pell-mell as an indicator of disintegration; this is what happens when Robert Wilson's staging overwhelms Heiner Muller's text; this is what happens when Peter Brook distorts the narrative structure of Indian mythology and of Chekhovian dramaturgy. The sense of imposition is omnipresent in these enterprises.
>
> (1989: 174)

Kathakali King Lear was an intercultural project conceived and developed with the full co-operation of leading *kathakali* artists. For senior actor Padmanabhan Nayar, developing the role of Lear was considered a consummate and appropriate acting challenge. With its collaborative process of creation, the meanings and experiences it made available were constrained by the limitations it imposed on itself – using *kathakali* techniques to elaborate a simplified Shakespearean narrative – and by the social, historical, literary, and aesthetic expectations its varied audiences had of both *kathakali* and Shakespeare's *Lear*. It did not, and could not, reach some hypothetically universal realm of communication.[15]

when marx met imperialism on the *kathakali* stage

INTRODUCTION

> *Kathakali* which once mainly functioned in the palaces of *rajas* and kings, has now stepped down and is performed among the common people. From this it is clear that *kathakali* is also an art of the people.
> (Aricatasumedharan 1987)

As unlikely as it might seem to anyone unfamiliar with the recent political history of Kerala, one day during 1987 in the town of Palakkad, Kerala, Karl Marx met Imperialism on the *kathakali* stage in the guise of a modern *kathakali* morality play pitting the evil demon-king, 'Imperialism' in his 'red beard' make-up, against the heroic lead, 'World Conscience' in his shining 'green' make-up. Entitled *People's Victory* (*Manavavijayan*), it was produced by the leftist cultural organization 'Kerala Art-House' (Kerala Kalabhavan). Unlike most *kathakali* experiments with non-traditional Western content such as *The Killing of Hitler*, *Faust*, *Hamlet*, or *Kathakali King Lear*, all of which had only one or two performances in Kerala, *People's Victory* was performed on numerous occasions during 1987 for often wildly enthusiastic left-front political audiences. Produced a full two years before the *Kathakali King Lear*'s first performance in Kerala in 1989 and its subsequent international festival tours and

notoriety, *People's Victory* was written and produced by the same well-known poet/playwright Iyyamgode Sridharan, who later, as Secretary of the Kerala Kalamandalam, translated and co-produced the first production and tour of *Kathakali King Lear*. And yet, unlike *Kathakali King Lear*, this leftist *kathakali* production has, with the exception of an earlier version of this chapter, been virtually ignored both by the English language press in Kerala and the UK, and by Indian and Western scholars, who have written with great vehemence and conviction about *Kathakali King Lear* (Awasthi 1993; Bennett 1996).

In his letter to the editor of a daily Malayalam newspaper, Aricatasumedharan applauded the overt political use of *kathakali* since he read the production as bringing *kathakali* 'down' from the loftly place of appreciation among Kerala's high-caste traditional patrons ('the palaces of *rajas* and kings' discussed in Chapter 2) to 'the common people' – such atypical *kathakali* audiences as the All-India Agricultural Workers Union, or the 1,000 members of the local Communist Party of India (Marxist) (CPI(M)) gathered for their annual meeting in Kannur, northern Kerala, by CPI(M)'s cultural wing, 'Organization for the Propagation of Modern Literature' ('Urugonoman Kalasahitya Sangham').

It would be as easy to dismiss this experimental leftist *kathakali* play as it would be to dismiss Currimbhoy's *The Dumb Dancer* as an anomaly, or as a didactic 'morality play' with its none too subtle 1980s stereotypes of America as Imperialism, the CIA as the 'Demons,' and the (then) USSR as World Conscience. But I have chosen to analyse precisely why and for whom *People's Victory*, and his more recent 1995 experiment, *Message of Love*, were performed for three reasons:

1   Focusing on leftist experiments helps locate *kathakali* within the contemporary Kerala and post-Independence India historical and socio-political landscapes, and allows us to see how the 1987 production became a site for the galvanization and performance of local, Kerala, communist ideology.
2   Unlike productions of non-epic content, such as *Kathakali King Lear*, *The Iliad*, or *Hamlet* which use Western 'classics' to gain the kind of cultural capital marketable in the transnational, global intercultural performing arts market associated with such international festival sites as Edinburgh, with its overtly didactic, political content, *People's Victory* in particular was a decidedly 'local' production with no aspirations of gaining access to this intercultural market-place, or to the discursive, critical modes of acclaim, disdain, or analysis which pass 'artistic' judgement on productions like *Kathakali King Lear*.
3   As a site of considerable local contest over meanings and interpretation, the debates that surrounded the production of *People's Victory*, and to some degree *Message of Love*, took place primarily in the local Malayalam newspapers. As such, the controversy throws into relief the 'internal cultural debates' circulating around the 'limits' to which *kathakali* can be used for the presentation of 'non-traditional' content for non-traditional audiences.

PEOPLE'S VICTORY: KATHAKALI FOR 'THE PEOPLE'

The story of *People's Victory* and its characters may be briefly summarized. In his unpublished English translation, Iyyamgode Sridharan lists each character, its make-up type, and the specific concept each type is intended to represent:

World Conscience	('Green' representing Virtue and Valour)
Imperialism	('Red-beard' representing Monstrosity)
People	(Two females representing Virtue)
Scientists	(Two sages representing Wisdom)
Devils	(Attendants to the Demon . . . representing docile followers of Imperialism).[1]

In the first scene two Scientists come before World Conscience to convince him of the dangers Imperialism poses to world peace.

SECOND SCIENTIST: The fiend raves through Nicaragua, Western Asia and Africa which are afflicted by his atrocious assaults. Make haste, O Lord, to halt the carnage and restore peace . . .
WORLD CONSCIENCE: I promise thee, (I shall set out at once) to face the foe that is out to destroy the earth with horrendous weapons, and will humble his pride with the blaze of Socialism.

To open the second scene, the vocalists introduce Imperialism as they sing a verse (*sloka*) in which they tell how 'even the stars are said to be scared of him.' After entering with the typical 'curtain look' (*tiranokku*) for the red beard/demon type character, Imperialism announces that all nations must

join my camp, or I will destroy you one and all. In star-war (sic), with weapons new and in a novel fashion, I will reduce the world to ashes. Those that hope to live shall fall prostrate at my feet or face extermination.

During the third scene the Scientists 'visit the demon's den' to try and convince him to make positive use of nuclear energy which is 'best utilised for the good of Man. May you steer towards this glorious goal!' Unconvinced by their arguments, and outraged by their reproof, Imperialism sends his attendants ('Demons') to capture the Scientists.

The fourth scene opens with World Conscience visiting the two female characters representing the peace movement.

FIRST FEMALE: Pray, lead us Lord, to work for Peace!

While millions languish in poverty
The affluent revel in luxury.
Let all wealth be shared by every one.
Let all exploitation be eradicated.

The peace workers convince World Conscience to confront Imperialism. In the fifth scene they fight a typical *kathakali* battle in which World Conscience defeats Imperialism, and in the closing scene the victorious World Conscience is 'received, felicitated, and coronated by the people.'[2] As part of the celebrations, the two female characters dance a *kummi*, the lyrical *kathakali* female dance in which joy and youthful gaiety are expressed. As the following song is sung by the onstage vocalists, there is a procession in which the red flag is brought to the stage:

May messages of Peace blossom!
May a new epoch dawn!
Down with arms and ammunitions!
May new ideas bloom.
May nuclear energy enrich the earth!
May the day be born without fear of war!
May brotherhood spread everywhere!
May we go forward singing songs of Man's victory!
May the Red Flag go up, proclaiming that the world is one!

In production the play lasted approximately two and a half hours, and was received with great enthusiasm by its target audiences – left-front political audiences. Although highly critical of the production in general, independent critic/journalist Gopalakrishnan described how the Kannur audience of over 1,000 'really enjoyed the production. Although there hadn't been much overt response during most of the production, when the red flag came to the stage, there was a tremendous response because of the political commitment of the audience . . . [T]he audience forgot themselves when they saw the red flag!' (interview, 1989).

PEOPLE'S VICTORY IN THE CONTEXT OF THE KERALA POLITICAL LANDSCAPE

It is not surprising that the red flag was brought to the *kathakali* stage at the conclusion of this production since it was in Kerala in 1957 that a communist government was democratically

brought to power for the first time when it collected 35 percent of the votes and won 60 of 125 seats up for election (Nossiter 1988: 65, 1982: 123). Given the vagaries of electoral politics in Kerala, since the declaration of Presidential Rule in 1959, which removed the communists from power after their initial two-year experiment, the communists have from time to time shared power in the form of left and democratic fronts, recently from 1987 until the 1991 elections when they were swept out of power following the assassination of Rajiv Gandhi, and then again in the elections in 1995.[3]

Whether communists have been in or out of the official seat of power, since the 1950s communist/socialist thought, discourse, and socio-economic policies have had an impact on the daily life of Malayalis. For example, the Agrarian Relations Bill, introduced by the Communist Party of India (CPI) but not passed until 1961 in a form modified 'to accommodate land interests' when the Congress-PSP ministry was in office, was nevertheless 'the first comprehensive measure of its kind attempted in India' and a self-conscious attempt by the CPI to abolish feudalism (Nossiter 1982: 149–50).[4] At least symbolically, if not actually, it helped dismantle the feudalistic house-land-ruler complex described in Chapter 2 where power and wealth had traditionally been concentrated, and from which *kathakali* had received its patronage until the 1930s when institutional patronage began with the founding of the Kerala Kalamandalam.

During Kerala's formative political years between the 1930s and 1950s, progressive thinkers, many of whom were from the educated higher castes and communities and who became part of CPI, helped foster both a desire for awareness and reassessment of the social ills of the old feudalistic order. To accomplish the goal, political parties and special interest organizations have had a long history of fostering educational, cultural, and artistic activities, usually under the guidance of the party or organization's 'cultural wing.' As early as the founding of the Congress Socialist Party in 1934, new dramas (*puthiya natakam*) were performed as one strategy of leftist/socialist political education (Nossiter 1988: 47–8). When the Kerala branch of the Communist Party of India (CPI) was born in 1939–40, along with other socialist parties it helped establish literacy programs in the form of reading rooms which made available modern literary works of members of the Progressive Writers' Association 'in whose work social criticism dominated', such as Kesava Dev's *From the Gutter* (1942), and Thakazhi's *Scavenger's Son* (1947) and *Two Measures of Rice* (1948) (Nossiter 1982: 95). The cultural wing of the Kerala branch of the CPI began to use social dramas both to raise consciousness about social ills, and to propagate potential socialist solutions for these ills, a strategy which led to the existence today of two major professional theater companies playing repertories of socialist dramas each performance season – the pro-Soviet Kerala People's Arts Company (KPAC) associated with the CPI, and the Kalidasa Kalakendra associated with the splinter CPI(M), pro-Chinese branch of the communist party (Richmond *et al.* 1990: 392–3, 402–3).[5]

Another CPI goal during these formative years was appreciation and preservation of 'a purely Malayali Kerala' (Nossiter 1982: 94–5). Although Indian independence was won in 1947, it was not until 1956 with the passage of the States Reorganization Act that the modern state of Kerala united Malayali speakers in a Malayali Kerala. As early as 1951 A.K. Gopalan, leader of the CPI in the Lok Sabha and a Malayali, 'asserted that "India's most important problem, the Communists' No. 1 goal" was the formation of linguistic provinces' (ibid.: 119). The Kerala CPI and other socialists contributed to the formation and preservation of a Malayali Kerala not only through its Malayalam literacy programs, but also by valuing the preservation of Kerala's traditional arts. The poet Vallathol's valiant campaign to 'save' *kathakali* from extinction, due to loss of traditional forms of patronage and simple neglect, helped establish *kathakali*, along with many other traditional arts, as a major bearer and symbol of Malayali culture.[6] As discussed in Chapter 2, part of Vallathol's strategy for preservation was to take *kathakali* outside of Kerala on national and international tours – a plan which not only brought badly needed revenue to an underfunded institution, but also brought increasing international recognition of *kathakali* as a performing art which could be appreciated by non-indigenous audiences as a great art form on a par with Japanese *kabuki* or *noh*, Peking opera, etc. As an 'international' art *kathakali* was a

fillip to developing a strong and distinctive pan-Kerala Malayali identity. These developments helped accentuate a linguistically and culturally based regional Malayali identity.

During this period there appears to have been no public recognition of what might be read from a Western liberal-humanist political stance as a 'contradiction' between progressive policies, such as attempts to redress the economic imbalances of the old feudalistic order through legislating land reform, and advocacy of government support for traditional arts like *kathakali*, which had been born in the crucible of that same feudalistic order. Among the CPI leadership there also appears to have been no public acknowledgment of the possible contradiction between simultaneously supporting the production of new consciousness-raising social dramas (*natakam*), and self-consciously preserving a traditional genre like *kathakali* since it was considered a totally different category of performance, i.e., not a new drama (*puthiya natakam*) but a performance which enacts (*attua*) stories (-*katha*). 'Saving' *kathakali* was thought of not simply as preserving the past, but as an act of resistance against the disintegration of Malayali cultural, linguistic, and political heritage brought by the imposition of false political boundaries imposed by colonial rule. Political and economic support of *kathakali* was actualized in fact when in 1957 the Kalamandalam, which from its establishment in 1930 had been on shaky financial grounds, was placed under Kerala State government management, and thereafter became a financial ward of the state receiving substantial subsidies whether those in power have been CPI, Congress, or a coalition of parties.

Although only further research can determine more precisely when this shift in thinking began to occur on the political left regarding their view of Kerala's traditional arts, it is certain that by the late 1970s the potential 'contradictions' between leftist progressive social analysis and their reading of the past as a feudalistic system with regressive ritual/religious beliefs began to be publicly articulated both in discourses about the traditional arts and in their use by leftist organizations. Founded in 1962 by a group of well-educated leaders in scientific fields in order to promote 'Science for Social Revolution,' the self-styled independent progressive grassroots, activist organization Kerala Shastra Sahitya Parishad (KSSP) began to use familiar folk stories, songs, and dances in new performance contexts on its all-Kerala processions (*jatha*) in 1977 in order to raise consciousness among the masses in Kerala's villages about a variety of contemporary social problems from environmental to educational to women's issues. As theater education scholar Sharon Grady has eloquently explained, rather than 'faithfully reproducing these stories and creating art for the sake of the gods, as was traditionally done, KSSP reworked these familiar tales to make art for the sake of social justice and political change' (n.d.).

In several articles, South Asian performance scholar Wayne Ashley and anthropologist Regina Holloman have documented how during the early 1980s Northern Kerala's most widespread form of traditional Hindu ritual/religious practice, *teyyam* (the generic name for the deities propitiated in calendrically determined ritual festivals, *kaliyattam*), began to be performed not only in its traditional ritual context, but also for 'Kerala Tourist week, as an entertainment for a biology symposium, as part of the Folk Dance Festival during the Republic Day celebrations, at the opening ceremonies of the 1982 Asian Olympics in New Delhi, and at the Village Art Festival in Kerala sponsored by the Ford Foundation' (1990: 148).[7] As *teyyam*'s low-caste performers themselves began to conduct *teyyam* outside its exclusive ritual context, others from outside the communities which traditionally held exclusive rights to perform and patronize *teyyam* began to use its stories and/or its representations of specific deities in new contexts. In 1981 the Natana Kala Kshetram, a theater company from Kannur, met violent opposition from one traditional *teyyam* patron community when it rewrote 'several sacred texts . . . of *teyyam* and turned them into popular dramas, complete with sound systems, smoke effects, flashing lights, projections, and painted backdrops' (ibid.: 149, 1982: *passim*). More important for purposes of my argument here, Ashley and Holloman also documented another non-traditional recontextualization of *teyyam* by the CPI(M) which, for the 1981 May Day rally,

> featured *teyyam* dancing after speeches were made against capitalism, corruption, and suppression. The plan to show *teyyam*

dancing was a conscious, well thought out attempt to strip the ritual of its efficacy by demonstrating that it could be performed out of context without rituals, priests or offerings. The Communist Party hoped to show, contrary to the villager's beliefs, that there would be no anger from the god, no consequences. *Teyyam* could be performed for fun. At the end of the dance, instead of calling important high caste members from the audience to come up and receive blessings, as the deity would do in the ritual context, he called local Communist Party members over the microphone . . .

> At the conclusion of his speech, the dancer told the spectators to turn their devotion to Namboodiripad, the general secretary of the Marxist Party, and to Nayanar, who was the chief minister of Kerala from 1980–81. The organizers of the rally told me they *would like to see* teyyam *performed as an art form, as something enjoyable to watch detached from any kind of belief system.* In their view, poverty, the continuing presence of a caste system, and the manipulation of the masses by an upper-caste elite, is intimately bound with the performance of and belief in rituals, which keep the proletariat passive and dependent on a force outside themselves.
> (1982: 71–2, emphasis added)

Even if, as South Asian anthropologist John Richardson Freeman persuasively argues, such contestatory uses of *teyyam* are the exception rather than the rule (1991), the incident reflects the shift in left-front views of and discourses on these traditional arts.

It is clear that by the early 1980s at least some leaders among the CPI(M) and other progressive leftist organizations had begun to reassess their view of the traditional arts and the role such arts could/should play in the life of their (ideal) modern socialist state. Leftist policy makers were faced with a difficult set of alternatives. If they summarily condemned traditional arts as a counter-progressive legacy of the feudal past, and therefore, as happened in radical Maoist China, banished 'feudalist' traditional arts from their (ideal) socialist state, they would be faced not only with the historical contradiction of their own position which supported the creation of a Malayali Kerala, but also with the enmity of those whose caste-specific identity is invested in the powerful, highly public symbols of caste-specific performances like *teyyam* or *kathakali*. In short, it would be political suicide simply to reject such traditional arts.

CREATING A NON-FEUDAL, DE-HISTORIZED, NON-SUPERSTITIOUS *KATHAKALI* 'FOR THE PEOPLE'

What gradually began to emerge was the argument that the traditional arts should continue to be valued and patronized, but only if they were historically decontextualized, shorn of the vestiges of the regressive feudalistic, superstitious belief systems of the past, and made accessible to 'the people' with new content. Iyyamgode Sridharan, speaking of the 1988 *Kathakali King Lear* experiment while on tour in Europe after he became Secretary of the Kalamandalam in 1987,[8] wrote in one of Kerala's daily newspapers *Mathrabhumi* for local consumption:

It is the need of the times to free our art from the clutches of religion and orthodox beliefs. The main culprits behind India's problems today are the activities of these disguised religious fundamentalists . . . In the birth and development of almost all art forms, religious rituals may have had a role. But these legacies have been thrown away by many of the art forms which are now expressing their own independence. The best example is *kathakali* itself where there is no difference between the gods, spirits, and demons. *Kathakali* considered Krishna and Rama only as *kathakali* characters which Hindus consider gods . . . Based on the fact that *kathakali* is a great art form, [Europeans] only consider its histrionic techniques . . . People from almost all parts of the world have come to know about *kathakali* not because this is a religiously bound art.

(1989)

In his more recent 1995 experiment, *Message of Love* (*Sneehasandesham*), Iyyamgode chose to bring such a new, 'independent interpretation of Krishna' to the *kathakali* stage.[9] In *Message of Love* he creates a highly charged counter-reading of Krishna's mythological past. Iyyemgode bases his interpretation of Krishna on the assumption that the 'dark' lord Krishna as he first appears in the Rig Veda belongs to the non-Aryan race, and therefore his original role should be read not so much as divine, but as a 'leader of the downtrodden.'

In the first scene of *Message of Love* Krishna returns to Mathura filled with fond memories of his childhood. His beloved Radha greets him, only to reveal with great pathos that while Dashakarma has been king enmity has been sown between the castes, untouchability has been introduced, and the number of major sacrificial rituals has been increased. Krishna goads his lethargic brother, Balarama, who has done nothing about the situation in his absence:

Now you're sleeping and taking liquor.
Why are you keeping silent about casteism?

Krishna reminds Balarama that the ritual and sacrifices favored by the high castes are nonsense, and that the truth is pursued through knowledge. The high castes instigate a fight among the lower castes, leading to the destruction of one of their temples. Krishna appears, advising them not to attack each other since the human body is the greatest temple. When King Dashakarma begins a major sacrificial ritual in which Lokayatha, the holy man who originally spoke out against the efficacy of such gaudy, expensive sacrifices, is about to be sacrificed himself, Balarama intervenes, killing both Dashakarma and his chief minister, and saving Lokayatha. Krishna and Radha appear in the final tableau, congratulating Balarama. Krishna describes his vision of a world without class, caste, prejudice, or discrimination.[10]

In stark contrast to his representation in all other *kathakali* plays such as *The Progeny of Krishna*, Krishna is presented not simply as a major devotional figure, but also as a leader of the socially downtrodden, and therefore as a voice of conscience. Although set in the mythological past, scenes and dialogue make specific reference to the contemporary political landscape, especially to the destruction of the Babri-Masjid temple, and the ascent and increasing influence of the Hindu, fundamentalist/nationalist right party (BJP: Bharatiya Janatha Party).[11] Iyyamgode sees *Message of Love* as another phase of his life-long 'fight against fanaticism' in the form of the Hindu right's fundamental nationalism.

> Revivalist forces are trying to divide people and this is why Indian democracy is having problems. So as an artist I wanted to work indirectly through art to help resolve this increasing division.
>
> (1993, interview)

In the contemporary socio-political battle over fundamentalism within India, Iyyamgode's *Message of Love* was one attempt in Kerala to provide a leftist interpretation of epic and puranic content as a counterpoint to the ascent and growing political influence of the Hindu right.

In his attempts to dehistoricize and decontextualize the traditional arts, Iyyamgode Sridharan assumes that the artistic ideal is the creation of (a modernist) 'universal' art, which leaves behind its cultural markings, is able to cross cultural boundaries, and shed its traditional religious associations. Sridharan's interpretation tries to uncouple *kathakali* from its Hindu religious roots. His discourse claims an exclusive spectatorial position which reads its characters *as characters*, leaving no room for those spectators who, as devotees of Rama or Krishna attending a temple performance, might still view and experience the appearance of Rama or Krishna with reverence and the ubiquitous gesture of obeisance to these gods with folded hands, even if such individuals are not part of the Hindu nationalist/fundamentalist right. He uses Western appreciation of *kathakali* as a justification for rejecting its traditional religious resonances, thereby accepting and projecting onto *kathakali* a (Western) dichotomy between the sacred and the secular – a dichotomy increasingly part of India's political landscape. In this intercultural circulation of modernist aesthetic and political discourses, for Iyyamgode Sridharan and some other leftists, *kathakali* has become what literary theorist Terry Eagleton describes as a commodity 'in the market place [which exists] for nothing and nobody in particular, and can consequently be rationalized, ideologically speaking, as existing entirely and gloriously for [itself]' (1990: 9).

This is the logic which gave birth to the Kerala Kalabhavan with its explicit agenda of not simply preserving the classical arts like so many other institutions such as the Kerala Kalamandalam, but rather bringing these classical arts 'to the people.' Its productions of Iyyamgode Sridharan's *People's Victory* in 1987, and of *Message of Love* in 1995 were experiments in realizing these goals. According to former CPI Chief Minister E.M.S. Namboodiripad, the initial 1987 revisionist production of *People's Victory* attempted to 'make *kathakali* a people's art,' by shearing it from its feudal, ritualistic past by cutting the preliminary ritual verses, dances, and lighting of the brass oil lamp, which traditionally began a *kathakali* performance, and by enacting a content based on 'present day issues' rather than 'themes mythological which [*kathakali*] usually enacts.'[12] Namboodiripad uses the poet Vallathol to authorize his point of view, claiming that because of Vallathol's involvement in the precedent-setting experiment, *The Killing of Hitler*, he had 'demolished the myth that *kathakali* could only depict stories from mythology and proved that *kathakali* could be linked with the present day issues.'[13]

LOCAL DEBATES AND CONTROVERSIES AROUND *PEOPLE'S VICTORY*

With the highest literacy rate in India (70 percent in 1981), and the largest circulation of Indian language newspapers in India (1.3 million in 1978–9) (Nossiter 1988: 57), after the opening of *People's Victory* in 1987 the Malayalam dailies were filled with debates about the production which reflected the fact that, as reception theorist Susan Bennett has asserted, 'within cultural boundaries, there are obviously different viewing publics' (1990: 101). No such discussions occurred in English language papers in India, which summarily ignored the production and the issues it generated. Iyyamgode Sridharan's *People's Victory* clearly postulated a particular Malayali political audience as its ideal public, and it was for that particular audience that its potential for meaning was most realized. As discussed in Chapter 9, public debate over the nature and limits of change and experimentation in *kathakali* has always defined itself as acceptable and even desired when taking place 'from within the tradition' (Kurup 1966–67: 25–31). *People's Victory* de-emphasized the pleasures of tasting the aesthetic delights of *rasa*, the experience of virtuosic realization of the nuance of technique, and precluded traditional narratological pleasure by substituting a contemporary political morality play for an epic story. Setting himself up as a spokesman for the 'average [i.e., traditional] *kathakali* audience,' Gopalakrishnan, while appreciating the vocalists singing of the text set to 'popular *ragas* . . . with beautiful efficiency,' criticized the production for the fact that 'the actors just don't have much to do', and argued that since *kathakali* is defined as 'playing a story,' and its literature is called *attakatha*, meaning 'a story (*katha*) for performing (*attua*)', this is a *kathakali* 'without any story!' (1987). S. Sunderdass critiqued the production for its lack of realizing the subtleties of characterization appreciated by *kathakali* connoisseurs:

> Although *kathakali* characters are types, nevertheless they are something more than a simple type. Is it because of this that Nala, Damayanti, Draupadi, etc. are living on the stage and in our minds? This truth they either forget or tried to forget. This is the failure of *People's Victory*. World Conscience and Imperialism never rise above the limitations of type.
>
> (1987)

The critique's emphasis on characters who live in the spectator's 'mind' and rise 'above the limitations of type' refers, as we have seen, to the current demand for performances which elaborate and emphasize the interior life of *kathakali* characters as exemplified in plays like *Nalacaritam* and *King Rugmamgada's Law*.

Both Sunderdass and Gopalakrishnan challenged the production's claim that it was making *kathakali* popular. Gopalakrishnan asked, 'Is it by changing the classical frames of this classical art that it will be made popular? Or will it lose its classical nature?' (1987). Gopalakrishnan and Sunderdass reached the similar conclusion that (in Gopalakrishnan's words) 'all contemporary events are another version of the stories of old with slight differences' (1987), and (in Sunderdass's words) that traditional epic characters like Ravanna

already represent concepts like Imperialism (1987). For these critics, to tout the potential 'loss' of what makes *kathakali* 'classical' stakes their claim to the high moral ground as they ostensibly 'protect' what they view as the essential nature of the art and its mode of appreciation.

In contrast, for those on the left, *People's Victory* contained many pleasures. *Mathrabhumi*'s critic described the production as 'a very successful effort to modernize *kathakali*' which, other than a few 'minus points . . . can be regarded as a beautiful epic'; accounted for that success by citing the playwright's ability to exploit *kathakali*'s use of representative character types in introducing contemporary concepts onto the stage; and finally hailed the production as 'changing the history of *kathakali*' (Asema 1987). For its ideal spectators – members of the political left – *People's Victory* self-consciously emphasized the pleasure of experiencing narratological elaboration of its single metanarrative – the triumph of a particular form of good (communism) over a particular manifestation of evil (imperialism). For these spectators, their superhuman heroes are not those of India's epic past played out with increasing emphasis on the subtleties of the interior life of its main characters, but of the (then) revolutionary 'epic' present. With communists and their activist organizations such as K.S.S.P. advocating 'science' in all its forms, including nuclear power, as the savior of 'the people,' as surely as epic heroes like Rama, Krishna, or Arjuna resonate for those whose referential universe still encompasses their righting of the cosmic wrongs of the universe in the cosmological *lila* (play) of the gods, just as assuredly in 1987 did World Conscience's victory over Imperialism resonate with the deeply profound cosmological 'truth' which inevitably brought this particular portion of the audience to its feet not for the appearance of Lord Krishna, but as the red flag, symbol of this metanarrative, was brought to the stage.

Given the collapse of communism in Eastern Europe, the 1987 production of *People's Victory* will no doubt remain a historical anomaly. Were it played again today, it would no doubt seem an anachronism, even to devout Kerala communists. Nevertheless, this 1987 production illustrates how certain specific cultural performances become arenas for socio-political contestation and debate at the particular moment of their production and reception. On this site leftist politicians and performers played out a melodramatic morality play in which their version of 'good' triumphed over 'evil' – at the geopolitical level Communism defeated Imperialism/Capitalism. This discourse and metanarrative melodramatically defines an 'us' as *different* from 'them.' Using *kathakali* to play out this cosmic battle not only theatrically reflects differences, but also further separates and establishes opposing socio-political factions in the Kerala political world. Given the political realities of 1987, the 'us' of the left-front state government was set over against the 'them' of Congress, which in turn was implicitly associated with both the central government and American imperialism. At the historical moment of this particular production, the *kathakali* stage became a platform for the expression of a spirited discourse of resistance to the center, and a moment of galvanization for Kerala's left.

CRITICAL RECEPTION OF *MESSAGE OF LOVE*: THE CONTINUING POLITICAL AND AESTHETIC DEBATES

Iyyamgode's 1995 production of *Message of Love* provoked nearly as much controversy as his first experiment; however, given *Message of Love*'s re-imagination of Krishna – perhaps India's most popular avatar of Vishnu – as representing the downtrodden, the attacks on the production came not only from *kathakali* critics, but also from the religious/political right. Similar in response to earlier leftist revisioning of *teyyam*, and as reported to me by Iyyemgode, at an open session for critical responses to the Palakkad production, P.Parameswaran, leader and theoretician of Kerala's far radical right/fundamentalist RSS, criticized the production for 'insulting Krishna by making him working class. Although I appreciate Iyyamgode's experiments, and certainly there are working class devotees of Krishna, making Krishna working class is insulting!'

Given Iyyamgode's use of traditional puranic source material for this production, the criticism from *kathakali* critics and journalists shifted from

content to characterization. V. Kaladharan began his review by commending Iyyamgode for the 'highly imaginative' first scene which enacted for the first time on the *kathakali* stage the reunion between Krishna and Radha (1993). Kaladharan praised the scene as a 'great achievement' for its dramatic exploration of Radha's state of pathos, performed within the confines of the traditional structure of *kathakali*. However, for Kaladharan, scenes after the first, and therefore the production as a whole failed to achieve Iyyamgode's revolutionary goal of 'creating a new consciousness for the audience' for several reasons. Using arguments similar to those garnered against *Kathakali King Lear*, Kaladharan asserts that '*kathakali* has its own form and structure' which fails 'to allow him to bring something new to communicate to people in this story.' More specifically, he argues that *kathakali*'s gestures, modes of expression, etc. are 'not appropriate' 'for conveying the feelings of a man (Krishna) who feels responsible for the working class' (ibid.: 16). Most significantly, Kaladharan thinks the production fails because each *kathakali* role has its own set of traditional associations for the audience which preclude the audience from seeing such traditional characters behave or have concerns which do not fit their traditional set of associations. As Kaladharan explains, the Krishna of *The Killing of Duryodhana* or the Balarama of *Subhadra Haranam*, when compared to the same two characters in *Message of Love*, are 'from two different worlds' – a fact which precludes 'the possibility of creating a new philosophy' (ibid.: 16).

Although Iyyamgode Sridharan's political and aesthetic voice is clearly far from the primary aesthetic interests and concerns of its most traditional audience of connoisseurs who continue to pursue an ever-evolving aesthetic founded on the fundamental principles of elaboration and appropriateness, his experiments – from his 1987 production of *People's Victory*, through his translations of *Kathakali King Lear* (1989) and *The Iliad* (1990) while Secretary of the Kalamandalam, to his most recent production of *Message of Love* (1995) – illuminate some of the ways in which a traditional art like *kathakali* is being negotiated within Kerala's contemporary socio-political environment. It is important to remember that Iyyamgode Sridharan's experiments have all involved some of the most respected *kathakali* artists, many of whom have willingly and/or enthusiastically been involved in these experiments, and some of whom see no contradiction between their performances in traditional plays and engaging in such experiments.[14] Although it is unclear whether these leftist experiments with *kathakali* content and interpretation will continue or not, what is definitely clear is that the debates fostered by such experiments are becoming increasingly acrimonious, the binaries increasingly oppositional, and the demons increasingly demonic.

Implicit throughout these last two chapters is the assumption that in a post-modern, post-colonial world our readings of non-Western performance traditions like *kathakali* must transcend the limitations of earlier narrowly defined genre-based studies which might accept at face value the hegemonic discourse of an aesthetic elite and their interpretation of their art as singular and natural. *People's Victory* and *Message of Love* both clearly illustrate how important it is to situate productions within the historical and socio-political particulars of each context so that the variety of subject positions from which interested discourses of theatrical practice, interpretation, *and* reception are constructed can be clearly identified, and the implicit ideologies of each position discussed.

whose gods, and whose demons dance?

[handwritten margin notes: x political tool, used to show power struggles + issues, relates 2 play, theatre as a political tool, cultural identity - kerala institutes, deeming whats appropriate]

Who are today's gods and demons that come to play on the *kathakali* stage? And who is defining what constitutes the *kathakali* 'stage' today? Answering these questions depends, of course, on one's perspective. As discussed in Chapter 2, *kathakali* has always been (re)shaped within the nexus of social, political, economic, and cultural formations which constantly impinge on its production and reception within Kerala. Chapters 9 and 10 detailed some of the inevitable encounters of a 'traditional' art like *kathakali* with newly emergent realities which have prompted/necessitated further shifts and changes. In contemporary India, amidst the increasingly 'global' market-place in which the *kathakali* stage is defined today, and from my perspective as a Western theatre-director/academic, these cannot but be open-ended questions to be constantly revisited.

Within Kerala's immediately 'local' spheres of influence, interpretation, and contestation, the gods and demons that play on the *kathakali* stage continue to be primarily those of the epic and puranic traditions. Even though their experiences of these epic gods, demons, and heroes are very different, the 'traditional' stories and characters are those favored by connoisseurs as well as Western tourists alike on the *kathakali* stages of Kerala. Cultural organizations and *kathakali* institutions like Margi, Drisyavedi, etc. continue to define the parameters of what can and should legitimately play on the *kathakali* stage within a fairly narrow range of 'what is appropriate.' Producers of tourist *kathakali* programs at Kovalam Beach and the port cities of Kochi/Ernakulam continue to play on Western tourist desires for a romance of an antique past as they package one-hour *kathakali* programs (Zarrilli 1977). Other cultural organizations, such as Iyyamgode Sridharan's Kerala Kalabhavan, or on occasion the Kerala Kalamandalam, with their quite different relationship to the contemporary political realities of Kerala, will continue to push at the edges of 'what is' or is not considered appropriate, and take *kathakali* to new content, and occasionally to non-traditional audiences, even within Kerala.

In the face of the stridency of the political realities shaped by an ever-hardening religious nationalism (van der Veer 1994), the 'play' of the gods is being revisited throughout India as well as in Kerala, whether in Iyyamgode Sridharan's reimagination of Krishna in *Message of Love*, or in Maya Krishna Rao's remarkable recent solo performance, 'Khol Do,' first performed in 1993. On 9 April 1999, I was fortunate enough to see Maya Krishna Rao's 'Khol Do' – an original dance-theatre performance inspired by the short story by Saadat Hasan Manto, and created out of her years of training and performance of *kathakali*.

Trained at the International Centre for *Kathakali* in New Delhi from a young age, Maya Rao learned *kathakali* from such excellent traditional masters as Guru Madhava Panikkar who came to the New Delhi Centre on its creation in 1960 (Zarrilli 1984a: 304-8). These master teachers introduced her to *kathakali*, not through the female roles, but rather through the strong male roles, providing her with a firm foundation in the 'strong' (*tandava*) aspects of playing *kathakali* characters. Only later in her training did she begin to learn, and discover the joys, of the repertory's female roles. Throughout her years of performance and teaching, often at the National School of Drama in New Delhi, Maya Rao's work has been inspired by and based on her *kathakali* training.

In her program note for a performance in Aberystwyth, Wales sponsored by the Centre for Performance Research in conjunction with the Performance Studies International conference, Rao relates the story behind her adaptation of 'Khol Do':

> 'Khol Do' is set in the riots that ended the division of India and the creation of a new state, Pakistan. Millions left their homes to cross the new border to make a new home. Sirajuddin was one such who left India and travelled by train to Lahore. By the time he got off, he was near unconscious. For days he sat on the platform staring at the dusty sky. Where was his daughter Sakina? When had he got parted from her? He could only remember the running crowd and Sakina's *dupatta* or veil, falling to the ground. When he turned to pick it up she had urged yelling in the melee, 'Don't bother with it.' In the refugee camp, the heavily armed eight young male volunteers had been solicitous. 'If Sakina is alive we will find her for you,' they had said reassuringly. How was old Sirajuddin to know they had already found her but they were not through with her, yet? (Rao 1999).

While inspired by this story, her performance – the first of a series of solo performances she began to create in 1993 – is neither an exercise in story-telling nor a *kathakali*-style enactment of the story. In this sense it is not *kathakali* in the way that *Kathakali King Lear*, *People's*

Victory or *Message of Love* are *kathakali* in technique and conventions, if not in content. As Rao explains, she is taking a different path through *kathakali*: 'here I am looking for a physical language, where every action may set off different signals of experience. The eventual form is not *kathakali*, yet it is inspired by it.'

But it is also not *kathakali*. Occasionally during the performance, specific *kathakali* gestures, facial expressions, and/or choreography emerge, but only as part of an integrated fabric of this totally physicalized performance developed out of a lengthy process of improvisation. During the creative process of devising the performance, 'I kept trying physical actions to generate that range of thought and emotions that are part of the atmosphere of the story. The result is, single gestures may have no particular meaning, but resonances that create multiple meanings' (Rao 1999). What is at the core of her process is *kathakali*'s mode of 'interior' acting – the total engagement of the performer's bodymind through the breath/energy in physicalization of the state/task/action at-hand. As discussed throughout this book, this is a non-psychologically based mode of engagement. It is Maya Rao's intuitive utilization of this mode of internal engagement in her process of improvisation and physicalization of action that gives her work its dynamism, and its contemporary resonances. Rao herself describes the problem and process of attempting to discover how 'to shift dance energy to a moment in a person's life when words are not being used to signal the transition' (Rao 1999).

Maya Rao's 'Khol Do' is an example of yet another new direction in experimentation with *kathakali* – the creative use of its interior, psychophysiological, preperformative base of engagement in the physicalization of action that does not need to be continuously marked by *kathakali* technique or traditional *kathakali*/epic content. Rao's strength as a performer rests both in her engagement wtih *kathakali*'s underlying psychophysiological technique and in her creative application of this base to new contexts and content – a content with strong resonances today in a world increasingly terrorized by the same forces of hatred unleashed during the period of partition. Rao's work is unrelenting in its acts of forceful physicalization, and in communicating through her body the pathos and terror of the experience of dislocation. Easier said than done. These contemporary demons dance on Rao's *kathakali* stage in their full terror, and some among the contemporary, primarily non-Malayali audiences that see 'Khol Do' will experience a destruction as complete as that of the goddess Kali.

kkk **appendix**

kathakali
performances
on video

Kerala 680 591 INDIA
Telephone: 91-488-452292

2   The Centre for Performance Research,
8H Science Park
Dyfed, Aberystwyth SY23 3 AH
Wales, UK
Telephone: 44-1970-622133
Fax: 44-1970-622132
email: cprwww@aber.ac.uk

3   Center for South Asia, Film/Videotape
Distribution Office
University of Wisconsin-Madison
203 Ingraham Hall
Madison, Wisconsin 53706
Telephone: 608-262-4884
Fax: 608-265-3062

One of the most important fully operational
and well-managed performing arts archives in
India. It houses an extensive collection of
ethnographic field documents in audio and
video formats, as well as a significant
collection of books and journals on the
performing arts of South Asia. For further
information contact:
Shubha Chaudhuri, Director
AIIS Archives and Centre for
Ethnomusicology
22, HUDA Institutional Area
Sector 32 Gurgaon, Harayana, INDIA
Telephone: 91–11–381384, 381424
email: rkiv@arce.ernet.in or
shubha@arce.ernet.in
fax: 91-11-4698150

PERFORMANCE VIDEOS FOR SALE

Of the above five videos available for rental, due
to copyright restrictions and permissions, only
Introduction to Kathakali and *The Killing of
Kirmira* are available for purchase from
Routledge and the Centre for Performance
Research (see 2, above)

ARCHIVAL VIDEOTAPES OF KATHAKALI AND OTHER KERALA PERFORMANCES

In addition to documentation of the
performances available for rental noted above,
also during 1993 and 1995, and in collaboration
with the Killimangalam Centre for the
Documentation of Kerala's Performing Arts, many
other performances were documented. A list of
these performances is provided below. Copies
either are presently, or will eventually be made
available at one of the following two archives:

1   The Centre for the Documentation of
Performing Arts, Kerala, India
Still seeking sufficient funds to open a fully
operable archive. For information about the
Center, its activities and needs, and what
documents and videos (PAL format) are
available at this time please contact the
President, K. Vasudevan Namboodiripad;
Secretary, M.P.S. Namboodiri; or Technical
Director, Kunju Vasudevan at the above
address.

2   The AIIS (American Institute of Indian
Studies) Archive for Ethnomusicology

ADDITIONAL *KATHAKALI* PERFORMANCES

1   *Lavana suravadham* 5/4/93
Location: Saastaamkadav, Aavanaav
meriyamana Trissur District
Featuring: M.P. Sankaran Namboodiri as
Hanuman

2   *Duryodhanavadham* 5/4/93
Location: Saastaamkadav, Aavanaav
meriyamana Trissur District

3   *Thoranayudham* 5/13/93 (two scenes only:
'Azhakiya Ravana' scene with Mandodari, and
Ravana/Sita/Mandodari)
Location: Killimangalam, Kerala
Featuring: Padmanabhan Nayar as Ravana

4   *Kirmīravadham* 5/14/93 (Lalitha/Panchali
scene)
Location: Killimangalam, Kerala
Featuring: Kottakkal Sivaraman as Lalitha
Kesvan Namboodiri as Panchali

5   *Kalakeyavadham* 5/14/93 (three scenes
only, including '*Swargavauranan*')
Location: Killimangalam, Kerala
Featuring: Padmanabhan Nayar as Arjuna

6   *Lavana suravadham* (two scenes only)
Location: Killimangalam, Kerala
Featuring: Keezhpadam K.R. Kumaran Nayar
as Hanuman
Kottakkal Sivaraman as Sita

7   *Rajasuyam* 5/14/93 (two scenes only)
Location: Killimangalam, Kerala
Featuring: Nelliyode Vasudevan
Namboodiripad as Jarasandha

8   *Bakavadham* (Bhima/Baka scene only)
Location: Killimangalam, Kerala
Featuring: Nelliyode Vasudevan
Namboodiripad as Baka
Kottakkal Unnikrishnan as Bhima

9   *Purappatu* and *Melappadam* 5/16/93
Location: Killimangalam, Kerala
Featuring: Gopalakrishnan and
Balasubramanian dancing
Vocalists: Gangadharan, Madambi
Centa: Unnikrishnan, Kottakkal Sasi
Maddalam: Narayanan Nambisan, Ravi

10   *Nalacaritam Day 2* 5/16/93
Location: Killimangalam, Kerala
Featuring: Gopi Asan as Nala
Kottakkal Sivaraman as Damayanti
Nelliyode Vasudevan Namboodiripad as Kali

11   *Balivadham* 5/16/93
Location: Killimangalam, Kerala

12   *Balivijayan* 5/17/93
Location: Killimangalam, Kerala
Featuring: Raman Kutty Nayar as Ravana
M.P. Sankaran Namboodiri as Narada
Kavungal Divakaran as Bali

13   *Santanagopalam* 6/19/93
Location: Tirtapatta Mandapam, East Fort,
Thiruvananthapuram

14   *Kirmiravadham* 7/17/93
Location: Tirtapatta Mandapam, East Fort,
Thiruvananthapuram

15   *Sitaswayamvaram* 11/28/93
Location: Killimangalam, Kerala
Featuring: Manojkumar as Viswamithra
Ettumanoor Kannan as Rama
M.P. Sankaran Namboodiri as Parasurama

16   *Prahladacaritam*
Location: Killimangalam, Kerala
Featuring: Vijayan as Hiranyakasipu
Pradeepkumar as Prahlada
Vadu Pisharody as Narasimha

OTHER GENRES

Mohiniattam and *Ottanthullal* 4/28/93
Kalamandalam Artists sponsored by David
Bolland, filmed at Old Kalamandalam
Mohiniattam:
Featuring: Leelaama and Hymavathi
Ottanthullul:
Featuring: Geethanandan
a. *Kalyanasaughandhikam* (selections)
b. *Kiratam* (selections)

Trissur Puram 5/1/93
Location: Trissur City

Teyyam 5/1/93
Location: Vellore, Payyannur, Kannur District
Includes:

1   Kelam Kulanghara Kandabhagavati Totam
2   Periyat Chamundi Totam
3   Vishnumurti Totam
4   Periyatt Kandar (Scholar) Totam
5   Bhagavati Teyyam
6   Make-up and Teyyam – Chamundi

Mohiniattam 5/16/93
Location: Killimangalam, Kerala
Featuring: Kalamandalam Sathyabhama
Vocalist: Ambika
Mridangam: Sivadas
Nattuvangam: Kalamandalam Leelamma

Ottanthullal: *Santanagopalam* 5/16/93
Location: Killimangalam, Kerala
Featuring: Kalamandalam Devaki
Vocalists: Guru Devakaran Nair Sarojini
Mridangam: Nelluvaya Nambisan

Kerala Shadow Puppet Performance 27 August
1993
Location: Killimangalam, Kerala
Featuring:
Vocalist: Vazhanath Balan Nair
Organizer: P. Unnikkrishnan
Performer: Chandran
Drummer: Gunasekharan

####### notes

1 AN 'OCEAN OF POSSIBILITIES'

1   Considerable differences of opinion exist among scholars of Malayalam literary history on Unnayi Variyar's precise dates. K.P.S. Menon suggests the provisional dates of 1675–1716, making him a contemporary of Kottayam Tampuran (1645–1716) (1957: 112), and C.V. Subramania Iyer gives his dates as 1674–1735 (1977: 13). K.M. George asserts that *Nalacaritam* was written 'immediately after the Kottayam works' (1968: 102), while Krishna Chaitanya posits a much later date, 'some time during the second quarter of the eighteenth century' (1971: 106).

2   Similar to commissioning a *Krishnattam* performance at Guruvayur Temple as an offering to Lord Krishna, at Panavalli Temple near Alleppey, *The Progeny of Krishna* is at least occasionally commissioned as an offering to the deity. It was at the Panavalli Temple that Kunju Nayar Asan used to perform the Brahmin role as a personal offering. When performing a role as a personal offering, the actor never accepts a fee for his performance, and only receives reimbursement for his travel.

3   For recent studies of South Asian folkloristics relevant to the issues raised here, and especially to context sensitivity and affect, see Appadurai (1991); Blackburn and Ramanujan (1986); Blackburn (1988); Blackburn *et al.* (1988); Claus and Korom (1991); Claus *et al.* (1987); Flueckiger (1988); Ramanujan (1990).

4   As Frederique Marglin points out, the category 'Indian Classical Dance' was invented as a result of turn-of-the-century social reform movements which helped create modern performing arts institutions: 'the adjective classical reflects the Western model of the reformers: Indian Classical Dance connotes a status on a par with Western Classical Ballet' (1985: 2-3). In part, this representation of some traditional arts as 'classical' was a response to the disparagement of these arts by a newly British-educated class. As discussed in Chapter 4 in detail and witnessed in *Kathakali: The Art of the Non-Worldly* (Nair and Paniker 1993), equally problematic is the representation of *kathakali* as exclusively appealing to a refined audience of connoisseurs.

5   The *purana*s are a diverse collection of wisdom and stories which, along with the epics, 'became the bibles of popular Hinduism' (De Bary 1958: 323). They are the sources of many modes of storytelling and performance. Of the eighteen major and eighteen minor *purana*s, the *Bhagavata Purana* is the most popular and widely circulated. Especially dear to devotees of

Vishnu, this *purana* tells the story of the life of Lord Krishna.

6   Although women (Nangyars) traditionally perform female roles (except for demonesses) in Kerala's *kutiyattam* and *nangyar kuttu*, for reasons to be discussed below, until the recent establishment of an all-women's troupe (Tripunithura Kathakali Kendra), women have only occasionally performed on the *kathakali* stage. For analyses of women *kathakali* performers and issues of gender in the performance of *kathakali*, see Daugherty and Pitkow (1991), and especially Pitkow's excellent Ph.D. dissertation, 'Representations of the Feminine in *kathakali* : Dance-Drama of Kerala, South India' (1998).

7   According to Patrice Pavis, a 'macrostructural narrative' is one which sums up either a scene or even an entire play (1989: 50).

8   Although kings, princes, and demon-kings are often represented as marshalling their armies for war, especially in the 'set' choreography of 'preparing for battle,' the vast majority of *kathakali* killings take the form of one-on-one (or occasionally one-on-two) combat. There are only a few plays in the repertory with 'war' and not 'killing' in their titles (*Banayudham* and *Toranayudham*).

9   The Malayalam word *vadham* literally means the act of killing, not 'death.'

10   For further discussion of the significance of kingship in South Asia see the essays in Richards (1981).

11   Warrier's recollection of the enthusiastic crowds attending performances in his youth must be balanced by other accounts, such as K.P.S. Menon who recalls that in spite of large crowds attending *kathakali* performances in the 1920s, 'it would be wrong to think that all those who flocked to see a *kathakali* performance, then held in the open air, appreciated the art. For one *kathakali* lover who can appreciate the beauty of the *choliattam* . . . there are hundreds who, insensible to such delights, are satisfied with gazing at actors doing their make-up or watching the drummers, or are fascinated by the noisy stage-entry of a *tadi* (bearded) character. Thus the masses, easily pleased, rule the hour' (1978: 84).

12   These gender and caste-based restrictions on intermingling precluded all but exceptional women from entering the *kathakali* stage. Pre-menstrual Nayar girls freely intermingled with boys as both trained in the martial art, *kalarippayattu* (Zarrilli 1998); however, as soon as girls began to menstruate they were considered polluting, could not enter the *kalari* while menstruating since it was a temple as well as training and healing space, and became 'dangerous' because of their sexually active state. For these and a variety of other reasons, as Marlene Pitkow argues, 'female purity was . . . essential to the well-being and prosperity of the *taravad* (extended family) and many social practices were designed to protect it' (Pitkow 1998: 60). Circumscribing female movement whether within the household proper, or when travelling, 'protected' the women of one's household, and therefore protected the 'prosperity'/purity of a household (see Moore 1983).

13   Like many other cities and towns throughout India, during British rule indigenous names like the capital city of Kerala, Thiruvananthapuram, were Anglicized in shortened and/or simplified versions such as 'Trivandrum.'

14   When Milton Singer first proposed the category 'cultural performance,' he applied it to discrete items of performance which encapsulate and exhibit 'elementary constituents of the culture' (1972: 7). The postmodern turn in anthropology has problematized the modernist notion of culture as a relatively stable category, as well as of cultural performances as 'encapsulating' 'elementary constituents.' It implies a fixed essence rather than the fluid process of creating meaning characteristic of any act of performance, or of cultural praxis.

15   I use 'social drama' in anthropologist Victor Turner's sense – units of 'aharmonic or disharmonic social process, arising in conflict situations' (1986: 74) and following a four-phase process of breach, crisis, redressive action, and

either reintegration or irreparable schism (1976: *passim*).

16   Another important qualification is necessary. Although individual and group identities are increasingly shaped in an interculture of juxtaposition and disjuncture characteristic of public culture today, a self-conscious awareness of this condition is primarily the discourse of an educated and/or artistic elite. Given my position as an academic 'elite' writing in the United States, this book's organization foregrounds the discontinuities of contested narratives, rather than the normative arguments of those 'traditionalists' in Kerala who construct *kathakali* in its 'pristine purity.'

17   Agatha Jane Pilaar recently published the first volume of her *Kathakali Plays in English* (1993) which includes translations of the most performed scenes from twelve different plays; however, these are inadequate and even misleading 'librettos' which Pilaar herself 'composed' loosely from verbal translations provided by her collaborators. They reveal no critical attention to textual issues and offer absolutely no annotation of the source texts from which these 'compositions' were generated. Although these 'librettos' may be useful to people attending *kathakali* performances, they are not very useful for textual or performance scholars.

18   Dr Sudha Gopalakrishnan is currently completing a much needed new English translation of *Nalacaritam* that includes the performance manual (*attaprakaram*) of the famous *kathakali* actor Kalamandalam Krishnan Nayar for the play. Dominique Vitalyos recently published a complete translation of *Nalacaritam* in French (1995). While concerned with the play-in-performance, existing translations rightfully focus on communicating the beauty of Variyar's language in translation.

19   Their translation of *Kalyanasaugandhikam* was limited to Scene 9.

20   In addition to Chapter 2, the commentaries in Chapters 5–8 elaborate these historical connections and concerns.

2 A SOCIAL HISTORY OF *KATHAKALI* PATRONAGE, CONNOISSEURSHIP, AND AESTHETICS

1   Difficult historical questions remain to be answered about the early history of *Ramanattam*, and the relationship of *Krishnattam* to the emergence of *kathakali*. Among the proposed dates for the composition of the *Ramanattam* plays by Kottarakkara Tampuran, the range varies widely from 1484 to 1660! I have chosen to follow D. Appukuttan Nair's dates of 1625–85 (1993: 25), making him a contemporary of Manaveda, the Zamorin of Kozhikode and composer of *Krishnattam* plays in 1650. Complicating the history of their dates and relationship is the following widely circulated legend about the birth of *Ramanattam*:

> Soon after its [*Krishnattam*'s] debut on the stage, Kottarakara Tampuran . . . made a request to the Zamorin to depute his *Krishnattam* troupe to Kottarakara to give a few performances. For certain considerations – maybe political, maybe personal – the Zamorin turned down this request and Tampuran, in a state of offended pride, decided to compose a new art form by himself, more or less on the same model. The result was the emergence of Ramanattam, which later came to be known as *kathakali*.
>
> (Raja 1964: 41–54)

Whether a legend or not, this story reveals the high degree of rivalry that existed among the rulers of Kerala's numerous petty principalities at the time.

2   Fuller traces how sovereignty is actualized at the 'local level' where 'the Indian village is "a reduced version" of the kingdom and "there is a homology between the function of dominance at village level and the royal function at the level of a larger territory . . ." The king's counterpart in the village is the headman' (1992: 139). In the larger households, the eldest male or *karanavan* in essence serves as 'lord' of the extended family.

3   'Caste' is a problematic mis-translation of *jati*. For a more complete account of the *jati* and caste structure in Kerala see Fuller (1976), Jeffrey (1976), Puthenkalam (1977), Gough (1961), and Moore (1983).

4 Betty Jones notes that the leader and master of the Vettattu Raja's *Ramanattam* troupe was one Shankaran Nayar who was 'also an officer of the Vettattu Raja's army' who 'won a memorable victory for the Raja' in 1705 (1983: 20). Two important masters in the early history of *kathakali* were Vellattu Chattunni Panikkar, in service of the Kottayam Raja, the Ittiri Panikkar, in service of Kaplingattu Namboodiri. Thurston (1975: 6, 54) and K.P. Padmanabha Menon (1983: 2, 426) have both noted that Panikkar was a title used for 'fencing-masters.'

5 Three of his seven plays were 'southern' versions of three of the Kottayam plays. The Kottayam versions remain favourites in the repertory, while his versions lost favor.

6 'Nalanunni' was the pseudonym given to Ramanunni since the actor was so widely known and appreciated for his performances of the role of Nala in *Nalacaritam*. The pseudonym itself further underscores the emphasis in the south on *rasabhinaya*.

7 While the *rasa/bhava* aesthetic and the *Natyasastra* can be described as pan-Indian, the therefore as formative in the history of Indian poetics and dramaturgy, the ways in which this aesthetic and its correlative concepts such as 'appropriateness' are realized are always context and genre-specific, and therefore are always unique and historically specific. Even though *kutiyattam* has played an extremely important role in *kathakali*'s development, each contribution from *kutiyattam* has been adapted, however subtly, to *kathakali*'s unique performance structure and version of this aesthetic. Therefore, I have been careful to use the key qualifying term, 'based on' because *kathakali*'s version of 'appropriateness' and the *rasa/bhava* aesthetic are unique. D. Appukuttan Nair provides a comprehensive discussion of the differences between *kathakali*'s realization of this aesthetic and what is found in the *Natyasastra* (Nair and Paniker 1993: 6–9). For general discussions of *rasa* see Chari (1990), Baumer and Brandon (1981: 209–57), and Miller (1984).

8 Kottarakkara Tampuran authored the still popular *Ramanattam/kathakali* version of this story as part of his eight play cycle on the life of Rama. Occasionally cultural organizations have sponsored back-to-back performances of the *kutiyattam* and *kathakali* versions.

9 Or at least this is how such changes are perceived and interpreted discursively. Interpolations in *kutiyattam* usually focus on a story-telling aspect of elaborating a character's predicament and/or character, while in *kathakali* many focus on the character's inner psychology in a more Western sense. The increasing number of interpolations in the twentieth century devoted to the character's inner psychology, like that of Ramunni Menon discussed above, may in part reflect a subtle Western influence. Typical of the style of criticism and assessment of acting during the 1950s and 1960s is the following excerpt from a brief anonymous review of the career and acting of Vazhenkata Kunchu Nair on the occasion of his sixtieth birthday in the *Kalamandalam Annual*:

> With his wide intellectual background, he is able to make a character and their changing interrelationships relevant to the progression of the plot. The result is that every character, however lifeless and stereotyped it may seem to be, is transformed into a full-blooded and easily distinguishable one when he handles it.
>
> (1969: 5)

The critical introduction of notions of 'progression of the plot' and concerns with 'full-blooded' or 'rounded' characterization no doubt stem in part from the introduction of Western, Stanislavskian-based psychological drama.

10 Extensive land reform and redistribution did not occur until after Independence and the formation of Kerala State in the 1960s.

11 See S. Sarma *et al.* (1978) for a broad overview of the importance of Vallathol as both poet and leader of Kerala's cultural renaissance.

12 In a recent publication, Vallathol's son C. Balachandran discusses the vagaries and difficulties of these early tours (Balachandran 1990).

13 See Scorpio (1996) for a discussion and analysis of some of these issues.

14   See Zarrilli (1984a: Chapter 7) for a more complete account of these other institutions.

15   Margi takes its name from the concept *margi*, meaning to transcend space and time.

16   One 'night' or evening of performance at Margi usually lasts approximately three hours. Therefore, three nights of performance at Margi would be equivalent to one traditional all-night performance. On average, Margi's productions are adding approximately one-third more performance time to the performance of a text.

3 KATHAKALI TEXTS IN PERFORMANCE

1   The contemporary Western discourse of experimentation, which demands that art appears to be created 'on the edge' or the 'fringe' in order to exemplify the artist's creativity and imagination, belies of course the conventional nature even of performances which construct themselves as 'new' or 'experimental.'

2   For examples of other *sloka* in performance see Zarrilli (1984a: 233ff.). Just as some *sloka* are enacted, so are some *dandakam*.

3   While performance of *padam* generally follows this two-fold format which, in its structure, is a form of double-acted elaboration of the text, there are even more lengthy and complex examples of elaboration of lines of a *padam*. One example is the lengthy choreographic elaboration of one line in Scene 3 of *The Killing of Narakasura* when, during another slow love scene between the demon-king Narakasura and his wife, he sees, and then embodies the peacocks in their garden. See Zarrilli (1984a: pp. 243ff.).

4   The style of singing was traditionally unique, and known as *sopanam*, but *kathakali*'s distinctive style of singing is gradually being subsumed by the ever-increasing influence of carnatic vocal styles (see Omchery, 1969, for a discussion of this unique style).

5   This point is argued more fully in the commentary in Chapter 8 when I discuss the relationship between ritual sacrifice and kingship in Kerala.

4 KATHAKALI ACTOR TRAINING AND CHARACTERIZATION

1   I have placed quotation marks around both 'external' and 'internal' since using the terms suggests a dualism that is inappropriate to the dialectic between these two modes of actualization – both equally integral to the actor's process.

2   An increasing number of teachers accept part-time students today, usually from middle-class families. Many of these students are girls who undergo a few years of training in *kathakali* rather than an all-women's dance such as *mohiniattam* as part of their 'cultural' education. Many college students learn and perform solo set pieces such as Puthana's transformation in *Puthana Moksha* for performances at college art festival cometitions. For a more complete account of part-time training see Zarrilli (1984a: 91–4).

3   These arguments are commonplace in spite the fact that in the past, as well as today, many Nayar girls trained with boys in Kerala's martial art (*kalarippayattu*) at least until the age of puberty if not occasionally beyond, as exemplified by the case of the infamous Unniarcha made famous in Kerala's northern ballads. In addition, girls train to perform a number of difficult genres of traditional performance including *Nangyar kuttu*, *kutiyattam*, *Mohiniattam*, etc. all requiring extensive stage time. It is clear that such arguments neglect taking account of these counter-examples of women's abilities and 'realities.' Such arguments reflect the traditional male fear that women are 'dangerous' once they reach the age of puberty and become sexually active, and that they must be controlled by males in their extended families. See Pitkow (1998) for an extended discussion.

4   For a complete description of all the exercises and training summarized here, see Zarrilli (1984a: 107–43).

5   The Kalamandalam is currently considering a new official syllabus of twenty-five plays.

6   Gopi Asan's view reflects the increasing emphasis on 'internal' or 'mental' conflict in

kathakali acting and aesthetics in the twentieth century. As noted in Chapter 2, Pattiyakkantoti Ramunni Menon (1881–1949) developed a number of more 'internally' focused interpolations, such as that of Bhima in *The Killing of Baka*. Gopi's view certainly reflects two important historical facts. First, roles like Nala and Rugmamgada were not so common, especially in central Kerala, until the noted actor Kunju Kurup (1920–72) began to popularize them. Since his technique was thought not to be as highly developed as his abilities in providing new interpretations of these two heroic roles, he began to probe the depth of their emotional states. Krishnan Nayar took up Kunju Kurup's mantle, and has passed it on to the current generation of senior actors, especially Gopi Asan, who is featured in these two roles. It is commonplace knowledge among connoisseurs that Krishnan Nayar based his own artistry on his opinion that conflict is much more interesting within a person than between people.

7   This is a relativizing connector used to join the words on either side of the connector.

8   This form of sequential playing of multiple roles is much more characteristic of *kutiyattam* than of *kathakali*. In *kutiyattam*'s *nirvahana* sections of performance, the actor playing the primary role sequentially enacts all the roles in the story he recounts without changing his costume through an entire evening of performance. By comparison, the *kathakali* version of this form of 'solo acting' of multiple roles is much more limited in time and scope.

9   I discuss the implication of *kathakali* structuring of performance for a 'task based' theory of acting elsewhere (Zarrilli 1999).

10   Perhaps the most vivid dramatic representation of this ability to 'discard' one's own body and 'enter a different body,' is the comic exchange of souls and bodies between the Courtesan and the wandering holy man, Parivrajaka, in King Mahendravarman's one-act farce, *Bhagavadajjuka* ('The Hermit/Harlot'). As the play unfolds, the recalcitrant student, Sandilya, constantly baits his teacher, Parivrajaka, and undoes his 'holiness' with his own il-logic. Relevant here are Parivrajaka's

attempts to explain the difference between the 'soul' and the 'body' to his student by differentiating between the 'subtle body which transmigrates according to Fate's decree,' and the 'active, gross, embodied self' which is the 'receptacle of suffering and pleasure' (Lockwood and Bhat 1994, Part II: 22). The student manages to twist his teacher's logic into the conclusion that 'nothing is real except Body' – a conclusion which allows him to indulge himself in 'wine, women, and song' rather than meditation. Finally, in order to teach his recalcitrant and wayward disciple a lesson, the holy man decides to 'show him the real power of yoga' by 'injecting my self into the body of this courtesan' (ibid. 1994, Part II: 30).

11   The analysis and translation that follow are based on the generosity of my colleague at the University of Wisconsin-Madison, Professor V. Narayanan Rao, whose expertise in Sanskrit and Sanskrit aesthetics made possible any useful insights which might follow.

12   I am defining *bhava* as the state of being/doing embodied by the performer/actor, as demanded by the dramatic context and interpreted within a particular lineage of acting.

13   I am defining *rasa* as 'flavor,' or 'taste,' arising out of the act or practice of spectating which involves as complete as possible an engagement of the spectator in experiencing what the actor 'brings forward' and embodies.

14   See Zarrilli (1998) for more detailed explanations of this relationship.

15   For a full discussion of the *kari* see Pitkow (1998, Chapter 5).

5 THE FLOWER OF GOOD FORTUNE (*KALYANASAUGANDHIKAM*)

1   Only Scenes 9 and 10 are included in the video version of the play on which this translation is based.

2   In addition to this *padam*, a text known as *nilappadam* is also used to accompany the

dance. This text is not part of the original composition and its author is unknown.

3   The following two *caranam* are not usually performed today:

caranam:
O you who are bound to the truth,
  along with your brothers you wander the forest
while Ambika's grandson, Duryodhana,
  that ocean of deceipt,
rules in Hastinapura with his retinue. [K]

caranam:
Because Arjuna is gone, here in the forest we are
  considerably weakened.
In fact, O King, for someone who is blind,
  what is the use of other parts of the body? [K]

(Editor's note: The somewhat illogical image in the final *caranam* may be one reason this passage is not usually performed today.)

4   This is a lengthy *astakalasam*.

5   The following three *caranam* are not usually performed today:

caranam:
Even if the Fire God abandons heat,
  and even if the Sun abandons the world,
O Son of Vayu, my younger brother,
  I am unable to transgress the truth.
Therefore, do not speak like this. [K]+[I]

caranam:
Did not Dasaratha, chief of the Sun clan,
  fearful of breaking a vow,
  send his sons to the fierce forest?
Doing so, his mind was full of grief.
  Consider this, and then decide. [K]+[I]

caranam:
Arjuna will soon return without difficulty,
  having secured the divine arrows.
For those who worship the Almighty who is
  worthy of worship,
others' evil acts will be rendered useless.
Therefore, don't be doubtful. [K]+[I]

6   The *sloka* includes many long vowel sounds and contains no consonant clusters – features

that contribute to the lyrically romantic (*srngara*) mood of the scene.

7   This *caranam* is sung to accompany the *iratti*.

8   The following two *caranam* were omitted at this performance:

caranam:
Because of the strength and speed of his thighs, a
  huge number of trees fall to the ground. [K]

caranam:
Lo! the deer, having become skittish, run about.
If one contemplates his expertise, it is very
  eloquent. [K]

9   In southern Kerala an *astakalasam* is usually performed after 'In my mind . . . .'.

10   This repetition of the *pallavi* accompanies the dancing of the *tonkaram*.

11   This and the subsequent change of *raga* are not noted in the Menon or Rediyar texts, but are part of current performance practice.

12   A *kalasam* begins this *caranam*.

13   This *caranam* is usually not sung, but its basic meaning is enacted in the *ilakiyattam* that follows.

14   This and the subsequent changes in *raga* are not found in the Menon or Rediyar texts, but are part of current performance practice.

15   This *sloka* is enacted. The following two *sloka* were omitted at this performance:

sloka
Vayu's son, Hanuman, showed his own body to
  Vayu's other son, Bhima, who was standing near,
anxious to see the frightening hard form
  Hanuman took when crossing the ocean.

sloka
After duly seeing the awe-inspiring form of
  Hanuman whose reputation is famous,
Bhima was overwhelmed with fear and fell at
  Hanuman's feet, saying . . .

16   The following *caranam* was omitted:

caranam:
Please know that I have shown this form of my
  body out of affection for you.
Alas, if mere mortals see it, they will faint and
  become helpless.

17   The following *caranam* was omitted:

caranam:
Please see this forest path, which is impossible
  to traverse for anyone but you.
O one of good conduct, go without delay,
  and relinquish any anguish in your heart.

18   The following *caranam* was omitted:

caranam:
O son of Vayu, O great-minded one, have
  great compassion for me.

19   This change of *raga* is not found in the
Menon or Rediyar texts, but is part of current
performance practice.

20   This particular *ilakiyattam* is known literally
as 'combined acting,' since it involves both
Bhima and Hanuman.

21   This use of 'vital spot' reflects both the
vernacular use of the term and Monier-Williams'
definition of the Sanskrit *marman*, 'the core of
anything, the quick' (1899: 791), i.e., the essence,
core, or heart of the matter.

22   For *katti* characters such as Ravana in *Bali's
Victory* or Bana in *Bana Yudham* their awesome
powers lead to an overweening pride which
ultimately leads either to death or to (temporary)
humiliation. In *Bali's Victory* Ravana self-
consciously displays his pride, heroism and
strength by lifting Mount Kailas. When played
by some of the best actors of *katti* roles such as
Padmanabhan Nayar this demonstrative act
makes all the more poignant his eventual defeat
and humiliation by Bali.

23   In *Kiratam* the entire play could be read as
dramatizing Arjuna's continuous humiliations at
the hands of Siva in disguise. This greatest heroic
sage among the Pandavas, who has attained
access to the subtlest powers available to martial
practitioners, is constantly and humorously

rendered impotent. Each time Arjuna attempts
another mode of accessing a special power to
overcome the Hunter, his adversary mocks and
defeats him. In addition to being read as the
lancing of a hero's pride, trials and tests such as
this, especially when administered by Siva
(*Kiratam*), Brahma (*King Rugmamgada's Law*), or
Vishnu (*The Progeny of Krishna*) can also be read
as a necessary test of heroic devotion through
which the hero achieves divine powers (the
Pasupata for Arjuna), release (for Rugmamgada),
or happiness and prosperity.

6 *The Killing of Kirmira* (*Kirmiravadham*)

1   The scene numbers are those used in K.P.S.
Menon's text.

2   In the Kerala Kalamandalam style of
performing this *padam*, the *pallavi* and
anupallavi are treated as a *caranam*.

3   This phrase is repeated after the performance
of the *kalasam*. This particular structure where a
kalasam is performed at the end of the first
phrase of a *caranam* is common in
Kirmiravadham. As in each *caranam* of this
padam, the initial phrase is always repeated by
the vocalists after the *kalasam* has been
performed.
  Where this performance structure occurs, we
have attempted to keep the initial phrase of each
caranam in the Malayalam text first in our
translation; however, this has not always been
possible.

4   In the K.P.S. Menon text this *caranam*
follows the next. Following the order of the
performance on 1 August 1996, we have placed
this *caranam* first since there is sufficient
dramatic justification for this inversion.

5   In the Kerala Kalamandalam performance
tradition the *pallavi* and *anupallavi* are treated
as a *caranam* in performance.

6   In the Kerala Kalamandalam performance
tradition this *caranam* is joined with the next to
create one *caranam* followed by a *kalasam*.

7   In the original text the *raga* is *savarasam* and the *tala* is *triputa*.

8   For this and the following *iratti*, the *pallavi* accompanies its performance.

9   The following *caranam* and *pallavi* are not usually performed:

caranam:
O charming friend, please listen to my words:
I wonder why my right eye trembles,
  and whether some misfortune is about to befall
  me.
The wind blows adversely.
I certainly should return home.

pallavi: Seeing this omen, fear comes,
              Have you seen it (the omen)?* [K]

*This and the next *pallavi* below have the same grammatical construction as the *pallavi* above, 'Seeing this forest, pleasure comes. Have you seen it?' As in our translation, single words are substituted within the basic construction of the *pallavi* marking the dramatic shifts in circumstances.

10   The following *sloka* is not usually performed:

sloka:
She whose tumultuous cry resembles that of a
  lion and instills great fear in the *devas*,
said all this from her growing anger.
At night-fall the demoness whose body terrifies
  (everyone),
satisfied from holding the hand of Panchali –
  that ornament of women – with her own,
  charred like firewood,
(and) angry from the killing of her husband, took
  Draupadi far away.

11   Menon records the *tala* as *triputa*.

12   The following three *caranam* are not usually performed:

caranam:
O my protector, son of the life of the universe,
  wild fire of the forest of demons,
please protect me and come without delay! [K]

caranam:
O husband, Arjuna – brave one,
  ocean of valor, handsome-bodied one –
because of my bad luck even you have forsaken
  your wife! [K]

caranam:
The demoness has the color of black clouds.
  She is as awe-inspiring as the final night.
O Nakula, the strong one, she will deliver me to
  Yama. Please protect me! Protect me! [K]

13   The following *sloka* is not usually performed today:

sloka:
Instructed by his guru to return first (from the
  Ganges River), having collected wood for the
  sacrificial fire,
on his way, Sahadeva heard from the interior of
  the forest
the wailing of their dear (wife)
  who had been spirited away by the demoness.

14   The *raga* in the original text is *suratti*.

15   The singing of the *pallavi* accompanies this *tonkaram* and the others performed in this *padam*.

16   The following *caranam* is not usually performed:

SIMHIKA:
caranam:
O you boaster! With confidence and skill
  I will certainly capture you with my hands and
  leave.

17   The following *sloka* is not usually enacted:

sloka:
Reacting like this, the demoness quickly released
  Panchali.
Then, with her own hand (the demoness)
  captured (Sahadeva), and began to run quickly
when Pandu's son cut her breasts with his sword.

18   Scene 12, translated below, has not been enacted within the memory of actors or spectators today. Dramatically, Scene 11's culmination with Sahadeva's cutting of Simhika's nose is continued with Kirmira's curtain look and Simhika's appearance before her brother in Scene 13.

Scene 12
[Pandavas, Panchali]
[*sankarabharanam* (*raga*); *cembata* (*tala*)]

sloka:
She whose round breasts were cut off by the
  scimitar's tip and showered with blood, cried
  out inarticulately with fear.
Having returned from the banks of the Ganges,
  the best among kings (Pandavas), hearing a
  sound
from the forest, spoke to their dear one:

PANDAVAS:
Living in this forest is extremely difficult.
  Certainly, this is the result of bad actions.
O good-natured one, why did you go into this
  terrible forest?
O dear one, with an unblemished mind, tell us,
  O young woman, why you seem to be so
  shocked.

PANCHALI:
When you went to the banks of the Ganges to
  worship the Sandhya (to offer *puja* at twilight),
  a cunningly disguised demoness came to visit me.
With her smile she enchanted my heart, and
  approaching me slowly, she held my hand.
O kings, no woman on earth has such skills.
Deceiving me, she took me away.
  Then Sahadeva came to the forest.
A terrible fight ensued for five or six hours.
During the fight the giant-sized one let me go,
  and grabbed Sahadeva.
Then I arrived here thinking that one of you
  would come running.

BHIMA:
Please do not worry. All of you should remain
  here. I am going to finish off the demoness who
  acted so cruelly.
This mace will help me.
Arjuna, protect our elder brother and all the
  others. Stand in the forefront holding your
  sword and arrows.
O one with an unblemished body,
  certainly I will kill her without the least
  hesitation.

SAHADEVA:
O elder brothers, do not worry.
O leaders of the Puru clan, I acted rashly.

All the demons will bring their armies to fight
  (with us).

DHARMAPUTRA:
After the demoness left, what thoughtless thing
  did you do because of your anger?
Our enemies will come to fight with numerous
  strategies.
Listen to their tumult!

SAHADEVA:
Remembering that it is inappropriate to kill a
  woman,
  I cut her nose and breasts.
Within half and hour the time will be ripe for a
  good fight.

sloka:
Yudhisthira and the others, skilled at arms stood
  there brandishing their bows, swords, and
  arrows, wearing chest-plates as defensive armor,
awaiting the arrival of the demons for the fight.

sloka:
Then Kirmira, becoming angry on hearing of the
  killing of his friend, Sardula,
graced the assembly, arousing his army which
  was like an ocean.

19   No *kalasam* are played or danced during
this *pudam*, perhaps because of the dramatic
circumstances.

20   The following *caranam* are not usually
performed today:

caranam:
Alas! (You) see, those suitable for being eaten
  have turned out to be (our) enemies!
Alas, Arjuna killed (my) husband.
  (You) must kill them or me. [K]

caranam:
Deciding that it was appropriate to take revenge,
  without hesitation I entered the forest.
Then (I) saw his consort in the forest – that
  impeccable decorative spot among women. [K]

caranam:
When separated from the Pandavas, I watched
  for an opportunity.

Without fear I approached her and captured her
  in the forest. [K]

  caranam:
O brave one, for whom no humiliation is
  possible, I wanted to give her as a gift to you.
Exhausted and frightened, she began to wail. [K]

21 The *anupallavi* and *caranam* are not usually
performed:

  anupallavi:
I will immediately annihilate that inimical mortal!

  caranam:
Put aside the sorrow in your heart. Rise up, O
  one with the elephant's gait.
I leave with anger in my heart, ready to send
  mortals to the world of the immortals!

22 The following *caranam* is not usually
performed:

  caranam:
While I live on the earth, you should not be sad
  because of (any) misfortune.
They will not be the target of my anger, but of
  my arrows.

23 At the performance on 1 August 1996 the
stage attendants neglected to come to the stage
with the curtain causing some confusion
onstage. Part of the ensuing *sloka* was then sung
with the curtain down, or only partially covering
the stage.

24 This and the other *kalasam* in this *padam*
are very short links to the ensuing *tonkaram*.

25 The *pallavi* accompanies the *tonkaram*.

26 Considerable disagreement exists over
whether the correct *raga* to perform here is
porvakalyam or *pantuvarali*. Menon records
pantuvarali. The two *raga* are very similar.

27 The following *sloka* is not usually performed:

  sloka:
Immediately, the two chiefs of the *ksatriyas* and
  demons girded their loins (and) challenged each
  other to fight.

Forgetting themselves, they raised their excellent
  maces and continued to hit each other repeatedly.
Enlocked arm-in-arm, they struck each other
  with their fists, and hitting the earth, they
  jumped, emitting sounds as they leaped.
Thus, they fought.

28 The following *caranam* are not usually
performed:

BHIMA
  caranam:
O demon's son, [K]
  who is ignorant of the truth, purity, etc.
  you will reach and 'enjoy' the town of the son
  of Sun (Yama)! [K]

    pallavi: Resist . . . [T]

  caranam:
You know that I am vicious. [K]
  Because of what you have done, like a bird you
  have entered the strong cage of my hands. [K]

    pallavi: Resist . . . [T]

  caranam:
Come here treacherous one, wicked worm! [K]
  You have a large arrow in your hand, but you
  can't fight with deception.
Fool! Nothing is possible against me! [K]

    pallavi: Resist . . . [T]

29 The closing scene, translated below, is not
usually performed. If it is included, immediately
after the killing, one or more of the ascetics
enter, perform the first *caranam*, and exit after
blessing Bhima.

  sloka:
Remembering the killing of his friend (Sardula),
  Kirmira became extremely angry,
and righting Bhima, attained death.

[*bhupalam* (*raga*); *cempata* (*tala*)]

sloka:
When Kirmira was killed, his attendants
  immediately hid themselves in different places.
The ascetics on the banks of the river Tapati
  arrived, and with delight each said the following:

MAHARSI:

> *pallavi*: O Bhima, ocean of valor,
> noble-minded one, our fear
> has vanished.

anupallavi:
King Bhima, one with great strength of arms,
  auspiciousness will always be with you.

   caranam:
Since you have killed the demons in battle to
  whom none are equal,
we can always live in this forest without fear.

   caranam:
We can stay on the beautiful banks of the
  Ganges performing the fire sacrifice (*Agnihotra*)
  with pleasure.

   caranam:
Protection of the pious is the most important
  duty of Bharata's clan.
Your birth has become fruitful. Let protection
  always be your duty.

   sloka:
Each of the sages showered Bhima with his
  blessings.
Then the Vidyadharas rained flowers on his head.

(The Vidyadharas are demi-gods overseeing and
reacting to the world's activities.)

30   Many other important issues implicit in
current stagings of *The Killing of Kirmira*
deserve further analysis. This and other
representations of *kari* characters like Simhika
could be read as a class/caste commentary on the
opposite of the educated, beautiful heroine, and
therefore as a stereotype of Kerala's darker,
'scheduled castes' and/or 'tribes.' Associated with
the untamed, dangerous, natural forest, Simhika
as protrayed in Nelliyode's opening interpolation
is represented as unwashed, unkempt,
unattractive and constantly aspiring toward the
ideal feminine which she cannot attain. She is
stared at by other women. When she attempts to
join in dancing *kaikottakali*, playing *kumi*, etc.
she tries to do everything an actor does who
plays such ideal heroines as Damayanti or
Draupadi; however, she is rejected, and must
'play' and 'dance' by herself – an out-caste. As a

satiric rendering of these aspirations to the ideal,
these portrayals can be read as mocking
'aristocratic' behavior, much as the 'failures' of
the epic heroes can be read as mocking their
male aspirations to fulfil the ideal. Although
Simhika is a stereotype, so in one sense are all of
kathakali's characters. Like other major roles, she
is complex, and cannot be reduced to this simple
stereotype. In her rage over her husband's death,
she represents the 'female' as active and not
passive. Indeed, her reaction to her husband's
death, as played by Nelliyode when he tears off
the *tali*, reflects the ideal behavior of a woman
mourning over her husband's death. Like other
representational sites, such as 'the heroic' where
behavior is explored in cultural performances,
Simhika is a place for the negotiation of images
and notions of character, behavior and, in this
case, the 'feminine.'

7 *THE PROGENY OF KRISHNA* (*SANTANAGOPALAM*)

1   For an English translation see *Srimad
Bhagavatam*, trans. Raghunathan (1976), pp
503–7. The date of the original puranic source is
uncertain, and ranges from as early as the fifth
to as late as the tenth centuries. The frame story
which begins the puranic account is not
dramatized, and in this respect *The Progeny of
Krishna* is similar to other *kathakali* adaptations
of stories from the *Bhagavata Purana*.

2   Yama appears in a special form of black *katti*
(*nedunkatti*) ('knife') with a rough design.
Chitragupta appears in *minukku*.

3   Chakra appears in *pacca* make-up.

4   Normally for dancing the *purappatu* there is
both a *sloka* and a series of *caranam* of a *padam*
describing the heroes. Here there are no such
caranam. If the *purappatu* is performed, *caranam*
are added from other sources. When the
purappatu is not performed, the entire *sloka* is
not sung and the performance begins with the
second *sloka* below.

5   Since Arjuna is a major role in the play, the
actor may decide to perform a longer elaboration
than the short one transcribed here. In this

elaboration he usually enacts the ten incarnations of Vishnu, and ends by summarizing the *Bhagavad Gita*, concluding that whenever there is injustice, (*adharma*) in the world, Vishnu appears in a form to set things right and regain a balance of *dharma*. If the actor playing Arjuna performs this longer interpolation, he simply goes ahead, and the actor playing Krishna takes his cues from Arjuna. The great *kathakali* actor Krishnan Nayar Asan is credited with introducing this interpolation. The dramatic justification, or 'sense of appropriateness,' for this longer interpolation rests in the fact that since Arjuna has not seen Krishna for a very long time, he wants to recount his greatness.

6   The following *caranam* is not usually performed today:

   caranam:
O son! Won't you cry even a little?
O one with a wonderfully-shining face.
For your father who is a great sinner,
has fate destined this? O son! Siva! Siva!

7   This *caranam* is only found in the Redyar text and not in Menon.

8   The following *caranam* is not usually performed today:

   caranam:
On the day your dearest's pregnancy comes to
   term, quickly come and inform me.
In the wondrous house of delivery made from my
   arrows, (where) your dear (wife) will deliver
   (your) son,
who in this world has the ability to take him
   away? [K]

9   There is another variant reading, not found in either the Redyar or Menon: *vadiccituvan satyam*. It means, 'I shall utter this promise.'

10   This scene often concludes with a long *ilakiyattam* between Arjuna and the Brahmin. The main purpose of the interpolation performed today is to foreground the importance of devotion to Lord Krishna. How this is done differs from actor to actor.
   One major version of the *ilakiyattam* was created by Kunju Nayar Asan. In it the Brahmin prompts Arjuna to vow on the name of Krishna

that he will jump into the fire with his divine weapon if he does not deliver the child as promised. It is intended to further subdue Arjuna's pride.

11   The *raga* in the original text is recorded as *gaulipantu*.

12   The following *caranam* is not usually performed today:

   caranam:
If Krishna, the one with eyes like the petals of
   the blue lotus,
the playful, the one with a dark body resembling
   blue clouds,
the one lying on the ocean of milk supports
   Arjuna, the son of Indra will protect this child.
O Hari, Lord, Krishna, embodiment of
compassion,
   please protect (us). [K]
This *caranam* is only found in the Redyar, and not in the Menon text.

13   The following *caranam* are not usually performed today:

   caranam:
My discomfort is increasing; my body is
   becoming weak; my stomach moves; the
   child plays.
It has become difficult for me to walk even one
   foot. [K]

   caranam:
Oh husband, everything I do seems to have been
   transformed. [K]

14   In the original text the *raga* is recorded as *sahana*.

15   This *pallavi* is not danced as an *iratti*, but simply delivered with hand-gestures.

16   This *pallavi* is sung but not danced.

17   The following *caranam* is usually not performed:

ARJUNA:
   caranam:
Please look with care and pleasure at the tent of
   arrows,

the good house (before whose) great height even
the tallest mountain peak must fold its hands.
Doesn't it also have great vastness and expanse?
It is not easy for even Yama with his ever-
increasing power to enter here.

O Brahmin, with brightness and great joy, let
that protector of your life – the lotus-eyed
pregnant one, surrounded by her close
attendants, gracefully enter.

18   The following *caranam* is not usually
performed today, and is only found in the Redyar
and not the Menon text.

caranam:
Now it is inappropriate for me to approach
Krishna to tell him what has happened, wail
aloud, or strike my head!
Powerless Arjuna, O best among fools, we have
now become refugeless because we trusted your
words, O leader of wrongdoers!

This *caranam* continues the Brahmin's tongue-
in-cheek thrashing of Arjuna for his overweening pride. Indeed, were this performed, it
would add to the humor of the performance
since it takes the Brahmin's over-emotional
displays of his sorrow and anger to their logical
conclusion, i.e., he can no longer publicly
display his grief for Krishna.

19   Arjuna's *pallavi* and *caranam* are only
found in the Redyar edition.

20   The following are usually not performed:

KRISHNA:
> *pallavi*: O Arjuna! Friend! O one
> compassionate to the
> good. [K]

anupallavi:
Please do not burn (your) body in the fire – (a
body) which gives pleasure both in this world
and the next, O great one! [K]

caranam:
O Arjuna, if you throw yourself into the fire
today and are consumed, how could I continue
to live without grief?
O Arjuna, Son of the Lord of the gods, your

unkindness is cruel.
O one who has conquered all enemies, while I,
your friend, am alive, things like this will
happen, O Partha. [K] + [I]

21   The remainder of Krishna's speech and the
first four lines of Arjuna's next *caranam* are not
included in the Redyar edition, and are only
found in Menon.

22   The following *caranam* is not usually
performed:

caranam:
O one with the color of black clouds, I know that
you and only you are the divine Lord who lives
in Vaikuntha.
Even in Siva's mind confusion reigns from all
the techniques of *maya* (illusion) with which
you charm the worlds.
O ocean of greatness, O one filled with *maya*, the
only remedy for the blemish to my honor,
brought by breaking my vow, is the pit of fire.
One full of illusion, ocean of greatness,
Hail to you, my Madhava, the only Lord of the
worlds. [K]

23   The following is not usually performed:
Both my purpose and vow were thwarted.
Dishonor has come to me.
(Therefore), don't stop my attempt to die.

24   The following is not usually performed:
You were born and raised to be a brave man
within the Puru clan.
As long as I live, no dishonor can come to you.
O brave one, let us set forth (to attain what you
desire).

25   The following is usually not performed:
This chariot of mine is driven by Daruka.
Climb into it calmly. Please come along with me,
O Paurava!
Once we have reclaimed the brahmin boys, we
will return.
We shall also, with great anticipation, meet the
Lord of the Worlds (Vishnu). [K]

26   This short interpolation provides a
dramative and narrative bridge to Scene 12
when Scenes 9, 10, and 11 are not performed
today.

27 Giving performances as offerings at temples is fairly common today and is by no means restricted to performances of *The Progeny of Krishna*. For example, well-known actor Kalamandalam Gopi Asan gave a performance of Bali in *The Killing of Bali* in 1996 at the Guruvayur (Krishna) temple.

28 The original story in the *Bhagavata Purana* gives very little attention to the human plight of the Brahmin.

29 There are also a few shorter interpolations, such as when the Brahmin enters in Scene 2, which allow the actor to emphasize the pathos of the Brahmin's dilemma.

30 The version of the *attam* I refer to is that of actors following Kunju Nayar Asan.

31 The importance of children, and especially sons, to Kerala's Namboodiri brahmin families is witnessed in such specific rituals as the performance of *Ayyappan tiyatta*, the propitiation of Lord Ayappan to ensure prosperity and 'wealth' (through progeny) of an extended family (see Zarrilli 1990a; Jones 1981).

32 On the importance and significance of funeral rites see Knipe (1991), and his more specialized study (1977).

33 On the problem of evil and suffering in Indian thought and mythology see Tiwari (1986) and O'Flaherty (1976).

34 Not surprisingly, in a modern Indian state like Kerala, which elected the first communist state government in India in 1957, it is important to note that in his study of 235 interviewees, Ayrookhuzhiel reported that 55 said they did not believe in concepts like fate (*vidhi*). As one interviewee asserted, '*Vidhi* is brought on man by himself,' (1983: 168–9).

35 Actors follow particular traditions of interpreting a role. For example, M.P. Sankaran Namboodiri, Vasu Pisharoti, and Nelliyode Vasudevan Namboodiripad (all trained at the Kerala Kalamandalam) follow Kunju Nair Asan's interpretation of the role of the Brahmin. It is this particular interpretation of the Brahmin that

is explained here through interviews with these actors.

36 On the relevance of this notion of the substantive, see McKim Marriott (1990).

37 *Kopam* is the more colloquial Malayalam expression. *Kopam* is uncontrollable anger. To have *kopam* is to have a degree of anger that will cause some kind of reaction against the cause of the anger. For the Brahmin, his *kopam* over the loss of yet another son is directed to Krishna as King since, according to the Dharma Sastras, a king is supposed to protect his subjects. *Kopam* also refers to a god's anger, as when a god or divine figure delivers a curse.

38 Although Namboodiri was using the English word 'realistic' here, as Rustom Bharucha suggests in his discussion of the *lokadharmi* element in *Krishnattam*, any use of the word 'realism' to translate *lokadharmi* 'needs to be qualified, of course . . . [in] that nothing in the traditional Indian theatre approximates "realism" in the European tradition' (1990: 238). As exemplified in Pisharoti's example of the specific stage business which he incorporates in playing the Brahmin, this is the *lokadharmi* or 'everyday' aspect of playing the role.

39 The *taravatu* refers to the extended joint families which, until the turn of the twentieth century, lived together in large house compounds. One's identity and well-being traditionally depended on one's extended family.

40 In some *kathakali* plays caricatures are played by senior actors. G.S. Warrier explains how and why the carpenter (*ásari*) role in *The Killing of Baka* is so enjoyable and important: 'Some of the great actors would be wonderful in this role! They had to translate it into the common man's language – measuring, etc. [doing all the easily identifiable things a carpenter does]. There was always some fun in it. He's got a coconut leaf he uses as a measure. He goes to cut the leaf, but almost cuts his head in the process! Or he's chewing *pan* and spits it into the audience, and everyone moves because it's so real!' Similar are the washerman and washerwoman, Mannan and Mannati, in *Lavanasuravadham* by Amritta Sastry (1815–77).

What differentiates the Brahmin from these roles is the depth of innocence and purity with which his everyday actions must be played in order to enhance sympathy for his pathos.

8 KING RUGMAMGADA'S LAW (RUGMAMGADA CARITAM)

1   The summary of the first seven scenes of the play is based on the Redyar edition. K.P.S. Menon's acting version includes a summary of these scenes. Menon's summary may be based on a slightly different version than Redyar since there are some substantive differences. His translation only includes the final three scenes. The translation of scenes 8, 9, and 10 is based on K.P.S. Menon's acting version (Vol. III, 1979).

2   This *sloka* is the original first *sloka* of the play, and is included in the Menon acting version. It was not sung at the Killimangalam performance, and is not usually performed today.

3   In the K.P.S. Menon version, scenes 8, 9, and 10 are listed as scenes 1, 2, and 3.

4   This *ilakiyattam* summarizes much of the content of the first seven scenes of the full play.

5   Although both the Menon and Redyar texts read '*atra sadaya sukham me*,' *sadaya* is doubtful. Given the context, a more likely reading would be *kalaya* for *sadaya*, thus rendering the line, 'Please do (something) to please me.'

6   In the following line, the tempo of *cempata tala* is increased slightly to enhance the dramatic impact of Mohini's demand. The tempo then returns to the original *cempata tala* speech with Rugmamgada's next lines. This pattern of slightly increasing and then decreasing the tempos is repeated throughout the following exchanges.

7   Both the Redyar and Menon read, '*pranayajana*,' ('people who have love'); however, this must be a mistake since only *pranatajana* ('people who bow down,' i.e., devotees) makes sense in the context.

8   This *kalasam* is not danced. Sometimes an *ilakiyattam* is performed here in which

Rugmamgada says, 'She is a demoness. Without knowing that, I trusted her and took the oath. I can now take refuge only at the feet of Lord Vishnu. How can I explain my position to my son and wife?'

9   For the type of *ilakiyattam* which follows, where so much improvisation is allowed the actor-dancer, the *centa* drummer must be able to read the actor's mind, and build toward the dramatic crescendo of the scene when he dances the N just before raising his sword to strike Dharmamgada.

10   This *kalasam* is not danced.

11   This form of Vishnu is especially sacred to Malayalis who worship Padmanabha at Sri Padmanabhaswamy Temple in Thiruvananthapuram. This is the temple associated with the Travancore ruling family at which performances of the play would have originated.

12   Other readings of the drama are also possible. The play could be read as enacting the conflict between eighteenth century Vishnavite devotionalism and the violent/dangerous powers of Dravidian tantric Saktism. As in Mantavappalli Ittiraricha Menon's *The Progeny of Krishna*, devotion to Vishnu prevails. This contrast is clearly marked in the differences between *mutiyettu*, which enacts the goddess' violent fury, and *Krishnattam*, where Vaishnavite erotic lyricism predominates (Caldwell 1995: 327).

13   Hart (1979, 1975), Hiltebeitel (1976, 1988, 1991), and Caldwell (1995) discuss the antique association of hair with 'power' in Dravidian culture. 'This inheritance is still seen in the loosening of women's hair during state of spirit possession, as well as in the *veliccappatu*'s (oracle) running of the fingers of his left hand through his long, loosened hair while in trance at Bhagavati temples. The running of the fingers through the hair, especially female hair, infuses the body with wild, natural sacred power' (Caldwell 1995: 184–5).

14   This state is clearly marked in *yakshagana tenkutittu* and, as David Gitomer records, in *The Catastrophe of the Braid* where Bhima is clearly

associated with ogres and demons: 'Bhima's interactions with the race of cannibalistic ogres in the epic lie behind his adharmic violence and voraciousness' (1999: 287–8). In *The Catastrophe*, as well as in the *yakshagana tenkutittu* version of the killing of Dussassana, an ogre must possess Bhima in order for him to drink blood:

> Bloodfield says, 'My master Wolfbelly has vowed to drink the blood of Dussassana. But I, the appointed ogre, must enter the body and do the drinking for him.'
>
> (ibid.: 94)

In both *yakshagana tenkutittu* and *The Catastrophe*, 'the depiction of *bibhatsa rasa*, the disgusting, often becomes comic, and emerges as a species of *hasya rasa*; the raksasas of the *Venisamhra* function as vidusakas (buffoons) in a play where there is no vidusaka' (ibid.: 286).

15   This reading of the dynamics of '*raudra*' as a state of heightened acuity from which dire consequences result is ubiquitous in Kerala, and has symbolic importance in the world communists have created to enhance consciousness about radical social change. In Bhaasi's *Memories in Hiding* the main character, Ceennan, during the Suranand Revolution in Kerala where many peasants and party workers died at the hands of the police, undergoes a transformation from life-long acceptance of his social position in service to his landlord/oppressor, to a state where his fury 'explodes': 'Tamburaan!' (*He stares at the landlord and stands up straight. The landlord is puzzled by the expression on his face. Nannu Naayar (the landlord's bodyguard) becomes afraid. Ceennan stares at him for a moment. In a firm declaration* 'I no longer have a Tamburaan! I am no longer a slave!' (1995, Act 4, Scene 1: 55). In the Kerala People's Art Club production, Ceenan is bathed in red light during this scene. A number of articulations exist between the goddess/terror/fury and the radical/revolutionary leftist movement in Kerala: the association of red with the 'heated' nature of the goddess, her fury and necessary blood-letting; the 'terror' society witnesses when the 'people' rise up in righteous/divine 'fury'; and the 'blood' it is necessary to shed to assuage this fury.

This reading is supported by the fact that just before this scene of revolt, in Act 3, Scene 4

during the chaotic melee in which the police are attacking the agricultural laborers and their families, Bhaasi has '*kathakali* drumming from the nearby (Bhagavati) temple' during a performance of *The Killing of Duryodhana* playing in the background. With Dussassana and Duryodhana both having been killed, the drumming from the performance comes to an end just as the fighting 'decreases and ends.'

9   ISSUES OF INTERCULTURAL PRODUCTION, PERCEPTION, AND RECEPTION IN A *KATHAKALI KING LEAR*

1   Unfortunately, I have not yet been able to locate a copy of the text of this *kathakali* experiment.

2   For a more complete account of some of these productions see Zarrilli (1984a).

3   Currimbhoy chooses to collapse Dussassana purposefully into Duryodhana for dramatic effect, and therefore calls Dussassana Duryodhana. For those who know the Mahabharata well, and/or *kathakali*, this choice is confusing.

4   Prior to this festive opening in Thiruvananthapuram, I also attended several rehearsals, including a dress rehearsal at the Kerala Kalamandalam. Before and after the opening I conducted interviews with a number of the performers and spectators.

5   The second production, no longer associated with the Kerala Kalamandalam, used a new Malayalam translation, several new cast members and some revisions in the staging. My analysis of the European performances is based on viewing a video of the Edinburgh production and the numerous reviews of the continental and Edinburgh performances.

6   McRuvie was referring to the fact that actors who play female roles receive special training in three modes of expression used exclusively for playing many female roles: a coy, 'pretended' shyness; a pouting contempt; and similarly, a pouting anger. In all three modes of expression there is clearly a set of quotation marks put

around each emotional state which says, 'this is pretended' or 'I don't really mean this.' Therefore, when a female character is enacting this special shyness toward her beloved, the subtext is, 'I'm just acting shy and you can really have me.' Although there are a few strong and less submissive female roles played in which shyness, contempt, and anger are expressed more directly without the quotation marks, they are the exception rather than the rule. Consequently, McRuvie's hesitancy about using a male *kathakali* actor for the role of Cordelia.

7   For a critique see Bharucha 1990: 94–120.

8   Somewhat in contrast to Brook, Eugenio Barba seeks a form of metacultural communication, but rather than erasing cultural distinctions he has his group of international actors each keep her distinctively enculturated movement vocabulary while developing the *mise en scène*, thereby seeking to reveal 'cultures . . . through cultures' (Pavis 1989: 53).

9   The question of what is or is not 'indigenous' or perceived as 'one's own' is highly problematic. Although Shakespeare's *King Lear* might be said to 'belong' to England, to whom can the tale on which Shakespeare based his play be said to 'belong'? As folklorist Peter Claus pointed out to me in a private correspondence, in contrast to the story of Cinderella, which is a type 510A colonial import to India, the Lear story is a type 510B tale which appears to have traditional forms in India. One version is the 'Woman of the Hut of Leaves' which tells the story of a king who had seven daughters, the youngest of whom he thought to marry to someone who might come and stay at his palace. At a palace festival the King asked, 'whose wealth are you enjoying?' The six eldest daughters all responded, 'We are enjoying the wealth earned by you.' When the youngest daughter said, 'As long as I am in your house I will enjoy your wealth, but when I go to my husband's house I will enjoy whatever is in my fate,' the King became outraged and banished her to a 'hut of leaves.'

10   For a comprehensive overview see Said (1978).

11   One of the earliest performance examples of our mystification of India is Ruth St Denis's creation of her 1905 'Radha' where she danced the role of this 'SPIRITUAL OTHER.' (See Erdman 1987.)

12   Ravanna and Rama are adversaries in one of India's two great epics, the *Ramayana*. Ravanna is the ten-headed demon-king of Lanka who captures Rama's wife, Sita, and whom Rama rescues with the help of the devoted monkey-god, Hanuman.

13   P.C. Namboodiri made the same point when he contrasted the historical characters who appeared in a locally initiated and produced World War II *kathakali* Hitler (the evil red beard), Roosevelt, Chiang Kai-Shek, and Stalin (the heroic beneficent 'green' character type) with epic characters:

> They are real human beings you have seen either in motion pictures or in photos. But you don't know what Siva is. People can only imagine what is his exact nature. The costumes fit only such characters. So realism in that [historical] way is not appropriate to a dance-drama like *kathakali*.
> (Hanna 1983: 162)

14   The only Sanskrit drama in which it could be argued that pathos plays a major role is Bhasa's play, *Urubhangam*. In the *kutiyattam* repertory, the style of acting Bali's death is filled with pathos, and may have served Padmanabhan Nayar as a model.

15   *Kathakali King Lear* played at Shakespeare's Globe Theatre in London from 6–17 July 1999. This most recent production is not discussed here.

10 WHEN MARX MET IMPERIALISM ON THE *KATHAKALI* STAGE

1   Iyyamgode Sridharan, *People's Victory* (manuscript, n.d.). All other quotations are from the five-page single-spaced manuscript.

2   *Manavavijayam Kathakali* (program, n.d.).

3   It is important to distinguish between the recently collapsed forms of Eastern European

bureaucratic communism/socialism, and this particular third-world, post-colonial, democratic communist/socialist experiment in non-adventurist policies attempted in Kerala. The long-term effect of the collapse of Eastern European communism on Kerala's communists is only now gradually unfolding.

4 On land reform in Kerala see also Hart and Herring (1977) and Herring (1980). Regina Holloman and Wayne Ashley note that 'the back of the traditional system was not broken in northern Kerala until 1972 when the Kerala Land Reforms Act was actually implemented in that area' (1983: 990).

5 On the split between the CPI and CPI(M) see Nossiter (1988, 1982).

6 It is important to understand that a *kathakali* text is known as an *attakatha* and *not* a *natakam*. *Natakam* would not be perceived as a totalizing category like our term 'drama,' which we might use to include both *kathakali* and socialist texts.

7 For the best analysis of *teyyam* as a popular form of Hinduism, see Freeman (1991).

8 Iyyamgode Sridharan's appointment was made in 1987 by the newly elected left-front coalition. He contined to serve as Secretary of the Kalamandalam until the 1991 election after which a new Secretary was appointed.

9 Iyyamgode's decision to return to 'traditional' content was in part prompted by the press attacks on the subject he had chosen for *People's Victory*. Even though in many respects *People's Victory* was successful in reaching 'new' audiences, it was the attacks from *kathakali* - lovers, and changing geo-political circumstances that led Iyyamgode to admit that 'epic, mythological stories, are more apt for *kathakali*' than contemporary politics (1993, interview).

10 There are several unique features to *Message of Love* as a *kathakali* play. First, Krishna is usually a relatively minor character, or at most plays an intermediate role in the repertory – like the intermediate role that Krishna plays in *The Progeny of Krishna*. In *Message of Love*, Krishna becomes a major role with scope for development by the actor. Second, his beloved Radha is virtually ignored on the *kathakali* stage. In *Message of Love*, Radha comes to the stage in the opening scene with Krishna for what critics (Kaladharan 1995) found to be a very satisfying scene since it follows the tenets of traditional *kathakali* structure, style, and characterization.

11 The BJP has come to power in the recent 1998 national elections as the leader in a coalition of primarily right/nationalist parties. It is precisely such a political development, and the attendant policies of the right that Iyyamgode was attempting to critique in this production.

12 *Manavavijayam Kathakali* (program, n.d.). It is unclear how often all of the preliminary rituals were dispensed with. S. Sunderdass noted in his *Kerala Kaumudi* review of 19 February 1987 that none of the rituals, including lighting the oil lamp, were performed. But according to Gopalakrishnan's account of the Kannur performance in *Kerala Kaumudi* (23 March 1987), although Iyyamgode Sridharan 'made clear that this *kathakali* was to be performed without the brass lamp, opening verses, and other rituals . . . everything was there except the opening verses.'

13 *Manavavijayam Kathakali* (program, n.d.).

14 To mention only a few examples: Raman Kutty Nayar planned and choreographed the fight scene, and selected some of the hand-gestures such as 'bomb' for the original production of *People's Victory*. Kalamandalam Vasudevan directed all the scenes for *Message of Love*.

⨳⨳⨳ bibliography

and
references cited

Alter, Joseph S. 1992 *The Wrestler's Body: Identity and Ideology in North India*. Berkeley: University of California Press.

Anonymous 1969 'Vazenkata Kunchu Nair,' *Kalamandalam Annual*, 5.
— 1989 'L'histoire du "Roi Lear" Contee en Kathakali,' *Canne Matin* (Nice-Matin), 26 November.
— 1989 'Le Roi Lear Version Kathakali: Un Spectacle Haut en Couleurs,' *Presse de la Manche*, 9 November.
— 1989 '"King Lear" in Kathakali,' *Hindu*, 13 January.

Appadurai, Arjun (ed.) 1991 *Gender, Genre, and Power in South Asian Expressive Traditions*. Philadelphia: University of Pennsylvania Press.

Appadurai, Arjun and Breckenridge, Carol A. 1995 'Public Modernity in India,' in *Consuming Modernity: Public Culture in a South Asian World*, (ed.) Carol A. Breckenridge. Minneapolis: University of Minnesota Press, 1–20.
—1988 'Why Public Culture?' *Public Culture*, 1(1): 5–9.

Aricatasumedaran 1987 Letter to the editor, *Kerala Kaumudi*, 28 March.

Asema 1987 'Modernity on the *Kathakali* Stage,' *Mathrabhumi*, 1 March.

Ashley, Wayne and Holloman, Regina 1990 'Teyyam,' in *Indian Theatre*, (eds.) Farley Richmond, Darius Swann, and Phillip Zarrilli. Honolulu: University of Hawaii Press.
— 1982 'From Ritual to Theatre in Kerala,' *The Drama Review*, 26(2):59-72.

Ashton-Sikora, Bush, Martha and Sikora, Robert P. 1993 *Krishnattam*. New Delhi: Oxford and IBH Publishers.

Awasthi, Suresh 1993 'The Intercultural Experience and the Kathakali *King Lear*,' *New Theatre Quarterly*, 9(34): 172-8.
— 1989 'Theatre of Roots,' *TDR: The Drama Review*, 33(4):48-69.

Ayrookhuzhiel, A.M. Abraham 1983 *The Sacred in Popular Hinduism: An Empirical Study in Chiralla, North Malabar*. Madras: The Christian Literature Society.

Ayyar, K.V. Krishna 1928-32 'The Kerala Mamakam,' *Kerala Society Papers*, 2, Series 6: 324-30.

Balachandran, C. 1990 'Memories of my father,' *Express Weekend* (Kochi), 10 November, iv-vi.

Balakrishnan, Sreevarahom 1997 'Blazes a new trail,' *The Hindu*, 24 January.

Barba, Eugenio 1967 'The Kathakali Theatre,' *The Drama Review*, 11(4): 37-49.

Barbosa, Duarte 1989 (1921) *The Book of Duarte Barbosa*, Vol. II. Trans. Mansel Longworth Dames. New Delhi: Asian Educational Services (reprint).

Bauman, Richard 1977 *Verbal Art as Performance*. Rowley, MA: Newbury Books.

Baumer, Rachel Van M. and Brandon, James R. (eds) 1981 *Sanskrit Drama in Performance*. Honolulu: University of Hawaii Press.

Bayi, Gouri Lakshmi 1995 *Sree Padmanabha Swamy Temple*. Bombay: Bharatiya Vidya Bhavan.

Benedict, Burton 1983 *The Anthropology of the World's Fairs*. Berkeley: Lowie Museum of Anthropology.

Bennett, Susan 1996 *Performing Nostalgia: Shifting Shakespeare and the Contemporary Past*. London: Routledge.
− 1990 *Theatre Audiences: A Theory of Production and Reception*. London: Routledge.

Bharucha, Rustom 1990 *Theatre and the World*. Columbia, MO: South Asia Books.

Bhat, G.K. 1984 *Rasa Theory*. Baroda: The M.S. University.

Billington, Michael 1990 'Empty Gestures of a Frustrating Lear,' *Guardian*, 17 August.

Blackburn, Stuart H. 1992 'Context into Text: Performance and Patronage in a Tamil Oral Tradition,' in *Arts Patronage in India*, (ed.) Joan Erdman. New Delhi: Manohar, 31-45.
−1988 *Singing of Birth and Death: Texts in Performance*. Philadelphia: University of Pennsylvania Press.

Blackburn, Stuart H. and Ramanujan, A.K. (eds) 1986 *Another Harmony: New Essays on the Folklore of India*. Berkeley: University of California Press.

Blackburn, Stuart H., Claus, Peter J., Fleuckiger, Joyce B. and Wadley, Susan S. 1988 *Oral Epics in India*. Berkeley: University of California Press.

Bolland, David 1996 (1980) *A Guide to Kathakali* (third edition). New Delhi: Sterling Paperbacks.

Boner, Alice 1935 'Kathakali,' *Journal of the Indian Society of Oriental Art*, 3: 61-74.

Bowers, Faubion, Meserve, Ruth L., Meserve, Walter J. and Srinivasa Iyengar, K.R. n.d. *Appreciations of Asif Currumbhoy*. Calcutta: Writer's Workshop.

Caldwell, Sarah Lee 1995 'Oh terrifying mother: The Mudiyettu Ritual Drama of Kerala, South India,' unpublished Ph.D. dissertation, Department of Anthropology, University of California at Berkeley.

Carlson, Marvin 1990 'Local Semiosis and Theatrical Interpretation,' in *Theatre Semiotics*. Bloomington: Indiana University Press.

Carriere, Jean-Claude 1987 *The Mahabharata*. New York: Harper and Row.

Chaitanya, Krishna 1971 *A History of Malayalam Literature*. New Delhi: Orient Longman.
− 1970 'The Aesthetics of Kathakali,' *Sangeet Natak*, 15: 5-10.

Chari, V.K. 1990 *Sanskrit Criticism*. Honolulu: University of Hawaii Press.

Chin, Daryl 1989 'Interculturalism, Postmodernism, Pluralism,' *Performing Arts Journal*, 12(1-3): 168-79.

Claus, Peter J. and Korom, Frank J. 1991 *Folkloristics and Indian Folklore*. Udipi, Karnataka: Regional Resources Centre for Folk Performing Arts, Mahatma Gandhi Memorial College.

Claus, Peter J., Handoo, J. and Pattanayak, D.P. (eds) 1987 *Indian Folklore*, Vol. II. Mysore: Central Institute of Indian Languages.

Clifford, James 1988 *The Predicament of Culture: Twentieth Century Ethnography, Literature, and Art*. Cambridge, MA: Harvard University Press.

Cohen, Anthony P. 1994 *Self Consciousness: An Alternative Anthropology of Identity*. London: Routledge.

Comaroff, John and Comaroff, Jean 1992 *Ethnography and the Historical Imagination.* Boulder, CO: Westview Press.

Coomaraswamy, A.K. 1957 *The Mirror of Gesture*, 3rd (edn.) New Delhi: Munshiram Manoharlal.

'Costumes and Accessories in Kathakali' 1961 *Census of India*, Vol. VII: Kerala, Part VIIA: 26-74.

Currimbhoy, Asif 1992 (1961) *The Dumb Dancer.* Bombay: Writer's Workshop Publication.

Damodaran 1996 *Annual Report for Margi.* Unpublished document.

Dasgupta, Gantam (trans.) 1993 'Dhanur Veda' chapters of *Agni Purana.* Unpublished translation.

Daugherty, Diane and Pitkow, Marlene 1991 'Who Wears the Skirts in Kathakali?' *TDR: A Journal of Performance Studies*, 35(2): 138-56.

Davis, M. 1976 'A Philosophy of Hindu Rank from Rural West Bengal,' *Journal of Asian Studies*, 36(1): 5-24.

De Bary, William Theodore 1958 *Sources of Indian Tradition.* New York: Columbia University Press.

De Marinis, Marco 1987 'Dramaturgy of the Spectator,' *TDR: A Journal of Performance Studies*, 31(2): 100-14.

Devi, E.H. 1975 'Medieval society as reflected in the ballads of North Malabar,' M.A. thesis, University of Calicut.

Drewal, Margaret 1991 'The state of research on performance in Africa,' *African Studies Review*, 34(3): 1-64.

Eagleton, Terry 1990 *The Ideology of the Aesthetic.* Oxford: Basil Blackwell.

Eck, Diana L. 1981 *Darsan: Seeing the Divine Image in India.* Chambersburg, PA: Anima Publications.

Eliade, Mircea 1957 'Time and eternity in Indian thought,' Papers from the Eranos Year Books. Bolingen Series XXX(3): 172-200.

Enros, Pragna Thakkar 1981 'Producing Sanskrit plays in the tradition of Kutiyattam,' in *Sanskrit Drama in Performance*, (eds) Rachel M. Baumer and James R. Brandon. Honolulu: University of Hawaii Press, 275-98.

Erdman, Joan L. 1987 'Performance as translation: Uday Shankar in the West,' *TDR: A Journal of Performance Studies*, 31(1): 64-88.
— 1978 'The Maharaja's musicians: the organization of cultural performance at Jaipur,' in *American Studies in the Anthropology of India*, (ed.) Sylvia Vatuk. Delhi: Manohar, 342-67.

Erdman, Joan L. (ed.) 1992 *Arts Patronage in India: Methods, Motives, and Markets.* New Delhi: Manohar.

F.C. 1989 '"Le roi Lear" en Kathakali!' *Progres*, 21 November.

Fabian, Johannes 1990 *Performance and Power: Ethnographic Explorations through Proverbial Wisdom and Theater in Shaba, Zaire.* Madison: University of Wisconsin Press.

Flueckiger, Joyce Burkhalter 1988 '"He Should Have Worn a Sari:" A "Failed" Performance of a Central Indian Oral Epic,' *TDR: A Journal of Performance Studies*, 32(1): 159-69

Foucault, Michel 1988 'Technologies of the self,' in *Technologies of the Self: A Seminar with Michel Foucault*, (ed.) Luther H. Martin. Amherst. University of Massachusetts Press.

Freeman, J. Richardson 1991 'Purity and violence: sacred power in the Teyyam worship of Malabar,' unpublished Ph.D. dissertation, University of Pennsylvania.

Fuller, C.J. 1992 *The Camphor Flame.* Princeton: Princeton University Press.
— 1976 *The Nayars Today.* Cambridge: Cambridge University Press.

George, K.M. 1992 'Asif Currimbhoy, A Preface,' trans. by T.M.P. Nedungadi. Calcutta: The Writer's Workshop.
— 1968 *A Survey of Malayalam Literature.* London: Asia Publishing House.

n.d. 'Asif Currimbhoy, A Preface,' [English translation of the Malayalam Introduction to the Malayalam edition of *The Dumb Dancers & Two Plays*] Calcutta: Writers Workshop.

Ghosh, Manomohan (ed. and trans.) 1975 (1957) *Nandikesvara's Abhinayadarpanam*. Calcutta: Manisha Granthalaya.
– 1967 (1951) *The Natyasastra* (Vols. I, II). Calcutta: Graanthalaya Private Ltd.

Gilles, Pierre 1989 'L'automne Indien du Roi Lear,' *Ouest France*, 15 September.

Gitomer, David 1999 *The Catastrophe of the Braid: The Mahabharata in Classical Drama*. New York: Oxford University Press.

Gopalakrishnan, K.K. 1993 'A mountain of sorrow for the artist,' *Malayalamanorama* (Malayalam), 24 January.
– 1992a 'Kalamandalam Gopi at 55: outstanding kathakali artist,' *Sruti*, 93/94: 35-9.
– 1992b 'After Diamond Jubilee, a new dawn?,' *Sruti*, 87/88: 23-30.
– 1987 *Kerala Kaumudi*, 23 March.

Gopalakrishnan, Sudha 1994 'Understanding *Kathakali*,' unpublished translation of *Nalacaritam*.

Gopinath, Mohan 1978 'Kathakali Music – An Appreciation,' *Malayalam Literary Survey*, 2(1): 55-62.

Gough, Kathleen 1961 'Nayar: Central Kerala,' in *Matrilineal Kinship*, (eds) Kathleen Gough and David M. Schneider. Berkeley: University of California Press.
– 1952 'Changing kinship usages in the setting of political and economic change among the Nayars of Malabar,' *Journal of Royal Anthropological Institute*, **82**, Pt. I: 71-88.

Grady, Sharon A. n.d. 'Do you know me? Activism for women's rights in Kerala, South India,' unpublished mss.

Grady, Sharon A. and Zarrilli, Phillip B. 1994 '. . . it was like a play in a play in a play! Tales from South Asia in an Intercultural Production,' *TDR: The Drama Review*, **38**(3): 168-84.

Grandmontagne, Cl. 1989 'Le "Roi Lear" par le Theatre Kathakali: Deroutant Mai Superbe,' *Telegramme*, 9 October.

Grayburn, Nelson (ed.) 1971 *Readings in Kinship and Social Structure*. Berkeley: University of California Press.

Gundert, Rev. H. 1982 (1872) *A Malayalam and English Dictionary*. New Delhi: Asian Educational Services.

Hanna, Judith Lynne 1983 *The Performer-Audience Connection*. Austin: University of Texas Press.

Hart, Henry C. and Herring, Ronald J. 1977 'Political conditions of land reform: Kerala and Maharashtra,' in *Land Tenure and Peasant in South Asia*, (ed.) Robert E. Frykenberg. Delhi: Manohar.

Hart, George L. 1979 *Poets of the Tamil Anthologies: Ancient Poems of Love and War*. Princeton: Princeton University Press.
– 1975 *The Poems of Ancient Tamil: Their Milieu and Their Sanskrit Counterparts*. Berkeley: University of California Press.

Hatch, Emily 1934 'Kathakali: the indigenous drama of Malabar,' unpublished Ph.D. dissertation, Cornell University.

Herring, Ronald J. 1980 'Abolition of land-lordism in Kerala: a redistribution of privilege,' *Economic and Political Weekly*, **15**(2), 28 June.

Higgins, Jon B. 1976 'From prince to populace: patronage as a determinant of change in South Indian (Karnatak) music,' *Asian Music*, **7**(2): 20-6.

Hiltebeitel, Alf 1991 *The Cult of Draupadi*, vol. II. Chicago: University of Chicago Press.
– 1988 *The Cult of Draupadi*, vol. I. Chicago: University of Chicago Press.
– 1976 *The Ritual Battle: Krishna in the Mahabharata*. Ithaca: Cornell University Press.

Holloman, Regina and Ashley, Wayne 1983 'Caste and cult in Kerala,' *South Asian Anthropologist*, **4**(2): 93–104.

Hopkins, Thomas J. 1971 *The Hindu Religious Tradition*. Encino, CA: Dickenson Publishing Co.

IIrdayakumari, B. 1974 *Vallathol Narayana Menon*. New Delhi: Sahitya Akademi.

Inden, Ronald 1986 'Orientalist constructions of India,' *Modern Asian Studies*, 20(3): 401-46.

Iyengar, K.R. Srinivasa n.d. (1975) 'The dramatic art of Asif Currimbhoy,' in *Appreciations of Asif Currimbhoy*, (eds) Faubian Bowers, Ruth L. Meserve, Walter J. Meserve and K.R. Srinivasu Iyengar. Calcutta: Writer's Workshop Book.

Iyer, C.V. Subrahmania (ed.) 1977 *Kerala Kalamandalam (Souvenir)*. Cheruthuruthy.

Iyer, K. Bharata 1966 'Krishnattam,' *Times of India Annual*, 71-80.
— 1955. *Kathakali: The Sacred Dance-Drama of Malabar*. London: Luzac.

Iyer, V. Subramania (trans.) 1977 *Nalacharitham*. Trichur: Kerala Sahitya Akademi.

Jacob, Paul 1990 'King Lear coming again,' *Indian Express* (Kochi edition), 5 August.

Jaffrey, Madhur 1979 'A total theatre filled with dance, music, and myth,' *Smithsonian*, 9(12): 68-75.

Jeffrey, Robin 1992 *Politics, Women and Well Being: How Kerala Became 'A Model'*. Delhi: Oxford University Press.
— 1976 *The Decline of Nayar Dominance*. Sussex: Sussex University Press.

Jenkins, Richard 1992 *Pierre Bourdieu*. London: Routledge Press.

Jones, Betty True 1983. 'Kathakali dance-drama: an historical perspective,' in *Performing Arts in India: Essays on Music, Dance, and Drama*, (ed.) Bonnie C. Wade. Berkeley: Center for South and Southeast Asian Studies, pp. 14-44.

Jones, Clifford Reis 1984 *The Wondrous Crest-Jewel in Performance*. New Delhi: Oxford University Press.
— 1981 'Dhulicitra: historical perspectives on art and ritual,' in *Kaladarsana: American Studies in the Art of India*, (ed.) Joanna G. Williams. Leiden: E.J. Brill, 69-75.
— 1967 'The Temple Theatre of Kerala: its history and description,' unpublished Ph.D. dissertation, University of Pennsylvania.

Jones, Clifford R. and Jones, Betty True 1970 *Kathakali: An Introduction to the Dance-Drama of Kerala*. New York: Theatre Arts Books.

Jung, Carl 1957 'Time and eternity in Indian thought,' *Papers from the Eranos Year Books, Bollingen Series*, 30(3): 172-200.

Kaladharan V. 1993 'Another tragedy in the (kathakali) repertory,' *Mathrabhumi* (Malayalam), 28 March.
— 1990 'Bitter-sweet days,' *Indian Express Weekend*, 10 November, 5-6.
— 1989 'The problems raised by *King Lear Kathakali*,' *Mathrabhumi*, 13 August.

Kale, Pramod 1974 *The Theatric Universe: A Study of the Natyasastra*. Bombay: Popular Prakashan.

Kannampilly, K.M. 1990 'Rebirth for kathakali,' *Indian Express Weekend*, 10 November, 1, 5.

Kareem, C.K. 1973 *Kerala Under Haidar Ali and Tipu Sultan*. Ernakulam: Paico.

Kathkali Mahotsavam 1993 Festival Program. (27 October–1 November 1993). New Delhi: Sangeet Natak Akademi.

Kathakali 1957 *Marg* (Special Issue), 11(1).

Kinsley, David R. 1979 *The Divine Player*. Delhi: Motilil Banarsidass.

Knipe, David M. 1991 *Hinduism*. New York: Harper Collins.
— 1977 '*Sapindikarana*: The Hindu Rite of Entry into Heaven,' in *Religious Encounters with Death*, (eds) Frank E. Reynolds and E. H. Waugh. University Park, PA: Pennsylvania State University Press, 111-24.

Krishnakaimal, Aymanam 1986 *Kathakalivijnanakosham* (Malayalam). Kottayam: National Book Stall.

Kulkarni, V.K. 1986 *Some Aspects of the Rasa Theory*. Delhi: B.L. Institute of Indology.

Kuppuswamy, B. 1993 *Source Book of Ancient Indian Psychology*. Delhi: Konark Publishers.

Kurup, C.G.R. 1968 'The International Centre for Kathakali,' *Kalamandalam Annual*, 21-5.
— 1966-67 'Kathakali on the modern stage,' *Natya*, 9(4): 25-31.

Kurup, Guru Kunju 1968 'The art of kathakali,' *Kathakali*, April–June, 8–10.

Kurup, K.K.N. 1973 *Cult of Teyyam*. Calcutta: Indian Publications.

LeDay, Annette and McRuvie, David 1989 *Kathakali King Lear* (program). Paris: Keli.

Logan, William 1951 (1998) *Malabar*. Madras: Government Press (reprint).

Lockwood, Michael and Bhat, A. Vishnu 1994 *Metatheater and Sanskrit Drama*. New Delhi: Munshiram Manoharlal Publishers.

MacCannell, Dean 1979 'Ethnosemiotics,' *Semiotica*, 27(1/3): 149-71.

McConachie, Bruce 1989 'Reading context into performance: theatrical formations and social history,' *Journal of Dramatic Theory and Criticism*, 3(2): 229-37.

McDaniel, June 1995 'Emotion in Bengali religious thought: substance and metaphore,' in *Emotions in Asian Thought*, (eds) Joel Marks and Roger T. Ames. Albany: SUNY Press, 39-63.

McRuvie, David 1989 'Kathakali King Lear.' Unpublished manuscript.

Marar, Kuttikrishna 1937 'The hand-symbols in kathakali,' *Modern Review* (Allahabad), 61: 680-5.

Marglin, Frederique 1985 *Wives of the God-King*. New Delhi: Oxford University Press.

Marriott, McKim 1990 *India Through Hindu Categories*. New Delhi: Sage Publications.
— 1980 'The open Hindu person and

interpersonal fluidity,' manuscript at session 19, 'The Indian Self,' 21 March, Association for Asia Studies.

Mathur, J.C. 1972 'Inside a temple theatre,' *Sangeet Natak*, 26: 20-32.

Mazo, Joseph H. 1981 'Dance from the edge of India,' *Geo*, 5(3): 40-60.

Mencher, Joan P. 1966a 'Kerala and Madras: a comparative study of ecology and social structure,' *Ethnology*, 5(2): 135-71.
— 1966b 'Namboodiri brahmins: an analysis of a traditional elite in Kerala,' *Journal of Asian and African Studies*, 1(3): 183-96.
— 1962 'Changing familiar roles among Malabar Nayars,' *Southwest Journal of Anthropology*, 18(3): 230-46.

Menon, A. Sreedhara 1972 *Kerala District Gazeteers: Cannannore*. Trivandrum: Government of Kerala Press.
— 1967 *A Survey of Kerala History*. Kottayam: Sahitya Pravarthaka Cooperative Society.

Menon, C.A. 1941 'The histrionic art of Malabar,' *Journal of the Indian Society of Oriental Art*, 9: 105-32.

Menon, Jisha 1998 'Dissembling dissemblance,' unpublished manuscript.

Menon, K.P. Padmanabha 1983 *History of Kerala*, Vol. I. New Delhi: Asian Educational Services.

Menon, K.P.S. (ed.), 1979 *Kathakali Attaprakaram*. Cheruthuruthy: Kerala Kalamandalam.
— 1978 'Vallathol's contribution to the art and craft of kathakali,' in *Vallathol: A Centenary Perspective*, (eds) S. Sarma *et al.* Trivandrum: International Vallathol Birth Centenary Festival Committee, 77-85.
— 1973 'Guru Kunju Kurup,' *Journal of the National Centre for the Performing Arts*, 2(1): 18-24.
— 1970 'Kalasams in Kathakali,' *Kalamandalam Annual*, 9–11.
— 1969 'Kruichi Kunhan Panikkar,' *Kalamandalam Annual*, 17-19.
— 1968 'Chengannur Raman Pillai,' *Kalamandalam Annual*, 9–11.

— 1957 *Kathakali Rangam*. Kozhikode: Mathrubhumi Printing.

Menon, Leela 1989 'Clown princes of Kathakali,' *Indian Express Weekend*, 15 April, 2.

Merton, Robert K. 1957 'The role-set: problems in sociological theory,' *British Journal of Sociology*, 8: 110-13.

Miller, Eric J. 1955 'Village structure in North Kerala,' *India's Villages*, (ed.) M.N. Srninivas. New York: Asia Publishing House.
— 1954 'Caste and territory in Malabar,' *American Anthropologist*, 56: 410-20.

Misra, Vidya Niwas and Sharma, Prem Lata 1992 'Loka,' in *Kalatattvakosa*, Vol. II (Concepts of Space and Time). New Delhi: Indira Gandhi National Centre for the Arts.

Monier-Williams, M. 1972 (1899) *Sanskrit English Dictionary*. Oriental Publishers.

Moore, Melinda 1983 'Taravad, house, land and relationship in matrilineal Hindu society,' unpublished Ph.D. dissertation, University of Chicago.
— 1982 'Nalukettu: the house as microcosm,' unpublished paper presented at the 11th Annual Conference on South Asia, Madison, WI.

Morgan, David 1998 *Visual Piety: A History and Theory of Popular Religious Images*. Berkeley: University of California Press.

Morris, Tom 1990 '*A Midsummer Night's Dream*,' *Times Literary Supplement*, 24 August.

Nair, C. Padmanabhan 1980 *Kathakali Vesham: Part I* (Malayalam). Trivandrum: State Institute of Languages, Kerala.

Nair, D. Appukuttan, and Paniker, K. Ayyappa (eds) 1993. *Kathakali: The Art of the Non-Worldly*. Bombay: Marg.

Nair, K. Ramachandran 1971 *Early Manipravalam, A Study*. Trivandrum: Anjali.

Nair, M.K.K. 1972 'Traditional disciplines in training,' *Sangeet Natak*, 24: 50-6.

— 1970 'Krishnan Nayar, Marvel of Kathakali Stage,' *Kalamandalam Annual*, 13-15.

Nair, P.K. Parameswaran 1970 '*Nala-caritam* – the attakkatha par excellence,' *Kalamandalam Annual*, 13-15.
— 1968 'Kathakali in India and Abroad,' *Kalamandalam Annual*, 17-20.

Nair, V. Madhavan 1990 'Cankers creeping into kathakali,' *Indian Express Weekend*, 10 November, 2.
— 1972 'Towards a better appreciation of kathakali,' *Sangeet Natak*, 24: 57-60.
— 1966 'Innovations in kathakali,' *Sangeet Natak*, 2: 86-91.

Nambishan, Tiruvangattu Narayanan (ed.) 1958 *Hastalaksanadipika*. Kozhikode: K.R. Brothers.

Namboodiri, M.P. Sankaran 1983 'Bhava as expressed through the presentational techniques of kathakali,' *Dance Research Annual* (CORD), 14: 194-201.

Namboothiry, E. Easwaran 1983 *Balaramabharatam: A Critique on Dance and Drama*. Trivandrum: Keralasamskritam Publications.

Natanson, Maurice 1973 *Phenomenology and the Social Sciences*, Vol. 1. Evanston: Northwestern University Press.

Nayar, Kalamandalam Ramankutti 1993 *Tiranottam*. Kottayam: D.C. Books.

Nayar, V. Madavan 1992 (1969) *Karnnasapatham*. Kottayam: D.C. Books.

Nedungadi, T.M.B. 1990 'In the beginning,' *Indian Express Weekend*, 10 November, 1, 5.

Neff, Deborah 1987 'Aesthetics and power in Pambin Tullal: a possession ritual of rural Kerala,' *Ethnology*, 26(1): 63-71.

Neuman, Daniel 1976 'Towards an ethnomusicology of cultural change in Asia,' *Asian Music*, 7(2): 1–5.

Nossiter, T.J. 1988 *Marxist State Governments in*

India. London: Pinter Publishers.
– 1982 *Communism in Kerala*. Delhi: Oxford University Press.

✦ O'Flaherty, Wendy Doniger 1988 *Other People's Myths*. New York: Macmillan.
– 1984 *Dreams, Illusions, and Other Realities*. Delhi: Motilal Banarsidass.
– 1976 *The Origins of Evil in Hindu Mythology*. Berkeley: University of California Press.

Omchery, Leela 1969 'The music of Kerala – a study,' *Kalamandalam Annual*, 7–15.

Pallath, Jaya Rani 1976 'Mamakam,' MA thesis, University of Calicut.

Panchal, Goverdhan 1984 *Kuttampalam and Kutiyattam*. New Delhi: Sangeek Natak Akademi.

Pandeya, Gayanacharya Avinash C. 1961 *The Art of Kathakali*. Allahabad: Kitabistan.

Paniker, K. Ayyappa 1993 'Textual sources for performances,' in *Kathakali: The Art of the Non-Worldly*, (eds) D. Appukuttan Nair and K. Ayyappa Paniker. Bombay: Marg.

Panikkar, Chitra 1993 'Patrons, troupes, and performers,' in *Kathakali: The Art of the Non-worldly*, (eds) D. Appukuttan Nair and K. Ayyappa Paniker. Bombay: Marg, 31–44.

Panikkar, K.M. 1919 'Some aspects of Nayar life,' *Journal of the Royal Academy*, 49.

Panikkar, Kavalan Narayana 1977 'Krishnattam,' *Malayalam Literary Survey*, 1(1): 33–43.

Parkin, D. 1978 *The Cultural Definition of Political Response*. London: Academic Press.

Paul, G.S. 1996 'Skilful (sic) use of theatrical elements,' *The Hindu*, 9 August.
– 1995 'Breaking the barriers,' *The Hindu*, Friday, 17 November, 26.
– 1993 'Doing a Hamlet,' *Indian Express Sunday Magazine*, 2 May, 6.
– 1990 'Puranic stories dominate,' *Indian Express Weekend*, 10 November, 6.

Pavis, Patrice 1989 'Dancing with *Faust*: a semiotician's reflections on Barba's intercultural mise-en-scene,' *TDR: A Journal of Performance Studies*, 33(3): 50.

Percival, John 1990 'Lear's heath at half-blast,' *Times* (London), 17 August.

Pichot, Nadine 1989 'Le Roi Lear en Theatre Kathakali: Intensite, force et feerie,' *Semaine Cote d'Azur*, 8 December.

Pilaar, Agatha Jane 1993 *Kathakali Plays in English. Vol. I: Tales from the Ramayana and the Mahabharata*. Kottayam: D.C. Offset Printers and Agatha Jane Pilaar.

Pillai, Narayanan 1992 'Kerala Kalamandalam: saviour of Kerala art-forms,' *Sruti*, **87-8**: 21-2.

Pitkow, Marlene B. 1998 'Representations of the feminine in *kathakali*: dance-drama of Kerala, South India,' unpublished Ph.D. dissertation, New York University, Department of Performance Studies.

Poduval, R.V. 1928 'The Malabar drama,' *Madras Christian College Magazine Quarterly Series*, **8**: 101-7.

Premakumar 1948 *The Language of Kathakali: A Guide to Mudras*. Allahabad: Kitabistan.

Puthenkalam, J. 1977 *Marriage and the Family in Kerala*. Calgary: University of Calgary, Department of Sociology (*Journal of Comparative Family Studies*).

Raghavan, V. 1993 'Natyadharmi and lokadharmi,' in *Sanskrit Drama: Its Aesthetics and Production*, (ed.) V. Raghavan. Madras: Paprinpack, 201-41.
– 1964-65 'Kudiyattam – its form and significance,' *Samskrita Ranga Annual*, **5**: 77-87.
– 1962 'Koodiyattam,' *Natya*, **6**(3): 21-2.

Raghunathan, N. (trans.) 1976 *Bhagavata Purana, Vol. II*. Madras: Vighneswara Publishing House.

Raja, K. Kunjunni 1974 'Kootiyattam,' *Quarterly Journal National Centre for the Performing Arts*, 3(2): 1–12.
– 1964 *Kutiyattam: An Introduction*. New Delhi: Sangeet Natak Akademi.

Rajagopalan, L.S. 1969 'Damayanti in *Nala Caritam Attakatha,' Sangeet Natak*, 14: 30-9.
– 1968 'Music in Kootiyattam,' *Sangeet Natak*, 10: 12-35.

Rajagopalan, L. S., and Subramanya Iyer, V. 1975 'Aids to the Appreciation of *Kathakali,' Journal of South Asian Literature*, 10(2–4): 205-10.

Ramanath, Renu 1996 'Never ending search for perfection,' *The Hindu*, 9 August, 27.

Ramanujan, A.K. 1990a *Who needs folklore? The relevance of oral traditions to South Asian studies*, South Asia Occasional Papers Ser., 1. Honolulu: Center for South Asian Studies.
– 1990b 'Is there an Indian way of thinking? An informal essay,' in *India through Hindu Categories*, (ed.) McKim Marriott. New Delhi: Sage, 41-58.
– 1989 'Where mirrors are windows: toward an anthology of reflections,' *History of Religions*, 28: 187-216.

Rangacharya, Adya 1996 *The Natyasastra: English Translation with Critical Notes*. New Delhi: Munshiram Manoharlal Publishers.

Ranganathan, Edwina 1975 'Krsnanattam: a traditional dance-drama concerning the life of Lord Krsna,' *Journal of South Asian Literature*, 10(2–4): 275-88.

Rao, Maya Krishna 1999 'Khol Do,' published program for a performance in Aberystwyth, Wales, Centre for Performance Research.

Rea, Kenneth 1978 'Theatre in India: the old and the new, Part I, Kathakali,' *Theatre Quarterly*, 8(30): 9–23.

Redyar, S.T. 1129 Malayalam Era (ME) *Attakathakal, Vol. I*.

Rele, Kanak 1992 *Mohini Attam: The Lyrical Dance*. Bombay: Nalanda Dance Research Centre.

Richards, J.F. (ed.) 1981 *Kingship and Authority in South Asia*. Madison: South Asian Studies, University of Wisconsin-Madison.

Richmond, Farley 1999 *Kutiyattam: Sanskrit Theater of Kerala*. Ann Arbor: University of Michigan Press (CD ROM).

Richmond, Farley, Swann, Darius L. and Zarrilli, Phillip B. 1990 *Indian Theatre: Traditions of Performance*. Honolulu: University of Hawaii Press.

Richmond, Farley and Richmond, Yasmin 1985 'The multiple dimensions of time and space in *Kutiyattam*, the Sanskrit Theatre of Kerala,' *Asian Theatre Journal*, 2(1): 50-60.
– 1978 'Rites of passage and *Kutiyattam*,' *Sangeet Natak*, 50: 27-36.

Roy, Arundhati 1997 *The God of Small Things*. London: Flamingo.

Rydell, Robert W. 1984 *All the World's a Fair*. Chicago: University of Chicago Press.

Said, Edward 1978 *Orientalism*. New York: Pantheon.

Sarma, S., (ed.) 1978 *Vallathol: A Centenary Perspective*. Trivandrum: International Vallathol Birth Centenary Festival Committee.

Sax, William S. (ed.) 1995 *The Gods at Play: Lila in South Asia*. New York: Oxford University Press.

Schechner, Richard 1986 'Talking with Peter Brook,' *TDR: A Journal of Performance Studies*, 30(1): 47–57.

Scorpio 1996 'Kalamandalam needs thorough overhaul,' *Indian Express Weekend*, 22 June.
– 1995 'And now, Tamil Kathakali,' *Indian Express*, 18 November.

Shankar, Rajendra 1958 'The mime of Kathakali,' *Modern Review* (Calcutta), 57: 348–54.

Sharma, V.S. 1982 *Thullal*. Madras: Higginbothams, Ltd.

Singer, Milton 1972 *When a Great Tradition Modernizes*. New York: Praeger.
– 1966 'Radha-Krishna *Bhajanas* of Madras City,' *Krishna, Myths, Rites, and Attitudes*, (ed.) M. Singer. Chicago: University of Chicago Press, 139-72.

Spencer, Charles 1990 'Hypnotic power of an Indian Lear,' *Daily Telegraph*, 17 August.

Sridaran, Iyyemkode 1996 *Snehasandesam* (*Message of Love*), unpublished manuscript (Malayalam).
– 1989 'King Lear kathakali and kalamandalam,' *Mathrbhumi*, 27 August.
– 1988 *Kathakali King Lear*, unpublished manuscript.

Stevenson, Randall 1990 'Beat of a different drum,' *Independent*, 18 August.

Stoller Miller, Barbara (ed.) 1992 *The Powers of Art: Patronage in Indian Culture*. Delhi: Oxford University Press.
– 1984 *Theatre of Memory: The Plays of Kalidasa*. New York: Columbia University Press.
– 1981 'Moving designs of masked emotions,' *Parabola*, **6**(3): 85–9.

Subramaniam, Radhika 1987 'Toward a semiotic of performance: the case of kathakali,' unpublished MS degree, Purdue University.

Sunderdass, S. 1987 Review of *Manavavijayam*, in *Kerala Kaumudi*, 19 February.

Surendran, Shyamala 1992 'Kerala Kalamandalam: views on its state & fate,' *Sruti*, **93/94**: 29–33.

Tampy, K.P. Padmanabhan 1963 *Kathakali: An Indigenous Art-Form of Kerala*. Calcutta: Indian Publications.

Tarlekar, G.H. 1975 *Studies in the Natyasastra*. Delhi: Motilal Banarsidas.

Thulaseedharan, K. 1977 '"Faust Moksham" Kathakali,' *Indian Express*, 13 January, 5.

Thurston, Edgar 1975 (1909) *Castes and Tribes of Southern India*, Vol. M–P. Delhi: Cosmo Publications.

Tiwari, Kapil N. 1986 *Suffering: Indian Perspectives*. Delhi: Motilal Banarsidass.

Trawick Egnor, Margaret 1983 'Death and nurturance in Indian systems of healing,' *Social Science and Medicine*, 17(4): 935–45.

Trombetta, Sergio 1989 'Le Roi Lear,' *Danse*, 3 October.

Turner, Graeme 1992 *British Cultural Studies: An Introduction*. London: Routledge.

Turner, Victor 1986 T*he Anthropology of Performance*. New York: PAJ Publications.
– 1976 *Dramas, Fields, and Metaphors*. Ithaca: Cornell University Press.

Ubersfeld, Anne 1982 'The pleasure of the spectator,' *Modern Drama*, **25**(1): 123–35.

Unni, N.P. 1977 *Sanskrit Dramas of Kulasekhara*. Trivandrum: Kerala Historical Society.

Unni, N.P. and Sullivan, Bruce M. (trans.) 1995 *The Sun God's Daughter and King Samvarana: Tapati-Samvaranam and the Kutiyattam Drama Tradition*. Delhi: Nag Publishers.

Varadpande, M.L. 1982 *Krishna Theatre in India*. Atlantic Highlands, NJ: Humanities Press, Inc.

Variar, Unnayi 1995 *Jours d'amour et d'epreuve: L'histoire de Nala*. Trans. Dominique Vitalyos. Paris: Gallimard.

Varryar, Unnayi (sic) 1975 *Nala Caritam Attakatha*. Translated and introduced by V. Subramanya Iyer, (ed.) Farley Richmond. *Journal of South Asian Literature*, 10(2–4): 211–48.

Varryar, Cerppattu Acyuta and Unni, V.K. Sridharan (eds) 1954, 1956 *Attakathakal* Vols. I, II. Quilon: S.T. Redyar and Sons.

Vatsayan, Kapila 1996 *Bharata the Natyasastra*. New Delhi: Sahitya Akademi.
– 1983 *The Square and the Circle of the Indian Arts*. Atlantic Highlands, NJ: Humanities Press.
– 1980 *Traditional Indian Theatre: Multiple Streams*. New Delhi: National Book Trust.
– 1974 *Indian Classical Dance*. New Delhi: Government Press.
– 1968a *Classical Indian Dance in Literature and the Arts*. New Delhi: *Sangeet Natak* Akademi.
– 1968b 'Kathakali – dance theatre of India,' *The World of Music*, 10(1): 22–35.

van der Veer, Peter 1994 *Religious Nationalism:*

Hindus and Muslims in India. Berkeley: University of California Press.

Venu, G. 1989 *Production of a Play in Kutiyattam.* Irinjalakuda: Natankairali.
— 1984 *Mudras in Kathakali: Notations of 373 Hand Gestures.* Irinjalakuda: Natanakairali.

Venu, G. and Panikar, Nirmala 1983 *Mohiniattam.* Trivandrum: G. Venu, Chittore House.

Vinita 1989 'The heart-rending King Lear,' *Deshabimani*, 5 February.

Viswanathan, Lakshmi 1996 'Festival of India's South,' *The Hindu*, 21 July: *Magazine*.

Warrier, Unnayi (sic) 1977 *Nalacharitham.* Trans. V. Subramania Iyer. Trichur: Kerala Sahitya Akademi.

Wijaya, Putu 1986 'Indonesian culture,' trans. Ellen Rafferty, unpublished manuscript.

Zaehner, R.C. (trans. and commentary) 1969 *The Bhagavad-Gita.* London: Oxford University Press.

Zarrilli, Phillip B. 1999 'Action, structure, task, and emotion: theories of acting, emotion, and performer training from a performance studies perspective,' *Performance Research* (in press).
— 1998 '*When the body becomes all eyes:' Paradigms, Discourses, and Practices of Power in Kalarippayattu, a South Indian Martial Art.* New Delhi: Oxford University Press.
— 1992 'A tradition of change: the role(s) of patrons and patronage in the *kathakali* dance-drama,' in *Arts Patronage in India: Methods, Motives and Markets,* (ed.) Joan L. Erdman. New Delhi: Manohar.
— 1991 'For whom is the king a king? Issues of intercultural production, perception, and reception in a Kathakali King Lear,' in *Critical Theory and Performance,* (eds) Janelle G. Reinelt and Joseph R. Roach. Ann Arbor: University of Michigan Press, 16-40.
— 1990a 'Ayyappan Tiyatta,' in *Indian Theatre,* (eds) Farley Richmond, Darius Swann, and Phillip Zarrilli. Honolulu: University of Hawaii Press, 151-65.
— 1990b 'What does it mean "to become the character . . ." ' in *By Means of Performance,* (eds) Richard Schechner and Willa Appel. Cambridge: Cambridge University Press, 131-48.
— 1987 'Where the hand [is] . . . ' *Asian Theatre Journal*, 4(2): 205-14.
— 1984a *The Kathakali Complex: Actor, Performance, Structure.* New Delhi: Abhinav.
— 1984b 'Doing the exercise: the in-body transmission of performance knowledge in a traditional martial art,' *Asian Theatre Journal* 1(2): 191-206.
— 1983 'A microanalysis of performance structure and time in *Kathakali* dance-drama,' *Studies in Visual Communication*, 9(2): 50-69.
— 1977 'Demystifying Kathakali,' *Sangeet Natak*, 43: 48-59.

ⰲⰲⰲ **glossary**

and
table of
transliteration

VOWELS

അ	ആ	ഇ	ഈ	ഉ	ഊ	
a	ā	i	ī	u	ū	
ഋ	എ	ഏ	ഐ	ഒ	ഓ	ഔ
ṛ	e	ē	ai	o	ō	au
അം	അഃ					
am	aḥ					

CONSONANTS

ക	ഖ	ഗ	ഘ	ങ	ച	ഛ
k	kh	g	gh	ṅ	c (ĉ)	ch
ജ	ഝ	ഞ	ട	ഠ	ഡ	ഢ
j	jh	ñ (ṅ)	ṭ	ṭh	ḍ	ḍh
ണ	ത	ഥ	ദ	ധ	ന	
ṇ	t	th	d	dh	n	
പ	ഫ	ബ	ഭ	മ	യ	ര
p	ph	b	bh	m	y	r
ല	വ	ശ	ഷ	സ	ഹ	ള
l	v	ś (ṣ́)	ṣ (š)	s	h	ḷ
ഴ	റ	റ്റ				
ẏ (ḷ)	ṟ (ṙ)	ṯṯ (Ṫ́Ṫ)				

The following glossary provides basic definitions of Malayalam and Sanskrit terms appearing in the text. Each term is fully transliterated according to the table of transliteration in the box on p. 242. The table of transliteration is a slight modification of Gundert (1982). Where modifications from Gundert occur, our transliteration is noted first, and Gundert's original version is in parentheses. A number of well-known Sanskrit words such as *tala, sloka*, etc. are transliterated in their familiar Sanskrit form rather than Malayalam. Nouns like *tala, sloka*, etc. ending in 'a,' add a final 'm' in Malayalam, i.e. *talam, slokam, sampradayam*, etc. Proper names are not transliterated. We have adopted commonplace, familiar spellings such as Krishna (Krsna), etc.

abhinaya: the audience's experience of a performance is 'carried toward' the audience through four elements: (1) *aharya* – the costumes, make-up and properties; (2) *vacika* – the vocal element; (3) *satvika* – the expressive, subtle, or 'internal' element of acting, and (4) *amgika* – the embodied, 'expressive' element of acting.

adbhuta rasa: the wondrous or marvellous.

adiyar: vassal.

ādyavasānan: major roles, nearly always played by the mature, senior, master actors.

āhārya: the costumes, make-up and properties element of performance.

akampati: a ruler's retinue of Nayars trained in martial arts and pledged to protect his rule.

Ambarīṣacaritam: one of four plays written by Aswati Tirunal Rama Varma (1756-94), and still in the active repertory.

āmgika: the embodied, 'expressive' element of acting.

Ampalavāsi: intermediate temple-servant castes including the performers of *kutiyattam*.

ānanda: a state of bliss itself.

anupallavi: the subrefrain of the dialogue portion (*padam*) of a *kathakali* play. The *anupallavi* may be omitted from particular *padam*.

araṅṅettam: inaugural performance by a student of *kathakali*.

Arayan: fishermen – among the lower polluting castes of Kerala.

asamyukta: single hand-gestures.

āsana: basic forms or postures of *hatha yoga*.

aśāri: a relatively high-ranking expert in the science of architecture traditionally consulted when building a house or other building.

Āścaryacūḍāmaṇi: ninth–tenth century Sanskrit play authored by Saktibhadra and still performed in *kutiyattam* style in Kerala.

atanta tāla: rhythmic cycle set in 14 beats.

āṭṭakkatha: literally, 'enacted story.' The technical term for *kathakali*'s play-texts.

āṭṭam: literally, 'to dance.'

āṭṭaprakāram: the performance manuals which actors compile while in training that are used to guide them in performing plays.

aucitya-bōdham: the 'sense of appropriateness' which guides performance choices by actors and often determines reactions by connoisseurs to actor's choices about how to perform a role.

Ayurvēda: literally, the 'science of longevity' or life. India's traditional system of humoral medicine which attempts to balance the three humors through positive/preventive means such as exercise and diet, and through treatment of illness or imbalances to the system.

Bakavadham: *The Killing of Baka* by Kottayam Tampuran. One of the formative four 'Kottayam plays' noted for its strict structure and importance in training performers.

Bālarāmābharatam: Sanskrit treatise on aesthetics and dramaturgy written by Kartika Tirunal and influential in the introduction of major changes to *kathakali*.

Bālivijayan: *Bali's Victory*, written by Kalloor Nambudirippad (1797-1835), the play features a major role for the demon-king Ravana.

bhakti: devotion, or the act of devotion.

bhava: state of mind, being, disposition. Refers to the actor's embodiment of a character's states of being/emotion.

bhaya bhāva: the actor's state of being/doing fear or the terrible.

bhayānaka rasa: the audience's aesthetic experience of fear or the terrible.

bībhatsa rasa: the audience's aesthetic experience of repulsion or disgust.

Cākyār: intermediate-ranking temple servants (Ambalavasis) who perform *kutiyattam* and a form of mono-acting in several of Kerala's temples.

campa tāla: a rhythmic cycle set in 10 beats.

cāpalyam: behaving with disregard for one's family and traditions.

caraṇam: the 'foot' of the dialogue portions (*padam*) of a *kathakali* play. There are usually several *caraṇam* in each *padam*.

cāṭṭam: jumps – part of the basic training of the actor-dancer for flexibility, balance, and control of the body.

cempaṭa tāla: a rhythmic cycle set in 8 beats.

ceṅkila: the hand-held gong played with a stick by the lead-singer to keep the basic rhythm in a performance.

ceṇṭa: equal in importance to the barrel-headed drum, this is a cylindrical double-headed drum usually played with two curved sticks, and occasionally with one stick and one hand.

Cēṟuman: one of the harijan or out-castes in Kerala.

cintā bhāva: the actor's state of being/doing reflection or remembrance.

citta: what is set by 'tradition' or 'convention.'

cittappeṭṭa: the rigid or tightly conventionalized structure required to perform certain roles and plays in the repertory, especially the four Kottayam plays.

cittapradānam: following specific essential conventions in performance of a role or play.

colliyaṭṭam: literally, 'to recite' and 'dance,' i.e., the rehearsal of plays in the classroom. The term encompasses both the vocalizing/learning of lines of the play, and learning to dance/enact each role.

Cōvan: among the low-ranking tenant farming castes of Kerala.

cuṇṭappūvu: the tiny crushed seed placed into each eyelid of the performer which allows the actor's eyes to become reddish as the veins are exposed, thereby accentuating a character's states as revealed in his facial expressions.

cuṭṭi: the white rice-paste and paper border which frames the face for certain characters.

cuvanna tāṭi: 'red beard' characters such as Dussassana are generally evil, vicious, and vile.

cuyippu: circling patterns which combine basic hand-gestures, rhythmic patterns, and specific use of the eyes as part of the basic training of the actor-dancer.

Dakṣayāgam: *Daksa's Sacrifice* authored by Irayimman Tampi (1783-1856).

dakṣina: traditional 'gifts' or 'offerings' a student gives to his teacher at the beginning and end of a course of training.

daṇḍakam: narrative passages, usually composed in third person, which serve the same function as *sloka*, but are set in special rhythmic patterns and metrical feet.

danyāsi: closing dance which ends a performance.

darśan: to have or take a glimpse of a deity in a temple. Implied in seeing the deity is a substantive exchange, and not simply a looking 'at.'

dharma: duty, law, the sociocosmic order of things as it should be, conduct, code, or customary observance. One's duty in upholding and/or maintaining that order. The maintenance of this order is literally played out in *King Rugmamgada's Law* when his son, 'the mace of Dharma,' insists that his father cut off his head to maintain the integrity of the family, and therefore uphold the divine sociocosmic order.

Duryōdhanavadham: *The Killing of Duryodhana*. Popular *kathakali* play authored by Vayaskara Aryan Narayanan Moosad (1841-1902) which enacts that part of the Mahabharata in which the Pandavas achieve victory over their cousins, the Kauravas when their leader, Duryodhana, is killed by Bhima on the great Kurukshetra battlefield.

ēklōchana: the expression of two different states of being/emotion in two eyes at the same time.

eṭa: untranslatable male addressive insult.

eṭi: untranslatable female addressive insult.

gada: mace or club, usually associated with Bhima.

guṇam: one's basic, inherent nature and behaviour. There are three basic *guṇam*, including goodness or truth (*satva*), passion/energy/dynamism (*rajasa*), and darkness/lethargy (*tamasa*).

Hastalakṣaṇadīpika: the Sanskrit manual of gesture language which came to serve as a sourcebook for much of *kathakali*'s hand-gestures.

hāsya rasa: the audience's experience of the comic, mirthful, or derision.

hṛdaya: heart/mind.

iḷakiyāṭṭam: literally, 'having moved/dance' – the performative interpolations into the original play text, composed and created by actor-dancers or their patrons to elaborate on the original literary text. When performed the actors 'speak' the lines of the interpolation only with hand-gestures, i.e., they are not sung by the vocalists. They have become one of the most important features of contemporary *kathakali* and feature star performers displaying their best abilities as actor/dancers.

ilattāḷam: bell-metal hand-cymbals played by the second singer.

iraṭṭi: dance compositions that come at the end of certain subrefrains, and set in a special rhythmic pattern (*cempata tala*).

iṭaykka: a small hourglass-shaped tension drum producing muted and melodious sounds used to accompany female characters.

Iyava: one name for the toddy tapping castes of Kerala.

janmam: proprietary rights given by one's birth within the traditional caste hierarchy. The rights to hold land, or perform certain rituals were restricted to particular high-ranking castes.

jīvan: life, individual soul, manifest in one's 'life force' (*prana vayu*).

jugupsa bhava: the actor's state of being/doing repulsion or disgust.

kacca: the long cloth wrapped around the abdominal/hip area to support the 'vital energy' of the practitioner in both martial art practice and *kathakali*. In *kathakali* performances the cloth is now used to wrap tightly the starched undergarments which are an essential part of the costume.

Kālakēyavadham: *The Killing of Kalakeya* authored by Kottayam Tampuran (c.1675-1725).

kāla: times or speeds within which rhythmic cycles are set.

kaḷarippayaṭṭu: a compound, technical term for Kerala's traditional martial art – the place (*kalari* – a pit dug out of the ground) where exercises (*payattu*) are practised. The preliminary exercises of this martial art and its massage system form the basis of *kathakali*'s intense psychophysiological training. Its ethos pervades the plays performed as part of the traditional repertory.

kalāśam: dance compositions that punctuate the stanzas of the text in performance and are danced according to the most appropriate mood of a scene.

kalivilakku: the large oil lamp which sits at center stage and traditionally provided the only illumination for performance. Lighting the oil lamp is part of the ritual inauguration of the performance.

kaḷiyōgam: a *kathakali* troupe or company fully outfitted for performance.

Kallaṭikkōtan: one of the early styles of *kathakali* performance.

Kalluvayi: the new composite style of *kathakali* developed by Unniri Panikkar in 1850 under the patronage of the famous Namboodiri brahmin household at Olappamanna Mana in central Kerala. It is one of the two remaining major styles of *kathakali* performance today, having synthesized elements of the earlier Kallatikkotan and Kaplinnatan styles.

kālsādhakam: footwork patterns learned as part of the basic training.

Kalyānasaugandhikam: *The Flower of Good Fortune* enacts the story of how Bhima retrieved the 'flowers of good fortune' requested by his common wife, Panchali, after journeying through a forest where he encounters his brother, Hanuman, as an obstacle in his path. One of the four 'Kottayam plays' authored by Kottayam Tampuran (c.1675-1725). Based on the Mahabharata, these four plays are considered to have extraordinarily fine poetry, and are crucial to the traditional training of the actor-dancer because of their tight and demanding structure of performance.

Kammāḷan: the artisan castes of Kerala – among the higher polluting castes.

kānakkāran: tenants who resided on lands owned by higher-ranking castes in return for services rendered to the land-owner.

kānam: those who worked the land for higher castes did so by tenure, i.e., they were in service to landholders.

Kaniyān: traditional astrologers and agricultural laboring castes of Kerala – among the higher polluting castes.

kaṇṇusādhakam: eye exercises performed as part of the basic training of the actor-dancer.

Kaplinnātan: one of the earlier styles of *kathakali*.

kāraṇavan: the eldest male member and ruler of extended families.

Karavadham: *The Killing of Kara* – one of the original *Ramanattam* plays recently revived by Margi.

kari: literally, 'black,' this class of make-up and characters includes the demoness Simhika. They are close to the black beards, and are also dressed in black, and wear oversized comic false breasts. They are considered the most grotesque of *kathakali* characters, and are a vivid and direct contrast to the idealized females of the 'radiant' category.

Karīpuya: one of the earlier, distinctive styles of *kathakali*.

Karṇaśapatham:. V. Madhavan Nair's 1967 play, *Karna's Oath*. Based on traditional epic sources, this is the most popular, though controversial, contemporary play authored in recent history.

karuṇa rasa: the audience's aesthetic experience of pathos or sadness.

karuttatāṭi: 'black beards' are evil, like red beards, but are also by nature schemers. They are primitive beings, and, like the hunter Kattalan, are associated with the forest and nature.

Kaṭattanāḍu: one of the distinctive earlier styles of *kathakali*.

kathakaḷi: literally, 'story play.' The name for Kerala's distinctive genre of performance which enacts stories from the epics and *puranas*.

katti: the 'knife' make-up refers to this type of character's distinctive stylized mustache. These characters are arrogant and evil, yet have some redeeming qualities – usually a streak of nobility.

Kaurava: led by Duryodhana, this clan tricked their cousins, the Pandavas, out of their claim to the crown of their kingdom, and sent them into banishment. The schism between the two clans is resolved at the great battle of Kurukshetra where Duryodhana and Dussassana are killed by Bhima. This is the story of the Mahabharata enacted in many *kathakali* plays.

kayca: traditional offering of gifts.

kēli: opening drum call for a kathakali performance. Part of the performance preliminaries.

keṭṭiccāṭṭam: jumping steps – part of the basic training.

Kirātam: *The Hunter*. *Kathakali* play authored by Irrattakulangara Rama Varier (1801-45) enacting that part of the Mahabharata in which the epic hero, Arjuna, goes to the Himalayas to perform penance to lord Siva as he seeks to secure from him the divine weapon (*pasupata*) needed to defeat the Kauravas in battle.

kirīṭam: crown or headdress.

Kirmīravadham: *The Killing Kirmira* was authored by Kottayam Tampuran (c.1675-1725). Based on the Mahabharata, it enacts the story of the disfigurement of the demoness Simhika, and the act of killing her brother, the demon Kirmira, by Bhima.

Kiṭangōr: the distinctive style of *kathakali* developed in Travancore, southern Kerala, and one of the two remaining distinctive styles of performance.

kōpam: colloquial expression in Malayalam for everyday anger.

Kottakkal: a major center for *kathakali* in northern Kerala. The location of the Kottakkal Ayurveda Sala and medical factory which patronizes one of the major *kathakali* troops and training centers today.

krōdha bhāva: the actor's state of being/doing fury, anger, wrath, or a 'transformative fury.'

Kṛṣṇagīti: cycle of eight dance-dramas composed by Manaveda, ruler of Kozhikode, and inspired by Jayadeva's Sanskrit work, *Gitagovinda*. This genre eventually became known as *Krsnattam*, Krishna's dance.

Kṛṣṇanaṭṭam (or *Krsnattam*): literally, Krishna's dance (*attam*). A cycle of eight dramatic episodes performed on eight consecutive nights that tells the story of Lord Krishna from his birth through his absorption into his divine form as Mahavishnu, and concluding on the ninth night with the repetition of the drama of Krishna's birth. Performances of this cycle of dramas were traditionally restricted to the Guruvayur (Krishna) Temple. The genre is one of the immediate precursors of *kathakali*.

kṣatriya: a member of the governing or ruling order – what eventually was considered the second highest ranking caste next to the brahmins or priests. Their duty was to uphold the sociocosmic order.

kūṭiyāṭṭam: literally, 'combined acting.' The term refers to Kerala's traditional form of staging acts of Sanskrit dramas in some of Kerala's temples where specially constructed theaters hold performances as 'visual sacrifices' for the major deity of the temple. The conventions, make-up, etc. of *kutiyattam* directly influenced the birth, growth, and development of *kathakali*.

kūttampalam: the specially constructed temple-theaters in which *kutiyattam* and Cakyar and Nannyar *kuttu* are performed at selected temples in Kerala.

lajja: shyness – one of three special female states of being/doing.

lalita: the celestial enchantress figure appearing in 'radiant' costume and make-up who is also a seductress. Demonesses like Simhika can take on this form temporarily, only to have their 'true' demonic nature revealed.

lāsya: graceful, soft, light, in contrast to the 'strong' (*tandava*).

Lavanāsuravadham: *The Killing of Lavanasura* – popular play featuring Hanuman.

līla: divine play.

lōkadharmi: the ordinary, concrete, or everyday from which the 'ideational' is abstracted.

maddalam: a two-headed barrel-shaped drum approximately three feet wide used to accompany any character or situation in a drama.

Mahabharata: along with the Ramayana, India's great epic which serves as a source of traditional oral narratives and teaching stories. It tells the story of the enmity and conflict between two sets of princely brothers, the Kauravas led by Duryodhana and the five princely Pandavas.

manaśśakti: literally, 'mental power.' Through practise of the martial art the master ideally gains superior mental power to be used in combat and/or daily life.

Manavavijayam: *People's Victory* – a leftist *kathakali* play by Iyyamgode Sridharan in 1987 which toured widely and played to enthusiastic, non-traditional, left political audiences.

mānipravālam: Kerala's heavily Sanskritized literary language especially important from the thirteenth to fifteenth centuries which influenced the writing of *kathakali* plays.

mārgi: to transcend space and time.

Markandēyacaritam: 1996 *kathakali* play by Kalamandalam Balasubramanian based on an incident performed as part of *The Progeny of Krishna*.

mātra: time units or beats within each rhythmic cycle (*tala*).

mēlappadam: the long vocal/percussion composition that is part of the preliminaries of a performance and provides both vocalists and percussionists ample opportunity to display their consummate musical skills.

meyyarappatavu: body control exercises – the preliminary training of the actor-dancer's bodymind.

minukku: literally, 'radiant' or 'shining,' this class of make-up and characters includes both idealized female heroines, such as Sita, Panchali, or Mohini, and the purest and most spiritually perfected males, including brahmins, holy men, and sages. The base make-up is a warm yellow-orange, with costumes relatively close to everyday traditional dress.

miśra: mixed hand-gestures, i.e., those that combine two different gestures.

Mōhiniyattam: 'Mohini's dance' – the traditional female 'classical' dance of Kerala.

mōksa: attaining a state of release or atonement for the eternal soul.

mudra: hand-gesture. *Kathakali's* gesture language includes twenty-four root *mudras* used singly or in combination literally to speak the dialogue of a play text, and also used decoratively during pure dance.

muriyatanta: 'half-*atanta*' – rhythmic cycle set in 7 beats (half of 14).

muti: the special crown, decorated with silver and worn by Krishna, Rama, and Lakshmana.

mutiyēttu: Kerala propitiatory ritual for the goddess Kali in her destructive form. Performed at only a few temples in Kerala as an annual propitiatory rite, this mode of performance probably influenced the development of certain aspects of *kathakali* costuming and performance.

nābhi mūla: literally, the 'root of the navel.'

nādi: the channels of the subtle body as understood in yoga philosophy and practice.

Nalacaritam: *King Nala's Victory* (*caritam*). *Kathakali's* enactment of the infamous Nala/Damayanti love story performed over four nights, and authored in four parts by Unnayi Variyar (c.1675–1716). The writing in the four plays is considered to be the 'highest peak in *kathakali* literature' (George 1968 102) since the poetry and imagery is considered to be the richest in the canon.

nālāmiratti: a fixed choreography used to

connect an interpolation to a scene, or to make an exit.

namaskāram: to pay respects or homage by the folding of the hands at the chest, and/or through prostration to an elder or deities. Also, the term for one of *kathakali*'s preliminary exercises in which the student stretches while performing an act of prostration on the floor.

Nampūtiri (*Namboodiri*): Kerala's highest-ranking brahmins.

Nampyār: the drummers who accompany the performances of Nannyars and Cakyars in temple performances of *kutiyattam* and *Nannyarkuttu*.

Nannyarkuttu: temple performances featuring women (Nannyars) as they interpret, elaborate, and enact epic and puranic stories through a form of mono-acting.

Nannyār: among the ranks of intermediate-cast temple servants (*Ambalavasis*) were Nannyars – the women who performed the female roles in the staging of Sanskrit drams (*kutiyattam*) and who also performed solo (*Nannyarkuttu*) as part of the ritual life of particular temples.

Narakāsuravadham: *The Killing of Narakasura* is one of seven plays authored by Kartika Tirunal Rama Varma Maharaja (1724–98). The play remains in the repertory and is still popular with connoisseurs.

nātyadharmi: the extraordinary, ideational which is elaborated, abstracted, transformed, and/or distilled in performance.

Nātyaśastra: the major work of Sanskrit dramaturgy ascribed to the sage Bharata and dated loosely between the 2nd century BC and 2nd century AD. It is an encyclopedic collection of techniques, conventions, practices, and aesthetics of Sanskrit drama-in-performance.

navarasa: the nine basic facial expressions which the *kathakali* actor learns as part of his training.

Nāyar: a distinct term, Nayar first appeared in the ninth century, and by the eleventh century it was commonly used to refer to a large indigenous group of non-polluting subcastes among Kerala Hindus. Although a few families became ruling lineages (such as the Zamorin of Calicut), the majority of Nayars were in service occupations providing military, personal, and managerial services for higher castes. Until the twentieth century,

Nayars lived in extended households, followed matrilineal descent, and children were raised in their mother's natal household. The first *kathakali* actors were Nayars in service to their ruling patrons as martial practitioners.

nōkku: to look or catch a glimpse.

onnām, rantām, mūnnām: first, second, and third speed within rhythmic cycles; *madhya, druta kāla*: middle and fast speeds

ōttantullal: a form of traditional mono-acting derived from *kathakali* and elaborating epic stories through solo performance with percussion accompaniment.

pacca: literally, 'green,' this class of make-up/characters includes divine figures like Krishna and Vishnu, kings like Rugmamgada, and epic heroes such as Rama and Bhima. The most refined among male characters, they are upright, moral, and ideally full of a calm inner poise – 'royal sages' modelled on the hero (*nayaka*) of Sanskrit drama whose task is to uphold sacred law.

padam: verses composed specifically as dance music for interpretation by the actor-dancer – the dialogue or soliloquy portions of the text 'spoken' through gesture language.

pallavi: the refrain section of the dialogue portion of a *kathakali* play.

pampin tullal: the worship of serpent deities understood to reside on extended family properties through annual ritual propitiation/possession dances.

pancāri tāla: rhythmic cycle set in 6 beats.

Pāndava: the five princely brothers of the Mahabharata led by Yudhisthira who fight their arch enemy cousins, the Kauravas, at the battle of Kurukshetra.

Panikkar: honorific title given to some practitioners of Kerala's martial art.

Parayan:among the lowest polluting castes of Kerala.

pāsupāta: divine weapon given by Siva to Arjuna after undergoing austerities.

Patapurappātu: an elaborate choreographical interpretation of 'preparations for battle.'

patiñña kālam: the slowest of the slow tempos used for love scenes and the elaboration of the erotic sentiment, with 56 beats.

Paundrakavadham: one of four plays authored by Aswati Tirunal Rama Varma (1756–94).

payuppu: using the same facial design as the 'green' make-up, this 'ripe' make-up of orange-red is used for characters such as Balarama, Brahma, Shiva, and Surya.

poṇḍi: a small club or mace used as a hand property in *kathakali* performances.

ponnāni: the lead singer who sets the mood and keeps the tempo of the performance as he keeps basic rhythms on his gong.

Prahlādacaritam: the *kathakali* play, *Prahlada's Law*, which enacts the story of how the demon-king Hiranyakasipu's son, Prahlada, became an avid devotee of Lord Vishnu and withstood his father's fury. Hiranyakasipu is eventually killed by Vishnu's man-lion incarnation. The opening scene is a famous love scene between the 'knife' character Hiranyakasipu and his beloved wife Kayati.

prāṇa vāyu: the breath(s) or wind(s) understood to circulate within the body. Also refers to the 'life force,' or 'breath of life.' Implicit in *kathakali* training since the actor must learn to circulate, control, and use the 'breath' or 'wind' when performing facial expressions, hand-gestures, etc. It is the 'enlivening' element of performance.

pūja: worship of Hindu deities through daily or special/seasonal offerings pleasing to each deity. *Kutiyattam* is performed as a 'visual sacrifice' to deities of particular temples, i.e., as an offering.

Pulayan: harijans or 'out-castes' of Kerala.

purāṇa: encyclopedic collections of traditional stories, lore, wisdom, techniques, etc. which, along with the two great epics, are the 'bibles' of Hinduism. Most *kathakali* plays which do not draw their stories for enactment from the two epics, base their narratives on stories from one or more of the *puranas*, especially those dealing with the life of Lord Krishna.

puṟappaṭu: the preliminary pure dance usually performed by students in full costume and make-up.

Pūtanāmōkṣam: *Putana's Release*. One of four plays written by Aswati Tirunal Rama Varma (1756–94). The role of the demoness Putana has become one of the most popular in the repertory, especially for performances of the interpolation in which Puthana enacts her death while suckling the baby Krishna.

rāga: musical modes to which verses are set by the author/composer. Each accentuates a particular mood.

rājasa: one of the three basic *gunam* categories,

'passion' or the energetic.

rājasic: the dynamic quality of certain characters, especially of 'knife' type anti-heroes such as Ravana and Narakasura.

Rajasuyam: one of seven plays by Kartika Tirunal Rama Varma Maharaja (1724–98). Along with *Narakasuravadham* it is still performed today.

Rāmanāṭakam: L.S. Rajagopal's 1995 adaption of the Tamil language 'Play of Rama' into *kathakali* style. The original Tamil work is by the great Tamil poet Arunachalam Kavirayar.

Rāmanāṭṭam: literally, 'Rama's dance.' A cycle of eight plays based on the Ramayana, and authored by Kottarakkara Tampuran (c.1625–85). The earliest dramas in the genre that eventually became known as *kathakali*.

Ramayana: along with the Mahabharata, India's great epic which serves as a source of traditional oral narratives and teaching stories. It tells the story of the trials and tribulations of Prince Rama, his wife Sita, and his brother Lakshmana. One of the principal parts of the epic story occurs when the ten-headed demon-king Ravana captures Sita and takes her to his island abode Lanka. The monkey-god, son of the Wind, Hanuman, leads the monkey armies as they assist Rama in securing Sita's freedom.

rasa: the goal of theater is to allow the audience to 'taste' aesthetic delight.

rasika: literally, a 'taster of *rasa*' – a connoisseur educated into appreciation of the nuances of *kathakali* poetry, imagery, gesture language, music, etc. and therefore able to achieve the ideal aesthetic experience when watching performances.

rati bhava: the actor's state of being/doing the pleasurable, the erotic, or love.

raudra: 'fury,' usually associated with the destructive power of the goddess, and the state of mind required to kill. One of the nine basic aesthetic states (*rasa*).

Ravaṇōtbhavam: play authored by Kallekkulangara Raghava Pisharody (1725–93) which features the major role of Ravana.

Rugmāmgadacaritam: *King Rugmamgada's Law* is one of two *kathakali* plays authored by Mandavappalli Ittiraricha Menon (1747–94). It enacts the story of King Rugmamgada's test by the enchantress Mohini.

Rugminīsvayamvaram: one of four plays authored by Aswati Tirunal Rama Varma (1725–94). Still performed as part of the repertory and featuring the role of Susupala.

śabdavarṇana: Kirmira's elaborate interpolation where he 'describes the sounds' which disturb him from his meditation in *The Killing of Kirmira*.

sahṛdaya: the ideal aesthetic engagement of the connoisseur whose 'heart/mind' has been entrained and cultivated into appreciation.

śakti: the active principle of power/energy. When defined as Sakti, the goddess, she embodies the dangerous, unstable female energy and is associated with the generation of a powerful, 'furious' heated condition and therefore inspires terror.

Sāmantan: titled high-caste royal lineages.

sama bhāva: the actor's state of being/doing at-onement.

sampradāyam: tradition, traditional method, lineage of practice, style.

Sampūrna Rāmāyaṇam: *Complete Ramayana* created by the P.S.V. Natyasangham company. A composite play pieced together from scenes from a number of different Ramayana scenes in order to create a 'complete' narrative enactment of the Ramayana epic.

saṃsāra: the eternal chain of rebirths in an infinity of bodies.

samyukta: combined hand-gestures where both hands make use of the same gesture.

sancaribhava: the secondary or subordinate state of being/doing, such as pride.

sānta rasa: the audience's aesthetic experience of atonement, union, or peace.

Santānagōpālam: literally, Krishna's (Santana) children, progeny, or prosperity (*gopalam*), i.e., *The Progeny of Krishna*. *Kathakali* play authored by Mandavappalli Ittiraricha Menon (1747–94).

sanyāsin: a renunciant.

satva: goodness or truth. One of the three basic *gunam* or substances. Usually associated with the high, purest priestly castes.

sātvika: the expressive, subtle, or 'internal' elements of acting.

Sētubandhanam: one of the original eight *Ramanattam* plays recently revived by Margi.

siddha: one who has become accomplished in a practice, usually through repetition, or by divine gift.

Simhadhvajacaritam: *kathakali* play authored by Utram Tirunal Maharaja (1815) who ruled Travancore during the mid-nineteenth century.

ślōka: metrical verse composed in stanzas, usually in the third person, which indicate the context and tell what is going to happen in the ensuing dialogue portion of the play.

śōka bhāva: the actor's state of being/doing pathos or sorrow.

sōpanam: *kathakali*'s unique traditional form of vocal music.

śrāddha: traditional funeral rites which an eldest son performs for his father.

sṛngāra rasa: the audience's aesthetic experience of pleasure, the erotic, or love.

śrutvā: literally, 'having heard.'

sthayibhāva: the nine basic, 'enduring' states of being/doing, eight of which were identified in the *Natyasastra*. The ninth state included in *kathakali*, at-onement was identified by the commentator Abinavagupta in the twelfth century.

strivēṣam: female roles in *kathakali*.

Subhadrāharanam: play authored by Manthredath Namboodiripad (1851–1906).

sūci: literally, 'needles,' or the splits performed as part of *kathakali* training.

Takayi: one of the earlier, distinctive styles of *kathakali*.

tāla: rhythmic patterns to which the dialogue portion of the texts (*padam*) are set and within which dances and dramatic action are performed.

tāḷavattam: the number of rhythmic cycles within which sections of dialogue are set for performance.

tāli: the chain necklace conventionally given when a woman formed an arranged relationship with a man as approved by the eldest male of her household – a traditional form of 'marriage.'

tāmasa: darkness/lethargy – one of the three *gunam* or fundamental types.

tamburān: an honorific title meaning lord or ruler.

tāṇḍava: the strong or energetic quality manifest in choreography.

tantētāṭṭam: one type of interpolation into the dramatic text, this is a set form of soliloquy acted by specific character types ('knife,' 'beard,' or 'black') after their entrances. They also take the form of an assessment of the situation a character faces.

tapas: austere meditation used to achieve higher powers.

tapassāṭṭam: Ravana's lengthy enactment of penance.

taṟavāṭittam: what is due to one's family home and therefore one's family name.

taṟavāṭu: extended family household presided over by the eldest male of the family.

tāṭi: literally, 'beard,' the general term covering three different classes of 'beard' characters, including 'white,' 'red,' and 'black'.

tattvāhini vēsi: one who is 'philosophically oriented.'

tēppu: a make-up class which is a catch-all or miscellaneous group of approximately eighteen characters from the active repertory that do not fit the other, standard types. Included here are the special bird-style make-ups and costumes of such famous characters as Garuda, Jatayu, and Hamsa (the goose in *Nalacaritam*); the goddess Bhadrakali in *Daksa's Sacrifice*, etc.

teyyam: traditional ritual performances of northern Kerala which serve as the locally most popular form of Hinduism through which hundreds of pan-Indian and local deities are propitiated, including local heroes.

tiranōkku: the 'curtain look' used for entrances of certain characters who, by their manipulation of the curtain, reveal certain enduring aspects of their inner-nature.

tiraśśila: the multi-colored *kathakali* curtain hand-held by two onstage attendants. Used for entrances and exits.

Tīya: one of the toddy tapping, higher polluting castes.

tōṅkāram: a short dance choreography similar to an *iratti* in that it too is performed to a *pallavi*.

tōṭayam: a lengthy piece of pure dance choreography taught during the student's first year of training, and including all the basic non-interpretive foot patterns, body movements, use of hands, and cycles of rhythm basic to performance.

triputa tāla: rhythmic cycle set in 7 beats.

utsāha bhāva: the actor's state of being/doing the heroic or the vigorous.

uyiccil: derived from Kerala's martial art, this vigorous full body massage is given annually to *kathakali* students as a part of their training process.

vācika: the vocal element of performance.

vadham: literally, the act of killing.

vandana ślōkam: singing of the opening verses that begins a performance, and contextualizes the story to be enacted.

vāyttāri: the verbal instructions or commands recited by a master as students perform exercises.

vellattāṭi: 'white beards' represent a higher, divine type of being, such as Hanuman, the wise and valorous chief of the monkeys.

vēṣam: a role the actor plays, or the 'covering' an actor uses to become the character, i.e., the putting on of costume, make-up, and character.

Vicchinnabhisekam: one of the original *Ramanattam* plays recently revived by Margi.

vidūṣaka: the stock high-caste brahman character of *kutiyattam* and Sanskrit dramas.

vīra rasa: the audience's aesthetic experience of the heroic. One of the nine basic aesthetic states (*rasa*) to be 'tasted' by an audience in *kathakali*. This state is particularly associated with the main heroic (*pacca*) characters of *kathakali*, and with the Nayar martial caste of Kerala who were protectors of 'cows and brahmins.'

vismaya bhava: the actor's state of being/doing the wondrous or marvellous.

vistarikkuka: a *tour de force* dance elaboration such as the 'peacock dance' in *The Killing of Narakasura*.

yakṣi: a special type of female ghost the unhappy women who die before having had sex or before marriage or giving birth.

yoga: from the root meaning 'to bind together, hold fast, or yoke.' Any ascetic, meditational, or psycho-physiological technique which achieves such a 'binding' of bodymind. Especially important for both brahmins and princes who model themselves on 'royal sages' and are supposed to overcome their emotions through such disciplines of practice.

TRANSLITERATION OF COMPLETE
PHRASES/PASSAGES QUOTED

Natan kathapātṛavumāyi tādātmyam
    pṛāpikkanam.
Natan kathāpatṛavumayi aliññu cērūnnu.
Māñcēl miyiyālē ninnāl vāñchitaṅṅaḷāyītunnor
    añcita saugandhikaṅṅal añcate
    koṇṭannītuvan.
Śaila mukaḷilennālum śakralōkattennākilum
    vēlayilla tava hitam vikramēṇa sādhippānum.

৵৵৵ Index